MANAGEMENT OF
Child Development
CENTERS

SIXTH EDITION

PATRICIA F. HEARRON
APPALACHIAN STATE UNIVERSITY

VERNA HILDEBRAND
EMERITA, MICHIGAN STATE UNIVERSITY

PEARSON

Merrill
Prentice Hall

Upper Saddle River, New Jersey
Columbus, Ohio

Library of Congress Cataloging-in-Publication Data
Hearron, Patricia F.
  Management of child development centers / Patricia F. Hearron, Verna
Hildebrand.—6th ed.
      p. cm.
  Includes bibliographical references and index.
  ISBN 0-13-171207-1 (pbk.: alk. paper)
1. Nursery schools—United States—Administration. 2. Day care centers—United States—Administration.
3. Early childhood education—United States. I. Hildebrand, Verna. II. Title.
  LB2822.7.H55 2007
  372.21—dc22

                                                                    2005032430

Vice President and Executive Publisher: Jeffery W. Johnston
Publisher: Kevin M. Davis
Acquisitions Editor: Julie Peters
Editorial Assistant: Michelle Girgis
Production Editor: Linda Hillis Bayma
Production Coordination: Thistle Hill Publishing Services, LLC
Design Coordinator: Diane C. Lorenzo
Cover Designer: Jeff Vanik
Cover Image: Corbis
Production Manager: Laura Messerly
Director of Marketing: David Gesell
Marketing Manager: Amy Judd
Marketing Coordinator: Brian Mounts

This book was set in Janson Text by Laserwords Private Limited, Chennai. It was printed and bound by Hamilton Printing.
The cover was printed by Coral Graphic Services, Inc.

Photo Credits: p. 1, Lori Whitley/Merrill; all other photos supplied by the authors.

Pearson Education Ltd.
Pearson Education Singapore Pte. Ltd.
Pearson Education Canada, Ltd.
Pearson Education—Japan

Pearson Education Australia Pty. Limited
Pearson Education North Asia Ltd.
Pearson Educación de Mexico, S.A. de C.V.
Pearson Education Malaysia Pte. Ltd.

10 9 8 7 6 5 4 3 2
ISBN: 0-13-171207-1

We dedicate *Management of Child Development Centers* to

all of the young children who share our small spaceship Earth,

to the families and caregivers who nurture them,

and to the managers of child development centers

whose commitment to high-quality programs

helps make that nurturing possible.

This edition of *Management of Child Development Centers*, like those that preceded it, is based on the premise that high-quality programs for young children are an essential support for families in today's world—a part of the family ecosystem. Therefore, managers charged with maintaining the quality of those programs must understand that ecosystem and the complex connections that exist between its components. Effective managers realize that neither the family nor the child development program is an island—that each affects and is affected by the other, as well as by countless forces within the community and society at large.

The challenges are many: As child development programs reflect society's increasing diversity, managers must strive to provide services that are culturally responsive and sensitive to a variety of family needs. As more centers embrace a philosophy of inclusion, serving *all* children, with and without disabilities, managers and staff members must collaborate not only with families but also with professionals from many other fields in order to help each child reach his or her full potential.

Framework of Core Competencies for Managers/Directors

Chapter 1 provides an overview of the context within which child development programs operate as we move into the 21st century. Chapters 2 and 3 describe the various forms those programs take and explore theoretical perspectives that inform the field. Chapters 4 through 16 respond to the increasing interest in the professional credentialing of early childhood managers by focusing on a single competency in each chapter. Derived from a review of current literature in the field, 13 core competencies for managers in the field are identified. Each chapter has been extensively updated for this edition.

1. **Personal and professional self-awareness.** The authors take the position that effective management requires more than technical expertise or formulaic responses to situations. Managers of child development programs must be reflective professionals, willing to analyze their own strengths and weaknesses and be open to new interpretations of received ideas.

2. **Organizational management.** Child development programs are complex systems of interrelated parts, which are, in turn, part of the larger social system. The manager's role

is to make the parts work together smoothly and to guide their programs' interactions with that system. Effective managers have a working knowledge of the many regulatory systems governing the operation of early childhood facilities, as well as a sense of the reasons for the regulations and an ability to operate their programs within those constraints.

3. **Fiscal management.** No program can survive unless its manager makes wise use of its financial resources. Managers must create realistic budgets, monitor expenses to align with those budgets, and know when to make appropriate adjustments. They must find ways to increase resources, including fund-raising or grant writing, and ways to economize without sacrificing quality.

4. **Personnel management.** Because child development facilities are labor-intensive operations, a large part of the manager's job is to recruit and hire employees with the greatest potential; to retain those employees in a profession with an annual turnover rate of approximately 40 percent; to monitor the employees' performance, providing feedback as needed and terminating employees when necessary; and, finally, to create a staff development plan that builds on the talents that employees bring to the job.

5. **Human relations.** An essential component of the manager's role is establishing and maintaining productive relationships with a variety of stakeholders: governing board members, families of enrolled children, employees, and representatives of businesses or community agencies. In addition to hiring, retaining, and developing the staff, managers must find ways to generate teamwork and motivation, drawing on a basic knowledge of group dynamics, communication styles, and conflict resolution techniques.

6. **Facilities management.** The manager is responsible for creating the spaces that support the day-to-day work of the employee team. This means designing, equipping, and arranging spaces that meet regulatory requirements and professional standards, spaces that incorporate sound principles of child development and environmental psychology.

7. **Managing health and safety issues.** Keeping children safe and healthy is a fundamental requirement of any child development facility. The manager's job is to establish policies and procedures that accomplish this goal and to see that they are carried out. We have added a checklist for recognizing symptoms of abuse and neglect.

8. **Managing food service.** Meeting the children's nutritional needs is another fundamental requirement. Managers must ensure that menus and food handling practices comply with the requirements of state licensing agencies and those of the U.S. Department of Agriculture if the program is receiving food subsidies. They must also think about how their program's meals reflect the cultures of the families they serve and what those meals contribute to the program's curriculum.

9. **Educational programming.** Although many managers are drawn from the ranks of early childhood teachers, managing a facility's educational program requires a perspective that looks beyond the individual classroom. Managers must have a working knowledge of the various curriculum models so that they can select and implement an appropriate choice and create the conditions necessary to support others doing the job. Developmentally appropriate assessment strategies, the inclusion of children with disabilities, and an antibias curriculum are all issues that concern managers.

10. **Family support.** Managers of high-quality programs for young children demonstrate a clear understanding that serving children means serving families. They possess an understanding of how family systems work, as well as an appreciation for diverse parenting styles. They can establish the types of open communication that help form partnerships with

parents. They know enough about their community to help families access those resources that promote family wellness.

11. **Marketing and public relations.** Managers must maintain a program's viability by developing a pool of potential clients. They must ensure that the community is aware of the program and, just as important, appreciates the program's high quality. This includes educating the public about what constitutes high quality in children's programs, as well as offering services that meet the specific needs of potential clients.

12. **Assessment and evaluation.** The last step in the management process is to determine how well an organization has met its objectives. Then, of course, the cycle begins again, with the manager adjusting practices to meet objectives more effectively, or setting new (perhaps higher) goals for the organization.

13. **Leadership.** Finally, managers functioning at the highest level of professional development are able to see beyond the day-to-day concerns of keeping their facility afloat. They have a vision of where they want their organization to go and the ability to marshal all of the resources at their command to attain that vision. They strive to influence spheres beyond their own organization—the profession at large and the well-being of children in general.

Features of This Text

The text presents a synthesis of current information in clear, reader-friendly language. Its organization is aligned with competencies identified by leaders in the director credentialing movement. Concepts and terminology are illustrated with examples drawn from the authors' experience, as well as by using charts, graphs, and photographs. In addition, the text includes a variety of practical tools, such as menu planning and evaluation forms and links to relevant websites. Each chapter contains the following elements to facilitate the instructor's class planning and student learning:

- **Decisions, Decisions** . . . features ask the students to reflect on topics discussed in the chapters and apply the information to real-life situations.
- **Questions for Review** at the end of each chapter help students identify and recall basic information.
- **Professional Portfolio** assignments help students create products that can be included in a portfolio to demonstrate their mastery of the core competencies. At least one portfolio assignment in each chapter incorporates the use of technology (e.g., Internet-based research; desktop publishing software), supporting the integration of these skills within the core competencies.
- **Resources for Further Study** provide students and instructors with a convenient list of up-to-date resources, in print as well as online, for a deeper investigation of the topics discussed in each chapter.

Changes for the Sixth Edition

In response to helpful suggestions from our readers and reviewers, we have incorporated several changes:

- We have expanded coverage of major issues affecting the field of early care and education, including state standards for preschool and national legislative initiatives such as No Child Left Behind and support for faith-based programs.

- We have added charts and checklists to facilitate understanding and application of information: characteristics of types of child development theories in Chapter 3; symptoms of stress level and strategies for preventing burnout in Chapter 4; a detailed grant proposal outline and a self-assessment of potential as a small-business owner in Chapter 6; a performance appraisal for teachers in Chapter 8; specific signs of various types of child abuse or neglect and a checklist for monitoring health and safety conditions in Chapter 10; a menu-planning worksheet (and links to sample menus online) in Chapter 11; and a chart comparing types of curricula and sample planning forms in Chapter 12.
- We have increased coverage of infant–toddler needs regarding space, scheduling, and programming in Chapters 9 and 12.
- A new *Online Instructor's Manual and Test Bank* has been created to augment student learning through assignments requiring the application of concepts. Instructors may ask their Prentice Hall sales representative for online access to this downloadable document.

Audience for This Text

This book is suitable for use in a variety of settings: in formal classes in 2- or 4-year college programs, in child development associate (CDA) training or inservice programs for practicing early childhood professionals, and as an independent study tool by individuals contemplating a move from classroom teacher or caregiver to center manager.

Management of Child Development Centers, Sixth Edition, is the product of the authors' combined experience over decades of working with children and their families, with young people anticipating a career in the early childhood profession, and with practicing professionals at many levels. Previous editions have been field-tested in university classrooms, and the present edition incorporates much of what has been learned during that process. Managers who apply this information will be well positioned to meet the growing demand for high-quality programs that are capable of serving all children.

Acknowledgments

We are indebted to the pioneering work of the late Dr. Beatrice Paolucci in the area of management and decision making; to Drs. Margaret Bubolz and M. Suzanne Sontag for their articulation of family ecosystems theory; and to the students (many of whom are now our colleagues) whose questions and insights provided inspiration for our work. Special thanks are due to the early childhood educators who have welcomed us into their centers and classrooms over the years, to the children in those classrooms, and to their families.

We gratefully acknowledge the skillful assistance of Angela Williams Urquhart at Thistle Hill Publishing Services, as well as the helpful suggestions from the reviewers for this sixth edition: Nancy Baptiste, New Mexico State University; Linda S. Estes, St. Charles Community College; Linda Huber, Ball State University; and Michele Parker, Glendale Community College.

The Prentice Hall Companion Website: A Virtual Learning Environment

Technology is a constantly growing and changing aspect of our field that is creating a need for content and resources. To address this emerging need, Prentice Hall has developed an online learning environment for students and professors alike—Companion Websites—to support our textbooks.

In creating a Companion Website, our goal is to build on and enhance what the textbook already offers. For this reason, the content for each user-friendly website is organized by topic and provides the professor and student with a variety of meaningful resources. Common features of a Companion Website include:

- **Introduction**—General information about the topic and how it will be covered in the website.
- **Web Links**—A variety of websites related to topic areas.
- **Timely Articles**—Links to online articles that enable you to become more aware of important issues in early childhood.
- **Learn by Doing**—Put concepts into action, participate in activities, examine strategies, and more.
- **Visit a School**—Visit a school's website to see concepts, theories, and strategies in action.
- **For Teachers/Practitioners**—Access information you will need to know as an educator, including information on materials, activities, and lessons.
- **Observation Tools**—A collection of checklists and forms to print and use when observing and assessing children's development.
- **Current Policies and Standards**—Find out the latest early childhood policies from the government and various organizations, and view state, federal, and curriculum standards.
- **Resources and Organizations**—Discover tools to help you plan your classroom or center and organizations to provide current information and standards for each topic.
- **Electronic Bluebook**—Paperless method of completing homework or essays assigned by a professor. Finished work can be sent to the professor via email.

To take advantage of these and other resources, please visit Merrill Education's **Early Childhood Education Resources Website.** Go to **www.prenhall.com/hearron**, click on the book cover, and then click on "Enter" at the bottom of the next screen.

Teacher Preparation Classroom

TEACHER PREP

MERRILL
PRENTICE HALL

See a demo at
www.prenhall.com/teacherprep/demo

Your Class. Their Careers. Our Future. Will your students be prepared?

We invite you to explore our new, innovative and engaging website and all that it has to offer you, your course, and tomorrow's educators! Organized around the major courses pre-service teachers take, the Teacher Preparation site provides media, student/teacher artifacts, strategies, research articles, and other resources to equip your students with the quality tools needed to excel in their courses and prepare them for their first classroom.

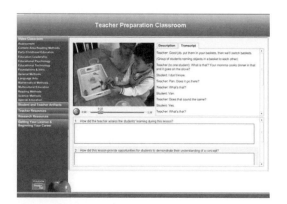

This ultimate on-line education resource is available at no cost, when packaged with a Merrill text, and will provide you and your students access to:

Online Video Library. More than 150 video clips—each tied to a course topic and framed by learning goals and Praxis-type questions— capture real teachers and students working in real classrooms, as well as in-depth interviews with both students and educators.

Student and Teacher Artifacts. More than 200 student and teacher classroom artifacts—each tied to a course topic and framed by learning goals and application questions— provide a wealth of materials and experiences to help make your study to become a professional teacher more concrete and hands-on.

Research Articles. Over 500 articles from ASCD's renowned journal *Educational Leadership*. The site also includes Research Navigator, a searchable database of additional educational journals.

Teaching Strategies. Over 500 strategies and lesson plans for you to use when you become a practicing professional.

Licensure and Career Tools. Resources devoted to helping you pass your licensure exam; learn standards, law, and public policies; plan a teaching portfolio; and succeed in your first year of teaching.

How to ORDER *Teacher Prep* for you and your students:

For students to receive a *Teacher Prep* Access Code with this text, instructors **must** provide a special value pack ISBN number on their textbook order form. To receive this special ISBN, please email: **Merrill.marketing@pearsoned.com** and provide the following information:

- Name and Affiliation
- Author/Title/Edition of Merrill text

Upon ordering *Teacher Prep* for their students, instructors will be given a lifetime *Teacher Prep* Access Code.

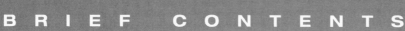

BRIEF CONTENTS

CONTENTS

PART II   CORE COMPETENCIES   59

CHAPTER 4   Reflective Management: Personal and Professional Self-Awareness   60

CHAPTER 5   Organizational Management   76

Note: Every effort has been made to provide accurate and current Internet information in this book. However, the Internet and information on it are constantly changing, so it is inevitable that some of the Internet addresses listed in this textbook will change.

Part I

INTRODUCTION

CHAPTER ONE

Managing Children's Centers in the 21st Century

Have you always dreamed of owning and managing a school for young children? Perhaps you expect to move up to managing the center where you now work, or you aspire to be the principal at the elementary school where you now teach kindergarten or prekindergarten.

What do you need to know to perform the manager's role adequately and efficiently? Will your experience as a successful teacher make a difference in your ability to manage a center? If you have an MBA (master's of business administration) yet have never been a teacher, could you manage a group of classrooms in a school or center? Are similar managerial skills and knowledge required in other human service organizations, such as a child-care referral service or a family counseling agency?

Defining Terms

This book focuses on management as applied in child development centers. Agreeing on definitions of key terms and concepts is essential. **Management** is the science of (a) setting goals, (b) allocating human and material resources judiciously for achieving the goals, (c) carrying out the work or action required to achieve the goals, (d) monitoring the outcome or product of the work or action based on established standards, and (e) making necessary adjustments or improvements to ensure that performance reaches or exceeds goals.

A child development center is a facility that provides out-of-home education and care for young children in groups, a service that supplements the education and care parents give their child. The term encompasses programs that are full- or part-day, profit or nonprofit, and programs known as preschools, child-care centers, kindergarten, prekindergarten, cooperative, Head Start, or variations of any of these.

Though the main focus of this book is on center- or school-based programs, many of the principles discussed are applicable to home-based family child-care providers. The definition of child development centers incorporates the concepts of education and care and asserts that the two are inextricably linked. A growing body of research, corroborated by the experience of parents and early childhood professionals, indicates that young children learn best in the context of a secure environment. Thus, the caregiving that creates that secure environment is the foundation upon which efforts to educate young children must be based.

Management is a science; some individuals spend their careers perfecting this science. Management has a background of theory, research, experience, applications, and knowledge that must be brought together by any individual who assumes the managerial role in an enterprise. Management of a center is complex—more complex than operating a single entity such as a home or a classroom. While many individuals are likely to have a stake in the outcome of a decision or action, the manager has the final responsibility for making decisions. President Harry S Truman had a sign on his desk that read "The buck stops here." In other words, as president, he was the ultimate decision maker, the manager.

Would you like being a manager? How will you know? Can someone else tell you whether you would like being a manager? What experience have you had that could make you a good manager? How many managers have you worked for? Were these "good" managers? What makes a manager good? What things that a manager does are especially enjoyable? What things are difficult? As you read this chapter, take some time to reflect on all of these questions and to answer them for yourself.

Decisions, Decisions . . .

What is your image of what a manager of a child development program does? What parts of the job do you think you would enjoy? What parts do you think you would find difficult? Does it take a certain type of personality to do well in the manager's role?

Stages of Professional Development

Where are you on your time line of professional development? Management of a school or center can give your professional life new challenges after you have had a number of years of successful experiences in teaching. Or you may feel that you need more teaching experience before taking on a managerial role. VanderVen (1999, pp. 196–197) identifies five stages in the development of early childhood administrators or leaders:

1. **Awareness.** As a newcomer to the profession, you might be so focused on the immediate concerns of your day-to-day interactions with children and families that you take little notice of the managerial work that makes it possible for you to do your job. Ironically, this is particularly true if you are fortunate enough to work with an effective manager. If that is not the case, you will most likely become aware of managerial tasks when you experience the results when they are not done or are done poorly. According to VanderVen, this managerial work is "ego alien" for you at this phase of your career: It just does not fit in with your image of yourself and your role.

2. **Induction.** As noted previously, your own dissatisfaction with the way things are done in your organization might be the catalyst that sparks a desire in you to change things. Whatever the reason, you are now ready to learn more about a new role.

3. **Competency.** Perhaps you are thrust into your new role as a consequence of the high rate of employee turnover in the field. Perhaps a promotion to management level is part of a carefully orchestrated staff development plan. Regardless of the route taken, as a new manager, you have a lot to learn—through classes or independent study,

supervised practice, and the inevitable trial and error that come with on-the-job experience. Eventually, your hard work will pay off in a rewarding feeling of competency, a deep-seated knowledge that you can do this job.

4. **Proficiency.** Do you remember learning to ride a bicycle? You probably gripped the handlebars with all your might as you wobbled down the sidewalk. Eventually, you got the feel of it and finally reached a stage where you could hop on your bicycle and take off with your mind on where you wanted to go instead of worrying about how or whether you would get there. Perhaps you even tried more complex maneuvers with your bike, riding "no hands," for example. You had reached the stage of proficiency in bicycle navigation. Seasoned child development administrators experience a similar transition. They find it takes less conscious effort to accomplish tasks that were originally very challenging (e.g., recruiting and hiring a new staff member) and they move on to more complex tasks (e.g., developing a long-range staff development plan to help retain the most qualified staff).

5. **Expertise.** You have arrived at this level and become an "expert" in your field when you can add creativity and innovation to all earlier accomplishments. At this point, you may be ready to move beyond managing one early childhood organization and assume a leadership role in your chosen profession.

Decisions, Decisions . . .

Imagine yourself 5 or 10 years from now. Where would you like to be working? What would you like to be doing? Where do you think you will be in VanderVen's sequence of administrative development? What steps can you take now to achieve those dreams?

Some people are pressed into the management role with little or no preparation when a manager leaves suddenly and they must look for quick management courses and advice. Whether you are already a manager, expect to become a manager soon, or have management as a future goal, learning about the intricacies of child development center management can add a new dimension to your professional career. Knowledge of managerial principles can make you more appreciative and supportive of managers with whom you work, even when you are happy that the buck still stops at their desk.

Child Development Centers: A Support System for Families

Families throughout the world have the primary responsibility for nurturing children. Nurturing may be done by the natural or adoptive parent or parents, extended family systems, or institutions. Families often decide to supplement the care and education they can give with assistance from institutions outside the family. Historical, cultural, political, and economic factors within each society affect their decisions. Access to child development services is very high in the industrialized world, but it is not universal. You may be surprised to learn that the United States lags behind many industrialized countries in developing policies to increase access and improve the quality of these services.

In 1999, a team of highly regarded early childhood experts compiled a snapshot of early care and education in the United States as part of an 11-country study sponsored by the Organization for Economic Cooperation and Development (OECD). In contrast to other countries in the study, the U.S. review team found higher rates of poverty and a greater concentration of poverty among children who were much less likely than their middle-class counterparts to participate in early care and education opportunities (OECD, 2000, July, p. 49). Policy recommendations growing out of this important study are addressed in chapter 16.

The child development centers considered in this chapter, including public school kindergarten, are, for the most part, optional services for families. Families may choose to use such facilities or to provide care and education for their young children in their own homes. Understanding the context within which families in today's world are living and rearing their children is essential if we are to effectively manage or administer such services as child development centers or any social service for families.

Population Trends: Getting the Big Picture in Focus

Knowing the current situation and trends in one's field of business is part of effective management. The development of the Internet in recent years has made this task much easier. As just one example, the U.S. Census Bureau maintains an extensive website, www.census.gov, where you can obtain information about patterns of childbearing, employment, education, child-

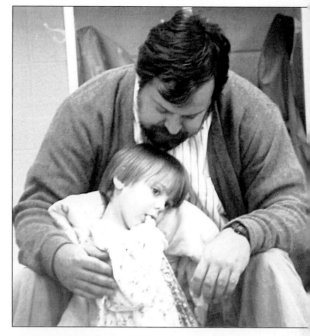

Child development programs are a support system for families, providing peace of mind for working parents and emotional security for children.

care arrangements, and a host of other topics. A wise manager makes a concerted effort to keep abreast of such national statistics and collects similar data regarding the community and state. Information on local employment trends is needed in addition to data showing a need for children's services. A local child-care resource and referral agency or a chamber of commerce can suggest the best source of local and state statistics.

Numbers and Characteristics of Children

At the time of the 2000 U.S. Census, there were about 19.2 million children under 5 years of age and 41 million children 5 to 14 years old. The average birthrate in the United States is about two births per woman. This rate, which is just below the rate needed to maintain the current population level, has remained fairly constant over the last 20 years. Several important changes are occurring within this apparently static figure, however. For example, about twice as many women in the 40–44 age range were childless as compared with women in that age group in 1976 (19 percent vs. 10 percent) (Downs, 2003, p. 1). Figure 1.1 illustrates some of the contrasts between these women and their mothers' generation.

Minority and Immigrant Populations. A closer look at that overall birthrate reveals another trend that will bring dramatic changes in the makeup of the population. In 2002 overall fertility rates for Hispanic women were significantly higher than those for non-Hispanic women: 78 versus 58 births per 1,000, with large differences most apparent in the 20–24 age range (Downs, 2003, p. 5). This means that in a few years, it will no longer be accurate to use the term "minority" in reference to non-White groups because White people will no longer comprise the majority population. The United States will become a nation in which the "majority" is actually made up of several "minorities."

FIGURE 1.1   *Comparing fertility patterns of women ages 40–44 in 1976 and 2002*

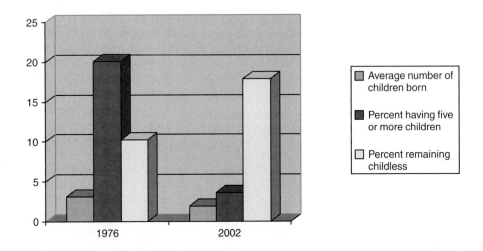

Source: Downs, Barbara (2003, October). *Fertility of American women: June 2002*. (U.S. Census Bureau: Current Population Reports, Series P20-548). Washington, DC: U.S. Government Printing Office. Retrieved from http://www.census.gov/population/www/socdemo/fertility.html

Another rapidly expanding sector of the U.S. population is composed of people born in other countries. Declining from a peak of 14.7 percent in 1910 to 4.8 percent in 1970, the percentage of foreign-born Americans has risen steadily since then. In 1994, 8.7 percent of the U.S. population was foreign born, while in 2003 that figure was 11.7 percent (Hansen & Bachu, 1995, p. 1; Larsen, 2004, p. 1). Immigration is only one reason for the rising numbers of foreign-born Americans. In 2002, 15 percent of all women of child-bearing age in the United States were foreign born, up from 11 percent in 1988. The fertility rate for those women was 71 births per 1,000, compared to a rate of 60 per 1,000 for native-born women (Downs, 2003, p. 3). These figures suggest that many children will be entering programs where the dominant language and customs are dramatically different from those they experience at home. Child-care facilities will face the challenge of helping those children learn new ways without cutting themselves off from their rich cultural heritages.

Children with Disabilities.   Other U.S. government statistics estimate that 9.1 percent of children from birth to 14 years of age have some sort of disability (e.g., difficulty seeing, hearing, or walking) and 1.1 percent have a severe disability (unable to perform one or more activities or needing assistance to do so). These percentages increase with age and vary across racial and ethnic groups, with higher rates among Black and Hispanic populations (U.S. Department of Commerce, Bureau of the Census, 1997). Some disabling conditions, such as Down syndrome, blindness, or cerebral palsy, can be identified at birth or in early infancy, while others appear somewhat later. Children with autism or pervasive developmental disorder, for example, may appear to be developing typically until about 18 months, when they begin to withdraw and engage in repetitive behavior (Greenspan & Weider, 1998, p. 7).

Still other conditions, such as delayed cognitive development or emotional impairment, may emerge as the result of environmental factors such as malnutrition, poverty, or abuse. Thus, when speaking of very young children, it is necessary to consider not only those with disabilities, but also those considered "at risk" for developmental delays or disabilities, a group estimated to comprise 5 percent to 15 percent of all infants born in the United States. The mother's health and nutritional status, her behaviors during pregnancy, prenatal care, the child's birth weight and gestational age, and the family's socioeconomic status are all factors that influence the level of risk (Widerstrom et al., 1997, p. 63). Of all mothers giving birth in 2002, only 83.7 percent received prenatal care during the first 3 months of pregnancy. Among Blacks, American Indians, and Hispanics, this percentage is even lower: 75.2, 69.8, and 76.7 percent, respectively. In the same year, 6.1 percent of all babies born weighed less than 5 lbs. 8 oz. (considered low birth weight); that figure was nearly double (11.4 percent) for Blacks (Martin et al., 2003, pp. 13, 21).

A rapidly expanding sector of the U.S. population is composed of people born in other countries.

Experts and national policy makers recognize that appropriate and timely intervention can help prevent a child considered at risk from actually developing a disability or lessen the severity of a disability resulting from a particular condition. Federal legislation supports the inclusion of children who have (or are at risk for developing) disabilities in programs for all children (Odom & Diamond, 1998, p. 3). This means that center managers are challenged to find ways to accommodate diverse needs and to view differences as potential strengths rather than deficits.

Poverty and Homelessness.   The problems experienced by society at large also impact children's programs. According to the Children's Defense Fund, one out of every five children in the United States is born poor, and one in three experience poverty at some time in their childhood (2001, p. xxxi). In 1999, poverty was defined as an annual income of less than $13,290 for a family of three, but the actual income of the average poor family was $4,000 less than that (p. xv). Housing becomes an increasing problem for poor families as the availability of low-cost rental units declines. A survey of 25 cities by the U.S. Conference of Mayors found a 15 percent increase in the demand for emergency shelter between 1999 and 2000—the largest increase in 10 years. This increase was even larger for families with children who made up over a third of the homeless people in the survey. Cities were unable to meet this increased demand and shelters had to turn away more than a quarter of the families with children who requested assistance (p. 14). In some cities, child-care facilities have been established to provide some measure of stability for young children in this stressful situation.

Teen Pregnancy.   The U.S. Department of Health and Human Services, which has tracked teenage pregnancy rates since 1976, reports that the birthrate among teenagers declined 13 percent between 1990 and 1997 and another 17 percent in the next two years. The pregnancy rate for young teenagers (ages 15–17) fell from 80.3 per 1,000 in 1990 to 63.7 in 1997, its lowest rate since 1976. The rates for older teenagers (ages 18–19) also declined, although not as sharply. Factors suggested as influencing this trend include increasing social pressure for abstinence and responsible behavior; easier, more effective methods of birth control;

expanded opportunities for all women, including teenagers; and social programs that help teens attain the goals made possible by those opportunities (Ventura et al., 2001, p. 3).

This decline is welcome news because teen pregnancy is often associated with a variety of risk factors, including a lack of prenatal care, low birth weight, and a lowered educational attainment for mothers. Nevertheless, among the 6.8 million births in 1997, 24,000 were to mothers under 15 years of age and another 872,000 were to mothers aged 15 to 19 (p. 8). This means that managers of child development programs will be challenged to meet the needs of these very young parents along with the needs of their babies.

Grandparents and Single Parents.   Although the numbers of children born to teenage mothers may be declining, the number of children living with grandparents is moving in the opposite direction. Between 1970 and 1997, the number of children living in households that included a grandparent increased from 2.2 million (3.2 percent) to 3.9 million (5.5 percent), with the greatest increase occurring among children living in what are termed "skipped generation" households, that is, with grandparents and no parent present, a trend attributed to a variety of social factors such as drug use, AIDS, and incarceration of parents. Compared with all children, those living in a grandparent-maintained household were substantially more likely to be poor, to lack health insurance, and to receive public assistance. Although this issue has attracted a great deal of attention from researchers and the news media, public policy has not kept pace, particularly in the areas of grandparents' rights and their access to public assistance (Bryson & Casper, 1999).

In addition to those children residing with grandparents, the number of children living with only one parent has increased markedly over the past two decades. In 1980, more than three-quarters (77 percent) of all children under 18 lived with both parents. That number had dropped to 68 percent by 1998. Although the majority of children living in a single-parent home live with their mothers only, the increase in this group has been more gradual, going from 18 percent in 1980 to 23 percent in 1998. During the same period, the percentage of those living with only their father more than doubled—from almost 2 percent to 4 percent (U.S. Census Bureau, 2001). Again, these trends suggest that the manager of children's programs in today's world needs a broad knowledge base and access to many resources to serve a wide range of family needs.

Demand for Child Care

The percentage of mothers of children under 6 in the labor force increased fivefold in the last half of the 20th century. It rose from 46.8 percent to 65.3 percent in the 20 years from 1980 to 2000. For married mothers, this number declined somewhat in 2003 to 57.6 percent, while it increased to 63.8 percent for single mothers (U.S. Department of Labor, 2004). Multiple factors probably contributed to women's increased participation in the workforce, as well as to the fact that married mothers appear only slightly less likely to stay home with their children than mothers in general. On the one hand, married mothers who might have stayed home with their children in an earlier era may have felt pressured to seek paid employment because of a rising cost of living or an economic downturn that eliminated their husbands' jobs. An increasing number of single mothers, divorced or otherwise, had to work to support themselves and their children. In addition, during the decades since 1960, career opportunities for women have expanded, thanks to the women's movement, with the result that working mothers became hesitant about giving up any job for more than a short maternity leave. As mothers became part of the workforce, they had to find alternate forms of care for their children: relatives, neighbors, or more formal arrangements.

U.S. government statistics show that the demand for organized child care outside the home has increased steadily since the 1950s, except for a brief downturn between 1988 and 1991, when there was a corresponding increase in the rate of care provided by fathers. This phenomenon was probably caused by an economic recession and a higher rate of unemployment for those fathers at that time. Recent government census data indicate that virtually all (98 percent) children under 5 whose parents are either at work or at school are in some form of care (Smith, 2000).

Organized facilities (i.e., child-care centers, nursery schools, and Head Start programs as opposed to care by relatives or in family child-care homes) provide care for 17 percent of those children, ages birth through 2 and 56 percent of those ages 3 through 6. Figure 1.2 compares the distribution of children of working mothers among various forms of child care in 1995 and 2001. Children of working parents are not the only ones receiving services, however. Nearly half (43 percent) of children whose parents are neither working nor in school are in some form of regular child care. This suggests that families expect programs to provide education and enrichment experiences beyond basic caregiving (Smith, 2000).

Both income and the mother's education level make a difference in the type of child-care arrangements that families select. Families enrolled in various government antipoverty programs are more likely to rely on relatives, while more affluent families are more likely to use centers or family child-care homes (Casper, 1997). Only 6 percent of children under 3 whose mothers have less than a high school diploma are in center-based care, as compared to 27 percent of those whose mothers have a college degree (Ehrle et al., 2001). One suggested reason for service workers and laborers not using organized child care is that the centers' hours of operation typically are daytime hours, which may not coordinate with the workers' schedules.

For most families, regardless of income or employment status, arranging child care is a juggling act: 44 percent of preschool children and 75 percent of grade-school children

FIGURE 1.2   *Comparison of child-care arrangements for children, birth to kindergarten, 1995 and 2001*

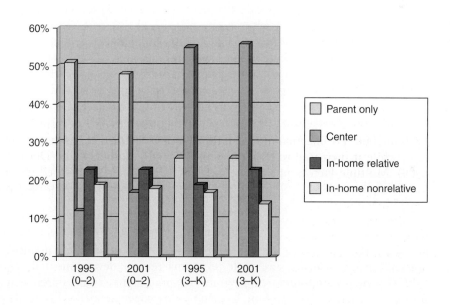

Source: Federal Interagency Forum on Child and Family Statistics. America's Children: Key National Indicators of Well-Being, 2005. Retrieved from http://www.childstats.gov/ac2005/tables/appendixa.pdf

spend time in more than one child-care arrangement each week (Smith, 2000). Most children whose mothers work full time spend 35 or more hours in care each week. Although, in general, children under 3 years of age are more likely than 3- and 4-year-old children to spend fewer hours in care, those of affluent families spend an average of 26 hours per week in care versus 21 hours for children of poor families (Ehrle et al., 2001). The pattern also varies across the country; percentages of children under 5 with employed mothers in full-time care ranges from 29 percent in California and Massachusetts to 56 percent and 59 percent in Alabama and Mississippi, respectively (Capizzano & Adams, 2000).

Historically, child-care centers were used primarily by poor parents and were considered a last resort in the choice of care of children away from home. Affluent families sent their children to nursery school for a few hours a week, seeking to provide socialization experiences or intellectual enrichment. However, as more educated and moderate- to upper-income mothers began working, more affluent families began seeking full-day child care. They expected the high-quality education they would receive in a nursery school. This increase in numbers and the shift in the child-care centers' clientele have created a demand for improvement in the quality of child care.

Kindergartens

Kindergartens today enroll over 95 percent of the 5-year-olds. A few states have made kindergarten a prerequisite to entering first grade; thus, the previously optional nature of kindergarten has been removed. Kindergartens in many states now have a longer day, equal to that of elementary school children. This change has doubled the demand for kindergarten teachers because one teacher no longer teaches two groups of children. The programs for before- and after-school care for elementary-age children have been increasing around the country.

Early Childhood Programs in Public Schools

Public school programs for 3- and 4-year-old children have become the norm. According to the National Institute for Early Education Research, 38 states provided such programs in 2002–2003, serving nearly 740,000 children, although only Georgia and Oklahoma offered universally available prekindergarten programs (Barnett et al., 2004). In addition to state-funded efforts, which target primarily 4-year-olds, some early childhood programs are funded by the federal government's Head Start program and the Individuals with Disabilities Education Act (IDEA) or Title I of the Elementary and Secondary Education Act, a program for children at risk for school failure caused by poverty, each of which serves 3-year-olds as well as 4-year-olds. Thus, the number of public school programs for young children is increasing, but the population they serve is, for the most part, limited to specific groups (children with disabilities or from low-income families). Many are part-day and do not fulfill the needs for child care when parents are working. Some require the parents to pay tuition.

As more states invest dollars in early education, there is a corresponding movement for states to establish standards for what young children are expected to know or be able to do after participating in early childhood programs. Managers of these public school programs are challenged to make sure their programs remain developmentally appropriate. The OECD review team found that programs for poor and at-risk children were more likely to use an "instructivist" curriculum, focusing on narrowly defined skills, while programs serving more privileged populations followed a "constructivist" model, emphasizing discovery and self-initiated learning (OECD, 2000, p. 49).

Head Start

Initiated under President Lyndon Johnson in 1965 as part of the War on Poverty, Head Start has retained its popular support under several presidents since then. Although it served 905, 851 children in 2004, the program still reached only about half of eligible preschool children (Children's Defense Fund, 2005a). Originally targeting 3- and 4-year-old children, Head Start has evolved to include services for infants and toddlers, as well as full-day programs and care for children of working parents. We will take a closer look at this program and its history in chapter 2.

Infants and Toddlers

The 1980s and 1990s saw a steady increase in the number of infant and toddler programs. The demand for these programs was partly fueled by changes in welfare policies that required mothers of young children to enter the workforce. Media coverage of research findings about the impact of early experiences on lifelong learning potential sparked widespread public interest in the quality of these programs. A national survey conducted in 1997 found that 73 percent of infants and toddlers with employed mothers were cared for by someone other than a parent. Of that number, about a quarter (27 percent) are cared for by relatives, 22 percent are in centers, 17 percent in family day care, and 7 percent are with nannies or babysitters (Ehrle et al., 2001). Standards for licensing and staffing these centers have been widely debated. Protection of the children is of primary importance to many child development specialists.

Child Care and Poverty

The 1996 Congress passed legislation to reform welfare, putting strict limits on the amount of time any family could receive government financial assistance. Over the next 4 years, the number of individuals receiving Temporary Assistance for Needy Families declined by 50 percent. The percentage of poor children receiving assistance fell from 57.3 in 1995 to 37.8 in 1999. According to a study by the Children's Defense Fund, most families work after leaving welfare, although their employment is often sporadic and low paying (Children's Defense Fund, 2001, p. 17). Clearly, the availability of affordable child care makes a difference in a family's ability to seek and maintain employment. However, in early 2001, state child-care administrators reported waiting lists for child-care assistance ranging from 2,000 children in Iowa to more than 44,000 children in Florida (p. 52), and budget cuts proposed in subsequent years threaten to exacerbate the problem.

No Child Left Behind

The No Child Left Behind (NCLB) Act of 2001, while not directly addressing early childhood programs, has generated concern among many early educators who fear that the push for accountability and mandated testing of elementary school children will fuel a drive toward an overemphasis on academics with a corresponding sacrifice of time for play or other activities long held to be beneficial for very young children. On the other hand, the law's emphasis on student achievement creates an opportunity for advocates to publicize information about the impact that high-quality early childhood programs have on subsequent school success (Kauerz & McMaken, 2004).

Two other components of NCLB apply directly to early childhood education. The Early Reading First initiative is intended to help low-income children enter school with the basic knowledge and skills they will need to become proficient readers by the end of third grade. Programs operated by school districts and public or private organizations, including private child-care providers, may apply for grants to fund literacy programs which use research-based curriculum and assessments.

The Early Childhood Educator Professional Development Program offers competitive grants to fund research-based professional development for educators working with children from low-income families in high-need communities. Grantees must be partnerships composed of at least one higher education institution, at least one public agency, and, if possible and not already included, at least one organization with experience in training early educators in the areas of behavior problems and/or child abuse. Funded activities include professional development to help early childhood educators apply recent research on child language and literacy development, and to work with children who have special needs, such as disabilities or limited English proficiency. Details, including the application form and abstracts of past awards, are available at the U.S. Department of Education's website: http://www.ed.gov/programs/eceducator/awards.html.

It is clear that NCLB offers both challenges and opportunities for early childhood educators. Managers of child development programs will be better prepared to meet the challenges and take advantage of the opportunities if they are well grounded in knowledge of child development, pedagogical research, and the complex issues involved in selecting, administering, and interpreting assessments of children's learning (Winter, 2005).

Core Competencies for Directors

This overview of trends in child development programs in the United States suggests a growing need for highly qualified managers who combine an awareness of broad demographic changes with the skills that enable their programs to respond to those changes. Historically, managers of child development programs have been promoted from the ranks of teachers, with little attention paid to the specific knowledge and competencies needed in their new role. Although the knowledge of developmentally appropriate practices is certainly essential to running a program for children, managers must know much more if they are to be successful. At least 14 states and the District of Columbia expect directors of child development programs to hold a credential attesting to their administrative competence (Rinker, 2001, November/December). Many of these programs are voluntary; however, the number of states requiring such a credential is increasing, with at least two states (North Carolina and Florida) offering graduated levels of credentialing. There is a push within the profession for a national credential (Culkin, 2000, pp. 13–15).

Various authors have tackled the job of enumerating and categorizing the skills and knowledge required by competent directors, and although each list varies slightly from the others, they all agree on certain basics or core competencies. (Table 1.1 compares several proposed lists of requirements for directors.)

Decisions, Decisions . . .

What skills and knowledge do you think are necessary for being an effective manager? Draw up your own list and compare it with those of your classmates.

The authors of this textbook propose the following slate:

1. **Reflective management based on personal and professional self-awareness.**
   Effective managers strive to know their own strengths and acknowledge their

weaknesses so that they can capitalize on the former and compensate for the latter. They have a strong commitment to ethical practice, and they are informed about issues that influence the early childhood profession as a whole. They continually reflect on what they learn through experience, as well as through formal study, and integrate both types of knowledge in their practice.

2. **Organizational management.** Child development programs are complex systems of interrelated parts. The manager's role is to make the parts work together smoothly. Child development programs are, in turn, part of the larger social system. Managers guide their programs' interactions with that system. They are not lawyers, but they must have a working knowledge of the many regulatory systems governing the operation of early childhood facilities: state licensing regulations, federal food program requirements, fire safety and sanitation codes, and laws governing fair employment practices are just a few examples. Perhaps more important, managers must have a sense of the reasons for the regulations and the ability to operate programs within those constraints.

3. **Fiscal management.** No program can survive unless its manager uses its financial resources wisely. This includes creating a realistic budget, monitoring expenses to align with the budget, and knowing when to make appropriate adjustments. Fiscal management also includes finding ways to increase resources, perhaps through fund-raising or grant writing. The other side of the coin, of course, is finding ways, such as buying supplies in bulk, to economize without sacrificing quality.

4. **Personnel management.** Child development facilities are labor-intensive operations. Personnel costs comprise the bulk of the expenditures, and it is important that these dollars be invested wisely. This means that managers must learn how to recruit and hire employees with the greatest potential. But their job doesn't end there. Retaining those employees is a constant challenge in a profession with an annual turnover rate of about 40 percent. In addition to attracting and keeping good employees, managers must monitor their performance, provide feedback as needed, terminate when necessary, and create a staff development plan to build on the talents those employees bring to the job.

5. **Human relations.** An essential component of the manager's role is establishing and maintaining productive relationships with a variety of stakeholders: governing board members, families of enrolled children, employees, and representatives of businesses or community agencies are only a few examples. In addition to the personnel functions described previously, managers must find ways to encourage teamwork and motivate their staff. This work requires a basic knowledge of group dynamics, communication styles, and conflict resolution techniques.

6. **Facilities management.** In addition to putting together a smoothly functioning team of teachers and support staff, the manager is responsible for creating the spaces that support the day-to-day work of that team. This means designing spaces that meet regulatory requirements, as well as professional standards, spaces that incorporate sound principles of child development and environmental psychology. It means implementing those designs by selecting the best equipment a program can afford and arranging it appropriately.

7. **Managing health and safety issues.** Keeping children safe and healthy is a fundamental requirement of any child development facility. The manager's job is to establish policies and procedures that accomplish this goal and then to see that they are carried out. Examples include establishing policies requiring each child entering the program to be fully immunized against communicable disease and teaching staff to follow safe diapering procedures. State and local regulations provide a framework for this task.

TABLE 1.1 *An overview of core knowledge and competencies for directors of child development programs identified by six sources with selected examples.*

State of North Carolina: Early Childhood Administration Credential (1998)	National Lewis University, Graduate Program in Early Childhood Administration Paula Jorde-Bloom (1999)	Bonnie and Roger Neugebauer (1998)
Leadership ■ Knowledge of community and professional resources ■ Self-assessment Program ■ Mission and goals ■ Family friendly practices Rules and Regulations ■ Creating policies and procedures to monitor compliance with licensing requirements ■ Planning to upgrade compliance status Financial Management ■ Budgeting ■ Fund-raising Staff and Organizational Management ■ Recruiting and hiring ■ Evaluation and professional development Public Relations and Community Outreach ■ Marketing ■ Publicity	Personal and Professional Self-Awareness ■ Tapping professional resources ■ Developing a management philosophy Legal and Fiscal Management ■ Budgeting ■ Fund-raising Staff Management and Human Relations ■ Recruiting and hiring ■ Evaluation and professional development Educational Programming ■ Child-centered, antibias curriculum ■ Inclusion and continuity of care Program Operations and Facilities Management ■ Creating spaces to meet needs of children and adults ■ Record keeping and risk management Family Support ■ Family-friendly practices ■ Appreciating diversity Marketing and Public Relations ■ Needs assessment and business plans ■ Publicity Leadership and Advocacy ■ Board relations ■ Evaluation and program improvement Oral and Written Communication ■ Correspondence ■ Presentations Technology ■ Selecting equipment and software ■ Using word-processing, graphics, spreadsheet, or e-mail	Leadership ■ Self-assessment and development ■ Advocacy Organizational Management ■ Business plans ■ Legal issues Financial Management ■ Budgeting and tracking money ■ Fund-raising Personnel Management ■ Policies ■ Recruiting, hiring, developing staff Program Development ■ Assessing quality ■ Working with parents Community Relations ■ Marketing ■ Publicity

Gwen Morgan (2000)	Nancy H. Brown and John P. Manning (2000)	Karen Hill-Scott (2000)
Ability to Plan and Implement Developmentally Appropriate Program for Children and Families ■ Knowledge of current research ■ Communication skills Ability to Develop and Maintain Effective Organization ■ Understand and comply with applicable regulations ■ Effective management philosophy Ability to Plan and Implement Administrative Systems to Carry Out Program's Mission, Goals, Objectives ■ Curriculum ■ Maintenance of physical facility Ability to Administer Program of Personnel Management and Staff Development ■ Hiring and supervision ■ Team building and staff development Ability to Foster Good Community Relations and Influence Policy ■ Knowledge of community resources and systems ■ Communication skills Ability to Maintain and Develop Physical Facility ■ Establishing procedures to monitor and maintain safety ■ Applying principles of early education and environmental psychology to space design Legal Knowledge ■ Child-care regulations ■ Labor laws Ability to Apply Financial Management Tools ■ Budgeting and tracking finances ■ Fund-raising	Knowledge of Others (Stakeholders) Knowledge About Organizations Knowledge About the External World (Community) Knowledge of Self (Reflective Knowledge)	Child Development and Curriculum Planning Staff Training Regulatory Compliance Developmentally Appropriate Practice Quality Control Systems Integration Operations and Efficiencies Corporate Liaison Interorganization Linkage Customer Service Planning and Forecasting Advocacy Human Resource Management Compensation Practices External Communications Internal Communications Financial Planning and Budgeting Evaluation and Accountability Technology Applications

8. **Managing food service.** Meeting children's nutritional needs is another fundamental requirement. State licensing authorities provide basic guidelines, and the U.S. Department of Agriculture spells out requirements for programs receiving federal food subsidies. Managers must make sure that menus comply with these standards and that food is handled in a safe and sanitary manner from the point of purchase to when it is served to the children. They must also think about how their program's meals reflect the cultures of the families they serve and what those meals contribute to the program's curriculum.

9. **Educational programming.** Because many managers arrive at their position after working as teachers in child development programs, this may be the area that feels most familiar and, therefore, comfortable for them. Nevertheless, managing a facility's educational program requires a broader perspective than that of a classroom teacher. It's one thing to carry out a particular curriculum yourself and another to create conditions that support others in doing that job. Managers need a working knowledge of the various curriculum models so that they can select and implement an appropriate choice. Developmentally appropriate assessment strategies are crucial, particularly in the light of the current emphasis on accountability reflected in legislation (the No Child Left Behind Act) and a growing movement to establish state standards for early childhood educational outcomes. The inclusion of children with disabilities and an antibias curriculum are both issues that concern managers.

10. **Family support.** A high-quality program for young children reflects the understanding that children do not exist in a vacuum. Serving children means serving families, and this requires an understanding of how family systems work and an appreciation for diverse parenting styles. It means establishing the type of open communication that helps the center form partnerships with parents. It means knowing enough about the community to help families access the resources needed to promote family wellness.

11. **Marketing and public relations.** No matter how high the quality of a particular program, it will not survive without continually enrolling new families. The manager develops a pool of potential clients by making sure that the community is aware of the program and, just as important, that it appreciates the program's high quality. (This may require educating the public about what constitutes high quality in children's programs.) Merely attracting potential clients is not sufficient, however. The program must offer services that meet the specific needs of its clients, and it is the manager's job to fine-tune this match.

12. **Assessment and evaluation.** The next step in the management process is to determine how well an organization has met its objectives. Then, of course, the cycle begins again, adjusting practices to meet objectives more effectively or setting new (perhaps higher) goals for the organization.

13. **Leadership and advocacy.** Finally, managers functioning at the highest level of professional development are able to see beyond the day-to-day concerns of keeping their facility afloat. They have a vision of where they want their organization to go and the ability to marshal all the resources at their command to attain that vision. They strive to influence spheres beyond their own organization, the profession at large, and the well-being of children in general.

Conclusion

The task of managing a child development center is complex and evolving. Child development programs must continually grow and change because families are defining and redefining what they need for their children. As a manager, you are on the front line of decision making that can be supportive of families. You can exercise leadership among your staff, among parents, and within your community and create a high-quality service that serves children in appropriate ways and helps them grow toward strong, skilled, and healthy citizens of the future.

This chapter has discussed population trends, such as family size and women's participation in the labor force, and government policies that impact child development services. Chapter 2 discusses the types of child development programs and the many forms of sponsorship supporting them. Chapter 3 reviews the theories that impact your work as a manager. Chapters 4 through 16 are each devoted to an exploration of one of the core competencies you need to succeed in the administrative role.

QUESTIONS FOR REVIEW

1. Define *management*. List the various aspects of management.
2. Define *child development center*.
3. Discuss the relationship between care and education in programs for young children.
4. Look at Figure 1.1. What information does a manager derive from this figure?
5. Look at Figure 1.2. What additional information does a manager gain from the figure?
6. Look at Table 1.1. What similarities or differences do you note between the various lists of administrative competencies? What competencies would you add?
7. What are the trends for incorporating infants and toddlers in early childhood programs?

PROFESSIONAL PORTFOLIO

Begin creating a professional portfolio (Campbell et al., 1997) to document your progress toward achieving the skills and knowledge you will need as an administrator of children's programs. In a large looseleaf notebook, label one divider for each of the competencies addressed in chapters 4 through 16 of this textbook.

Alternatively, your instructor may suggest different headings for each section of your portfolio, or you may live in a state where the licensing agency has established specific categories of portfolio assignments as requirements for a director's credential. Whatever labeling system you use to organize your portfolio, as you complete the assignments associated with each chapter select those that you feel best demonstrate your mastery of a particular competency and place them in the appropriate section. Create a cover sheet for each assignment that explains why you have included it and what you think it shows about your managerial abilities.

RESOURCES FOR FURTHER STUDY

Print

Chang, H. N., Muckelroy, A., & Pulido-Tobiassen, D. (1996). *Looking in, looking out: Redefining child care and early education in a diverse society.* San Francisco: California Tomorrow.

Culkin, M. L. (Ed.). (2000). *Managing quality in young children's programs: The leader's role.* New York: Teachers College Press.

Wolery, R. A., & Odom, S. L. (2000). *An administrator's guide to preschool inclusion.* Chapel Hill, NC: Frank Porter Graham Child Development Center.

Internet

National Child Care Information Center

http://nccic.org

National Child Care Information Center is a service of the Child Care Bureau, which describes itself as a "national clearinghouse and technical assistance center that links parents, providers, policy-makers, researchers, and the public to early care and education information. Click on "popular topics" to access organizations, resources, and publications (many in PDF format) on topics such as child-care arrangements, child care as a business, federal policy, licensing regulations, and tiered quality strategies.

Kids Count

http://www.aecf.org/kidscount

Kids Count is a project of the Annie E. Casey Foundation, which gathers information on several measures of child well-being at the local, state, and national levels in an annual census, available in hard copy and PDF format. Findings are also presented in searchable online databases as well as in tailored summaries addressing specific ethnic or demographic populations (e.g., newborns, teen parents, Southwest border residents).

Federal Interagency Forum

http://www.childstats.gov

The Federal Interagency Forum on Child and Family Statistics produces the annual federal monitoring report, *America's Children: Key National Indicators of Well-Being.*

2

Types of Child Development Programs

The previous chapter discussed the broad context within which the field of early care and education is growing and changing. You read about trends within society and the profession that will shape your career as a manager of child development programs. This chapter narrows the focus just a little to examine the universe of child development programs.

This universe is complex. It seems that no matter what classification scheme is used, few programs fit neatly into a single category. Distinctions based on the age of children served don't work for long: infant–toddler, preschool, and school-age programs often exist under a single roof. The hours of operation is another way of distinguishing programs. There are training conferences, professional organizations, and "how-to" articles targeting child development personnel in half-day, full-day, and after-school programs, suggesting that each type has its own set of needs and interests. A common distinction is made between for-profit and nonprofit programs based on the corporate status of the organization. The authors have chosen to categorize child development programs in two ways. We use the term *type* to capture a program's central mission, often a direct outgrowth of its historical roots. The term *sponsorship* refers to financial resources and the governance structure associated with that revenue. As you will see, there is a great deal of overlap between these categories.

Five Types of Child Development Programs

What do all types of child development centers have in common? First, they serve young children. Second, the children are served outside their homes less than 24 hours a day. Third, the centers must be managed by an appropriate set of principles to protect the children and deliver services of the quality promised.

Child development centers are organized as part of the public social service system, the education system, the philanthropic system, and the business system. The breadth and depth of service varies considerably among the centers, and such philosophical differences guide management decisions. Though the breadth and depth of programs differs, the principles of managing the centers remain substantially the same. Child development centers offer families child-care and education services that they need and want for their young children, services that will enhance life for both children and parents. Generally speaking, the various philosophies have as common elements a stress on nurturing and educating young children and on accepting their individual differences in development. Parents selecting a program for their child may find five basic program types available. Depending on their primary needs and interests, parents may choose one rather than others. The six basic program types are as follows:

1. Investment in human capital
2. A consumer service for working parents
3. Supplement to care and education provided by families
4. Remedial or compensatory service
5. Research and teacher preparation

The distinctions between program **types** represent a different concept than program **sponsorship,** though the two ideas are often entangled. Sponsorship refers to the funding source and governance of organizations, while program type refers to the central mission or purpose of the organization. Each type of program described here can be funded in a variety of ways, and a program funded in any particular manner can function in ways that could place it in more than one of these categories. For example, programs to supplement care provided by families are funded through parent fees, through state or federal government subsidies, through corporate sponsorship, or (most likely) through some combination of these and other resources. A single program, such as a family child-care home, might originate as a supplement to family care (Type 3), aiming simply to keep children safe and happy while their parents work. The same family child-care provider might enter into a collaboration with a local agency serving children with disabilities and enroll one or more children whose placement in inclusive care is part of their Individualized Family Service Plan. The family child-care home thus blends aspects of a Type 4 program as well (offering remedial or compensatory service). Of course, any facility that provides a developmentally appropriate program is fulfilling the function of investing in human capital (Type 1).

Although it is tempting to assert that these program types are merging into a single concept of developmentally appropriate practices that apply to all programs, the reality is that the distinctions can affect the level of services provided, families' perceptions of a program, and the way program managers and staff envision their mission. Families who pay for nursery school as a consumer service may expect—and be willing to pay for—more "frills" than families who purchase 8 or 10 hours of supplemental care each day while the parents are at work. Families in subsidized programs, whose children are deemed at risk for school failure, are probably more likely to accept testing and evaluation of their children as part of the package than are families who have elected to pay either for an enriching nursery school program or full-day child care while they pursue careers. Staff members who view their job as "just babysitting" are likely to feel less professional, and to interact differently with children, than staff members who see themselves as partnering with parents to foster a child's optimum development.

Type 1: Investment in Human Capital

Skills, talents, knowledge, and abilities are a person's **human capital.** When enrolling a child in a child development center with the objective of enhancing the child's abilities or human capital, parents expect that this investment will pay off later in terms of better performance in school and better job performance beyond school. It is likely that most public school programs for young children (kindergartens or pre-K) have been supported because of a belief that an investment in children's education has future payoffs.

Project Head Start, which was initiated by the U.S. government in 1965, is an example of such an investment in children's human capital. Head Start was designed for disadvantaged children as part of President Lyndon Johnson's War on Poverty. The emphasis on giving young children a "head start" arose when it was observed that children of the poor had more difficulties with later school performance than more advantaged children—particularly when many of the advantaged children had had a preprimary school experience or had parents who provided many types of intellectual stimulation. The argument for Project Head Start was that an earlier start in preprimary school with more educationally oriented programs would decrease the number of later school dropouts and also decrease the number of children entering special education. Such a desirable outcome would indicate a wise investment.

Studies of the outcomes of Head Start indicated that the hopes of the early planners did materialize (Ryan, 1974). Gains for parents and older siblings of Head Start children also resulted (Lazar et al., 1982; McKey et al., 1985). An analysis of studies conducted over time has found that low-income children with preprimary experience were less likely to be held back a grade or placed in special education than children from similar backgrounds with no early education. Managers will find this information helpful in gaining support for their programs from public agencies, private organizations, parents, and the general public.

Major—and controversial—changes to Head Start were introduced in 2003. First, as part of Head Start's reauthorization in 2003, the president proposed channeling funds to states, rather than to community agencies. Advocates fear that such a shift will weaken the program, arguing that states faced with mounting budget deficits will use the funds for their own preschool initiatives, which are less comprehensive and are not bound by the quality assurances that have governed Head Start throughout the program's history (Children's Defense Fund, 2005b). Also, beginning in the fall of 2003 all 4- and 5-year-olds in Head Start are tested twice a year, using the National Reporting System (NRS), which consists of subtests that measure English-language competence, receptive vocabulary, knowledge of letter names, and mathematics. The test has been severely criticized by prominent early educators as biased and developmentally inappropriate (e.g., Meisels & Atkins-Burnett, 2004). Advocates argue that the emphasis on narrow academic goals to the exclusion of social and emotional concerns will shift Head Start's focus from its holistic approach to development that has been its hallmark since its inception and, because it runs counter to what we know about how children learn best, will be counterproductive in the long run (Raver & Zigler, 2004).

Type 2: A Supplement to Care and Education Provided by Families

Supplemental care extends the strengths and talents that parents have for caring for and educating their children. We contend that all early childhood education and care should be considered a support service for families. Supplemental care arrangements support parents by nurturing and educating their children in the hours during the day when they must be at work or school or when they are otherwise unable to provide such care themselves. If child-care providers truly understand that they simply provide the nurturing that parents would provide for their children if the parents were available, they will make every effort to serve as a support for each family system. This means they must highly value parent-child bonding and attachment and work to strengthen, never to undermine, these crucial emotional relationships. In addition to filling in during parents' absence, sensitive child-care providers can provide information, guidance, and emotional support to enhance parents' ability to fulfill their role. Supplemental care must never become a substitute for parental nurturing and educating.

FIGURE 2.1   *Child-care arrangements for children ages 0–4 with employed mothers, 2002*

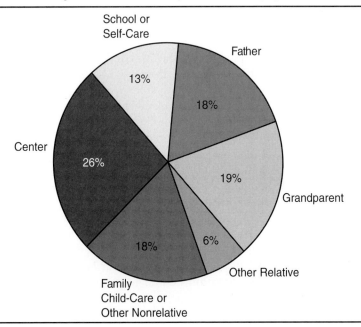

Source: America's Children: Key National Indicators of Well-Being 2005, Appendix A, Table POP8.B. Retrieved 12/2/05 from http://childstats.ed.gov/americaschildren/xls/POP8b.xls

As indicated in an earlier discussion, the need for supplemental care for children has grown with the increasing participation of women in the workforce over the past several decades. Between 1977 and 1985, the proportion of children under 5 in organized care facilities nearly doubled, going from 13 percent to 23 percent; it has remained at or near that percentage since 1985. Figure 2.1 shows the enrollment of children ages 0–4 in child-care programs.

Figure 2.2 shows the before and after school care arrangements for children in kindergarten through 3rd grade. These children were sometimes called **latchkey children** because of the keys to their houses that they carry on a string around their necks and use to let themselves into their empty homes. Many accounts of fires and other mishaps during a child's self-care periods have alerted the country to the problems resulting from children having several hours a day alone at home. Programs are increasing for the before- and after-school care and summer care of elementary-age children.

Child-care centers developed in the United States and Europe during the early 1800s to protect children while their mothers and siblings worked in factories. These were primarily custodial situations limited to physical care. Child-care centers continued to have a second-class status compared with programs designated as educational. In recent years, this distinction has faded as programs have made a concerted effort to incorporate an appropriate educational component. Many factors have contributed to this development: media attention to recent research findings on brain development in the early years; rising expectations of families, particularly educated professionals, who rely on child care; and state licensing regulations designed to improve the quality of full-day care.

Children can spend as much as 10 hours a day and 260–300 days per year in child care, compared with about 3 hours for 180 days in kindergartens or nursery school programs. Certainly children in the longer-day settings need enriching and educational experiences as much as or more than their counterparts in the partial-day programs.

FIGURE 2.2 *Before and after school child-care arrangements for children kindergarten through 3rd grade, 2001*

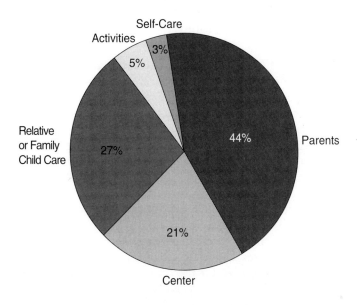

Source: America's Children: Key National Indicators of Well-Being 2005, Appendix A, Table POP8.C. Retrieved 12/2/05 from http://childstats.ed.gov/americaschildren/pdf/ac2005/appendixa.pdf

While many countries have concluded that child care with appropriate educational components is a social utility essential for improving the well-being of society as a whole (Kamerman & Kahn, 1988), the United States has not yet reached such a conclusion. The establishment of 4C (community coordinated child care) organizations, the development of the CDA (child development associate) certificate for child-care workers, and federal initiatives for more tax support for increased and improved child-care services may be steps toward our country's acknowledgment that child care and early education are inextricably intertwined (Brauner et al., 2004).

As a supplemental service to families, child-care centers continually evolve ways to respond to families' needs, including extended hours of operation to accommodate second- and third-shift workers; drop-in, irregular, or half-day enrollment for families that don't need full-day care; and after-school, summer and back-up (e.g., snow-day) care for school-age children. Accommodating families' needs for care when their children are mildly ill is another example of such efforts.

Care for Mildly Ill Children.   In the typical half-day nursery school of many years ago, a child with even a minor illness was routinely required to stay home. Full-day programs adopted the same policies even though this meant financial hardship and a threat to the livelihood of parents who had to stay home from work when their children were sick. In the 1980s, this pressure created a demand for child development centers to establish facilities for the care of mildly ill children. Some communities created entire centers for this specific purpose. The American Public Health Association and the American Academy of Pediatrics (APHA and AAP) have established standards for this type of care (2002). (The health and safety needs of children are further discussed in chapter 10.)

The Family and Medical Leave Act of 1993 may decrease the need for this type of care and also affect infant care. Under this act, a worker may take up to 12 weeks per year, without pay but with job protection and continued insurance benefits, to care for a sick child, a newborn, or a newly adopted baby (Hildebrand et al., 2000).

Family Child-Care Homes.   Family child care is another form of supplemental care popular with parents. Often, the family child-care home is in the neighborhood where the family lives, making it a convenient option. Some parents prefer family child care because it is provided in a smaller, more homelike setting and offers a closer match to the values and caregiving style experienced by the child at home.

Family child-care providers as a group are working toward a more professional status through affiliation with organizations such as the National Association for the Education of Young Children. Frequently, people who begin by providing child care in their homes move on to become managers of centers as their business grows. Some center managers work out cooperative arrangements with nearby family child-care providers to pool resources and purchase supplies in bulk or refer families to another member of the group when needed services are beyond the scope of a particular provider. For example, a center that is licensed to care for children ages 2.5–5 might develop a pool of nearby family child-care providers to care for younger siblings. Or the center might make an arrangement for certain family providers to accept those mildly ill children whose parents are unable to keep them at home. Such cooperation is appropriate and desirable.

Type 3: A Remedial or Compensatory Service

Certain centers may enroll children to remediate or compensate for particular difficulties the child has. These programs have their historical roots in the special schools for blind, deaf, or physically handicapped children that originated in the 19th century (Bailey & Wolery, 1984), and in the programs for economically disadvantaged children that grew out of the War on Poverty in the 1960s. A more recent trend is toward the inclusion of children with disabilities in programs for children who are developing typically. This trend is an outgrowth of several federal laws, beginning with PL 90-538 of 1968, which set the stage by establishing the Early Education Program for Children with Disabilities and provides funding for model programs from which we can learn more about serving young children with disabilities and their families (Wolery & Wilbers, 1994, p. 18). Six years later, PL 93-644 (1974) reserved 10 percent of available spaces in Head Start programs for children with disabilities. In 1975, PL 94-142, the Education for All Handicapped Children Act, established the right to a free public education for children with disabilities from age 3 to 21 and mandated the use of an Individualized Education Program (IEP).

States were encouraged to make plans for extending the scope of services to include children from birth to age 5 when PL 98-199 (1983) provided funding for this purpose. In 1986, PL 99-457 instituted the Individualized Family Service Plan (IFSP) for infants and toddlers with, or at risk of developing, disabilities, and it offered states incentives to provide services for them. In 1990, PL 101-576, the Individuals with Disabilities

High-quality child development programs serve all children—those with and those without disabilities.

Education Act (IDEA), reauthorized PL 94-142 and further extended services by adding autism and traumatic brain injury to the list of recognized disabilities. When the law was reauthorized as PL 108-466, the Individuals with Disabilities Education Improvement Act of 2004, it extended services to homeless children and their families as well as children who are wards of the state. Other changes included provisions requiring states to ensure that service providers are appropriately qualified and that intervention methods are based on peer-reviewed scientific research.

The Americans with Disabilities Act, PL 101-336 (1990), prohibits discrimination against individuals with disabilities and requires that public and private services (including child development facilities) make reasonable accommodations to provide equal access to children with disabilities (Wolery & Wilbers, 1994, pp. 18–19). As a result of this legislation, children with typical as well as atypical patterns of development are being served together in the same child development programs, with distinct advantages resulting for both. The child with a disability acquires a group of peers to emulate and the satisfaction of play and friendship as rewards for progress. The children without disabilities learn social skills and compassion.

As the movement toward inclusion gains momentum, many centers formerly reserved for children with disabilities are now actively recruiting children without disabilities to be included in those settings. Problems with funding arise, however, because priorities in this country designate subsidies for early education for only those children with specific disabilities or those determined to be at risk for developmental delays.

Once again, this focus of resources on deficits is in contrast to European countries, such as France and Italy, where a belief in the "universal need" for high-quality care and family support services prevails, with the result that "priority may be given to children or parents with special needs, but the programs are not designed for this purpose or limited to this population" (Kamerman & Kahn, 1994, p. 76).

Type 4: Research and Teacher Preparation

Some centers are specifically organized to provide a group or groups of children for research in child development, child psychology, and early childhood education. At times, these centers are also combined with teacher preparation programs to give university students an opportunity to learn the various skills necessary to interact with young children. Although these centers give services to the children and families involved, the primary objectives are research and teacher preparation. This distinction can have several implications, creating both advantages and disadvantages for families served (McBride & Hicks, 1999). For example, programs designed to support research might not admit children on a first-come, first-served basis, but rather establish enrollment criteria to ensure equal numbers of boys and girls. Families served by programs whose primary aim is teacher preparation benefit from the level of quality created as these programs strive to model best practices for their teachers-in-training. At the same time, the staff in these programs largely comprises student teachers who possess varying degrees of skill and who come and go with each semester. In addition to these staff fluctuations, families must often accept the inconvenience of locating alternate care when the programs close during breaks in the academic schedule. As funding sources tighten or university

University lab programs provide opportunities for young men and women to gain experience working with children.

objectives change, these centers often face challenges to their continued existence (Freeman & Brown, 1999).

Type 5: A Consumer Service

Because it is often purchased by families, child care is sometimes perceived (by families, by providers, and by the public at large) as a consumer service. This view is problematic for many reasons, but largely because it oversimplifies a very complex phenomenon. Who is the consumer, for example? The parent who pays, or the child who receives care? What exactly is purchased? Is it merely a certain number of hours of freedom from responsibilities for tending to a child's safety and well-being? Certainly that may be what some providers intend to deliver and what some families hope to purchase, but child care involves much more, and high-quality child care yields much more. Thus we would argue that even child care viewed as a consumer service is likely to be an investment in human capital and a service to families.

For example, early private nursery schools and kindergartens were used by parents as a service that was "nice to have if one could afford it." Private early childhood programs were the province of the middle and upper classes, and parents took pride in having a child enrolled in a prestigious school. Occasionally parents were required to reserve a place for their child during infancy to be assured of a space when the child was ready at age 3 or 4.

Parent cooperative nursery schools, which grew out of parents' desire to access a nursery school experience for their children at a price they could afford, are a good example of how a consumer service can also fit into other categories of child care. Parents pooled their money and hired a professional teacher. All other labor was provided by parents.

The middle-class families that were served by co-ops were future oriented and upwardly mobile. Many parents likely saw this schooling as an investment in their children's future educational success, suggesting an obvious overlap with Type 1 programs. Parents also enjoyed and learned from their involvement in the co-op classroom and on governing boards. They liked the social group of friends they built around the co-op experience. Thus, co-ops served a valuable function as a supplement to family care and as part of a support system in highly mobile communities where grandparents or other support groups were unavailable to the family.

The persistent view of child care as a privately purchased consumer good, distinct from education, which is recognized as a social good, is one of the barriers to creating a system of child care that is high quality, affordable, and widely accessible (Brauner et al., 2004).

Decisions, Decisions . . .

What experience have you had with any of the types of child development programs? Which type, or combination of types, seems most ideal to you? Why?

Three Ways of Financing Child Development Programs

You have read how child development programs can be classified as one or more of five distinct types, based on their central purpose or objectives. Now, we turn our attention to the ways that programs are funded. Whatever a program's purpose, it cannot be accomplished without financial resources to pay for staff, rent, utilities, equipment, and supplies. The source of those dollars influences not only how well a program is able to fulfill its mission, but often the nature of that mission as well. Basically, child development services can be funded in three ways, each of which spreads the cost over a successively wider base. (1) The narrowest base of support occurs when the cost is entirely shouldered by the individual families who are direct consumers of the services. (2) The base of support widens somewhat when costs are shared by social agencies that sponsor programs for philanthropic reasons or by corporations with vested interests in doing so. (3) Finally, costs are spread across society as a whole when tax-supported initiatives at local, state, and federal levels fund programs. This last scenario is analogous to the system of funding public education for children over 5 years of age. Everyone who pays taxes helps pay for public schools, not just the parents with children in those schools, because everyone in a democratic society benefits from having a well-educated population.

In reality, many programs are funded by a combination of methods. Centers relying on parent fees for the bulk of their budget might supplement those fees by applying for grants from private foundations or by participating in the government-sponsored Child Care Food Program.

Lally (2005) argues that the various funding methods reflect distinct views of society's responsibility and children's rights. He uses the term *economic rationalism* to characterize the view that parents bear sole responsibility for their children and, thus, for providing substitute care when they are unavailable. Another view, *instrumentalism*, holds that a society acts in its own best interest when it funds child care programs to counter the likelihood that abused or poor children will grow up to become burdens on society. According to Lally, neither approach recognizes children as citizens with rights in the present: "the right to be, the right to become, the right to enjoy, and the right to choose" (p. 45). This view, which Lally terms a *social enrichment* perspective, underlies the generous child-care policies in Europe, Australia, and New Zealand.

Family Payments for Child Care

It may seem logical that child development programs derive their financial support by charging families a fee for the service, just as any other business charges its customers. A restaurant, for example, sets its prices for meals by calculating the costs of the food, salaries for kitchen and waitstaff, and overhead such as rent, utilities, laundry, and cleaning costs. If there is a deficit, the restaurant either raises the prices for its meals or lowers expenses, perhaps cutting corners on laundry costs by substituting paper napkins for table linens. Either option risks driving away customers, whether those who object to higher prices or those who prefer their filet mignon served on fine china and damask tablecloths. In the end, though, the restaurant's income must exceed its expenses or the business will founder.

Making ends meet in a child development center can be more difficult. One reason is that child care is a labor intensive operation, meaning that staff salaries comprise the bulk of any program's expenses. Although a restaurant might economize by finding a less expensive source of vegetables, for example, a child development program can hardly cut down on staffing costs when the average child-care worker already earns less than $16,000 per year.

Child care is expensive, and many families are already devoting substantial portions of their annual income to it. In 1999, for example, average weekly child care costs ranged from $64 for families with incomes less than $1,500 per month to $89 for families with incomes of $4,500 and over. While low-income families appear to pay less for care, in reality they must devote a proportion of their monthly income almost six times greater than that paid by those with higher incomes. See Figure 2.3. In many urban areas, the average annual cost of care for a 4-year-old child is higher than (sometimes even double!) the cost of college tuition (Children's Defense Fund, 2001, pp. 50–51). It must be noted, however, that tuition

FIGURE 2.3 *Percentage of monthly income spent on child care by employed mothers of children under 14, Spring 1999*

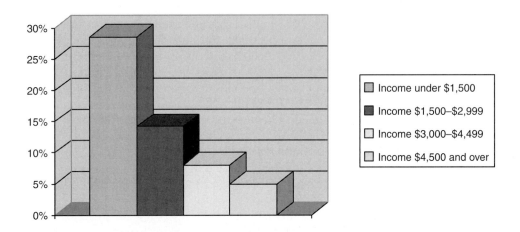

Legend:
- Income under $1,500
- Income $1,500–$2,999
- Income $3,000–$4,499
- Income $4,500 and over

Source: U.S. Census Bureau (2003). Who's Minding the Kids? Child Care Arrangements, Spring 1999. Detailed Tables (PPL-168). Retrieved from http://www.census.gov/population/www/socdemo/child/ppl-168.html

and fees account for less than one-fourth of the total cost of college. State tax dollars, grants, endowments, and other sources comprise the bulk of revenue for public higher education. In contrast, fees paid by families comprise nearly two-thirds of the revenue stream for early care and education nationwide (Child Care Action Campaign, 2001).

Decisions, Decisions . . .

What do you think child-care personnel should earn? Why? How much do you think families should pay for child care? As a manager of a child development center, how might you go about balancing these two factors?

Thus, it is nearly impossible for child development programs to charge fees high enough to support living wages for their staff. This situation is called the child-care "trilemma." They are caught between three equally desirable and complexly interrelated, but competing or mutually exclusive, goals: program quality, fair compensation, and affordability. If they charge fees that parents can afford, they are unable to pay adequate salaries. If they keep salaries low, they are unable to attract highly qualified employees—or keep them when they do—and program quality suffers. Yet, raising rates to reflect the true cost of high quality places that quality outside the reach of most families. Even programs that rely on parent fees for the bulk of their income are likely to supplement that revenue with various fund-raising activities. The unspoken truth is that their underpaid employees are subsidizing the program with their own labor. Many early childhood professionals and child advocates have concluded that high-quality child care will be impossible to achieve unless the costs are spread beyond families to a wider segment of society.

Sponsored Programs

Recognizing a need for services for young children, and the fact that families—particularly poor families—are unable to shoulder the full cost of such services, religious and civic organizations have a long history of either providing or underwriting the costs of programs (Rose, 1999). In fact, since the 1830s, charitable institutions have provided most of the center-based child care in the United States (Neugebauer, 2000b, p. 6). While these organizations may have had philanthropic motives, business organizations also have found reasons to sponsor programs for children. Maria Montessori, a renowned innovator in early childhood education, began her work in Rome in 1907 when a group of Roman entrepreneurs hired her to keep children from vandalizing the housing developments they were attempting to renovate. Her Casa dei Bambini (Children's House) eventually became the model for the thousands of schools around the world that bear her name today (Goffin & Wilson, 2001, pp. 38–45). Enlightened corporations have continued to recognize that sponsoring child-care initiatives has benefits for the corporation, as well as for the children and families served.

Church-Sponsored or Faith-Based Programs.   Between 1997 and 2000, the number of child-care programs housed in churches increased by 26 percent, a growth rate outpacing that of centers operated by for-profit chains (14 percent), as well as those operated by public schools (20 percent) (Neugebauer, 2000a, p. 6). With the implementation of federal policies to encourage and fund faith-based initiatives, these numbers are likely to grow even more. Although exempted from licensing regulations by some states, religiously affiliated programs are encouraged to become licensed voluntarily in order to demonstrate their adherence to the external standards, to reassure parents, and to access higher reimbursement rates (Child Care Bureau, n.d.).

Over the last two decades, church-sponsored initiatives have begun to coalesce at the national level with the creation of the Ecumenical Child Care Network. This organization recognizes high-quality church-sponsored programs and supports that quality through its conferences and publications. Neugebauer (2000b) cites four major trends among programs affiliated with churches: (a) Denominations are paying more attention to child-care services, assigning specific individuals or divisions to the issue and taking steps to increase both the supply and quality of services. (b) Although there is variation among denominations, church-affiliated programs as a whole are increasing more rapidly than other sectors of the child-care industry, and this phenomenon is even more pronounced outside the United States. (c) Churches are becoming more directly involved with running the child-care programs that they sponsor. (d) Perhaps as a consequence of the increased interest and involvement at the national level of the various denominations, more church-sponsored programs are citing "spiritual development" as a goal and many publish curriculum materials with religious themes (Neugebauer, 2000b, pp. 18–20).

Recent federal initiatives have given churches and religious organizations new access to government resources. In January 2001, President George W. Bush established a White House Office of Faith-Based and Community Initiatives to expand and encourage such programs. The Center for Faith-Based and Community Initiatives within the U.S. Department of Health and Human Services states that its mission is to "create an environment within HHS that welcomes the participation of faith-based and community-based organizations as valued and essential partners with the Department in assisting Americans in need" (www.acf.hhs.gov).

Corporate Support for Child Care.   Employer-supported child care is not a new phenomenon. An early venture into industry-connected child care occurred during World War II when a federal law, the Lanham Act, financed centers to provide child care for children of women needed in the war industries. These were known by many as the Lanham Act Nursery Schools. Advisers to the government for these schools were people prominent in the field. Many centers had state-of-the-art facilities, equipment, and programs. After the war, most of these centers were abandoned, though their influence continues to be felt. In a survey conducted to mark the turn of the century, prominent leaders in early childhood education noted that the creation of these centers marked society's new acceptance of women working outside the home. The training materials they produced are still used in some centers (Neugebauer, 2000d, pp. 35–36).

Employer-supported child-care initiatives blossomed again in the 1970s and 1980s when women born during the Baby Boom years entered the workforce in great numbers. Many programs were the result of collaboration between employee unions and employers, including those in the private sector (e.g., the automobile and garment industries), as well as public sector employers at local, state, and federal levels (Hildebrand, 1993, pp. 221–224). These accomplishments signaled an emerging and irreversible trend toward (1) the acknowledgment of child care as a core, rather than a peripheral, concern of employers as well as employees; (2) the acceptance of child care as a legitimate matter for negotiation at the bargaining table and for cooperative problem solving outside formal collective bargaining; and (3) the realization that the invention of constructive solutions can be beneficial to management as well as labor, assisting employers to recruit and retain a stable and productive workforce, while aiding unions to be responsive to their needs.

The trend for businesses to enter the child-care arena for their employees' children increased by 2,000 percent from 1978 to 1988, going from 105 to 2,500 centers and programs (U.S. Department of Labor, 1988, p. 125). Still, employer-supported facilities constituted only 3 percent of all child-care centers in 1998 (Hill-Scott, 2000, p. 208), and the increase in their number has leveled off in recent years, with 4 percent growth in 2002 and 2003, followed by zero growth in 2004. Among the largest employers providing child care is the U.S. government with initiatives for federal employees and for military families (Neugebauer, 2005a, p. 66–68).

In addition to providing on-site centers, employer support for families' child-care needs can include contracting with existing programs to purchase child-care "slots" for employees, providing or contracting for child-care referral services, and offering options such as flexible scheduling or job sharing. Most common, and least costly for the employer, is the "flexible spending account," which allows employees to set aside pretax dollars to cover child-care expenses. (This is classified more properly as a combination of family payment and public support. On the one hand, families are spending their own dollars to pay for care; on the other, they are enjoying a tax savings, the true cost of which is actually spread among all taxpayers.)

At the next level, employers might provide assistance in the form of child-care resource and referral services that help parents locate and evaluate the quality of child-care facilities. Figure 2.4 shows that in 2000, employees in organizations with 5,000 or more employees were 10 times more likely to have this option available than those in establishments with fewer than 100 workers (U.S. Department of Labor, 2000, December 28).

At a deeper level of involvement, employers provide child-care assistance in one of three ways: (1) They pay, or reimburse families, for all or part of the cost of care, wherever that care is provided; (2) they operate a child-care facility at the work site; or (3) they manage a facility in another location, either alone or in collaboration with other employers. According to the Bureau of Labor Statistics, which has been tracking the numbers since 1990, employers providing these types of support are a distinct minority. Just as the case with resource and referral services, employees in larger establishments are more likely to have access to these benefits than those in smaller organizations, with employees of state and local governments falling in between (U.S. Department of Labor, 1998, 2000). Figure 2.5 illustrates this pattern. Furthermore, both large and small businesses are more likely to extend these benefits to employees in professional or technical jobs than to those in clerical, sales, or blue-collar positions (U.S. Department of Labor, 1999, April and September).

FIGURE 2.4 *Worker access to child-care resource and referral services*

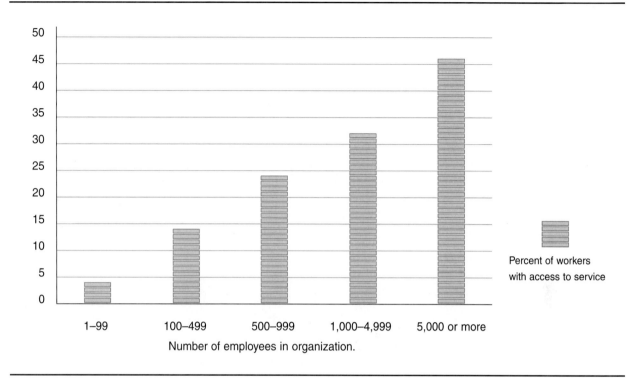

Percent of workers with access to service

Number of employees in organization.

Source: U.S. Department of Labor, Bureau of Labor Statistics, 2000.

The expansion of employer-supported child-care programs has tapered off considerably (Neugebauer, 2005a). Nevertheless, even though such programs are few in actual number, their high visibility and connections to the influential world of business means that their potential impact on the field as a whole is substantial. Hill-Scott, for example, sees these programs as an important factor in the movement toward establishing a credential for administrator (2000, pp. 208–209). Thus, whether or not you find yourself working in a corporate-sponsored program, you will want to keep an eye on this phenomenon, which will surely influence your management career.

Why, some might ask, should employers become involved in the child-care arena? There are several reasons. First, in a tight labor market it makes sense for employers to try to attract the widest possible pool of highly qualified potential applicants. This means that they must attract women as well as men and, although the picture is changing somewhat, child care is still largely viewed as a woman's issue. In addition, today's workforce increasingly expects management to show more concern for family life by providing child care and maternity and paternity leaves. In addition to the recruiting edge described above, employers receive several benefits from providing help with child care, according to the Department of Labor (1988, pp. 128–130).

Retention. Keeping key employees, especially high-level administrators, scientists, women, and minorities, is a goal of many employers. In studies, employees stated that they would not move because of the child-care center for their child.

Public Relations. Companies find that concern for employees' families is good for their public image. The child-care provisions offered by certain industries have attracted national media attention.

FIGURE 2.5   *Percentage of employees with access to child-care benefits in the private and public sectors*

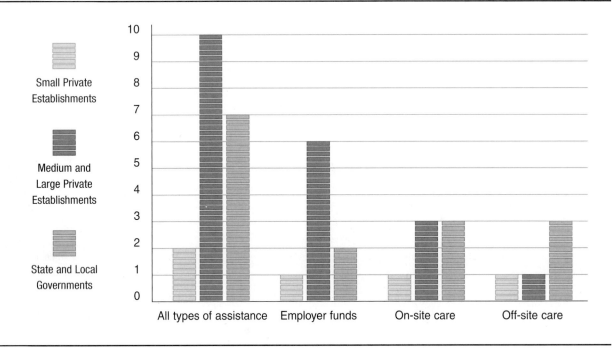

Source: U.S. Department of Labor, Bureau of Labor Statistics (1999, April). *Employee benefits in small private establishments, 1996,* Bulletin 2507 (1999, September). *Employee benefits in medium and large private establishments, 1997.* Bulletin 2517 (2000, December). *Employee benefits in state and local governments, 1998.* Bulletin 2531. (Note: Data from the annual Employee Benefits Survey may be accessed at http://www.bls.gov/ncs/ebs/home.htm.)

Productivity.   A 2005 study by the Iowa State University Extension, Center for Family Policy, cited productivity of both the current and future workforce as one of the economic benefits of high-quality child care (Larson et al., 2005). In the short term, the stress of worrying about unsatisfactory child care arrangements or searching for replacements siphons parents' energy and attention from the workplace. In the long term, the children who languish in poor-quality care are far less likely to develop the emotional and cognitive qualities that will make them desirable employees in the future. In other words, employers are acting in their own interest when they help their employees access high-quality child care.

Turnover.   Once employees are recruited and specifically trained for the company's work, these employees have received a considerable investment of the company's time and money. The retention of such employees makes sense to dollar-conscious employers.

Absenteeism.   Absenteeism and tardiness have been reduced by the child-care assistance programs. On-site child care, sick-child care, and other provisions are very helpful to working parents. When before- and after-school services are unavailable, parents have to arrange for their children to be cared for by an older sibling or a neighbor, or they may be forced to allow the children to stay home alone. The period from 3 p.m. to 6 p.m. has been recognized as the most worrisome to parents; that is, when their children are at home alone. Suitable child-care programs have considerably reduced workers' absence from the job.

Morale. Employers and employees alike report improved morale as the workplace becomes more friendly to parents and their children. Studies show that when child-care arrangements break down, workers become stressed in ways that affect their health and work. Both men and women feel this stress; however, men ranked a nonsupportive supervisor more seriously than they ranked child-care worries.

In his 14th annual status report on employer child care, Neugebauer (2005a) identified several trends in employer support for child care, including consolidation of major providers, increased interest in providing services tailored to local requirements of a workforce that is distributed nationwide, and flexibility to meet changing family needs such as support for telecommuters and emergency back-up care.

Decisions, Decisions . . .

Form a team with two or three classmates and prepare a proposal to convince a large employer in your community to provide one or more services that will help employees with child-care needs. Be sure to consider the benefits to the employer as well as to the employee, and any costs to the employer. Present your arguments to your classmates.

College- and University-Sponsored Child Care.   Community and 4-year colleges, technical schools, and universities are in the child-care business to varying degrees. Most serve both students' and employees' children and have a sliding-fee scale to adjust for income differences. Some of the programs are especially designed to help maintain student enrollments. Some are used by state social service programs to provide care for children of parents who are receiving state assistance to participate in training programs that will help the parents become financially independent. The programs range from full-day child care to drop-in care during the daytime or evening while the student parents attend a class. Many of the programs operate with grants from the college for the building and its maintenance. Other grants help with subsidies for low-income students.

Hospital-Sponsored Child Care.   Hospital and medical school complexes typically have a child-care center for their staff and students. Hospital centers in some localities have responded to the flextime options for employees by extending the permitted hours a child can remain in child care. Some have instituted sick-child care, which taps their medical and nursing expertise. Another type of program is a playroom or "child life program" maintained by some medical facilities to serve children and their siblings while they await treatment or the results of tests.

Military Child Care.   The U.S. military has become a major component of the employer-sponsored child care field with on-site care at bases around the world, serving nearly 200,000 children in 900 centers and 9,000 family child-care homes, in more than 300 locations. The centers are financed by a combination of government support and parent fees. An effort was started in 1989 to increase the quality of the centers (Neugebauer, 2005, p. 31). The Caregiver Personnel Pay Plan offers employees salary increases as they obtain additional training and demonstrate competence. Child-care workers are, therefore, treated more like other military workers and are less dependent on what parents can afford to pay for their compensation. Not surprisingly, these efforts have greatly reduced staff turnover at the centers (Bellm et al., 1994).

Government Support for Child Care

As mentioned earlier, tax credits for working families represent one way that the government subsidizes the cost of child care, in this case by foregoing a certain amount of revenue. More direct forms of government financial backing for child development programs come through the Child Care and Development Fund (CCDF). The Child Care and Development Block Grant of 1990 authorized $750 million for this purpose in fiscal year (FY) 1991. This amount has increased over the years, reaching $4.8 billion in FY 2003. States receive a share of these funds according to a formula that takes into account the number of children under 5, the number of children receiving free or reduced-price lunches, and the state per capita income. Although there is no requirement for state matching funds, the federal dollars must augment, not replace, the state and local monies already designated for child development programs.

Temporary Assistance for Needy Families Block Grant (TANF). In 1996, Congress enacted a welfare reform law with the overall goal of ending adult dependence on public assistance, as well as preventing such dependence in future generations. In order to receive TANF funds, states had to ensure that welfare recipients met minimum work requirements. At the same time, states were given considerable leeway in using TANF funds so long as the programs they set up were compatible with four purposes:

Purpose One: Provide assistance to needy families so that children may be cared for in their homes or in the homes of relatives.

Purpose Two: End the dependence of needy parents on government benefits by promoting job preparation, work, and marriage.

Purpose Three: Prevent and reduce the incidence of out-of-wedlock pregnancies and establish annual numerical goals for preventing and reducing the incidence of these pregnancies.

Purpose Four: Encourage the formation and maintenance of two-parent families. (National Governors' Association for Best Practices, 2000)

Thus, in addition to providing temporary, direct financial assistance to needy families, states have the option of creating or expanding programs to support the overall healthy growth and development of children. They might use TANF dollars to establish home-visiting programs to enhance parenting skills and prevent child abuse, alternative education programs to help teen parents complete high school or GED requirements, or programs aimed at building self-esteem in young men and women. Probably of greatest interest to you as a manager of a child development program is the fact that many states use TANF funds to create or expand before- and after-school child care, Head Start, and Early Head Start programs. TANF dollars also support initiatives such as TEACH (Teacher Education and Compensation Helps) which provides scholarships and salary increases for professional development by child development staff (National Governors' Association for Best Practices, 2000, pp. 4–10).

Universal Pre-K. Another form of state-level sponsorship for early childhood programs is gaining momentum and will likely have a substantial impact on your work as a manager of a child development program. Noting that the number of public school programs for 3- and 4-year-old children has increased fourfold in the last 20 years, the Child Care Action Campaign has targeted Universal Pre-K (UPK) as one of its advocacy goals. With a primary focus on the UPK movement in New York state, this group seeks to advance the cause through research that documents existing programs, competitive grants to encourage the development of new programs, and policy forums to promote strategic alliances between stakeholders. All of their efforts focus on collaboration between child-care programs, Head Start, and public schools (Child Care Action Campaign, 2001). Some early childhood leaders predict that the collaborative aspects of the UPK movement will reinforce the concept that "it takes a village to raise a child" and spur improved compensation and training for early childhood personnel. Others argue that new public school initiatives could absorb all 3- and 4-year-olds, so that existing programs would serve infants and toddlers exclusively (Neugebauer, 2000b, p. 8). This could burden those existing programs with the high cost of infant-toddler care and deprive them of the opportunity to balance those costs with less expensive program components for older children.

Decisions, Decisions . . .

What do you see as outcomes if Universal Pre-K becomes a reality? Will it mean a loss of clientele (and revenue) for programs in the private sector? Will it mean more or fewer job opportunities for you as a manager of early childhood programs?

Institutional Collaboration

The foregoing discussion gives you a picture of the range of child development programs and their funding sources. It also points to a new era in early childhood care and education, one that you will want to follow closely. For many years, several institutions in the United States have worked independently to provide some early education and care for children in various sectors of the population. The differences in philosophies, services, and funding that parents confront are often confusing.

Ideally, the many varieties of early childhood services would collaborate to reduce duplication and maximize returns on society's investments. Zigler and Lang (1991) propose such a collaborative model in their "School of the 21st Century," centering on the public school districts across the country. This arrangement is attractive, economic, and efficient. These schools already pay an installed administrative hierarchy and need only leadership from a qualified educator to set up high-quality early childhood education of the type needed for all families in the district. In addition, the districts often have space that can be made available. The proposal suggests that tuition from parents could help finance the endeavor, at least at the beginning. With this coordinated effort, early education and care could be provided for all children who need it (pp. 190–214).

The first School of the 21st Century was established in Independence, Missouri, in 1988. Since then, more than 500 programs nationwide have followed suit and at least two states (Connecticut and Kentucky) have adopted legislation modeled on the concept. Yale University's Bush Center in Child Development and Social Policy continues to spearhead the movement, providing consultation, training, and evaluation for programs (School of the 21st Century, 1998). The Center for Best Practices of the National

By collaborating across institutional and agency boundaries, child development programs are often able to provide individualized attention that would not otherwise be possible.

Governors' Association (NGA) notes that several states have either established coordinating councils for early care and education or supported such coordinating bodies at the community level. The goal of these councils is to reduce wasteful duplication, while expanding services to more children and families. An expected outgrowth of the expanded services for all children is the elimination of segregated programs for children who are poor or have disabilities (National Governors' Association, Center for Best Practices, 1997, p. 2). Like the Child Care Action Campaign mentioned earlier, the NGA Center for Best Practices sponsors a number of initiatives to advance state-level coordination of early care and education programs, including technical assistance, sponsorship of policy forums, and evaluation projects.

Another force for coordination and collaboration is the National Association of State Boards of Education, which launched the Early Childhood Network in 2001. The goal was to help states articulate a vision for their early education system, develop research-based standards for prekindergarten through grade three, assess program performance, and make high-quality curricula and training more widely available for practitioners (National Association of State Boards of Education, 2005).

Conclusion

This chapter has outlined several types of child development centers, including investment in human capital, supplemental care, remedial or compensatory research and teacher preparation, and consumer service. Individual programs often represent a combination of two or more of these types. Funding models for child development programs range from complete reliance on parent fees to varying degrees of government or corporate subsidization. While the United States tends to lag behind most of the developed world, having ignored the needs of families for many years, managers of child development programs should certainly feel encouraged to see the momentum of support for child care as it is developing in this country. A number of factors, aspects of the human ecological system that will be discussed in the next chapter, suggest that society is on the verge of moving toward a higher status for child development services. Managers of child development programs are in a unique position to help make this happen.

QUESTIONS FOR REVIEW

1. Name and describe five types of child development centers that you might manage. Explain how each serves a particular need for children, families, or society.
2. Describe the various ways that child development programs are funded.
3. Explain the trends in workplace child-care service. Describe the benefits that employers derive from providing assistance with child-care needs.
4. Describe trends in church involvement in child care.

PROFESSIONAL PORTFOLIO

Collaborate with your classmates to compile a list of potential funding sources for child-care programs in your community. Write a brief summary of each resource, including appropriate contact information, and enter this list in the Fiscal Management section of your administrative portfolio. Remember to add a cover sheet explaining what the list documents about your administrative competence.

RESOURCES FOR FURTHER STUDY

Print

Campbell, N. D., Appelbaum, J. C., Martinson, K., & Martin, E. (2000, April). *Be all that we can be: Lessons from the military for improving our nation's child care system.* Washington, DC: National Women's Law Center.

Click, P. M., & Parker, J. (2002). *Caring for school-age children* (3rd ed.). Albany, NY: Delmar.

Internet

Families and Work Institute

www.familiesandwork.org

The Families and Work Institute is a nonprofit organization, founded in 1989, whose research on trends in family, work, and community life is aimed at encouraging the development of equitable, flexible, family-friendly policies in the workplace. The executive summary of the 2002 National Study of the Changing Workforce can be downloaded at no cost, while the full report as well as the data files allowing comparison between findings for 1992, 1997, and 2002 may be purchased.

National Institute of Early Education Research

www.nieer.org

The National Institute of Early Education Research, originated at Rutgers University's Graduate School of Education and funded through a variety of private and governmental sources, collects and disseminates research on a variety of topics such as teacher qualifications and interpretation of test results. The site includes link to a comprehensive report in PDF format, *The State of Preschool: 2004 State of Preschool Yearbook*, which provides state-by-state snapshots summarizing spending, accessibility, and quality of state funded programs for 4-year-old children.

Florida Children's Forum

http://www.centraldirectory.org/uploads/inclusion.pdf

Understanding Inclusion and the Americans with Disabilities Act (ADA), an online publication of the Florida Children's Forum, answers questions frequently asked by child-care providers and provides an overview of the team approach to caring for children with disabilities. It includes a list of resources, definition of terms, and information about specific disabilities.

CHAPTER THREE

Applying Theories in Managing a Child Development Center

You may feel that theory is something for scholars and outside the practical concerns of the manager of children's programs. However, any time you make a decision based on what you think the consequences of your actions will be, you are operating on a theory, whether consciously or not. Theories help human beings make sense of all the fragmented bits of information that confront them. As a manager of a child development program, you will be confronted with countless ideas and recommendations for how to accomplish the components of your job. Theories are frameworks that help answer the question of why one recommendation or course of action might be preferable to another, why it might work better to accomplish your aims.

In formal terms, a **theory** is an organized set of related ideas, concepts, and principles that describes a particular area of knowledge. A good theory fulfills three criteria. First, it is carefully defined in writing. Second, it is published in the public domain so other scholars can evaluate it carefully. Third, it has been tested by independent scholars and practitioners, with the results published in the public domain. Theory is not a fact. Once it becomes a fact, it no longer is called a theory.

When you read about theories, you should realize that people are still working on them, testing them, and polishing them. New theories are proposed as information accumulates. You can assist in the work of theory development by thinking about and testing theories in your day-to-day work. Perhaps you can refine or develop a new theory. Certainly, you can question a theory or ask whether it applies to your situation. You can make suggestions for modifications in light of your experience. Then, you and other scholars and practitioners in the field can test these ideas to bring the activity into the realm of a science, with useful predictable outcomes arising from given procedures.

Theories from Multiple Areas of Knowledge

Managers of child development centers must coordinate information—and theories—from several areas of knowledge. First, they must think about how children grow and develop and how environments and activities help or hinder that development. Then, they need to remember that children do not exist in a vacuum; each child comes to the center with a complex history and set of relationships with his family and community. Center directors, therefore, should consider how families relate to the center and how both relate to other systems within the larger community. Finally, directors must think about the best ways of managing complex organizations, like child development centers, in order to achieve their goals for children and families.

Experts in each of these broad areas of knowledge have developed a number of theoretical frameworks to organize ideas and create a rational basis for predicting outcomes. This chapter begins with a brief discussion of **developmental theory** to help managers focus on the needs of children enrolled in their centers. Then, the **ecosystems framework** is presented, focusing on families and the interaction of the child development center with the other systems that comprise the families' environment. Finally, a brief review of **management theories** is presented.

Developmental Theory

Managers of child development centers need a theoretical basis for understanding and planning for children. Information about children's growth and development has provided a consensus that a developmental theory is a sound basis for decisions about children, although it is important to remember that this theory represents only one way of looking at the issue. The document, *Developmentally Appropriate Practice in Early Childhood Programs Serving Children from Birth Through Age 8* (Bredekamp, 1987) is a case in point. Published in 1987 by the National Association for the Education of Young Children (NAEYC), this work by a commission of professionals spelled out how developmental theory could be applied to the operation of early childhood programs. Based on research showing the step-by-step development of children, it described in practical terms the state of the art of applied child development at the time it was published. It was widely discussed and extremely influential in shaping programs for children in all types of child development centers, as well as public school settings. Other researchers applied the concept to early childhood special education (Fox, Hanline, Vail, & Gallant, 1994) and to standards for school-age child-care programs (Albrecht & Plantz, 1991). Some early childhood specialists criticized the document, however, because it seemed to present only one "right way" of doing things and appeared to favor White, middle-class patterns of child rearing. They argued that the practices defined in the document did not apply as easily to children from minority cultures or to children with disabilities (e.g., Mallory & New, 1994). NAEYC leaders listened to these concerns, and the revised edition (Bredekamp & Copple, 1997) addressed them by presenting a range of options for the early childhood practitioner to consider when making decisions.

Our ideas about developmentally appropriate practice incorporate the work of many scholars who tried to explain one or more aspects of human development. Jean Piaget, Lev Vygotsky, Howard Gardner, Benjamin Bloom, and B. F. Skinner focused primarily on cognitive, or intellectual, development. Erik Erikson studied social-emotional development. Arnold Gesell explored connections between cognitive and perceptual-motor development. Urie Bronfenbrenner examined the links between human development and its larger social contexts. Today's programs for young children reflect the thinking of all these and many other people, although some programs may operate without being aware of their theoretical bases. Because they are working with human beings and complex interactions, early childhood professionals cannot slavishly adhere to a single theory. They constantly refine their understanding and adjust their practice as they attempt to provide the best for each child in their care. Nevertheless, as the manager of a child development center, you should be familiar with the people and theories whose ideas have helped shape your profession.

Types of Theories of Human Development

Some scholars classify theories of child development as belonging to one of four types. **Maturationist** theories emphasize that growth and development come largely from within the child and follow a predictable timetable. **Environmentalist** or behaviorist theories focus on the ways that growth and development can be influenced from the outside. **Interactionist** theories explore the ways that inside and outside forces interact to create change, suggesting that children with different backgrounds experience the same environment in very different ways. **Ecological** theories consider the individual within the context of all the systems that make up his environment (e.g., Thomas, 1992). Table 3.1 summarizes some of the distinguishing characteristics of these four types of child development theories.

A maturationist, for example, when confronted with a 4-year-old who cannot (or will not) repeat a simple rhyme might suggest simply waiting until the child has time to mature and develop greater language skills. An environmentalist might try using drill and practice sessions with rewards, such as stickers, for successful performance. An interactionist might consider internal factors, such as the child's previous language experience and interest in the project, as well as external factors, such as the cultural relevance of the rhyme or the manner in which the activity was presented. An ecologist might look at family and social contexts for this particular ability.

B. F. Skinner is known for his work on the behaviorist theory and its emphasis on reinforcement. People who have never even heard of Skinner are following one of his premises when they believe that a reward helps a child learn the behavior that is rewarded. What has also been explained by the behaviorists is that to eliminate a behavior (i.e., extinguish it), the behavior must never be rewarded. Intermittent rewards, even when far apart, are still reinforcing. Benjamin Bloom, another behaviorist theorist, contributed to the concept of behavioral objectives in education, based on the belief that children achieve greater success if all tasks are broken down into manageable steps. Bloom's early research led him to state quite strongly the importance of the early years for later development, arguing that the most significant learning takes place during the first 5 years of life. Although scholars have disagreed with the emphasis Bloom placed on the early years, the concept of critical periods in development has received new attention as the result of recent research on brain development (Shore, 1997).

Postmodern Critiques of Child Development Theory

A discussion of developmental theory should also acknowledge that a number of writers are critical of the fact that child development theories have been so influential in shaping our professional practices and our view of children. They argue that the theories are not based on objective knowledge, but are instead embedded in—and perpetuate—particular social systems. This **postmodern** perspective asserts that theorists cannot discover "reality" or "truth" because there is no such thing apart from our beliefs and perceptions. Furthermore, those beliefs and perceptions are dominated by those in power at particular times and places. Postmodernism, as the term suggests, grows out of a critical reaction to a worldview characterized as modernism. Child psychologist David Elkind summarizes the modernist view as resting on three basic beliefs: (a) that social progress is possible and tied to increasing scientific knowledge, (b) that nature is governed by universal principles that can be discovered and explained, and (c) that natural phenomena are regular and predictable.

TABLE 3.1   *Characteristics of four types of child development theories*

	Maturationist	Environmentalist or Behaviorist	Interactionist	Ecological
Major Theorists	G. Stanley Hall Arnold Gesell	J. B. Watson B. F. Skinner	Jean Piaget Erik Erikson	Urie Bronfenbrenner Lev Vygotsky
Focus of Study	Predictable patterns of growth and development within individual	Relationships between external factors and observable changes in behavior	Mental or psychological constructions resulting from individual's interaction with physical or social environment	Relationships between and among individual and multiple environments
View of Human Development	A genetically determined process	Tabula Rasa or blank slate shaped by accumulated responses to environment	Combination of internal drives and environment	Mediated by culture and society
What Impels Development	Assuming that basic needs are met through caregiving, nutrition, etc., development unfolds over time; cannot be rushed	Stimuli elicit behaviors which are reinforced or extinguished by pattern of consequences experienced	Adaptation occurs as individual encounters new experiences which either become assimilated into existing mental frameworks or provoke creation of new ones	Caring relationships with more experienced individual leads to widening sphere of understanding and control
Adult Role	Meet basic needs; observe and support transitions to next stages	Break learning goals into sequential steps; reinforce progress through those steps	Provide an environment that nourishes intellect and/or emotions; assist and support children	Provide an environment that nourishes intellect and/or emotions; assist and support children; be aware of and mediate outside influences

41

Postmodernism questions the ability of science and reason to solve all human problems because scientific objectivity is not possible (Elkind, 1994, pp. 17–21). Postmodern critics of child development theories indicate that those theories are rooted in the Western, middle-class experience and not necessarily applicable to other groups (Dahlberg, Moss, & Pence, 1999). They also argue that too often theories are flawed because they purport to explain or predict aspects of groups or individuals without considering the ideas and perceptions of the people being studied. This is particularly likely to occur when the scientific establishment studies less powerful segments of society, such as children, poor people, or individuals with disabilities (e.g., Pugach, 2001). A modernist might try to explain, for example, how child care differs from preschool and define the particular skills needed by caregivers as distinguished from teachers. A postmodernist, on the other hand, would argue that the idea of child care and the idea of early education are just that: ideas. Each emerged to serve certain social purposes at particular times in history (e.g., Zigler & Lang, 1991). You will encounter the concept of postmodernism again when we look at theories of management later in this chapter.

Examples of Developmental Theories

Piaget.   Piaget's theory represents a particular type of interactionist theory, often referred to as *constructivist*, because it holds that children must construct knowledge for themselves as they experience the environment. The idea is that children are not blank slates or empty containers to be filled with information. Instead, they are like scientists with their own hypotheses about the world, which they constantly test and refine as they move about in that world. For example, Piaget demonstrated that very young children (in what he called the preoperational stage) did not realize that an amount of water stays the same when poured from a tall, narrow container into a short, wide one. Nor, he argued, can adults teach them that this is so. Each child must discover this through countless experiences with pouring. Piaget's concepts help early childhood professionals understand children's thinking more clearly. Managers can use the theory to help teachers and parents appreciate the intelligence that goes into what appear to be "wrong" ideas.

Vygotsky.   The work of Lev Vygotsky, a Russian psychologist, has recently come into prominence, in part because of its application in the preschools of Reggio Emilia, Italy, which gained worldwide fame through the traveling exhibit "The Hundred Languages of Children." Vygotsky adds to Piaget's idea of the child constructing knowledge by suggesting that when more advanced learners—adults and older children in the culture—communicate with a child who is learning, they aid the child's thinking and learning. This concept is called the **social construction of knowledge.** Also of interest to Vygotsky is **private speech,** in which a child may be observed audibly talking through a problem-solving situation, such as, "I'll put the big block here to keep this roof up." The private speech may be addressed to no one in particular. Vygotsky's theory is called **dialectical,** meaning that thinking and reasoning proceed through dialogues and social interaction.

Seymour Papert (1993), the creator of Logo, a computer language for children, has added to Vygotsky's ideas about the social construction of knowledge by suggesting that children interact with the things they make or build and get feedback that helps them generate or modify their ideas in much the same way as feedback from adults or older children. Papert calls his version of this idea **constructionism** to distinguish it from constructivism.

Erikson.   Erik Erikson, another theorist in the interactionist category, turns our attention from the realm of the intellect to social-emotional development. Erikson's theory of the

Eight Stages of Man conceives of development as the individual's navigation through a series of stages, each of which is defined by two opposing outcomes. The task is to achieve an appropriate balance between the two: trust versus mistrust in infancy, autonomy versus shame and doubt in toddlerhood, initiative versus guilt in the preschool years, and so on through the life span. Erikson worked to refine his theory throughout his life, adding a ninth stage describing the conflict and resolution culminating in old age when he himself was 86 years old. Thus, teachers in infant programs are borrowing from Erikson when they talk about responding promptly to babies' cries so that the infants feel secure and gain a sense of trust. When we notice toddlers' insistence on feeding themselves, or their fondness of the word "no," we are confirming observations that Erikson made years ago about the origins of autonomy. The practice of offering 3- and 4-year-old children large blocks of time for free (or self-initiated) play reflects Erikson's belief that children of this age are working on building a sense of initiative.

Importance of Social–Emotional Development. In spite of Erikson's strong influence on what we know as developmentally appropriate practice, child development professionals worry that too many contemporary programs for young children have shoved aside concerns for social–emotional development in response to demands that they prepare children for academic success (e.g., Caldwell, 2001). Ironically, an emerging body of research and theory suggests that neglecting social–emotional issues in the push for academic excellence is actually counterproductive. Mental health experts tell us that "children who do not begin kindergarten socially and emotionally competent are often not successful in the early years of school—and can be plagued by behavioral, emotional, academic, and social development problems that follow them into adulthood" (Child Mental Health Foundations and Agencies Network, 2000). The brains of children, we have learned, are still under construction in the first few years of life. They need a rich variety of experiences to create new neural connections (in other words, to learn), but they also need to feel secure and connected to their caregiver in order to absorb those new experiences. When young children experience chronic stress, their bodies produce more of the chemicals that inhibit connections between neurons (Shore, 1997, pp. 15–35).

Goleman. Psychologist Daniel Goleman argues that emotional intelligence is more important than IQ for success in life, that adults who are unable to recognize, express, and manage their feelings are more likely to fail at both relationships and careers. Furthermore, he says that children acquire emotional intelligence in "the crucible of the family," where parents model as well as teach these important abilities, but only if they themselves have achieved a level of understanding and mastery of their own feelings. Stanley Greenspan, a prominent child psychiatrist, takes issue with Goleman's separation between intellectual and emotional intelligence. He theorizes that the two are inextricably intertwined, that the roots of cognitive development are embedded in emotional attachments.

Greenspan. Greenspan describes six levels of the mind's development. In the first stage, the infant struggles to organize myriad physical sensations to achieve what Greenspan calls "global aliveness." At the next stage, "the related self," infants begin to form a connection with another person and develop a sense of shared humanity. In the next two stages, the infant's actions become more intentional, and in the last two stages, the child acquires the ability to think symbolically.

Gardner. Howard Gardner's theory of multiple intelligences can be seen as another example of interactionist theory in its assertion that particular characteristics of individuals cause them to perceive and interact with their environment in different ways. His theory also challenges the customary distinction between cognitive, social–emotional, and perceptual–motor development. Gardner argues that humans are capable of at least seven ways of knowing the world: language, logical-mathematical analysis, spatial representation, musical thinking, the use of the body to solve problems or to make things, an understanding of other individuals, and an understanding of themselves. Each individual has a particular "profile of intelligences" resulting from his unique pattern of strengths and weaknesses across the seven areas. In Gardner's view, traditional concepts of intelligence have focused too narrowly on language and logical–mathematical thinking, with the result that our educational system has not supported the development of individuals with strengths in other areas.

In reviewing these theories of development, you might notice that it is extremely difficult to "slice up" the various domains of development. The traditional categories of physical, cognitive, social, and emotional development seem to overlap and blend into each other within every individual. To make matters even more interesting (you might say complicated), it also can be argued that individual development cannot be examined apart from its social context. Erik Erikson, for example, addressed the interaction between stages of an individual's development and the larger social forces at work during his lifetime.

Bronfenbrenner.   Uri Bronfenbrenner takes a closer look at these interactions. His ecological model of human development depicts the infant as nested within a series of concentric rings, or systems, beginning with the family (the microsystem) and culminating with the society at large (the macrosystem). For him, development consists of the child's increasing competence within, and understanding of, these increasingly wider spheres, and he holds that this growth results from challenging and supportive interactions at each level. A recent report by the Committee on Integrating the Science of Early Childhood Development, pulling together the most recent information about development from a broad spectrum of sources, is a good example of human ecological theory applied. The committee concluded that healthy child development depends on factors at every level of the family ecosystem, from the physical and emotional nurturing that occurs within the family microsystem to the social policies and programs or macrosystem supporting that nurturing. The committee argued that the nation should support healthy development of all children both because it is the right thing to do and because it is an investment in the human capital that sustains democracy (Shonkoff & Phillips, 2000).

The Challenge of Applying Theories of Development

Because they reflect the complex nature of the human beings involved, child development programs rarely embody a single theory in its pure form, although one type or another has seemed to predominate at various periods in the history of early childhood programs (Thomas, 1992, pp. 473–489). The NAEYC's Developmentally Appropriate Practice, noted earlier, incorporates ideas from all four types of theorists, with a particular emphasis on constructivism, a specific form of interactionist theory (Bredekamp, 1994). And, as mentioned previously, some theorists are already at work modifying and extending the ideas of constructivism.

Further complicating matters, members of other professions working with young children have been trained according to different theoretical frameworks, and these frameworks have evolved, just as they have in the field of early childhood education. Bruce Mallory, for example, describes the theoretical models that shape early childhood special education as developmental-interactionist, functional (or behaviorist), and biogenetic, and he argues that a "triangulated" approach, using ideas and methods based on all three, is necessary to serve children most effectively (Mallory, 1994). Now imagine the even greater challenge created by this variety of perspectives when a child with a disability is included in a program based on constructivist views of typical child development. All of the professionals involved must work together to develop a common vocabulary and function effectively as a team.

Finally, theory is always in a state of flux until it becomes accepted as fact, but solid facts are seldom found in the arena of human development and behavior. You might feel that these complicating factors and continual changes make the study of child development theory too confusing and time-consuming for a busy program manager.

How Managers Apply Theories of Development

Nevertheless, there at least three compelling reasons for you to learn about theories of child development. First, the theory (or theories) that underlie your program influence the ways you see children and families and all of the decisions you make as you interact with those children and families. Theory is behind action even if it consists of only the informal theories we all learn in the process of growing up. Ask a staff member or parent, for example, "What makes a 2-year-old hit another child?" and the answers you receive reveal a wide range of theories.

Second, even though theory is often difficult for beginning teachers and caregivers to apply to their work, one of the manager's tasks is to help staff apply more advanced ideas as they gain experience and ask questions that show they are thinking about what and how children are learning. Teachers have teachable moments, just as children do. You can be prepared to help teachers and caregivers explore children's development in more depth when you recognize one of these teachable moments. Learning a few terms from those who have made the study of behavior and development their life's work will help you discuss these opinions more intelligently.

Finally, studying theory will make your own work with children and families more exciting as you see examples of what the theorists mean in the behaviors before your eyes, or when you find possible explanations for things that have puzzled you. As a future manager of child development programs you will, no doubt, be taking additional courses in early childhood curriculum where you will learn more about these and other theorists. Some additional resources are listed at the end of this chapter, or you can consult your library to find others.

In applying developmental theory, you start with a general knowledge about the way children grow and develop to plan environments and activities for them. If you know you have a 5-year-old group, you plan activities and organize the environment according to what research and experience says 5-year-old children are like. Then, you look at the particular individuals in your group and adjust your generic planning to fit the developmental needs of these children. That is, if Emma is reading, you find books for her to read. If Peter needs climbing practice that does not match the typical 5-year-old, you see that he is able to practice climbing skills. Finally, you take into account the families and communities in which your particular group of children grow and develop, so that your program incorporates and respects their particular patterns of child rearing. Thus, there are three dimensions to developmental planning: (a) the typical characteristics of the age group, (b) the particular or personal characteristics of the children you enroll, and (c) the unique qualities of the families and communities of the children you serve.

Decisions, Decisions. . .

Consider a child development program where you have worked or observed. List the theory or theories that seem to form the basis for its practices with children and families.

Management Theory

As individuals, we all live and work within families, agencies, and groups. All of these entities have goals for their existence, use resources, and serve the needs and desires of the individuals within the society. All groups need an activity or process that coordinates individual efforts toward achieving goals, allocates resources effectively, and serves needs. That activity is called management.

Management is needed in every effective group to attain the desired goals with the least expenditure of time, energy, and money. Whether the operation is an agency, school, business, or family, whether it is operated for profit or on a nonprofit basis, management is needed. A manager is the person who applies management theory and uses management techniques. A manager may also be called administrator, executive, chief executive officer (CEO), supervisor, director, or boss.

A management theory is an organized set of related ideas, concepts, and principles that attempt to describe the process of managing an organization. Although management is widely recognized as a science, some would argue that it is an art because it encompasses creativity and requires new approaches and new ways of looking at old procedures. However, even the most creative manager must use management science as a basis for action. Just as you have seen in the case of child development theory, there have been a number of management or organization theories and volumes of studies designed to test those theories. Different theories appear to apply better to one type of organization than to another. There is not total agreement on the most desirable management theory to use. This can also be said about the child development theories, so this condition of inconclusiveness should not bother you.

Historical Evolution of Organization Theory

A review of the evolution of organization theory reveals four successive stages, each influenced by the work of scholars from many disciplines (Hatch, 1997, pp. 5–55):

- The first half of the twentieth century was dominated by the **classical** view, which drew heavily on the sciences of economics, engineering, and sociology, particularly the ideas of Adam Smith, Karl Marx, Emile Durkheim, and Max Weber. According to this view, organizations are like machines, designed to accomplish specific purposes, and managers are like engineers, who create and operate the machines.

- The **modern** perspective developed about 1950, incorporating knowledge from the emerging disciplines of political science, ecology, industrial sociology, and social anthropology. The writings of Talcott Parsons, Alfred Gouldner, and Ludwig von Bertalanffy helped shape the image of the organization as an organism, a living system adapting to its environment as needed. The manager, in this view, is one of the components of the system, interdependent with all of the others.

- According to the **symbolic-interpretive** view of the 1980s, an organization is a concept, like culture, created by human thought with no objective existence, though it is treated as real by the mutual consent of society. By extension, then, the manager is also a social construct, perhaps a symbol for the organization. The writings of Erving Goffman, Roland Barthes, and Kenneth Burke, as well as other ideas drawn from cultural anthropology, folklore, semiotics, and linguistics, contributed to this view.

- The **postmodern** perspective emerged on several fronts in the 1990s, including architecture, literary theory, and culture studies. As you saw in the discussion of child development theory, postmodern theory focuses more on how knowledge is created than on the content of that knowledge, and it is often critical of that process. Ideas drawn from the writings of Michel Foucault, Jacques Derrida, Mikhail Bakhtin, and others contributed to the idea that organization theory is like a collage (or a theory), combining bits of past knowledge to create new ways of viewing things. The manager, then, is akin to the artist (or theorist).

Theoretical Paradigms

Lemak (2004) argues that this chronological approach fails to capture the essential distinctions among a rapidly growing array of theories. Instead of focusing on when they emerged, he examines theories for their underlying assumptions about people and organizations. Every theory rests on assumptions, or ideas accepted as given. In his review of management literature, Lemak found six key assumptions that can be characterized as implicit answers to the following questions: Should one study individual workers, groups, or systems to understand how organizations work? What motivates workers? Are people basically rational, or are they controlled by emotions? Should managers be concerned with what workers do or with what they think and feel? What is the goal of the organization, and what function does the manager fulfill in accomplishing that goal? Lemak found that three distinct clusters of theories emerged, each representing a particular paradigm or conceptual model:

- The classical paradigm views the individual worker as the unit of analysis and assumes that monetary rewards will be effective motivators because those workers are rational beings. With efficiency as the main goal, the manager's job is to lay out the steps of production and then supervise workers to make sure they follow procedures.

- The behavioral paradigm focuses on the group rather than the individual and views social connections and the resulting job satisfaction as more powerful than economic motivators. Social change rather than profit is seen as the goal, and the manager's role is team building. (Note that the descriptor, *behavioral*, is a term used within the field of organizational management and not to be confused with *behaviorist*, which applies to psychological theories discussed earlier in this chapter.)

- The systems paradigm stems from the concept of cybernetics (i.e., automatic control systems), developed during the Second World War. The idea is that any system, whether animal, machine, or organization, must continuously adapt in response to feedback from its environment. The unit of analysis in this paradigm is the system as a whole, which must maintain equilibrium or balance within a constantly shifting environment in order to survive. The goal is to transform inputs into outputs as efficiently as possible, and the manager serves the dual function of taking in and interpreting feedback while helping to coordinate the system's responses to that feedback.

While acknowledging that each model developed within a particular historical context, Lemak asserts that ideas from one period often have roots in earlier eras or may be echoed in writings of theorists who ostensibly belong to a later school of thought. Thus, the chief proponents of the classical paradigm emerged during the second half of the nineteenth century and drew ideas from engineering and physical science. The behavioral paradigm is frequently presented as a later development, most closely associated with the depression of the 1930s, although its tenets can be traced to writings that appeared a half century earlier criticizing social ills brought on by the Industrial Revolution.

Applying Management Theories

Just as no individual program is likely to be a "pure" example of one type of child development theory, management approaches often reflect elements of more than one paradigm. This textbook is no exception. It is organized around a framework of managerial processes that, as Lemak points out, are derived from the classical paradigm (p. 7), while incorporating concepts about family systems (which we discuss later in this chapter) that share much in common with Lemak's third paradigm. You, too, are likely to find ideas from many types of management theories useful in your work, depending upon the particular situation. Lemak suggests that the three paradigms be considered analogous to management styles and that individual managers will gravitate toward theorists whose assumptions about human nature and the like most closely resemble their own (p. 15).

Total Quality Management

One approach to management that has gained increasing popularity in the United States recently is **total quality management.** This approach is based on the ideas of two westerners, W. Edwards Deming and Joseph Juran, who developed it in Japan more than 40 years ago when U.S. industries were entrenched in the opposite, "top-down" approach to management. Japan's achievements in gaining a large share of the world market for automobiles and electronic equipment prompted U.S. manufacturers to take a closer look at Deming's theories. The Ford Motor Company hired him as a consultant in 1980, and his ideas caught on from there.

Total quality management contrasts with traditional management methods in several ways:

1. Power is shared. Ideas flow upward from the people actually doing the work and downward from the organization's leaders.
2. Responsibility is shared. Everyone is expected to understand and be committed to the organization's mission, spot problems, propose solutions, and take appropriate action to solve the problems.
3. Customer satisfaction is the central focus.
4. Quality is achieved by doing even the small things right the first time. When products or outcomes are faulty, the process is examined and altered as needed.
5. Successful businesses do not rest on their laurels but strive for continuous improvement.

According to Dorothy Hewes (1994), who has studied the history of educational management systems, total quality management may have seemed revolutionary to U.S. industry when it came into vogue in the 1980s, but it should sound very familiar to those of us in the field of early childhood education, where prominent leaders have been espousing self-government and bottom-up management for over a century. In fact, the accreditation process of the National Association for the Education of Young Children begins with a detailed self-study by all of the people involved in a child development center, followed by self-initiated movements toward greater quality. This process is discussed in greater detail in the next chapter.

Ecological System Framework

We turn our attention now from theories about child development and organizational management to a framework for understanding the ecosystem in which both families and child development programs operate. A manager of a child development center has three main goals: (a) to understand the families needing and desiring child development center services, (b) to understand the intricacies of a child development center operation, and (c) to integrate families' and children's needs, child development center operations, and societal standards. A useful approach to help achieve such goals is to find a framework for analysis—that is, a theory for examining the various parts and the whole. You encountered the topic of systems in our discussion of management theory. In this section we will look at how systems theory can be applied to families and child development programs.

Systems theory is based on the idea that every phenomenon comprises interrelated parts within itself at the same time that it makes up a part of some larger system. The human brain, for example, is a complex arrangement of cerebellum, cerebral cortex, and other specialized parts, each comprising cells, which are in turn made up of atoms. The brain is also part of the larger central nervous system, which governs all bodily functions. In the social realm, the various departments of a large corporation are all examples of systems, in that they are smaller units or individuals who must work together to function effectively, and together they make up the larger system, the corporation. Ecology is a branch of science concerned with the interconnections of organisms and their environments. Thus, an ecosystem framework looks at the connections between systems and the contexts in which they operate.

The biological sciences have long used an ecological system framework to explain the interdependence between biological organisms and the encompassing environment. For example, scientists can show that the quality of a field of grass depends on many factors (e.g., the variety of grass present, photosynthesis, soil fertility, insect infestations, moisture, competition from other plants, length of the growing season, and the traffic or feeding in the field by animals). Scientists can measure the effect of a specific input—say, additional moisture—on the increased production of grass. You will note the solar energy inputs implied in this example and that an appropriate combination, balance, or equilibrium between the various inputs is required for the grass to grow well.

According to the ecosystem framework, social systems, such as families or child development centers, require energy and use feedback from the environment to achieve equilibrium just as biological systems do. Human energy is derived from food, and nonhuman energy is derived from fossil fuels.

Bubolz and Sontag (1993) proposed a family ecosystem framework that examines interactions within and across three environments:

1. The physical–biological environment refers to the environment formed by nature, such as soil, climate, and natural resources.
2. The human-built environment entails the environment that human beings have constructed or altered to fit their needs, such as factories, roads, farms, and pollution.
3. The social–cultural environment includes other people as well as the more abstract results of interactions between people, such as cultural values and institutions.

The child development program comprises part of the family's human-built environment (e.g., building, equipment, materials), as well as part of the family's social–cultural

Child development programs can help children appreciate and care for the physical–biological environment.

environment (e.g., the social institutions that fund and regulate child care and education, and the human interactions that take place between children, staff, and families at the center). The child development program interacts with other parts of the human-built and social–cultural environments, as well as the physical–biological environment.

The Physical–Biological Environment

The physical–biological environment affects the operation of a child development center in many ways, both obvious and subtle. For example, centers located in extremely hot or cold climates spend more on heating and air conditioning; a Head Start program located in a rural area must budget for higher transportation costs because of the distances between children's homes; and all centers should plan for coping with natural emergencies such as tornadoes. Natural resources also relate directly to the wealth of the community and individuals within the community. The presence of many natural resources provides productive jobs for the parents of children, increases the amount of income they receive, and stimulates their desire for early childhood education for their children. On the other hand, an absence of natural resources is likely to be correlated with unemployment or low-paying jobs for parents and an inability to pay for high-quality service.

The amount and quality of natural resources influence the funding available to pay for operating the child development center—salaries, facility, utilities, and supplies. People in oil-importing countries who are familiar with the recent dramatic increase in the price of oil realize this fact all too well. Inflation and unemployment occurred in areas short of oil. Child-care center costs also rose during this period; then, enrollments dropped as out-of-work parents economized by withdrawing their children. Tax collections also decreased, damaging publicly financed centers.

The Human-Built Environment

Natural resources become more valuable economic resources as they move through factories, businesses, farming enterprises, and into retail consumer markets—all aspects of the human-built environment. Jobs for citizens result from such enterprises. Some of the holders of these jobs are the parents of the children in our child development centers.

Although the human-built environment depends on the physical–biological environment, it transforms that environment in many ways. Some transformations are purposeful, while others may be accidental by-products of human actions. The results of such transformations might be beneficial, apparently neutral, or at times harmful. The child-care center itself is a part of the human-built environment: a physical structure built to serve specific human purposes. Good roads and efficient public transportation systems make it easier for parents to get their children to the center and themselves to work.

Some changes wrought by humans are less benevolent, as in the case of air or water pollution. These might seem like issues far removed from your role as manager of a child development center, but people in a child development program breathe the same air and drink the same water as people elsewhere in the community. High concentrations of automobile exhaust in a city can result in pollution levels that keep everyone indoors for several days. An emergency resulting from the bacterial contamination of a city's water supply can mean that a center must purchase bottled water, spend extra energy boiling a supply of drinking water, or perhaps suspend services until the situation is brought under control.

Interactions flow within the center, as well as between the center and other parts of the human-built environment. For example, public utilities provide water and energy supplies and remove waste. This flow of interaction requires a great deal of both human and non-human energy to operate.

The Social–Cultural Environment

The social–cultural environment is the product of people interacting with one another and with elements of their environments, forming relationships and creating cultural patterns and social and economic institutions. The extended family and neighborhood network of friends are two examples of social-cultural environments. The teachers, caregivers, cooks, and custodians at child development centers interact with children and parents to create another social-cultural environment. Just as in the human-built environment, interactions within the cultural environment require energy—emotional and intellectual energy, as well as physical energy.

Social expectations regarding people's roles are another aspect of the social–cultural environment. In the 1950s, for example, women were expected to stay home and take care of their families. Although attitudes have changed to the extent that working mothers are considered commonplace, ambivalence persists about how much society should support families with low-cost, high-quality child-care options. In addition to a cultural tradition of self-contained, independent nuclear families, the economic institution of a market economy is part of the social–cultural environment for families in the United States. Child care is often viewed as a service to be purchased by the family rather than as a family support and an investment in human capital that benefits society as a whole. This view is in contrast to that of countries such as Italy, where child-care and family-support services are considered a right of all families. So, although more working parents create a greater demand for child-care services, a lack of funding means tight budgets for those centers.

Regardless of how they are funded, child development centers are established by human beings to provide physical care and to foster the individual development, growth, and education of children coming from the family systems. The child development center supplements the efforts of the children's parents and is obligated to help further develop the child's human resources—strengths, knowledge, skills, abilities, and the like. Such attributes are often called **human capital.** With a higher level of human capital development, a person can make a larger contribution to society. Conversely, without human capital development, a person may become a burden to society. Evidence suggests that an investment by a country in early childhood education yields a high return.

A country's economic base depends on factors from all three environments: the natural resources from the physical-biological environment (e.g., fossil fuels, arable land, and suitable climate); the facilities within the human-built environment for transforming those resources, such as factories and organizations; and the country's willingness and capacity to invest in educational opportunities for its citizens, an aspect of the social–cultural environment. Japan, for example, is a country that has minimal natural resources but has invested wisely in human capital—the education and skills its citizens needed to develop high-technology products. This output, in turn, brings economic wealth to the inhabitants.

Historically, countries that have developed strong economic bases have evolved institutions that give more services to family members. For example, there are more medical, educational, and social services for families in economically developed countries than in the less-developed countries.

Government or corporate support for child care and social trends such as women entering the workforce or deciding to have fewer children, which you read about in previous chapters, are all aspects of the social–cultural environment. Throughout this book, you will repeatedly recognize the social–cultural environment when topics such as parent–child relations, staff relations, teacher-child relations, professional relations, or public relations are discussed. Interactions with people, such as vendors, bankers, licensing officials, or fire safety officers, are examples of a manager's involvement with the social–cultural environment.

Equilibrium and Energy in the Ecosystem

Striving for an equilibrium or balance is an important characteristic of the human ecological system. Families create an internal family ecosystem and also interact with environments outside the family; they attempt to maintain equilibrium between themselves and the other systems. A child development center interacts with numerous systems, and it too must seek equilibrium.

Feedback from one environment may make adjustments in others necessary. The manager of a center acknowledges the feedback and makes adjustments to help maintain some balance, equilibrium, or stability. For example, increases in the number of children require proportionate increases in the number of adults as well as in the amount of food and supplies purchased. Licensing regulations from the political system set certain standards for child–adult ratios that managers must follow. When a health problem arises, the manager seeks appropriate advice for corrective measures from the community's health system.

Moving toward energy equilibrium is an important aspect or tendency of all ecological systems. In the example of the field of grass mentioned earlier, water, soil, and solar energy were identified as major inputs. In a child development center, nonhuman resources, such as fossil-fuel energy, natural raw materials, and solar energy, are used in the structure and to heat and cool it. Nonhuman resources are organized and activated by human energy—the energy people derive from food. Human energy, represented by skill and know-how, is needed in every aspect of the child development center operation. Much of the knowledge and skills present in staff members result from energy expended in other systems—their homes, schools, and colleges. This point illustrates how an investment in the human being (in human capital) at one time often pays off at another time.

Many printed resources are used in a child development center—books for children and professional books for staff members. Printed material requires human energy to prepare, produce, and distribute. In addition, some natural materials, such as paper, glue, and ink, are required for making the physical objects containing the printing.

A human service, such as a child development center, can be called energy intensive, requiring high-energy inputs from many people. The child development service supplements parental energy. The children's energy is channeled into exploring their own learning activity and helping with some of the center's work. For example, children learn to pick up after themselves and take care of their own needs, reducing the demand on teachers for energy inputs. The quality of human-energy inputs is represented by costs to the community and the family. One can readily hypothesize that the quality of programs for children is related to the available energy of teachers and caregivers for each child. Energy includes the knowledge, skills, and stamina to carry on the work. Studies have suggested that if there are more than 18 children in a group, the children receive an inferior program because of inadequate individual attention. In recognition of this fact, professional organizations such as the National Association for the Education of Young Children, as well as many state licensing agencies, have set standards establishing maximum group sizes and required adult-child ratios for each age level.

Applying the Ecosystems Model

The human ecological systems model is useful in planning and coping with problems that arise. Simply checking to discover which environment is the major source of the problem is a first step toward a solution. For instance, if children are not eating the food prepared for them, use the model in the following way. First, check the physical–biological environment to see whether the food is produced with adequate quality and flavor. Second, check the food storage and handling (the human-built environment), because improper storage and handling may result in a loss of quality. Finally, check the food service personnel's procedures (the social–cultural environment), because their lack of skill or knowledge may result in unappetizing or culturally inappropriate food combinations, excessively large servings, or inaccurate recipe calculations. Once the manager determines the source of the problem, corrective solutions can be selected. Note that none of these examples suggests doing anything with or to the children. The human ecological system framework serves as a useful tool for suggesting avenues to check for possible solutions. In general, solutions dealing with things rather than people are more easily implemented and should be tried first.

Decisions, Decisions . . .

Consider another problem from the human ecological systems perspective: Suppose that nap time in the center where you work is chaotic, with children crying and fussing instead of resting peacefully. List the elements you might check in the physical–biological environment, the human-built environment, and the social–cultural environment in order to make nap time more peaceful.

Management Processes

If you are going to be a manager of a child development center, what will you be doing? How will your job differ from the teacher's job that you may have been performing previously? How will your tasks relate to licensing regulations enacted by your state and local governing bodies and to the accreditation standards established by your professional organization, the National Association for the Education of Young Children?

As you study the managerial processes and approaches, reflect on all of the managers you have known. How did they work? How did they relate to employees? How did they delegate assignments? How did they reward unusual performance? How did they correct inadequate performance? By watching other managers, you can learn some things about managing. Wherever you are presently, begin thinking about service and organization from a manager's viewpoint.

It may look like child's play, but all aspects of the managerial process are required for assembling the time, materials, and adult support that make such positive interactions possible.

All managers use five basic processes regardless of what enterprise they manage:

1. Planning
2. Organizing
3. Staffing
4. Leading
5. Monitoring and controlling for quality

These processes are integral to every managerial task, and managers are evaluated both formally and informally on their ability to perform them. When evaluating the manager informally, parents or staff may refer to personality characteristics and the way the manager interacts with them. However, as important as interpersonal communication is, managers must carry out many other tasks. When the sponsoring agency or industry evaluates the overall success of the child development center, the manager's handling of all managerial processes is on the line.

These five basic managerial processes are examined in greater detail in later chapters. In the following brief overview, we relate each to the role of a child development center manager.

Planning

Planning can be defined as creating a mental image of what you want to accomplish and how you will go about doing so, a road map of where you want to go and how you will get there. Andrew DuBrin defines three levels of planning. **Strategic** planning is the organization's "overall master plan that shapes its destiny." **Tactical** planning breaks that master plan down into specific goals, assigning them to various parts of the organization. **Operational** planning spells out the specific procedures or steps that it will take to meet the goals (DuBrin, 2000, p. 95). When designing and building a house, for example, the strategic plan is represented by the architect's drawings. Tactical planning occurs when a contractor hires the electricians, plumbers, carpenters, masons, and other professionals needed to work on the many interdependent components of the house. Each of these professionals engages in operational planning as they figure out how to lay the foundation, build the walls, or install the wiring and plumbing.

Organizing

Organizing is defined as arranging elements (e.g., people, supplies, and equipment) and coordinating joint activities so that all of the interdependent parts contribute effectively to the desired goal. This critical process begins after planning and requires assembling the people, physical space, equipment, and materials in an orderly process so as to accomplish the center's goals. Some people are very good at suggesting ideas or even at writing plans, but they fall short when the time for implementation arrives. If you see this occurring, you may need to step in and guide them. It is through organizing that the dreams begin to materialize as the hard work of the center gets done.

In the organizing process, the manager delegates and organizes units to facilitate conducting the programs stipulated in the goals. An internal logic and consistency should be applied to the delegation of duties. Also, the manager assembles and uses space, facilities, materials, and equipment effectively to accomplish the work of the center.

Decisions, Decisions . . .

The family of a child who is blind has asked to enroll the child in your center, beginning next month. Your center's stated philosophy is that *all* children are welcome, and you know that some changes will be needed to accommodate this child. List the steps you will take to prepare for this child's arrival and the people you will involve. Discuss the resources (e.g., equipment, materials, knowledge) needed.

Staffing

People make the major difference in any service institution. The importance of people is indicated by the statistic that salaries for the personnel of a center often consume over 70 percent of the operating budget. **Staffing** is a process of recruiting, developing and deploying the human resources (human capital) required to perform the functions of the center.

The staffing process begins with recruiting and selecting the individuals most well qualified to carry out the center's goals efficiently. High standards begin with high-quality staff. Once staff members have been hired, it is the manager's job to orient them to the center's policies and procedures and ensure that they are thoroughly informed about their specific duties as well as the standards for performance of those duties.

Staff members agree to their job description, which serves as the basis for the evaluation. Careful evaluations during a staff member's probationary period and at least annually thereafter help the individual make corrections in practices and are a wise investment of a manager's time. Because there is so much to learn about this vital field of service that deals with vulnerable human beings, a dynamic and ongoing plan for building human capital through staff development is another wise investment.

Leading

Leading is a process of directing and influencing others through example, talent, information, and personal interaction skills. A leader anticipates developments based on broad knowledge of the field at the national as well as the local level and communicates those possibilities to all members of the organization. The leader inspires enthusiasm and helps individuals maintain a holistic and dynamic picture of their responsibilities, minimizing problems of burnout. A leader makes decisions, takes actions, and assigns responsibilities necessary to transform possibilities into realities. Finally, a leader reaches out beyond the center and assumes responsibility for professional activities at the community, state, and national levels.

Monitoring and Controlling for Quality

Monitoring and controlling are defined as the evaluation and action functions of maintaining high quality in the promised services. In other words, after a plan of action has been developed and put into action, the manager must check regularly to ensure that the plan is actually being carried out and meeting its intended aims.

Standards are the measuring sticks used to determine how well the center is accomplishing its aims. A good manager establishes personal standards based on professional knowledge and individual experience, as well as the standards provided by one or more outside sources. All centers must adhere to licensing standards. These are minimum requirements established by the state for the protection of children when they are not in their parents' care. Wise managers understand that the rules are minimum standards and that they are the result of a collaborative effort of many people just like themselves. They ensure that their centers adhere to the rules and do not try to "get around" them. They also understand that they can have a voice in improving rules that need to be changed as new needs arise or new information develops. In other words, the manager of a child development center works in partnership with the licensing agency to establish a baseline of quality.

In addition to licensing standards, some centers are required to meet standards established by their funding bodies. Some states, for example, fund programs for 4-year-old children in public schools, and, in order to qualify for the grants, school districts must comply with specific guidelines. Federally funded Head Start programs have another set of detailed guidelines to follow. In each case, these regulations are above and beyond minimum licensing standards and must be followed consistently in order for the center to maintain its funding.

Any center, regardless of funding source, can elect to meet a further set of standards designed to establish a benchmark of quality beyond the minimum welfare and safety considerations of licensing regulations. Accreditation is a distinction awarded to early childhood schools and child-care centers that have met the standards established by the National Academy of Early Childhood Programs, a division of the National Association for the Education of Young Children. These standards were agreed to by early childhood professionals and parents from across the nation before they were accepted by the NAEYC board. One section of the criteria pertains to the administration of centers.

A standard is a measure of the quality or quantity of a service or a product. To achieve high quality, you must be aware of the standards or criteria of quality.

Conclusion

Management of a child development center requires an integration of theories and principles from child development, organizational management, and human ecology. A theory is an organized set of related ideas, concepts, and principles that describe a particular area of knowledge. A theory must be stated as clearly as possible, published in the public domain, and tested by independent scholars who also publish their results in the public domain. A theory provides explanations for *why* a course of action might be desirable. Individuals may find particular theories more convincing or compatible with their own assumptions, but no one theory can be said to explain everything. Managers who understand a range of theories can choose the one that best fits a particular situation.

All managers use five basic processes regardless of what enterprise they manage: planning, organizing, staffing, leading, and monitoring and controlling for quality.

QUESTIONS FOR REVIEW

1. Define *theory*, and state three requirements of a good theory.
2. Look for more information about one of the developmental theorists mentioned in an encyclopedia, library, or online database. List ideas that the theorist proposes that relate to children in a child development center.
3. Define human ecological systems theory.
4. Name and describe each of the three environments of the ecological systems model and give examples of how each environment contributes to operating a child development center.

5. Define management theory. List the three major paradigms that characterize management theories.
6. Explain how theory differs from fact.

PROFESSIONAL PORTFOLIO

Consult the website for the National Association for the Education of Young Children, http://www.naeyc.org, to learn the steps involved in accreditation. Develop a plan that a center could follow to accomplish each step and achieve accreditation. For each step, describe what must be done, who will be responsible, when it should be completed, and what resources might be helpful. Include this plan in your administration portfolio in the section labeled Assessment and Evaluation. Be sure to add a cover sheet describing what the plan shows about your competency as a manager of programs for young children.

RESOURCES FOR FURTHER STUDY

Print

Edwards, Carolyn Pope (2002, Spring). Three approaches from Europe: Waldorf, Montessori, and Reggio Emilia. *Early Childhood Research and Practice*, 4:1. Online at http://ecrp.uiuc.edu/v4nl/edwards.html

Hersey, Paul, Blanchard, Kenneth H., & Johnson, Dewey E. (2001). *Management of organizational behavior: Leading human resources*, (8th ed.). Upper Saddle River, NJ: Prentice Hall.

Shonkoff, J. P., & Phillips, D. A. (Eds.). (2000). *From neurons to neighborhoods: The science of early childhood development.* Washington, DC: National Academy Press.

Internet

Academy of Management

http://www.aom.pace.edu/omt/omt.html

Website of the Organization and Management Theory division of the Academy of Management (affiliated with Pace University and the Lubin School of Business, New York); provides links to nine professional journals on organization theory and several online resources for managers. The division's mission is "to attract, develop and serve academics and practitioners who wish to advance understanding of organizations and organizing."

MAP for Nonprofits

http://www.mapnp.org/library/mgmnt/skills.htm

A list of interactive links to resources on a number of topics, including the basic management functions discussed in this chapter. This site is part of a free management library compiled by management consultant Carter McNamara and hosted by Management Assistance Program (MAP) for Nonprofits in St. Paul, MN.

Part II

CORE COMPETENCIES

CHAPTER FOUR

Reflective Management: Personal and Professional Self-Awareness

As you learned in the previous chapter, administrators of children's programs draw on a complex, continually evolving body of knowledge in at least three areas: child development, family ecosystems, and management. Building a solid understanding of current thinking and finding ways to stay up to date in each of these areas are essential components of your preparation for a management role. It is not sufficient, however. Effective management is not a question of learning a few "right" techniques and simply applying them. As you have seen, there is no agreed-upon right answer! Furthermore, managing always involves human interactions, whether the facility managed produces computer parts or a human service such as the care and education of young children. This makes managing a complex undertaking, requiring professional judgment and the ability to think on one's feet.

Reflective Practice

Managers must absorb a great deal of information from the "experts" as well as from the situation at hand, and they must be able to select and apply that information in the way that makes most sense to them at the time. They observe what happens, and what they learn from experience becomes part of their knowledge base for future decisions. This entire process of looking back and making sense of your experience is called **reflection.** Another term for reflection is critical thinking. It is an activity essential to any type of learning beyond simple rote memorization. In the "Decisions, Decisions" segments that appear in each chapter, this textbook asks you to engage in reflection—to think about what you are reading in the context of your own experience and to apply your thinking to some new situation.

Seibert and Daudelin (1999) traced the history of reflection in education back to the Greek philosopher Socrates and argued for its application to management theory and practice. They distinguished between two types of reflection, believing that successful managers must use both types, and offered suggestions for enhancing each. **Active reflection** occurs in the situation, "on the fly in the midst of challenging experiences." All managers engage in active reflection—that is, they ask themselves questions about what is happening, what they should do, and what might happen as a result. They answer their own questions by interpreting what they observe. Managers can enhance this active reflection process by becoming more aware of it. They can listen to themselves and try to generate more probing questions, always remembering that their interpretations of situations are not necessarily final. They should find ways to capture the ideas that occur to them in the heat of the action and use spare moments throughout the day to mull over current problems (pp. 206–207).

In **proactive reflection,** managers take time away to reflect on their experience, often after completing a particular task or project. They review what happened, compare it to their other experiences, formulate explanations, and make plans for what they might do differently another time (p. 148). **Community reflection** is a particular type of proactive reflection in which a group of managers approaches similar questions under the guidance of a facilitator. Some managers report that they not only learn more through this collaborative approach, but they also develop feelings of greater closeness with their colleagues (p. 205).

Managers, like children, need time to pause and reflect about what they are doing.

Knowing Yourself

Seibert and Daudelin (1999, p. 18) pointed out that the Latin root of the word *reflection* is *reflectere*, which means to bend back. And, as you read in the preceding section, managers do "bend back" in their thinking as they review what has happened and formulate new ideas. Another, perhaps more common, association with the word reflection is the image that looks back at you from mirrors or other shiny surfaces. Managers look into metaphorical mirrors to acquire **self-reflective knowledge,** which is an understanding of one's purpose or mission and of one's strengths and weaknesses in relation to that purpose. Brown and Manning (2000, pp. 84–85) considered self-reflective knowledge one of four types of core knowledge for directors of children's programs. Common sense tells you that you must have a strong sense of who you are and what you believe, as well as the humility to acknowledge what you do not know, if you are to be credible and effective in a leadership role. The "mirrors" that managers of child development programs use are self-assessment tools; feedback from colleagues, employees, and families; and self-reflection within a context of professional knowledge. A review of Table 1.1 in chapter 1 reveals a high level of agreement between the writers who have tried to spell out what directors should know. Terms such as self-assessment, personal and professional self-awareness, self-development, and knowledge of self appear on four of the six lists.

Some people aspire to managerial positions because they enjoy being responsible for a large operation. They like a major role in making things happen and enjoy the give and take that is required. Some people like the thoughtful solitude that decision making requires. They can tolerate the dissonance that may arise at times when all of the staff members are not completely satisfied. Some people are challenged when helping solve problems and conflicts. Others, oriented excessively toward a love of power and higher managerial salaries, may not be the most effective in providing needed managerial services. People who are organized enough to become good managers are needed in many fields. Consider seriously your own personality and preferences as you study how to manage a child development center.

What Will Be Your Management Style?

Recall that chapter 3 presented an overview of three paradigms, or conceptual models of management. If you have some work experience, you have probably already witnessed the application of at least one of these models. Some managers use concepts of cost and increased efficiency. They analyze jobs and figure out the "best way" for the job to be done and expect that the job should be done that way. These are often called **classical managers.** In another approach, the manager recognizes that the way workers feel about their jobs, both individually and as a group, has profound effects on job outcome. The people-oriented approach (classified as "behavioral" by management theorists) gives employees more independence and helps them take more responsibility and develop maturity in their job. In the third approach, based on a systems theory of organizations, a manager strives to understand the "big picture" and help all the parts work together so that the organization as a whole can adapt to changing situations within the larger environment.

In addition to reflecting your ideas about organizations and human nature, your management style will be influenced by aspects of your personality, such as power orientation, ways of dealing with conflict, reaction to stress, and psychological type (Benfari, 1999).

Power and Conflict

You might think of power, for example, as based on fear of punishment or a desire for reward. You might see it as based on respect for either the position itself or the expertise of the individual holding that position. Or you might see power as something based on subordinates' personal admiration and affection for the person in authority (Zeece, 1998). Your basic approach when confronted with conflict can range from simply pretending the issue doesn't exist or capitulating to avoid a fight to defending your position at all costs. In between these two extremes, you might seek a solution in which both parties settle for something less than they wanted, or ideally, collaborate to find a solution that satisfies everyone and may even be better than what either had imagined.

Stress

Your reaction to stress can vary from time to time, just as it varies from that of other individuals. One manager may need predictability and stability while another thrives on the challenges of opening new programs and juggling special fund-raising activities, all while handling the day-to-day operations of a center. The second manager, in fact, may become bored without the added stimulation, yet an illness or family crisis could change that picture quite suddenly. In other words, stress can be viewed as an interaction between external conditions or events, your perceptions of those conditions, and your inner reserves for dealing with them. Chronic stress overload leads to burnout or the inability to function—in work or in life in general.

The key is to recognize signs of overstress in yourself and take action before burnout sets in. Your goal is to thrive, not merely survive. In order to do that you will need to distinguish between the essential and the trivial and let go of the expectation that you can be all things to all people (Bloom, 2005). While it may seem contradictory, delving more deeply into your work can be as effective at preventing burnout as letting go. Linda Yaven, who teaches in the Graduate Design Program at California College of the Arts in San Francisco, was inspired by documentation she witnessed in the preschools and infant–toddler centers of Reggio Emilia and began applying the concept to her own work with adults. Over the next four years she taught—and learned along with her students—how to use photographs, drawings, and written records to make their learning visible.

FIGURE 4.1 *Recognizing and coping with stress*

Symptoms of Stress	
Physical	Emotional
• Loss of appetite • Frequent indigestion • Fatigue • Difficulty sleeping • Sweating, faintness, nausea (without apparent cause) • Frequent colds	• Feeling inadequate, incompetent • Sense of hopelessness • Overreacting (crying or extreme irritation) • Loss of interest in pleasurable activities • Inability to let go of problems and relax at end of workday
Strategies for Coping	
Eliminate or Reduce Causes	Strengthen Inner Reserves
• Regular physical exams to discover and treat health problems that can add to stress • Pare down or postpone commitments at work and/or at home • Delegate tasks where possible • Set realistic goals and timeframes for achieving them • Distinguish between what you can change and what you cannot; focus on the former and let go of the latter	• Exercise vigorously several times a week • Choose a healthy diet • Meditate or practice yoga • Cultivate a relaxing hobby • Spend time with family and friends • Establish a relaxing bedtime ritual • Begin to eliminate unhealthy habits (smoking, junk food) • Seek professional help from a counselor or physician

Sources: Fontana, David. Professional Life Stress Scale. Retrieved July 4, 2005, from http://honolulu.hawaii.edu/intranet/committees/FacDevCom/guidebk/teachtip/stress-t.htm and Rose Medical Center, Denver. How to fight and conquer stress. Retrieved July 4, 2005, from http://www.rosemed.com/healthcontent.asp?page=/hic/stress/index.

She writes, "The fact that I looked forward to coming to class each day did not go unnoticed by me. There are teachers in Reggio who have been teaching there for decades without burnout. I had glimmers while there what that might be about" (Yaven, 2005, p. 10). Figure 4.1 lists symptoms of burnout and offers suggestions for reducing and/or dealing with stress.

Psychological Type

Psychological type refers to a concept introduced by Carl Jung in the 1920s that became the basis for a widely used instrument developed by Isabel Briggs Myers in the 1940s. The Myers-Briggs Type Indicator (MBTI) seeks to determine an individual's basic preferences in four areas, each identified by a particular letter: (E) *extraversion* or focus on the outer world versus (I) *introversion*; (S) *sensing* or focus on information versus (N) *intuition* or focus on interpretation; (T) *thinking* versus (F) *feeling*; and (J) *judging* or decisiveness versus (P) *perceiving* or postponing judgment. These preferences interact to create 16 possible combinations or personality types, each designated by a four-letter code. Individuals characterized as INTJ, for example, lean toward the inner world, interpret rather than accept information at face value, rely on thought and logic, and would rather settle on a solution than keep matters open (Myers & Briggs Foundation website, http://www.myersbriggs.org).

No single type is superior to another, and in fact it is desirable to have many types represented within an organization because the strengths of each will complement the others. Understanding variations in personality types can help you as a manager think about adjusting the ways you interact with individuals in your organization. For example, while you may prefer a logical approach, your well-articulated arguments are likely to be ineffective if addressed to someone who focuses more on feelings.

Leadership Styles

As you recall from chapter 3, management is defined as the process that coordinates individual efforts toward achieving goals, allocates resources effectively, and serves needs. Leadership is one of the five functions of management, defined by DuBrin (2000, p. 232) as "the ability to inspire confidence and support among the people who are needed to achieve organizational goals." In other words, leadership is the human element of management. The subtle distinctions between management and leadership are discussed in greater detail in chapter 16. For now, it is probably safe to assume that when people refer to someone's style of *management*, they are often thinking about that person's *leadership* style.

DuBrin identified three leadership styles (2000, pp. 244–245). His categories may be familiar if you have read about parenting styles in your child development classes. **Autocratic leaders** hold most of the authority in their organizations and focus on getting the job done rather than on people's feelings. At the opposite extreme, the **free-rein leader** relinquishes authority to the group, expecting its members to figure out the best way to accomplish a given task. Steering a middle course between these two styles, **participative leaders** involve group members in decision making; however, not all such leaders involve group members to the same degree. At the level of least group involvement, **consultative leaders** merely seek the group's opinions before making the final decision themselves. **Consensus leaders** facilitate discussion to arrive at some level of agreement or consensus among all group members and base decisions on that. **Democratic leaders** listen to everyone's ideas and let the group vote on the final decision. Note that in a consensus decision, discussion continues until everyone can agree on an issue, at least to some extent. In democratic decisions, everyone listens to the discussion, but in the end, the majority rules. Xavier (2005) characterizes effective managers as those who can navigate a path between these extremes, tapping the resources and expertise of all their staff members, but always accepting responsibility for making the hard decisions needed to keep the organization going.

Decisions, Decisions . . .

Which type of leadership (autocratic, free rein, participative) seems most effective to you? Why? Do you believe that your preferred type is best for all situations? Can you think of circumstances that would change your opinion? Discuss this with your classmates.

Emotional Intelligence

Xavier (2005) argues further that successful managers not only adapt well to change and avoid crucial errors, but they also exercise high degrees of **emotional intelligence**, a concept that has been popularized by Daniel Goleman (1995). Emotional intelligence includes four areas of competence: self-awareness, self-management, social awareness, and relationship management.

Self-Awareness

In essence, self-aware individuals know themselves. Their confidence in their abilities stems from realistic notions of their strengths and weaknesses. They recognize their feelings and understand how those feelings might color their perceptions and judgments.

As a manager of a child development program, you need to realize that you don't have all the answers, that human development is complex, and that our understanding is in a constant state of flux. This is partly because new discoveries mean there is more to learn, and partly because the more we learn, the more we realize that what appeared simple and straightforward is actually subtle and complicated. Knowing you are fallible and do not have all of the answers should not paralyze or discourage you, however; instead, it should moti-vate you to study and challenge your ideas about what is best for children.

As you struggle with a shoestring budget and the mundane daily realities of lost mittens or clogged toilets, you may at times feel overwhelmed by feelings of discouragement and frustration. Self-awareness means recognizing these emotions as temporary states rather than objective assessments of the situation. Today's catastrophe may well become the kernel of a hilarious story in weeks to come.

Self-Management

Recognizing your feelings is a foundation for the next component of emotional intelligence, which is to manage those feelings. This means keeping things in perspective rather than indulging in emotional extremes in reaction to circumstances. It also means being able to rise above one's personal feelings for the good of a common goal rather than venting frus-trations on those around you. You need patience, or emotional self-control, to encourage children, families, and staff members to strive to learn when you are tempted to provide ready-made, but perhaps inadequate, solutions to problems. If you have patience, you do not expect instant results from children, families, staff, or yourself.

Managing your feelings means maintaining a positive outlook in the face of adversity and summoning the energy to tackle a job even though you are tired. It means standing up for what you believe rather than taking the path of least resistance. You can accommodate families' needs, for example, without allowing yourself or your program to be taken advan-tage of. Clearly formulated policies, discussed with each family on enrollment, help you avoid unwanted situations; for example, parents who decide to do a few errands on their way to pick up their children and arrive late, causing tired staff members to be even later than usual in getting home to their own children. Setting fees at a level that allows you to pay staff a living wage requires no apology—although it may require some effort to help fami-lies who cannot afford the rates locate financial assistance. These are simply examples of healthy assertiveness, without which you are less able to fulfill your mission of service.

Managing your emotions will be easier if you remember that your own energy requires replenishment from time to time. A healthy diet, exercise, time with family and friends, hobbies, and outside interests all help you give your best. The trick is to give your best when you are at work and then leave that work behind at the end of each day. Remember that although your work is important, it is not the only important thing in your life.

Social Awareness

In addition to understanding and managing their own feelings, effective managers understand and care about the feelings of others. They derive satisfaction from helping others, and they are sensitive to the complex nature of human relationships.

People who work in child development centers are entrusted with the task of helping parents nurture and educate their children. They are expected to love and care for these children as though they were their own beloved offspring. As manager, you are expected to care about each individual; work to allay conflict; and maintain an atmosphere of peace, love, security, trust, and respect. To accomplish this enormous task, you need the professional dedication to view your work as more than "just a job."

Socially aware managers recognize that institutions should serve people—never use them. Their ultimate goal is to strengthen children and their families. Their role is to supplement, never supplant, the care that families give their children. Because families are often in desperate need of child care, they can be vulnerable to programs that assume unwarranted power over them. Professional ethics demand that you avoid this possibility. Following are examples of how a program takes advantage of its power over people who need its services:

- Demanding that children arrive by 9:00 a.m. or be turned away even though a parent must take another child to school several blocks away and cannot get back to the center before 9:30.
- Accepting only a particular style and color of athletic shoe, even though the cost is a burden to a family's budget.
- Expecting all of the children at the center to participate in a religious observance when not all of the families share that particular religious orientation.

Parents, already pressured by their multiple roles, scarcely need the extra pressure of unrealistic demands from the child development center.

Relationship Management

This aspect of emotional intelligence includes what are commonly called "people skills": inspiring, motivating, and convincing others; bringing out the best in people; getting them to work together; and helping them work through disagreements.

Given the sheer number of people and the myriad complex relationships involved in a child development program, it's easy to see how crucial this aspect of emotional intelligence is to a manager's success. It is the manager who communicates the program's vision to families and staff and who works out strategies for attaining that vision. These strategies can include planning dynamic professional development activities for staff or helping families understand and accept rate increases needed to prevent staff turnover. When inevitable conflicts or disagreements arise—with families or among staff members—the manager must help the parties hear one another and arrive at satisfactory solutions. All this may seem to require superhuman qualities, but relationship management also involves reaching out for help from policy and advisory boards, staff members, outside consultants, families, community members, and the children themselves, recognizing that all of them are potential sources of new ideas and creative solutions to the challenges faced.

Stages of Personal and Professional Development

In chapter 3, you learned that child development programs are complex systems. They are part of a highly interrelated social structure at the same time that they themselves comprise many interrelated entities. You also read about Bronfenbrenner's ecological model of human development, which views the individual as gradually gaining greater understanding and influence over increasingly wider spheres or embedded systems. Infants have a mighty impact on the family microsystem even as they struggle to master their tiny world. As an example at the other end of the developmental continuum, mature adults have an understanding of how social institutions (or the exosystem) influence their lives, and they are capable of interacting effectively with those institutions. VanderVen (2000) applies systems and human ecology theory to create a five-phase model of early childhood administrators' professional development.

Novice Phase

The Novice Phase applies to entry-level practitioners, such as teachers' aides with very limited administrative responsibilities, who work directly with children in the classroom with little or no formal training. Thus, their focus is confined to the microsystem, and they have little understanding of, or influence on, the larger system.

Initial Phase

Practitioners in the Initial Phase still have very limited administrative duties and remain focused on what happens in the classroom microsystem; however, they are beginning to acquire and apply knowledge from the wider sphere of the early childhood profession.

Informed Phase

An administrator in the Informed Phase is likely to hold a 2- or 4-year degree and to have been promoted to an administrative position as a reward for teaching performance—although with little formal preparation for the new role. A key quality marking this phase is a move away from a narrow classroom focus to a growing appreciation for the many influences on human development.

Complex Phase

Practitioners in the Complex Phase may continue working directly with children, modeling higher levels of expertise for teachers, or they may have moved completely into an administrative role. As they enter this phase, their focus begins to move from the classroom microsystem to their program's interactions with the families and community they serve (i.e., Bronfenbrenner's mesosystem). With increasing experience, these administrators gain an even wider perspective. They appreciate how things such as welfare, employment, and the education system (part of the exosystem) impact children, families, and their centers and become more proactive. While a professional at an earlier phase might have bemoaned the lack of funds to provide adequate salaries for staff, an administrator in the complex phase might write to legislators and the media, informing them of the problem and arguing for higher child-care subsidies.

Influential Phase

With sufficient experience, and a capacity for reflective thought, administrators arrive at the Influential Phase. This phase is marked by an understanding of the complex overarching system of values that shape society (i.e., Bronfenbrenner's macrosystem). The influential administrator has a vision and the ability to translate that vision into a reality that both embodies ideals and transmits those ideals to succeeding generations of children and families.

The general pattern, then, is that administrators move from a narrow to a successively wider frame of reference as they progress through the phases of career development. You might compare the novice director to someone who has just taken up the hobby of hunting for morel mushrooms. He walks through the woods, eyes glued to the ground, searching in vain for even one of the delicacies. A more seasoned mushroom hunter takes a broader view and, knowing that morels grow particularly well in the soil of old apple orchards, scans the landscape for clusters of apple trees before concentrating his search. As his skills become more complex, he might consult county maps and real estate records to locate old farmsteads where old orchards are likely to be found. At the Influential Phase, he might join a group that advocates for the preservation of old farmland.

Decision Making

Decision making is the central activity of the manager of any organization. It is a mental activity that may require hours of sitting at your desk reading relevant materials, making calculations or drawings, and developing draft copies of plans until the best possible plans have finally evolved. In some ways, decision making is a lonely activity. It certainly requires time. To some of your staff, who are busy getting things done, it may seem like loafing—after all, you are just sitting there at your desk with a pencil in your hand. When the right decision is made and the right direction is taken, things look rosy. On the other hand, conditions may be gloomy if the wrong decision is made and the wrong direction taken. Dissonance frequently occurs as decisions are made. Your task is to reduce dissonance to a minimum and guide it toward constructive change. Each of the basic functions of management—planning, organizing, staffing, leading, and monitoring and controlling—requires decision making.

Decision Types

DuBrin (2000, p. 114) describes two types of decisions. **Programmed decisions** are those that are made so frequently that they become routine and involve simply following prescribed procedures. For example, managers of those programs with established admission policies need not agonize over which family on the waiting list should be offered the next opening; they simply apply the procedures in place. In contrast, **nonprogrammed decisions** are made when new or more complicated situations arise. What should a manager do, for instance, when a highly competent teacher, with a long history of excellent performance, suddenly begins missing work or treating children inappropriately? Before answering this question, the manager needs more information about the reasons for the sudden change. The manager also must know what options might realistically be considered available in a climate of acute teacher shortage. And, perhaps most important, the manager may have to use creative or original thinking to make this nonprogrammed decision.

The more programmed decisions you face, the easier your job as manager. You can increase the proportion of programmed decisions by establishing ground rules or general principles that apply in all similar cases. Recall the discussion of reflection and use proactive reflection to generate the ground rules or principles. Take some time to look back on an experience and learn from it what can be applied to future situations.

Consider the following problem confronting the director of a small, two-classroom center. Although she had hired sufficient staff to maintain appropriate adult–child ratios, as well as "extra" help to cover for absences, the system was stretched beyond its limits when several people happened to be out at the same time. In addition to unplanned absences because of illness or family emergencies, the director had to plan for coverage when staff took well-deserved vacation days. Approving the requests for vacation time case by case was a nonprogrammed decision. The director had to think through every request and consider all other planned or unplanned absences that might occur on the requested days, what might happen to staff morale if requests were denied, and issues of fairness in deciding whose request took priority. After several experiences of active reflection (while coping with days when both lead teachers were on vacation and a substitute called in sick), the director stepped back to think about things, to use proactive reflection. In fact, she and the teachers used community reflection to arrive at a general principle that shifted the decision of approving or denying requests for time off from the nonprogrammed to the programmed realm. They decided that the two lead teachers could not take the same days off, nor could the lead and the associate teachers in one classroom take the same day. Following this decision, the staff simply had to consult one another before requesting approval for time off and the director no longer had to spend undue time trying to decide whether to grant the approval.

Perhaps you are thinking that this sounds like a lot of trouble to go through for an apparently simple problem. You might think the director could have simply decreed the policy from the beginning. In the realm of human relations, however, nothing is as simple as it might seem. One of your challenges as a manager is to know which decisions can be programmed or routine and which should be nonprogrammed or handled creatively. In the interest of saving your time—and your sanity—handle as many decisions as possible with established procedures. However, an organization can become rigid, stifling creativity and growth, with too many established procedures. The refrain "But we always do it this way" has killed countless good ideas in the brainstorming stage and discouraged budding innovators who may have had a better way in mind. To make matters trickier, new developments can occur in an issue that seems routine and has always been treated as a programmed decision. Suppose, for instance, that the lead teachers in the previous example found themselves in conflict because both, for very good reasons, wanted the same day off. All of a sudden, the director's nice, neat procedure no longer works and the group is confronted with a nonprogrammed decision. More community reflection at this point might lead to a new, more encompassing guiding principle. Instead of asking teachers to coordinate their vacation days, the teachers and director could decide that teachers must come up with the way to resolve conflicts over scheduling. This principle might then become applicable to other conflicts between staff, further reducing pressures on the director.

Decisions, Decisions . . .

Mrs. Parker explained her shortage of funds for her daughter Jackie's weekly fees. As manager of the center, you explain that you can allow a 1-week grace period before discontinuing care. Is this a programmed or nonprogrammed decision? Can it be classified as either? Is it preferable to treat it as one type or the other?

Interrelated Decisions

Decisions are often interrelated in complex ways.

Chain Pattern.   One pattern of decision making is called a **chain pattern,** characterized by a straight line, each decision being dependent on the preceding choice (Paolucci, Hall, & Axinn, 1977, pp. 108–109). The chain can stop and recommence at any point. An example of chain-pattern decisions in a child development center might be as follows:

- Decision 1: The policy board decides to organize a child-care center.
- Decision 2: The board members decide the first year to enroll only 3- and 4-year-old children.
- Decision 3: They decide to establish a 4- and 5-year-old group the next year from the previous year's enrollees and continue the first classroom by enrolling $2\frac{1}{2}$- and 3-year-olds.
- Decision 4: The following year, they decide to add a new group for kindergarten children who need a place to go before or after their half-day of regular school.

Each decision is based on the experience gained from the preceding decision.

Central–Satellite Pattern.   In the **central–satellite** type of decision making, a central decision is followed by several satellite decisions that are dependent on the central decision (Paolucci et al., 1977, pp. 106–108). For example, in a center, a board policy decision to start an infant care unit is a central decision. Then, numerous satellite decisions follow, such as housing, equipping, staffing, and organizing the unit. If the central decision is different, the satellite decisions likewise change.

One might conceptualize several central decisions as being strung together in a chain, with all decisions being related to the overall goals of the center. The satellite decisions for each central decision may relate only minimally to those of the other central decisions. For example, is providing only one type of service more cost-effective or efficient than providing several services? Also, are the expanded services consistent with the central goal of the center?

The Decision Process

Four steps make up the decision process:

1. Identifying the problem
2. Developing alternatives
3. Analyzing alternatives
4. Making the final decision

Identifying the Problem.   Just as decisions can be categorized by type, so too can problems be categorized as to when they arise. Type 1, routine problems, arise because of a breakdown in something that should be regular or routine. Type 2, nonroutine problems, arise when things are less structured and, thus, less predictable. When a problem arises, you can quickly determine whether it is a Type 1 or Type 2. With the routine type, such as having problems with deliveries, the problem might arise repeatedly, perhaps every day. Immediate attention to the sequence of events heads off trouble. At times, stopgap measures must be taken, but routine is desired and is the goal.

Decisions, Decisions . . .

Center XYZ has 240 children enrolled. At 10 a.m., just when foods requiring the oven were ready to bake, the power goes off. A call to the power company reveals that it will be off at least an hour. What type of decision is required? What would you do?

The nonroutine problems often have elements that can be programmed or made routine in advance. For example, the problem in the preceding example is 240 children who must have food at noon. This problem can be foreseen to some extent, making the solutions somewhat routine, though stress producing nonetheless.

Developing Alternatives. Possible alternative solutions can be determined by stimulating the creative thinking of everyone involved. Staff members can be very helpful with generating alternatives if a climate of trust exists such that their creativity can emerge. One way is to brainstorm among the staff for alternatives—even seemingly impossible alternatives are recorded and valued as a contribution. Any idea may have usable elements or stimulate thinking that leads to better ideas. Avoid premature evaluation. As manager, you can offer several alternatives, showing that you trust the process.

Information is essential to developing alternatives. Your staff has information accumulated through years of experience. Various readily available publications have relevant information. Sometimes you may wish to bring in consultants or contact a consultant for specific information. For example, information on children's diets can come from a dietitian. You can obtain information about employee insurance by getting bids from a number of companies and by questioning other child development center managers regarding their solutions to the problem. Information gathering generally has a cost, in time or money, that the organization must bear if the best possible decision is to be made.

Analyzing Alternatives. In a group discussion, allow each staff member to state the pros and cons of the various alternatives. By consensus, you can begin to erase some from the list that are not right for your situation at this time. Listen carefully to staff members and value each one's contribution.

Making the Final Decision. Soon, only a few alternatives remain, and these can be voted on or decided by consensus. Improved decisions result when staff members have a voice, particularly in person-centered organizations such as child development centers. Normally, a problem has many aspects and talking things over helps the manager gain perspective on the problem. Obviously, there is very little substance to the decision-making process if at least two alternatives are not considered.

Decisions, Decisions . . .

Pressure is mounting for your center to lower the age of admission from $2\frac{1}{2}$ to 2. The often-heard pro argument is that parents who need or want care for their 2-year-olds will choose a competing center that accepts them. Then, when the child is $2\frac{1}{2}$, parents will not bring their child to your center because the child is already happily adjusted to another center. Describe the decision process.

Rationality in Decision Making

Decision making in a human services organization, such as a child development center, is rational in some respects and extrarational in other respects. **Rational decision making** is considered to be objective, logical, based on hard data, and useful for **technical decisions.** For example, concerning the center's physical plant maintenance, you decide on the floor covering, the quality of paint, or a parking lot covering based on objective criteria such as the cost of

Rational decision making requires considering all options and being open to information from other points of view.

installation, the cost of its upkeep, and its predicted longevity. These are all technical decisions.

Extrarational decisions require judgment or wisdom in addition to available objective facts. Extrarational decisions are often **social decisions.** Paolucci et al. (1977) said that social decision making occurs when there is a conflict in values, goals, or roles. Social decisions occur frequently in children's classrooms as the values, goals, and roles of parents, teachers, and children become integrated into the human service that is child care. Teachers use social decision making repeatedly during each day as they mediate the interaction between children.

Ethical Decisions

The National Association for the Education of Young Children (NAEYC) developed a code of ethics to help guide early childhood professionals in their interactions with children and families. Recognizing that the manager's responsibilities encompass more people and relationships than those of the classroom teacher, a group of educators began in 1997 to develop a supplement to the NAEYC Code of Ethical Conduct for administrators (McCormick Tribune Center for Early Childhood Leadership, 2005 June). If approved by the NAEYC Governing Board, this document will supplement—not replace—the original code.

Both the original code and the supplement consist of a set of basic ideals and principles regarding responsibilities to children, families, colleagues, and society developed by members of the profession (Feeney & Kipnis, 1995; McCormick Tribune Center for Early Childhood Leadership, 2005). Sometimes a situation creates a conflict between two or more basic principles. This is called an **ethical dilemma,** and it can be resolved only by careful reflection and discussion that involves all parties. Ideally, they find a way to sustain the spirit of both principles; if not, they have to decide which principle takes precedence.

For example, a parent might demand that a caregiver use spanking to control a child's behavior. The center adheres to the basic principle of cooperating with parents and respecting their individual child-rearing style. However, the center also follows a fundamental principle of using positive guidance techniques with children, which means that all forms of corporal punishment are prohibited. Because a state licensing regulation prohibits corporal punishment, you might argue that the center can make this a routine decision, simply by citing that regulation when denying the parent's request. But that solution does not resolve another conflict between two ideals regarding ethical responsibilities toward families: respecting families' ideas about child rearing, while sharing information that enhances parenting skills.

Thus, the center finds itself in an ethical dilemma. The manager, teacher, and parents should talk openly and try to come to some understanding of the reasons for each position. In this case, the parents might lack information about other, more effective, methods of getting their child to "behave." They might view the center's positive guidance techniques as spoiling the child. If, after honest and open discussion, the parents and center cannot come to some agreement, it may be necessary for them to "agree to disagree," and the family may decide to withdraw the child.

Whatever the final outcome, the thoughtful manager realizes that ethical decisions like this are complex, requiring the consideration of several competing ideals and principles.

Laws against corporal punishment may make this dilemma seem fairly simple to solve. Other situations may involve more gray areas (Feeney & Freeman, 1999).

Time Management

Time is a valuable, nonrenewable resource. Managing this resource carefully is essential if you are to achieve the goals set forth in your plans. If you are moving up in the ranks from a teaching position, you may have difficulty delegating some of the responsibility and may tend to do things that your teachers or other staff can do for themselves. You must learn to let others do their share of the work and to leave your time for the managerial and leadership functions that are now your responsibility.

Effective managers use a variety of time management tools to plan ahead and avoid crises.

Prioritizing Tasks

Management expert Stephen Covey (1989) said that the essence of time management is to "organize and execute around priorities." He suggests that managers determine priorities using the criteria of importance and urgency:

1. Activities that are both important and urgent
2. Activities that are important but not urgent
3. Activities that are urgent but not important
4. Activities that are neither urgent nor important (p. 101)

As a center manager, you may find yourself constantly dealing with crises of minor importance unless you manage to allocate significant amounts of your time to activities that, in Covey's language, belong to the "second quadrant"—that is, they are important but not urgent. Planning your center's public relations strategy, for example, may seem insignificant compared to a broken water pipe, but neglecting it may lead to larger problems, such as declining enrollment.

Using these criteria, you might decide to take the time to recruit and train a volunteer to do routine tasks like sorting mail, knowing that your investment will pay off in many hours saved later on. Even tasks that qualify as both important and urgent can be delegated if you have selected your staff wisely and explain the task carefully. A staff member, for example, can keep children's time records and generate invoices or send reminders to parents, freeing you to work on a feasibility study for a new infant–toddler component. Activities that may seem unimportant, such as having lunch with key board members or individual staff members, can promote valuable relationships and help your organization develop a clear, unified vision. Knowing your priorities helps you decide which activities to tackle, which to delegate, and which to put off for another time as you face your weekly or daily "to-do" list.

Managing Meetings

Meetings may appear frequently on your list of activities. Plan ahead for those meetings that are your responsibility. Give people an agenda several days ahead of time so they can be prepared with thoughtful information and opinions on the various items. Follow your agenda and keep it moving along. Occasionally, people take more time than an item seems to warrant, preventing the group from moving to the other items. It may help to put a time limit on the discussion for each item and agree to table any item if it is not completed when the time is up. Keep minutes of your meetings, and send copies to members as early as possible. Do all informal visiting before or after the meeting.

You may be invited to numerous meetings because of your role as manager. After each meeting, make a careful analysis to determine whether a particular meeting really warrants the time you just gave to it. You may decide to pass it up another time and just read the minutes.

You will soon become aware of the cyclical periods when certain reports are due, requiring a larger time input. Learn to anticipate those periods in order to even out the work over a period of time.

Put a picture of your family or other reminder of your life outside work on your desk so that you remember to get things accomplished efficiently in order to have time for them. To be fresh and inspirational as a manager requires that you spend some time in a pursuit that revitalizes your psychic energy. Time is a precious, nonrenewable resource. Use it wisely and guard it appropriately.

Conclusion

This chapter described the role of reflection in your personal and professional development as an early childhood administrator. Active and proactive reflection are the means by which managers learn from experience. Self-reflective knowledge, an awareness of one's strengths and weaknesses, is essential when managing groups of people. Management style reflects both your basic beliefs about people and organizations and personal factors, such as psychological type and emotional intelligence. Management styles vary in their emphasis on accomplishing tasks versus motivating people and in the degree to which subordinates are involved in decision making. Bronfenbrenner's ecological model of human development and the ecosystems theory are useful for conceptualizing the professional development of early childhood managers as their awareness and influence expand beyond the classroom to society at large. This chapter outlined the steps of the decision-making process, a central activity of management, with special attention to ethical decisions. The material focused on the core competency of personal and professional self-awareness as the foundation for all of the other competencies required for effective management. You now turn your attention outside yourself to the management of the human and nonhuman resources that comprise the child development program.

QUESTIONS FOR REVIEW

1. Define the following terms:
   a. active reflection
   b. proactive reflection
   c. ethical decision
   d. classical manager
   e. participative manager
   f. emotional intelligence

2. List the steps in the decision-making process and give an example using all of the steps.

3. Define and give examples of programmed and nonprogrammed decisions.

4. Divide a sheet of paper into four sections. Label the top left section "urgent/important," label the top right section "not urgent/important," label the bottom left section "urgent/not important," and label the bottom right section "not urgent/not important." Think back over your activities during the past 24 hours and write each in the appropriate section. What conclusions can you draw about your time management effectiveness?

PROFESSIONAL PORTFOLIO

1. Select a tool to use to assess your strengths and weaknesses as a manager or potential manager of an early childhood program. (Your instructor may give you some suggestions, or you can consult the Resources for Further Study at the end of this chapter.) After completing your self-assessment, develop a plan for capitalizing on one or more of your strengths and a plan for addressing at least one of your weaknesses. Include the specific strategies you will use and develop a timeline for completion. For example, if you have a weakness in the area of budgeting and finances, you might attend a workshop on financial management by a specific date. If relating to families is a strength for you, you might capitalize on this skill by looking for ways to involve families at a deeper level in your program. Your strategy might be to conduct a focus group seeking families' input on the issue.

2. Make a list of several time-management strategies and describe how you will use each in your role as an early childhood administrator. Examples might include creating a daily to-do list, prioritizing tasks and using your peak energy times to focus on the most important, or using computer technology to maintain your work calendar and track appointments.

RESOURCES FOR FURTHER STUDY

Print

Carter, M., & Curtis, D. (1998). *The visionary director: A handbook for dreaming, organizing, and improvising your center*. St. Paul, MN: Redleaf Press.

Goleman, Daniel, Boyatzis, Richard, & McKee, Annie. (2002). *Primal Leadership: Realizing the power of emotional intelligence*. Boston: Harvard Business School Press.

Internet

Myers & Briggs Foundation
http://www.myersbriggs.org
Website of the Myers & Briggs Foundation; provides extensive information about the purpose, development, and uses of the Myers-Briggs Type Indicator, with explicit cautions that the instrument must be administered and interpreted by a qualified professional in order to obtain valid results.

6 Seconds
http://6seconds.org
Website of a nonprofit California corporation founded in 1997 to promote the role of emotional intelligence in schools and organizations; contains more than 175 articles as well as links to other resources regarding Emotional Intelligence.

CHAPTER FIVE

Organizational Management

In this chapter, our attention shifts from *knowledge of self* to *knowledge of others*—in particular, to knowledge of the stakeholders involved in early childhood programs (Brown & Manning, 2000). A **stakeholder** is defined as a person or group who stands to benefit (or suffer) in some way as a result of an organization's success or failure. Children and families are, of course, the primary stakeholders in a child development program. If you recall what you learned about the human ecosystems perspective in chapter 3, it should come as no surprise to learn that the stakeholders in child development programs extend far beyond the children and families directly served by the program. Teachers, legislators, corporate sponsors, members of society in general all have a stake in how well a child development program functions. We have chosen the term **organizational management** to encompass all of the activities involved with aligning a program with the interests of these broadly defined stakeholders. This chapter, then, focuses on stakeholders beyond the immediate program participants. The relationships with staff and families as stakeholders are discussed in later chapters. Organizational management competency includes (a) a working knowledge of the many regulatory systems governing program operation, (b) an understanding of the reasons for the regulations, and (c) the ability to manage the program within those constraints.

Working with the Systems

Licensing

One of the first legal systems you encounter as a program director is licensing. You may be tempted to view licensing rules as a bothersome list of petty details. Perhaps, you feel a certain amount of anxiety when the licensing agent comes to inspect your program and breathe a sigh of relief when you "pass" for another year. If you think about it a little more deeply, though, you may begin to see things differently.

Licensing is the mechanism by which the state acts on behalf of its citizens to protect their interests when it is impossible for individuals to do so for themselves. With licensing, a state prohibits a particular activity or enterprise and then selectively lifts that prohibition for individuals or organizations who meet specific requirements. In the case of child-care licensing, the state assumes responsibility for safeguarding the health and welfare of children whose parents are not present. Although most states make exceptions for small numbers of children or particular circumstances, such as limited time in care or care provided by religious organizations, they essentially declare that no one may care for groups of other people's children unless specific requirements are met. The requirements, which are established by state agencies concerned with health and welfare issues, set forth minimal levels of safety and protection for children. They are mandatory, meaning that they have the force of law, and the state empowers its licensing agency to enforce the regulations by imposing penalties when providers violate the rules. Recently, some states have attempted to encourage programs to exceed the minimum standards and to acknowledge those that do by offering a range of licensing levels. Programs still must meet minimum standards, but they may earn higher levels by meeting stricter requirements. North Carolina, for example, has a system of awarding 1- to 5-star licenses based on staff education levels, a history of regulation compliance, and program quality indicators.

Who are the stakeholders represented by licensing? Certainly, parents want to know their children are kept safe in their absence. The legislators who enact the laws requiring that programs be licensed and the licensing agencies who enforce those laws have an interest. In a broader sense, every element of society is a stakeholder in the regulation of child care because when children are harmed, society bears the cost. Long-term costs include the loss of human capital when children are prevented from growing up to be healthy, functioning, productive adults. Short-term costs include lost time at work or lowered productivity for parents, additional strain on families, and extra burdens on health-care systems.

You, too, are a stakeholder in the licensing system, as director of a single program and as a member of the early childhood profession. From the administrator's perspective, licensing regulations help level the playing field by requiring all programs to meet at least minimum standards for health, safety, staff training, adult–child ratios, nutrition, and the like. This reduces the possibility that unscrupulous program operators are able to gain an unfair advantage—for example, offering reduced prices because they have cut corners on these basic elements. Your status as a member of the early childhood profession means that, in addition to a concern for your own program's survival in the marketplace, you care about (i.e., have a stake in) the well-being of all children. Therefore, you want to support strong licensing systems to protect that well-being.

Other Governmental Regulations

A number of other governmental regulations govern your program's physical facility and your interactions with employees and the children and families you serve:

- **Zoning** laws in many communities determine where a business may be located and may dictate how much parking space you must provide or the type of fencing you may install around your playground.
- **Building codes** address issues such as fire safety and sanitation. If you are the manager of a program that is building a new facility, you will want to work closely with those inspection agencies during the planning phases. It is far easier to install an adequate number of exits in the proper location initially than it is to revise these

features once the mortar is set. If you inherit an existing facility when you take on the manager's role, your concern is to ensure that the building remains in compliance with codes. Buildings deteriorate, occupants become careless (e.g., obstructing exits or propping open doors that are intended to prevent fires from spreading), and codes change. Sometimes modifications to a building or changes in the way a building is used triggers additional requirements.

- **The Americans with Disabilities Act** applies when buildings are renovated and to new construction. It requires features such as ramps in addition to stairs and wider bathroom doors with levers instead of knobs. Some changes in use may trigger act requirements—for example, moving a wheelchair-using toddler into an older classroom may require the installation of a ramp to allow the child to enter the room easily.

You must have up-to-date information and persistent vigilance to meet these challenges. As with licensing, it is helpful to understand the reasons for the regulations and to form cooperative working relationships with the various agency representatives who enforce them.

Labor Laws. In addition to laws and regulations governing the physical plant and program operations, managers must be familiar with numerous **labor laws.** Those addressing hiring and compensating staff members are discussed in chapter 7 (Personnel Management). Other laws govern payroll deductions and safe work environments:

- The Federal Wage Garnishment Law sets restrictions on the amount of an employee's earnings that may be deducted in any one week through garnishment proceedings. It also regulates terminating employment because of garnishment.
- The Social Security Act of 1935 and Federal Insurance Contributions Act provide retirement, disability, burial, and survivor benefits to eligible employees and self-employed individuals.
- Federal income tax laws require employers to collect employees' income tax and deposit it in a federal depository. The failure to comply is a criminal offense.
- The Occupational Safety and Health Act of 1970 requires that employers furnish employees a safe place to work.

Rights of Children and Families

Your role as manager also requires a familiarity with laws that address the rights of children and families.

IDEA

The Individuals with Disabilities Education Act (IDEA) of 1991, as amended in 1997, affirms the right of all children, including those with disabilities, to an appropriate education, and the rights of families to participate in developing plans for that education. The individualized family service plan (IFSP) for infants and toddlers addresses all domains of the child's development as well as family concerns, resources and priorities, while the individualized education plan (IEP) for children age 3 and older focuses more narrowly on the child's educational performance. You will encounter these plans again in subsequent chapters.

TANF

The Temporary Assistance for Needy Families (TANF), created under the Welfare Reform Law of 1996, provides federal dollars to fund state programs that meet any of the law's purposes:

- Assisting needy families so that children may be cared for in their own homes
- Reducing the dependency of needy parents by promoting job preparation, work, and marriage
- Preventing out-of-wedlock pregnancies
- Encouraging the formation and maintenance of two-parent families (Administration for Children and Families, 2004)

Some states use their funds to pay for child care so that parents can work or attend training.

Family Educational Rights and Privacy Act

The Family Educational Rights and Privacy Act (FERPA), passed in 1974, prohibits releasing information about a child to any person or agency without the consent of a parent. An exception to the confidentiality requirements exists when a child development professional has reason to suspect that a child is being abused.

Child Abuse Prevention and Treatment Act

This law, which was passed in 1974 and reauthorized in 2003 as the Keeping Children and Families Safe Act (CAPTA), mandates all 50 states to establish laws that require certain professionals (including teachers and child-care providers) to report suspected abuse. The laws also protect those who make such reports from any liability stemming from the report.

Because state and local laws vary considerably, managers should seek information through their legal advisers, accountants, and licensing agency to ensure that they are aware of and in compliance with the laws that relate to their center. Discussions with other center managers may help clarify certain regulations and the appeal procedures available.

Business Concerns

Tax-Exempt Status

The corporate status of a child development facility has several implications for you as the manager. Some organizations are granted 501(c)3 tax-exempt status by the Internal Revenue Service, meaning that charitable contributions they receive are tax deductible for the donors. Applying for tax-exempt status can be complicated and expensive, but it may enable the center to tap into particular funding sources such as grants or charitable foundations. Nonprofits are also more likely to involve a board of directors composed of representatives from several sectors. As a manager of a nonprofit program, you should develop grant-writing skills, as well as the skill to relate well to many "bosses." As the owner–manager of a small for-profit center, your life may be somewhat simpler because you are able to make decisions without consulting a board. It is also riskier, however, because you are responsible for the center's success. Larger for-profit programs are often operated as part of multisite franchises or have contracts with corporations to provide child care for employees. In either case, the director functions more as a middle manager, answerable to the corporate chain of command. Obviously, a goal of the for-profit program is to make a profit, but even nonprofit centers must pay attention to the bottom line; consequently, directors of either type must have financial-management skills.

Insurance

Whether you manage a for-profit or nonprofit program, you must purchase several types of insurance to protect the organization's assets. Property insurance is necessary to cover losses caused by theft, fire, or other disaster. If the program provides transportation, it must have vehicle insurance. Liability insurance protects the organization, as well as you and your employees, from claims that result from accidents or injuries. Cohen (1999) cautions directors to consider several issues when purchasing insurance:

- Check the status, rating, and track record of the insurer—cheapest is not always best.
- Get written confirmation of exactly what the policy covers and what it excludes, and be sure you understand how the policy defines each item.
- Update your coverage as you acquire new equipment or take on new responsibilities (e.g., transporting children) that might invalidate a policy.

The Manager's Job: A Juggling Act

In chapter 3, you learned about five management processes used by all managers: planning, organizing, staffing, leading, and monitoring and controlling for quality. You may find it tempting to view these as an orderly sequence of activities: The leader of a student group, for example, draws up a plan to build a float for the homecoming parade. The leader then organizes the resources needed to fulfill that plan—perhaps a truck bed, chicken wire, tissue paper, and paint. Next, the leader finds people to carry out the plan and leads them through the construction process. While the plan is underway, the leader continually checks the group's progress and makes adjustments as needed so that the finished product matches the planned objective. The reality of managing a child development program—or any complex human enterprise—is somewhat less tidy. First, you are juggling more than one of these processes at any given time as you attend to the many components of your job. Second, within each component, you move through the five processes in a cyclical, rather than a linear, manner.

Planning and organization are required in making sure that lunch for these toddlers is nutritious, on time, and served in an attractive setting that supports their independence and enjoyment of the meal.

Competency Areas and Management Processes

Let's explain. The 13 competency areas that were discussed in chapter 1 represent the components of the manager's job (and comprise the major headings for your Professional Portfolio). Think about which of the five management processes are involved in just the first area, Personal and Professional Self-Awareness. To be even more specific, think about what you did—or what you might do—to complete the portfolio assignment regarding self-assessment. Your initial *planning* may have consisted of checking with your instructor or the list of suggested readings to learn about some of the self-assessment tools available. You then had to *organize* your time and energy to locate the selected tool and complete it. Because you were the only person involved in this task, neither *staffing* nor *leading* played much of a role. On the other hand, the entire task of self-assessment can be seen as part of *monitoring* and *controlling for quality* because it required that you identify some of your strengths and weaknesses and make concrete plans to enhance the former and remedy the latter. In other words, you had to revisit the planning and organizing processes and begin the cycle again.

As you proceed through the remainder of this text, you will see that each of the competency areas involves most of, if not all, five management processes, although specific competencies might emphasize one process more than the others. Your job as a center director does not afford you the luxury of choosing which competency to exercise. Certainly, the manager who "loves people" and "hates numbers" cannot spend all available time on staff development and ignore the budget. From time to time, however, the demands of one area might pull your attention from others. When you are trying to meet a deadline for preparing next year's budget, for example, you are less able to find time for reflection and self-assessment. In other words, fiscal management crowds out personal and professional self-awareness for the time being. If this happens consistently, however, and you continually neglect one or more areas, your program will suffer. So you see, the manager's job is a juggling act. Think of a circus performer keeping 13 plates spinning atop 13 poles. The juggler propels each plate with a vigorous shove and moves on to the next. Any plate that loses momentum falls unless the juggler comes back to give it another spin; therefore, the performer must move along the row quickly and continually. Now, imagine that you are that juggler and that each pole is one of the manager's competency areas. The spinning plates represent your movement through the cycle of the management processes—from planning to monitoring and controlling for quality. If you don't keep all of your "plates" spinning (i.e., recycling through these processes), they will fall.

The Planning Process

As a teacher, you have made daily plans, monthly plans, yearly plans, lesson plans, and children's plans. If you have taught in a small center, you may also have experience doing some of the managerial tasks described in chapter 3. If you become a manager, you can expect to move beyond planning for a single group to planning a center operation with a number of classrooms, a greater number of children and families, a larger staff, a bigger budget, and perhaps more varied services.

Managers are frequently involved with such activities as planning an expansion of programs, planning to reorganize existing programs, and planning the coordination of several centers throughout a city or region. In addition, managers must assist, monitor, and suggest improvements in the planning done by unit staff members.

In chapter 3, we defined **planning** as creating a mental image of what you want to accomplish and how you will go about doing so, a roadmap of where you want to go and how you will get there. We also identified three levels of planning: **strategic planning** or the organization's "overall master plan that shapes its destiny"; **tactical planning**, which means breaking that master plan down into specific goals and assigning them to various parts of the organization; and **operational planning**, which spells out the specific procedures or steps that it takes to meet the goals (DuBrin, 2000, p. 95). In other words, a plan describes what should be done and how it is to be done. Because plans, particularly strategic plans, are most effective when developed in collaboration with stakeholders, we view the management process of planning as most closely aligned with the competency area of organizational management.

Strategic Plan and Central Concept

Initially, a strategic plan requires clear agreement on the statement that sets forth the center's central concept. This statement (which may also be called a vision or mission statement) describes the program's ultimate goal in general terms. A center may have a central concept statement when the manager is hired or one may have to be developed as the work proceeds. The wise manager collaborates with all of those who hold a stake in the center's operations when developing this statement: members of the policy board, parents, and staff. Involving parents helps the center better understand and serve the needs of its customers; involving staff helps ensure that they are committed to the center's ultimate goals. The central concept may be a simple statement such as "The ABC Center will provide high-quality, developmentally appropriate care and education to children 18 months to 6 years of age on a full-time, year-round schedule." Part of your job as manager is to interpret, with input from your stakeholders, the meaning of this policy. You might, for example, define "high-quality" as achieving a certain numerical score on an instrument such as The Early Childhood Environmental Rating Scale (Harms, & Cryer, 2005). Or you could determine that "developmentally appropriate" means meeting the accreditation standards of the National Association for the Education of Young Children (2005). A "full-time, year-round schedule" could mean operating round-the-clock to accommodate several work shifts or it could mean remaining open from 7:30 a.m. to 5:30 p.m. and closing for two weeks each summer.

Often the central concept includes additional elements. An early childhood laboratory program on a college campus provides developmentally appropriate care and education, but its major focus typically is to provide experience with children for college students preparing to enter the field of early childhood education. An employer-sponsored child-care center in a hospital also provides developmentally appropriate care and education, but its major focus is often to provide a convenient service that helps the hospital attract and retain skilled medical staff. Yet another child development center might be operated as a franchise of a large corporation with at least part of its purpose being to make a profit for stockholders. Ideally, the central concept statement is reviewed by all stakeholders at least every five years, and the strategic plan for fulfilling that central concept is reviewed annually. Documenting these reviews in writing, perhaps with minutes of relevant meetings, is part of the manager's responsibility (Talan & Bloom, 2004, p. 38–39).

Tactical Operational Plans

As the strategic plan is translated into tactical operational plans, the administrator must apply licensing and professional standards to the services proposed. Operational planning means ensuring that staff members understand the standards and follow them. Licensing standards vary from state to state, so it is important to have accurate information about the specific standards that apply in your state. For example, some states allow as many as 12 infants or toddlers or 20 4-year-olds per caregiver. Regulations in other states come closer to the NAEYC recommendations of no more than 4 infants and toddlers, or 10 children, ages 3 through 5, per caregiver (Children's Defense Fund, 2001, p. 138). You can learn the specific licensing requirements for your state by visiting the website for the National Resource Center for Health and Safety in Child Care, listed under "Resources for Further Study" at the end of this chapter.

Goals and Objectives

Planning involves developing goals and objectives for the center that are both appropriate and realistic. To many, goals and objectives are synonymous. To others, objectives spell out the steps for arriving at the goal. For example, the goal of having happy, well-adjusted children might imply objectives addressing staff retention because children who are able to form secure long-lasting relationships with their caregivers are more likely to be happy and well adjusted. However you define the two terms, you have to help your staff and others clarify the meaning of the goals and the method of determining when they have been achieved.

Because a great deal of time and energy goes into agreeing on goals and objectives, it follows that they should form the basis of decisions. The manager develops, evaluates, and revises plans as needed. This responsibility is continuous from the first to the last day of a manager's tenure. As you enter the position, record a baseline of statistics—for example, on the number of classrooms, staff, and children; the amount of the budget; and the breadth of services offered. These data provide a benchmark for evaluating program developments that you implemented. In a sense, you are making an audit of the enterprise as you find it. Do not rely on your memory.

Decisions, Decisions . . .

Suppose you are the manager of a child development center that accepts children ages 3 through 5 years. You have received several calls recently requesting care for younger children and wonder if your center should expand its services. How would this change be influenced by your center's strategic plan? What modifications to your tactical and operational plans might be needed? How can you "produce the best thinking of many individuals" at each level of planning? What individuals do you want to involve? How should you approach them?

The Policy Board

The policy board is usually the ultimate authority in an organization that makes plans for services, hires the individuals to carry out the plans, and monitors the provision of the services. If you direct a child development program that is part of a public school system, an elected board of education fulfills these functions. In other child development centers, the board may derive its authority from private or public sources. Community people usually make up boards of this sort, and sometimes the funding agency mandates that specific groups be represented on the board.

When you are hired to manage an existing center, the policy board is already in place—it made the decision to hire you. If you are hired to direct one of many centers owned by a large corporation, you may have little or no dealings with the policy board. If, however, you are fortunate enough to participate in the establishment of a new policy board, you must be aware of the political strategy to use when encouraging people to run for or be appointed to the board. The strategy of getting many groups involved, informed, and supportive of the child development services necessitates that people from the community's groups should serve on the board. That is, people from the community's labor unions, businesses, or farm organizations reflect the needs and views of these groups. Having professionals from child development and health organizations as members will facilitate some of the board's technical planning. Of course, parents, as consumers of the service, should be represented, including parents of children with disabilities and ethnic or cultural minorities. The board should reflect the diversity of the population served by the center so that there is a good fit between the center's policies and the needs of its clientele.

Whether you have a voice in creating a policy board or are hired by an existing board, your job as manager is to carry out decisions made by the board. You can help the board make the best decisions by providing your expertise in child development, as well as information about the center's operations. You are an intermediary between the policy board and the center's staff, children, and families. This means that you have to develop your communication skills to a high degree, cooperating when possible and being assertive enough to stand up for what you believe to be right when necessary. It is important that you and the board have clearly stated expectations of each other from the beginning, so that you do not waste energy trying to do each other's jobs.

Decisions, Decisions . . .

A member of your policy board has suggested that your child development center begin using a popular commercial phonics instruction program with the 3-year-olds. The issue has been placed on the agenda for the next board meeting. What will you do to prepare for the discussion? What will you say at the meeting?

Bylaws

The primary functions of the policy board are to write the bylaws and set broad policies for the center, leaving the day-to-day details to the manager. Bylaws are rules adopted by the organization to spell out how the board is established and maintained, how decisions are made, and how changes can be made. Figure 5.1 is an example of bylaws that may be adapted to fit the particular circumstances of any child development center. The bylaw amendment procedures should be somewhat complex to help maintain the organization's stability. Items that may change periodically, such as enrollment figures and tuition fees, are not included in the bylaws—such decisions are made by the policy board at its meetings.

The Advisory Board

If a policy board's function is to create policy, it follows that an advisory board exists to give advice. It may be formally or informally organized. You can simply select a few people to be your eyes and ears in the community, to provide feedback on innovations you are considering, or to provide insight on problems. This type of group can be very useful in your somewhat lonely authority role of manager.

As a manager of any enterprise, you need a method of keeping in touch with people in other organizations who might have connections with families or children's services. Try to identify people in city government, civic organizations such as the League of Women Voters or Chamber of Commerce, the school board, health or mental health providers, the media, labor unions, churches, or a cooperative extension service. Choices might include parents of formerly enrolled children. An advisory board composed of members of such groups gives you a different and larger perspective from that of the parents and teachers you see daily. It also widens your circle of influence in the community, with each member becoming an ambassador for your center within his or her own sphere.

FIGURE 5.1 *Sample bylaws*

BYLAWS

XYZ Child Development Center

Article I. Name

The corporate name of the center is the XYZ Child Development Center located at 123 Rightway, Child City, Michigan 48823.

Article II. Purpose

The center aims to promote child development

2.1 Through the operation of group child care services.

Article III. Policy Board

3.1 The corporate powers of the center are vested in the Policy Board.

3.2 The Policy Board shall consist of a minimum of five (5) and a maximum of nine (9) members.

3.3 One Policy Board member shall be selected from each of the following community groups: business, labor, parents, community services, and early childhood education. Four at-large board members may be appointed by the Policy Board.

3.4 The Policy Board shall meet a minimum of eight (8) times a year.

3.5 The Policy Board, by resolution adopted by a majority of the members, may delegate to the Executive Committee the management of the affairs of the XYZ Child Development Center.

3.6 A quorum of over one half of the duly constituted Policy Board shall be able to transact business.

Article IV. Officers

4.1 The Policy Board shall elect annually from their number a President, First Vice President, Second Vice President, Secretary, and Treasurer who shall constitute the Executive Committee.

> 4.1.1 The offices of President, Second Vice President, and Treasurer shall be filled by election in odd-numbered years. These officers shall serve for two years.
>
> 4.1.2 The offices of First Vice President and Secretary shall be filled by election in even-numbered years. These officers shall serve for two years.
>
> 4.1.3 Each officer may serve only two consecutive terms in an office.

4.2 The President shall preside at all meetings of the Policy Board and of the Executive Board.

4.3 The First Vice President shall preside and perform the duties of the President in the President's absence.

4.4 The Second Vice President shall preside and perform the duties of the President in the absence of both the President and First Vice President.

4.5 The Secretary shall record and preserve the minutes of all meetings of the Policy Board and of the Executive Committee.

4.6 The Treasurer shall keep the Policy Board informed of the financial status of the center. The Treasurer shall countersign checks in excess of an amount designated by the Policy Board. The Treasurer shall be a member of the Finance Committee. Auditing shall be done yearly.

(Continued)

FIGURE 5.1 *Continued*

Article V. Staff

5.1 The Policy Board shall appoint the manager of the XYZ Child Development Center.

5.2 The manager shall employ such staff as required to carry out the purposes and objectives of the XYZ Child Development Center in accordance with policies established by the Policy Board.

> 5.2.1 The manager shall keep the Policy Board fully informed of all aspects of the XYZ Center's program.

> 5.2.2 The manager shall keep a record of all information of value to the XYZ Center and shall be the intermediary between all units of the XYZ Center and the Policy Board.

Article VI. Organization

6.1 The work of the XYZ Child Development Center shall be organized under the standing committees named in Article VII of these Bylaws and under such other committees as shall be authorized by the Policy Board.

6.2 The members of all committees, excluding the Executive Committee, shall be appointed by the President.

Article VII. Standing Committees

7.1 *Committee on Personnel.* This committee shall be headed by the Second Vice President.

> 7.1.1 This Committee shall recommend the appointment of the manager of the XYZ Child Development Center.

> 7.1.2 This Committee shall serve as the screening group for center staff.

7.2 *Committee on House and Grounds.* This committee shall be headed by the First Vice President.

> 7.2.1 This Committee shall handle problems related to equipping and maintaining the facility of the XYZ Child Development Center.

> 7.2.2 This Committee shall make recommendations for any improvements, expansions, or renovations.

7.3 *Committee on Finance.* This Committee shall be headed by the Treasurer.

> 7.3.1 This Committee shall prepare the budget with the manager.

> 7.3.2 This Committee shall assist in obtaining the funds necessary for the operation of the center.

7.4 *Committee on Programs.* This Committee shall handle problems dealing with the childcare services program.

7.5 *Committee on Nominations.* This Committee shall be headed by the President.

> 7.5.1 This Committee shall prepare the slate of officers to fill any vacant positions or list those rotating up for election.

> 7.5.2 New board members shall take office at the January board meeting.

Article VIII. Amendments

8.1 Amendments to these Bylaws may be proposed at any regular meeting of the Policy Board having a quorum present. The vote on the proposed amendment shall be taken at the next meeting of the Policy Board and requires a two-thirds majority to pass.

Start with a small group that you can afford to invite to a simple dinner to get acquainted. Keep meetings short with planned agendas so as not to infringe heavily on people's schedules. If you want to keep things informal, you may keep dated notes on your organization's activities, participants, and accomplishments rather than a set of bylaws. Once you become acquainted with these individuals, you can call them for advice as particular situations arise.

Decisions, Decisions . . .

Your center's policy board, in an effort to accommodate the needs of working parents, has decided to offer an additional service that would allow mildly ill children to continue coming to the center rather than exclude them, as has been the practice. How will you tap the expertise of your advisory board to help you carry out this plan?

The Value of Planning

The owner of a winning baseball team once said, "Luck is the residue of design." In other words, success does not occur by accident. It results from careful planning. Planning charts a course by which goals can be reached most effectively. You meet with the responsible employees in each unit to plan their work and to delegate work to them. Some beginning-level employees may require very specific assistance as they learn to plan. One cannot assume that if given the time, the new employee will produce the necessary written plans—lesson plans, activity plans, menus, maintenance plans, record-keeping plans, and the like.

When planning is undertaken by staff members and the course is outlined so that all clearly understand and reach agreement, then everyone can follow the directions required for success. Everyone will know what must be done to contribute to the organization's goals. Plans for exigencies should be posted—for example, when inclement weather prevents the children from using the play yard or when the head teacher is absent.

Planning helps develop an esprit de corps among staff members. Not only do they get better acquainted when working together to formulate plans, but they also develop a common sense of purpose. Consequently, they feel a joint obligation to work toward the fulfillment of those plans.

Planning specifies in writing what is to be accomplished. For example, your center's plan to add a new classroom becomes a goal that can be measured during the process of controlling (discussed in chapter 15). Planning requires many steps and numerous preliminary drafts. Forms for planning can be provided. (See chapter 12 for forms for planning children's curricula.)

Planning together helps develop an esprit de corps—a common sense of purpose—so that staff members feel more willing to work toward fulfillment of plans.

Time for Planning

Planning is very time consuming, and time set aside for planning is often eaten away by what seem like more pressing concerns. The wise manager, however, recognizes that planning is an investment that saves future time and energy. If you hope to be efficient, you must protect your planning time from interruptions by telephones or casual visitors. Effective planning is closely related to high-quality outcomes. When you, as manager, are allocating the staff's time for tasks, you should realize that they, too, need planning time if they are to accomplish the professional job you expect. If planning time is scheduled, then you, the teachers, the food service personnel, and others are paid for the time spent planning. Teachers' planning, menu planning, and health planning are covered in later chapters.

Finding time for planning in a busy child development center requires careful management. Because planning is so essential to the achievement of goals in high-quality programs, one of your first tasks is to create time for planning. Once scheduled, it is essential that the time actually gets used for planning. This may mean an evening meeting or a weekend retreat at center expense for centerwide planning. It can mean simply 2 or 3 hours of designated time each week for teachers to make classroom plans while someone else manages the children. Of course, such arrangements are costly in terms of time and dollars, but unplanned programs are also costly because they are far less likely to deliver the quality of services promised to the children and their families.

Managers often discover that staff members need assistance with planning. Managers should meet with small groups to generate curriculum ideas, discuss interaction processes, perform evaluations, and so forth. At other times, staff members need help planning for individual children, understanding behavior, and discovering ways that changes in the curriculum can help alleviate a problem the teachers face in the classroom.

Pairing less experienced staffers with the more experienced and clearly stating your intent that the latter assist the former with planning and organizing the unit can facilitate cooperation. Without this verbal assignment in the presence of both parties, one may feel that it is not appropriate to advise the other.

Of course, once planning is done, materials must be assembled, rooms and the play yard arranged, and other actions taken—activities that take time and are more efficiently done when children are not present. The time spent having everything ready for the children is one of the best ways to prevent behavior problems and conserve adults' energy in the long run. Some of the staff's paid time should be scheduled for these organizational tasks. According to a national study, teachers in state-sponsored early childhood programs report an average of 4.1 planning hours per week, ranging from 1.6 to 7.9 hours (Gilliam & Marchesseault, 2005, p. 13).

Steps in the Planning Process

Step 1. Define the Central Concept of Your Child Development Center

What services will your center provide to society? How will your center create those services? Will your center have some distinctive services or methods of creating services? The policy board and the manager take this step together. For example, you can state, "The ABC Center shall provide, for 10 hours a day, developmentally appropriate care and education for children 18 months to 6 years of age."

Step 2. Establish the Goals That Your Center Will Pursue

A goal is defined as a specific achievement to be attained at a future date. For example, "Within 2 years from [date], an infant care center will be in operation." Your center's objectives or goals are based on the central concept statement. For example, one objective might be to provide a full-day child development program for 40 3- and 4-year-olds.

Goals must first state clearly what service the organization is chartered to perform. Organizations may have numerous goals that are being pursued simultaneously, for example: to increase employee benefits within 1 year and achieve greater diversity in both staff and families served within 2 years.

Step 3. Develop Planning Assumptions and Forecasts

Do you know how many young children there are in your community? Population and birthrate figures help you estimate or forecast the potential demand for your child development services. Do you know how many centers there are in your community and the extent of their services, costs, locations, and other details? Are industries or labor unions becoming involved in children's care? How many centers have been established recently or have gone out of business? This information should be available through licensing officials and will help you make judgments regarding the need for a new service.

Considering the ecosystem framework presented in chapter 3, what is the current number of jobs for parents of young children in your community? Is the region attracting new businesses? If so, where are they locating and what is the potential job market forecast? Is there an educational institution where parents are enrolling young children that need child care? What is the community knowledge base regarding early childhood programming? Do families prefer one program or philosophy over another? How much can parents afford to pay? These questions are important to planning regardless whether your center is a profit or nonprofit institution.

Forecasting the number of children needing child development services is often of concern to managers and boards of directors. Perhaps you are considering the purchase of a child development center, or your local board president has suggested starting a new service in your present center or moving to a new site. It is to the manager's advantage to know a lot about the neighborhood and how it has changed over time. Perhaps you conclude that the neighborhood has become a community with few young children. Thus, you might decide not to add a new service or not to buy the center from owners who may have forecast that their enrollment is expected to drop and are hoping to sell their center to some unsuspecting person.

Needs Assessment.   The public schools generally carry out a school census each year to enable them to forecast the need for classrooms and teachers for each age. You may have access to the public school data, or you may want to conduct your own survey using a **needs survey** or **needs assessment.** By using a form similar to Figure 5.2 and questioning neighborhood residents, you can discover the number, ages, and present care and education arrangements of the community's children. A needs survey can be useful to any group—for example, a religious congregation considering opening a child-care facility using the church buildings. The questionnaire is easily inserted in a weekly newsletter, to be returned the following week. Besides serving the needs of the congregation's families, services for others can be planned by surveying the needs of nonmembers in the surrounding neighborhood. A church may consider a child-care program to be a helpful community service and part of its ministry. Some churches view their child-care programs as recruiting tools to attract members.

Accurate forecasting based on reasonable assumptions is indispensable to the planning process. For example, when predicting enrollment for a new center, it is important to remember that it takes time for the reputation of a center to become known and for parents to begin using it. Overly optimistic projections that ignore this reality are bound to result in disappointment.

FIGURE 5.2 *Sample needs survey*

This survey is being distributed to families whose children attend Green Hills Elementary School. The purpose is to determine the need for education and/or child-care services for young children or for school-age children outside of regular school hours.

Please indicate by age the number of children not yet in school for whom you need or would like a child-care or education program:

_____ under 1 year   _____ 2 years   _____ 3 years

_____ 4 years   _____ 5 years

Indicate the days and hours that you would need or prefer this service:

_____ Monday through Friday   _____ 7:30 a.m. to 6:00 p.m.

_____ Other (explain)   _____ Other (explain)

_____   _____

Please indicate by age the number of school-age children for whom you need or would like a child-care or education program:

_____ 5 years   _____ 6 years   _____ 7 years

_____ 8 years   _____ 9 years   _____ 10 years

Indicate the days and hours that you would need or prefer this service:

_____ Before and after school on regular school days (beginning 7:30 a.m.; ending 6:00 p.m.)

_____ Full day during school vacations, on snow days, school holidays and/or teacher work days (circle all that apply)

_____ Other (explain) _____

Please provide the information below if you would like to be informed of the results of this survey or be contacted in the event that a new program for children is developed.

Name _____   Telephone _____

Address _____   Email address _____

_____

We appreciate your cooperation in completing the survey and give assurance that your individual responses will remain confidential. Please return the survey in the self-addressed, stamped envelope provided.

Step 4. Evaluate Resources

Resource types include financial, managerial, personnel, building and yard space, and equipment. Based on your evaluation, some programs or expansions may be more or less feasible. For example, if you have someone who is familiar with infant care, if space is available, and if you already have cribs and other equipment and adequate financial backing, then planning to add an infant care unit may be relatively simple. If one type of resource is absent, the project faces added difficulties.

Step 5. Develop Alternatives

Alternatives or options must be present for real choices to be made. Creative thinking develops alternatives. One of the most important managerial tasks is to establish and maintain a climate that encourages the creativity of individual board and staff members. The essence of effective decision making is ascertaining and testing promising options or alternatives.

A wise manager uses groups and committees to help develop alternatives. When staff members participate in generating alternatives, they tend to accept the resulting choice. Remember that parents have insight, expertise, and connections that make them a fertile source of ideas. Ask them to help, too.

Step 6. Test Alternatives Against the Resources, Goals, and Central Concepts of Your Center

During brainstorming for alternatives, a wide range of ideas may be put forward; yet, to make realistic decisions, you must weigh each alternative against your center's central concept, resources, and goals. Timeliness may also be a consideration. For example, in times of economic prosperity, expansion alternatives may be considered; during an economic downturn, alternatives related to cutting back may be necessary.

Step 7. Decide on a Plan

After making sure you have the available facts, you are ready to make a decision on a plan. Talk over the issues with everyone in your center to ensure that you have heard all points of view. Sort out and clarify your own thoughts and feelings. Knowing that personal moods can adversely affect a decision, delay decisions to another time if you or others are tired or grouchy. (Recall the discussion of emotional intelligence in chapter 4.) Avoid flatly declaring that a decision is final. An overstatement may box you into a course of action that you would like to change later. Recognize each individual's personal values, and be open to what others say.

Step 8. Implement the Plan

Implementing the plan is the action stage and the exciting one. Organizing material resources, staffing the project with qualified people, and providing leadership as the plan moves ahead are all necessary.

Step 9. Evaluate the Plan

Checking up on every step as the plan is being implemented is the evaluative or controlling function of a manager. It is essential to see that the plan is carried out and to check for quality—whether it is the quality of a floor covering or of a human relationship. Evaluations and corrective actions are essential in every enterprise.

Planning in Response to Change

The world changes, people change, needs change, and plans must, therefore, change. Conduct periodic reevaluations to ensure that all aspects of the plan fit today's conditions and can be readily changed to fit tomorrow's. Managers must be in the forefront of change and must be looking ahead to be ready.

The movement to establish prekindergarten programs in the public schools in order to provide better academic preparation for children creates increased competition for existing community child-care facilities. Will some centers just give up and quit? Or will the centers shift with the times and capitalize on the fact that they can offer more comprehensive services than the public school programs? The longer daily schedule of a child development center, for example, is more convenient for working parents and does not leave them without child care during the summer and holiday seasons. In addition, by providing care for children younger than those accepted by the public schools, centers offer the convenience of one dropoff and pickup point for all of the children in a family. Some centers have even been able to contract with public schools to set up before- and after-school programs in the school buildings. Other centers have worked out agreements with corporations, using either a vendor approach or a corporate group-rate approach. In the first instance, the corporation guarantees direct payment to one or more centers for a specific number of child-care spaces; in the second, the corporation pays a fee in return for reduced rates for their employees.

Types of Planning

You can expect the planning for your center to have several phases. Circulate as many rough drafts as are needed among the staff for feedback before final budgeting and funding take place.

Directional Planning. This type of planning means giving the staff the broad direction in which they are expected to move. **Directional planning** is a characteristic of human service organizations. Plans calling for expanding services or retrenching are examples of directional planning.

Management by Objectives. In contrast with directional planning, **management by objectives (MBO)** is "a systematic application of goal setting and planning to help individuals and firms be more productive" (DuBrin, 2000, p. 111). Management by objectives is a particular type of strategic, tactical, and organizational planning. It consists of a sequence of steps that closely parallel the more general "Steps in the Planning Process" discussed earlier:

- Step 1: The policy board or top administrators establish broad goals and map out each unit's responsibilities necessary to meet the overall goals.
- Step 2: Mid- and lower-level managers translate the organization's general goals into specific goal-oriented objectives for their respective units. The objectives spell out what is to be accomplished in concrete, measurable terms, with specified timelines for completion. Ideally, they are established with team input. The objectives are realistic enough that competent workers can meet them, but are sufficiently challenging to inspire workers to aim a little higher than usual.
- Step 3: Individuals set their own objectives and propose methods for meeting the goals assigned to their units.
- Step 4: Managers either accept the plans submitted by team members or negotiate workable compromises.
- Step 5: Once they reach an agreement, the participants develop the action plans necessary to achieve their objectives.
- Step 6: Performance reviews are conducted at specific intervals (e.g., every 6 or 12 months) to determine whether an individual has met most of the established objectives and to examine possible causes for any that are not achieved. New objectives are set then, because the end of one review period marks the beginning of the next, and the cycle is repeated.

Innovative Planning.   **Innovative planning** is a technique that gathers concerned people together to brainstorm possibilities for a new service or a new direction. Innovative planning can be used for retrenchment, as well as for an expansion into new programs. The manager or board president generally sets the stage for brainstorming by providing information about forthcoming possibilities. Getting small discussion groups involved in making extensive lists of creative ideas, without regard to the reality of present restraints or structures, leads to ideas triggering other ideas.

Getting small discussion groups involved in brainstorming often results in one idea triggering several other creative ideas.

SWOT Analysis.   One way to evaluate the alternatives that emerge during brainstorming is to conduct a SWOT (strengths, weaknesses, opportunities, and threats) analysis of each idea (DuBrin, 2000, pp. 104–106). Suppose, for example, that a center faced with declining enrollment pulls together a planning team to brainstorm possibilities for revitalizing its recruitment. Expanding to a 24-hour operating schedule is proposed as a way to tap the market of second- and third-shift workers who need child care. A strength of this option, in addition to enlarging the program's customer base, is the fact that the center already has invested in space and equipment that is not being used during part of every 24-hour period. Weaknesses or drawbacks include the need to invest additional money in beds (as well as finding space to store them during the day) and the potential difficulty of recruiting staff to work during the later shifts. The plan does present the opportunity to increase enrollment, leading to increased revenue. Being the first in the community to offer such a unique service may enhance the public's awareness of and regard for the center, leading again to higher enrollment and the accompanying financial gain. If the center goes forward with the plan, one potential threat is an insufficient enrollment to recoup the expense of the new beds and additional staff. It may be that dressing the children and transporting them to the center, where they will sleep all night, simply does not seem practical to parents working the night shift. Before moving forward with the plan, the center should minimize this threat—perhaps by providing equipment and staff for the smallest feasible number of children before investing more heavily.

Following these brainstorming sessions, a committee may group the ideas into categories. Additional discussion sessions may follow. Perhaps one committee has met to devise a sample needs survey, and another committee has met to explore the costs, locations, services, human skills, and so on needed for some of the proposed major categories. Openness is desirable at all stages. People who are involved feel more committed to the final outcome. When planning child development services, professionals should involve parents who represent the user-consumer perspective. Eventually, tentative and specific proposals can be developed by representative committees or task forces. If funding does become available, the reports on the work already accomplished provide a basis for a final proposal to develop a new program or revise an existing one. (For information on writing funding proposals, see chapter 6.)

Unit Planning.   Regular planning specific to each unit's operation occurs in food service, the classrooms, the transportation unit, and so on. Staffing patterns determine the authority in each unit. As manager, you delegate the planning responsibility to qualified staff members. Your role is to coordinate the various units by establishing a system by which each unit communicates its plans. Using a specific system ensures that each unit's plans are attuned to the center's overall standards, policies, and procedures. The total ecological framework within your center comes into focus as the units use space and resources to meet the needs of children and their parents.

Time, Scope, and Cycling of Plans

Plans differ as to how much time they cover. In some centers, a long-range plan covers only 1 year; in another, it might cover 5 years. Some plans that are called short-range may cover a year or less.

The scope of plans differs, too. A comprehensive plan may cover the entire child-care center or elementary school. Plans can be narrow in scope, covering only one classroom or one service.

The level of the planning also influences the plans' scope. Classroom teachers develop plans that are implemented only in their classrooms, while the manager develops plans covering all of the center's classrooms. If several centers function within one organization, a superplan may be made to cover them all.

Repetitiveness is also a feature of plans. A skeleton plan may cover a center's regular routine, with teachers filling in details on a weekly and monthly basis. Cycle menus and curriculum cycles are examples of planning for repetitive tasks. Contingency plans for emergencies can be repeated and should be made to aid decision making. For example, during inclement weather, the playground may be unusable; a general plan for sharing an indoor space for a large motor activity avoids confusion for both adults and children because necessary changes in a routine are known in advance. A contingency plan for coping when illness strikes staff members is essential. Evacuation plans, used in the event of fire, hurricane, or tornado, are required, often by law.

Policies, Procedures, and Rules

Policies are "general guidelines to follow in making decisions and taking action" (DuBrin, 2000, p. 110). Generally, the policies in a child development facility are established by the policy board after careful, thoughtful deliberation. Policies should be stated in general terms to allow the flexibility necessary to deal with specific situations. They should be stated in writing and given to board members, staff, and parents. Once established, policies must be followed consistently. If they prove unworkable or if evolving circumstances warrant it, changes may be made by formal board action. Finally, policies should be as complete as possible, covering all relevant categories: services to be provided, administration, and dealings with staff, children, and families. Some policies are required by state licensing regulations. Michigan, for example, requires that centers provide parents with written policies for admission and withdrawal, food services, discipline, and the operation schedule.

Suppose, for example, that you are the manager of the ABC Center. The center's central concept is to "provide high-quality, developmentally appropriate care and education for children 18 months to 6 years of age on a full-time, year-round schedule." Because your goal is to provide high-quality, developmentally appropriate care and education, and research has established a link between staff training and the quality of care (e.g., Bowman, Donovan, & Burns, 2001) you and your board establish the policy that the center will hire only those individuals whose education, experience, and personal characteristics equip them to work with young children. In order to apply this policy, a manager has to determine what specific education, experience, and personal qualities are needed for each particular job. A candidate whose temperament and skills are ideally suited for an infant classroom may not be successful in an after-school program, for example. Although your policy application criteria might specify formal course work or degrees, you must still exercise your independent judgment because a degree in "early childhood education" may or may not include specific training pertaining to the developmental needs of specific age groups.

Your center must have the procedures and rules necessary to implement each policy. Procedures specify how to handle certain tasks. According to DuBrin (2000, p. 110), a procedure "guides action rather than thinking." Rules state in particular detail how a procedure is carried out. The procedure for implementing your staffing policy, for example, might state: "For each teacher opening, a job specification must be developed that sets forth the requirement that a candidate must hold a valid early childhood certificate or an endorsement with course work and/or experience pertinent to the job requirements. Job specifications are to be circulated to the placement centers in state colleges and universities that offer early childhood teacher preparation programs and to those state associations where experienced teachers are likely to see the notice."

Any search for new employees invokes another policy regarding nondiscriminatory hiring practices—not only because it is the right thing to do, but because it is required by law. The center's policy in this area might state that "Center XYZ does not discriminate on the basis of race, color, creed, gender, age, ethnicity, or disability." A more proactive nondiscriminatory policy might add, "Center XYZ actively seeks to increase the diversity of its staff." The procedures for implementing such a policy must require that all references to race on application forms be removed and stipulate that job openings be posted where they are most likely to reach a diverse pool of candidates.

The following rule spells out in detail how the manager is to ensure compliance with the center's stated policy and procedure regarding teaching staff:

> The manager personally reviews each candidate's college transcripts and teaching license, checks employment references to verify the person's qualifications, and determines whether the candidate fits the job requirements.

Written policies, procedures, and rules encourage consistent and timely decision making, while discouraging those decisions made without sufficient information. They constitute the blueprint for achieving the established goals of the center.

Decisions, Decisions . . .

What procedures should the ABC Center develop to implement its policy that it "accepts all children, families, and employees on a nondiscriminatory basis without regard to race, color, creed, gender, ethnicity, or disability"?

Conclusion

Child development programs do not operate in a vacuum. They are part of the larger social system. In order to function effectively, a manager must understand how that system governs the operation of the facility. The term *organizational management* refers to all of the activities a manager uses to align a program with the interests of the stakeholders representing the larger system. We view this broad understanding of where a program fits in the bigger picture as a requirement of effective planning, which is a primary task of managers. Depending on a program's corporate structure, plans start with a policy board, a business partnership, or an individual entrepreneur—the center's central concept is established, money is allocated, and a manager is hired. The manager has the overall responsibility for planning, organizing, and delegating responsibilities to other staff members. Staff members participate in planning, especially where their units are involved. The manager, knowing that monitoring and controlling for quality are integral parts of management, fits a control function into all plans to help ascertain when a plan has effectively been carried out. The manager may periodically report on the center's progress to the policy board. The nine steps in planning and policies, procedures, and rules were discussed, and directional planning, management by objectives (MBO), innovative planning, and unit planning were defined. The concept of planning as it relates to other aspects of the manager's job, such as fiscal or personnel management, is discussed in the later chapters.

QUESTIONS FOR REVIEW

1. Define stakeholder.
2. Define and give examples of strategic, tactical, and operational plans.
3. Describe the purpose of bylaws for the policy board. What are the methods for changing the bylaws?
4. Define an advisory board and explain how it differs from a policy board.
5. List and define the steps in the planning process.
6. Explain what a needs survey is and describe its components.
7. Define and give an example of a policy, procedure, and rule.

PROFESSIONAL PORTFOLIO

1. Write a strategic planning statement for a child development program. Remember that a strategic plan is an organization's "overall master plan that shapes its destiny."
2. Write three policies translating your strategic plan into operational terms. Write out the procedures that must be followed to implement one of your stated policies.

RESOURCES FOR FURTHER STUDY

Print

Bess, G., & Ratekin, C. (2000, November/December). Orienting and evaluating your board of directors. *Child Care Information Exchange*, 136, 82-87.

Bloom, P. J. (2000). *Circle of influence: Implementing shared decision making and participative management.* Redmond, WA: Exchange Press.

Internet

National Resource Center for Health and Safety in Child Care
http://nrc.uchsc.edu/STATES/states.htm
National Resource Center for Health and Safety in Child Care; provides links to child-care licensure regulations and changes for each state, as well as contact information for licensing agency, and other child-care contacts within the state.

An Administrator's Guide to Preschool Inclusion
http://www.fpg.unc.edu/~publicationsoffice/pdfs/AdmGuide.pdf
An Administrator's Guide to Preschool Inclusion; authors Ruth Wolery and Sam Odom provide in-depth coverage of all aspects of managing programs for young children with and without disabilities.

6

CHAPTER SIX

Fiscal Management

A child development program, just as any business or, for that matter, any family, cannot survive unless the manager makes wise use of its financial resources. This includes creating a realistic budget, monitoring expenses to align them with the budget, and knowing when to make appropriate adjustments. Fiscal management also includes finding ways to increase resources, perhaps through fund-raising or grant writing. The other side of the coin, of course, is finding ways, such as buying supplies in bulk, to economize without sacrificing quality. Managing monetary resources requires that you, as manager, objectively perform all of the managerial functions: planning, organizing, staffing, leading, and monitoring and controlling. Your goal is to keep your center on firm financial ground. You must balance a tough head for understanding, monitoring, and controlling the budget with a tender heart for giving children loving care and education.

Whether a program is for-profit or nonprofit, its financial practices are subject to scrutiny by several sources, including the Internal Revenue Service and auditors that might be required by funding sources. Accreditation criteria of the National Association for the Education of Young Children (2005) require that a child development center be fiscally sound in order to serve the needs of children and families effectively and efficiently. Sound budget planning and accounting practices are also addressed in the Program Administration Scale (Talan & Bloom, 2004), a tool designed to complement widely used classroom rating scales.

Types of Resources

A resource is defined as a means—a person or thing—through or by which an end or goal is attained. Money is the medium of exchange for purchasing the resources needed to provide child development center services—the end or goal desired. Resources are dormant until human ideas and human energy organize and use them to achieve goals.

MESH Formula

Resources required for a child development center can be grouped in four categories: materials, equipment, space, and human energy, abbreviated as **MESH.** Your task as manager is to mesh or synchronize these resources to meet your program goals. The MESH categories may be expanded as follows:

- *Materials* include all of the physical items and information materials used in the center.
- *Equipment* includes all toys (large and small), kitchen and office equipment, furnishings, and transportation.
- *Space* includes buildings, playgrounds, and interior arrangements; and the organization, decoration, and utilization of the space. Insurance expenses also fit in this category.
- *Human energy* or human capital includes the knowledge, skills, and abilities of all adults involved in developing and delivering the service, as well as that of the children, families, and volunteers.

Figure 6.1 illustrates how the MESH formula can be used to generate a detailed list of the resources required to operate a child development program.

FIGURE 6.1 *Using the MESH formula to identify the resources required to establish and maintain a child development center*

Materials

Most of the listed materials are consumable and must be frequently restocked:

- Teaching and child-care supplies
- Food and food service supplies
- Maintenance supplies
- Clerical supplies
- Postage
- Materials for newsletters and other reports

Equipment

- Classroom furnishings: tables, chairs, shelves, and lockers
- Play equipment for indoors and outdoors
- Furniture and equipment for kitchen, office, staff lounge, and workroom
- Maintenance equipment and tools
- Vehicles:
  Rental and purchase
  License plates and insurance—both liability and accident
  Maintenance and servicing
  Depreciation
  Chauffeur's licenses

Space

Start-Up Costs:

- Capital costs for land, building the facility, developing the playground, or renovating existing space

FIGURE 6.1   *Continued*

- Connection fees and deposits for electricity, sewer, gas, water, and telephone
- Incorporation fees related to establishing the center
- Special tax assessments related to the building process
- Parking spaces

Operating Costs:
- Rent or mortgage payments
- Property taxes
- Repairs and maintenance
- Decoration—art and artifacts
- Insurance—fire, liability, and vandalism

Human Energy
Start-Up Costs:
- Planning services before opening—a needs survey, location study, and so on
- Legal services—setting up structures for operation, taxes, liability insurance, building and land contracts, employee contracts, and so on
- Accounting services—setting up regular accounting and auditing systems
- Public relations—preparing copy, giving talks, and printing brochures
- Advertising—recruiting employees and children

Operating Costs:
- Staff salaries—administrator, bus driver(s), caregivers and teachers, clerical staff, cook, and custodian
  Consultants—health, parent educator, and social services
  Substitutes for absent employees
- Benefits—Social Security, workers' compensation, child care, maternity, health insurance, unemployment insurance, holidays or vacations, retirement, and bonding
- Staff development—inservice training (consultant), professional publications and resource books, fees and support for staff to attend conferences, and dues for professional associations
- Public relations
- Recruitment of children
- Publicity, publications, and appearances

Money is required to obtain most resources—materials, equipment, space, and the human capital of teachers, cooks, custodians, and others. Human capital includes the energy of children and their parents as well as that of program staff. When the children's energy is directed toward hanging up coats, tidying up rooms, and serving and feeding themselves, less adult energy has to be expended on those tasks. More importantly, children are learning significant skills. One of the main objectives of early childhood education is the channeling and directing of the children's energy into developing skills, talents, and independent behavior, including self-care.

Parents contribute their time and energy when they help with field trips or special projects or when they volunteer for particular tasks such as building a playhouse for outdoor play, tilling a plot of land for the children's garden, or typing a newsletter. In one center, the parents organized themselves to give teachers a "gift of time" in lieu of the more typical items usually purchased for staff at holidays. Each teacher received a handsome certificate indicating that a particular parent would serve as a classroom substitute for a four-hour period on a mutually agreeable date.

Funding Sources

As noted in chapter 2, child development centers are funded in a variety of ways:

- The children's families may pay the total cost through tuition fees.
- Philanthropic donors may make contributions, or an organization, such as a business or church, may give in-kind support such as space, utilities, and custodial services.
- Local, state, and/or federal taxes may partially or completely fund a center.

The picture is complex, however, and most programs need a combination of funding sources to survive, largely because there are differences between a center's **expended costs** (cash outlays) and the **full cost** of providing child development programs. A 1995 study of centers in four states found that parents who paid full tuition provided about 90 percent of the amount centers expended in providing care. When the cost of the care for children in government-subsidized programs is included, the average contribution from parent payments goes down to about 70 percent. Cash payments from government sources and philanthropic donations from businesses or churches, for example, provide the remainder (Cost, Quality, and Child Outcomes Study Team, 1995).

Parent Fees

Although they do not cover the full cost of child care, parents find that they must devote increasingly greater portions of their paychecks for that care. According to the latest available U.S. Census figures, employed mothers paid an average of $94 per week, or 8.6 percent of their monthly income for child care in 1999, up from 6 percent in 1986. Child care takes an even bigger bite from the budgets of families with incomes below federal poverty levels (34 percent versus 7.5 percent for the wealthiest families) (U.S. Census Bureau, 2003).

Government Subsidies

Many child advocates believe that families are already paying as much as they can for child care. They argue that government has a responsibility to help families shoulder the burden because a good beginning for every child is in society's best interest. Government subsidies, however, whether direct or indirect, are subject to shifts in the country's political mood, and many hard-fought gains for children stand to be lost in the currently popular move toward cost reduction through welfare reform.

Supplementing the funds from family payments, the federal government contributes 19 percent of the total cost of child care through some 90 programs within 11 agencies. Examples of these programs, which were described in greater detail in chapter 2, include Head Start, the Child and Adult Care Food Program, and the Child Care and Development Block Grant. State governments must often match these federal contributions, and all but 10 states allocate additional funds for their own initiatives such as public school prekindergartens. These forms of public support target specific groups (i.e., children in poverty, with disabilities or considered at risk for school failure) rather than applying to all children (Barnett, Brown, & Shore, 2004).

Foregone Wages

Unfortunately, in the United States, child development programs depend on another unspoken source of funding support because they must skimp on teachers' pay. According to the 1995 study cited earlier, providing even mediocre child-care services requires $127 per week per child, while the average amount actually spent is only $95 per week. Donated goods and volunteer time make up a small part of the difference between the two amounts, but the foregone wages of the teachers and assistant teachers, who earn even less in child care than they would in other female-dominated professions, comprise the remainder, or 19 percent of the full cost of programs (Cost, Quality, and Child Outcomes Study Team, 1995). This appallingly inadequate compensation for a job with such heavy responsibility is—not surprising—the main reason so many early childhood professionals leave the field (Whitebook & Bellm, 1999, pp. 38–41).

Setting Fees

Establishing fees for the services provided by your center requires a constant balancing between what it costs you to provide the care and what price the market in your community will bear. As you will learn in the next section, the largest component of a center's operating costs is labor. Factors influencing your labor costs include the types of services you provide, the level of quality you hope to maintain, and the current job market for teachers in your community.

Infant–toddler programs are more expensive to operate because they require one teacher for every three or four babies, while programs for older children can meet NAEYC standards with one teacher for as many as ten 3-, 4-, or 5-year-olds. As you aspire to offer a high-quality program, you want to hire teachers with appropriate education and experience and they expect higher salaries than employees without such qualifications. Competition from other child development programs (or from jobs outside the field entirely!) may raise this figure even higher.

Because average fees vary from one community to another (with the highest fees generally occurring in large urban areas), the best way to determine the fee level that the market in your community will bear is to find out what other programs in your area charge for various types of service. Your local child care resource and referral agency may be able to provide this information. You should gather information about several programs to make sure you are not comparing apples and oranges in your final analysis (e.g., do not compare infant–toddler rates in one program with rates for older children in another). The study conducted by the Cost, Quality, and Child Outcomes Study Team (1995) found that the average fee charged by centers for full-time monthly care for infants was about $450 (or about $2.50 per hour); for preschool children the fee was about $370 (or about $2 per hour).

Another method of establishing a ballpark figure for your fees is to check with your local Department of Social Services, or whatever agency handles subsidy payments for child care, and ask about the maximum allowable fees established for each category of care: full and part day, infant, toddler, preschool, school-age. (You can find out what agency handles child-care subsidies in your state by visiting the website of the National Child Care Information Center, http://nccic.acf.hhs.gov/). Note that both of these methods might lead you to underestimate the actual cost of providing care by a substantial margin. Local subsidy rates are usually based on the "market rate" that is calculated annually by surveying providers to learn what they are charging. If providers in a given community maintain unrealistically low rates, whether out of sympathy for parents or a fear of competition, the market rate reflects these unrealistic figures rather than the true cost of service, and the problem is perpetuated. The good news is that the number of states using tiered quality strategies (TQS) under which programs receive higher reimbursement rates or special licensing ratings for maintaining higher levels of quality has more than doubled since 1999, going from 16 to 36 (National Child Care Information Center, 2004).

Fees and Quality

Artificially depressed rates can impact the *quantity*, as well as the *quality*, of the services. Take rates for infant–toddler care, for example. As you have learned, the staffing requirements for this age group are more than twice as high as the requirements for older groups. The logical implication is that fees for infant–toddler care should be more than double those for older children. Logical or not, this difference would price many, if not most, families out of the market for infant–toddler care. Consequently, center operators choose to charge less than the true cost of infant–toddler care. Some providers simply absorb the loss; others structure their fees so that programs for older children actually subsidize the infant–toddler components, an option that will become less available as more 4-year-olds are absorbed by state-funded prekindergartens. The unintended consequence is that many providers simply opt out of the unprofitable business of caring for babies, and the shortage of care for this age group is perpetuated.

How Funds Are Spent

Let's imagine that you are the manager of Rainbow Place, a medium-size child development program that serves 100 children, ages 6 weeks through 5 years. To keep our example simple, let's also assume that you have *not* filed for 501 (c) 3, tax-exempt status, and your program is *not* affiliated with any school, religious group, or corporate child-care chain. This means that you must pay for staff salaries, rent, utilities, cleaning and other services, food, and all other equipment or supplies out of the fees you take in each month, or you must find other sources of revenue to make up any shortfall. According to Neugebauer (1999), the typical cost of operating a center for 65 children is approximately $5,000 per child, so we can assume that the expenses for your (somewhat larger) Rainbow Place are $500,000. If your center is typical of for-profit programs, your single greatest expense (60 percent) is staff salaries and benefits, amounting to $300,000. Mortgage or rent payments and other occupancy costs, such as heat and lighting, total $95,000 (19 percent). Another $70,000 (14 percent) is spent on equipment, supplies (including food), and services. Miscellaneous expenses comprise 2 percent or $10,000, leaving a profit of $25,000 or 5 percent as a return on your investment (subject, of course, to federal, state, and local taxes) (see Figure 6.2).

Calculating Staff Costs

Let's take a closer look at how you will distribute that $300,000 salary budget. One way to approach this problem is to calculate the number of "teacher hours" you need those dollars to cover. Assume that you want your program to meet or exceed the NAEYC standards for group size and adult–child ratios for each age group. Furthermore, because you are concerned about the vulnerability of very young babies in group settings, you decide to meet the even more stringent standards established by the American Academy of Pediatrics for your youngest infants. Assume, also, that your center operates 10 hours per day.

Table 6.1 illustrates how you might calculate the total number of teacher hours needed to serve the 100 children enrolled in your center. Note that the total number of teacher hours needed is greater than the sum of two teachers per classroom. This is because you can expect each individual teacher to be present in the classroom no more than 8 hours per day, meaning that you require additional staff to cover all 10 hours of service. Assuming that a full-time employee is paid for 2,080 hours per year (52 weeks × 40 hours per week), the

FIGURE 6.2   *Typical distribution of expenses in a for-profit program serving 65 children*

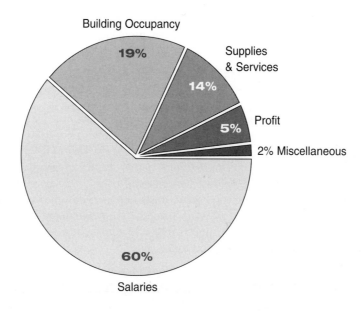

Building Occupancy

Supplies
& Services

Profit

2% Miscellaneous

Salaries

Source: Neugebauer, R. (1999). The cost of center-based child care. In Child Care Information Exchange, *Inside child care: Trend report 2000* (pp. 27–30). Redmond, WA: Exchange Press.

TABLE 6.1   *Calculating the number of teacher hours needed*

Classroom	Number of Children	Number of Teachers	Total Teacher Hours per Day @ 10 hrs/day	Total Teacher Hours per Week @ 5 days/wk	Total Teacher Hours per Year @ 52 wks/yr
Infants	6	2	20	100	5,200
Infants	6	2	20	100	5,200
Toddlers	8	2	20	100	5,200
Toddlers	8	2	20	100	5,200
3–5-Year-Olds	18	2	20	100	5,200
3–5-Year-Olds	18	2	20	100	5,200
3–5-Year-Olds	18	2	20	100	5,200
3–5-Year-Olds	18	2	20	100	5,200
TOTALS	100	16	160	800	41,600

total number of teacher hours calculated in Table 6.1 represents 20 full-time employees (FTEs). In order to staff your program at these levels, your $300,000 budget allots an average of $7.21 per hour for each teacher, or roughly $15,000 per year. Note, however, that this does not account for salaries for a director or other support staff (e.g., cook, secretary, or custodian), meaning that your actual teacher salaries have to be considerably lower.

Decisions, Decisions . . .

Study the calculations in Table 6.1. How would the figures change if you decided to eliminate one of the rooms for 3–5-year-olds in order to open another room for infants?

Child care is a labor-intensive enterprise, meaning that personnel costs are the greatest expense for any child development program.

Of course, your salary expenses are not distributed so evenly across all of the employees in your program. The study conducted by the Cost, Quality, and Child Outcomes Study Team (1995) showed that the average hourly wage for teachers was $7.22; for assistant teachers, $5.70; for directors, $11.33. Staff benefits add roughly 25 percent to these salary figures. Calculating total salary costs becomes complicated as you decide how many teachers and assistant teachers are needed and whether you (the director or manager) are figured into the adult–child ratio. Your state licensing standards will help you make these decisions.

Importance of Increasing Teacher Salaries

The National Day Care Study (Ruopp, Travers Glantz & Coelen, 1979) indicated that 69 percent of an average child-care program's budget went for personnel in the late 1970s. Given the present effort by the NAEYC to bring the salaries of child development services personnel up to a living wage with adequate benefits like other employees, the appropriate percentage is probably more like 90 percent of programs' budgets. The salaries of child development professionals must be raised to appropriate levels for several reasons:

- Workforce demands. As you learned in chapter 1, increases in the number of women in the workforce, dual-career families, and single parents all point to an increased demand for child-care services, meaning an increased demand for personnel to provide those services.
- Population trends. The rising number of immigrant families, the movement toward greater inclusion of children with disabilities, and social problems such as homelessness and drug abuse mean an increased need for special skills and sensitivities on the part of child development professionals. In other words, the need is not just for more personnel, but for more highly qualified personnel.
- Research implications. Media attention to the research findings on brain development has raised public awareness of the importance of high-quality early childhood programs and heightened parent expectations. Again, this underscores the need for more highly qualified staff.

In order to attract and keep well-qualified staff, managers must take the lead in improving salaries, benefits, and working conditions. Nearly two decades ago, the NAEYC established the basic principles that compensation of early childhood professionals should include salaries and benefits commensurate with those of other professionals with comparable training, experience and responsibilities and not be dependent upon the type of setting or age of children served (Willer, 1990). Still in 1997, the U.S. Bureau of Labor reported that median salaries for child-care professionals compared unfavorably with those for data entry keyers, secretaries, or bus drivers. Family child-care providers and personnel identified as "child-care workers" earned less than parking lot attendants. Wide disparities within the field remained as well, depending on job setting and age of children served. Those designated as "preschool teachers" earned more than twice as much as family child-care providers and about 15 percent more than "child-care workers," but less than half as much as kindergarten teachers cited in Whitebook & Bellm (1999, p. 38).

Strategies for Increasing Teacher Salaries

The Center for the Child Care Workforce offers a useful starting point for those interested in working toward the goal of economic parity for child care professionals (Whitebook & Bellm, 1999). It suggests that centers compare staff wages with the cost of living in their community and establish a salary schedule with "living wage" as a minimum for entry-level employees and parity with elementary school teachers as an ideal (pp. 118–119). Using this information to establish target salaries, a manager can formulate a plan for reaching those goals and develop a coalition of parents and community advocates to create strategies for doing so.

Participation in programs such as the TEACH Early Childhood Scholarship project is one way programs can augment the funds available for salary increases. This program, with nearly $22 million in private and public funding, operates in 22 states. It provides stipends for individuals who complete educational requirements and commit to staying in the field, as well as for the programs that employ them. The resulting impact on stability in staffing is evident in the fact that turnover rates for scholarship participants in associate degree programs averaged less than 10 percent for the 2003–2004 fiscal year (Russell & Rogers, 2005).

Fund-Raising

As you have no doubt concluded already, locating and maintaining funding for a center requires a good deal of your attention, unless you direct a program funded entirely by state or federal dollars. Even in that case, your challenge is to cope with fluctuating allocations and the possibility of budget cuts from year to year. If you manage a program with a policy board, the responsibility for raising money might fall to a finance committee. In fact, board members are sometimes selected because of their connections with a funding source.

To continue with the example of our hypothetical Rainbow Place, you can expect parent fees to cover about 94 percent of your total costs, meaning that you have to find other ways to raise the remaining 6 percent. Your fund-raising objectives might include capital investment dollars, ongoing operating expenses, or a one-time special purchase (e.g., revamping the outdoor play area).

Small amounts of money may be raised with the support of parents and the community. Possibilities include sponsoring bake sales, rummage sales, or concerts. In addition to raising funds, such events can rally the support of parents and the community, as well as generate valuable media attention.

In-Kind Donations

In the quest for funds, directors should not overlook the possibility of in-kind donations. Businesses may publicize a center as part of their community outreach, or they may be willing to donate used computer hardware or office furniture when they upgrade or redecorate.

Others may have regularly discarded materials (e.g., wood scraps from a lumberyard) that can be used in a variety of ways. A civic club or church may provide space or a number of hours of its members' labor if the center becomes its cause to support. Use the combined imaginations of your board members and staff to generate creative possibilities for new resources, as well as uses.

Grant Proposals

Seeking funds may be as simple as writing a letter to a civic club requesting scholarship funds for a child or two. Such a request can be an unsolicited proposal—just a shot in the dark, or you might develop a more systematic approach by actively searching for funding opportunities offered by government agencies, philanthropic organizations, or corporations. These entities regularly issue **requests for proposals (RFPs),** or announcements outlining specific goals and inviting applications for funding from individuals or agencies whose projects align with those goals. A directory of foundations in your state, usually available at libraries, is a good source of information about the foundations' particular interest areas and currently available RFPs. When you locate one or more with interests that seem to match your own, you can write and ask for details about eligibility requirements, deadlines, and application process. You can also check Internet sources, such as that for The Foundation Center (http://fdncenter.org), described in "Resources for Further Study" at the end of this chapter.

When you locate an RFP that seems to match your needs, you and your board can decide whether you have the time and talent to develop a proposal and, if it should be funded, whether you have the appropriate staff to carry out the proposal. **Proposals** are documented requests that show your expertise and ability to fulfill the proposed project and your timetable, budget, and procedures. It is essential to follow directions and meet the deadlines set by the funding agency. Proposals can be simple or complex depending on the dollar size of the request, the funding agency, and the accounting requirements. Writing your first proposal is the hardest because you are collecting many materials for the first time. However, if you are careful to save the various components in digital format, you will have the information readily available to use in future proposal writing. If the funding agency has a specific proposal format, as many do, be sure to follow it as exactly as possible. Your ability to adhere to form is one measure of your ability to execute your plan successfully. Figure 6.3 outlines components of a typical proposal's contents.

Careful preparation is the key to success. Ask a close friend who is both knowledgeable and frank to check over the proposal and help you eliminate any errors and unsound information or ideas. Use a word processing program to give your final version a professional appearance and ensure that the required number of copies are received at the address listed in the RFP before the deadline.

The review process your proposal undergoes may explain some of the requirements regarding format and deadlines. Funding agencies often establish panels of reviewers to read the proposals and rank each one according to established criteria. These reviewers may include recognized experts, practitioners from the field, potential consumers of the service, or other stakeholders. You may be invited to serve on such a review panel some day! Agency staff members are the gatekeepers of the review process. They screen proposals that have arrived by the announced deadline and distribute only those that meet requirements to the reviewers. Thus, attention to seemingly small details can be the difference that gets your proposal the consideration it deserves. All of your hard work creating the proposal is wasted if it is eliminated before the review process because you used the wrong format, submitted too few copies, or mailed it at the last minute and missed the deadline. Following the prescribed format also helps the individual reviewers who are looking for specific elements in your proposal.

FIGURE 6.3 *Components of a typical proposal*

Title Page. Project title, organization's name, applicant's name, related addresses, agency to which it is submitted, total budget, appropriate signatures, and date submitted.

Executive Summary. Imagine that you have been granted a 15-minute interview with a busy executive during which you want to convince her that your project is worthwhile and that you can deliver the proposed solution. Address four points in one page:

1. **Problem.** A paragraph or two stating the problem
2. **Solution.** What will happen? Where and how? Who will do it? Who and how many will benefit? How long will it take?
3. **Funding Requirements.** How much money is needed? Do you plan to obtain any part of the funding from sources other than the granting agency? Is this a one-time expense, or do you anticipate needing continued funding. If so, where will that come from?
4. **"Fit".** Why is your program uniquely suited to do what you propose? What is your history, purpose, track record?

Rationale. In no more than two pages, spell out why the problem matters, both to society and to the funding agency. Support your arguments with relevant facts and statistics from experts as well as from your own experience, but avoid "padding" or overstating the problem so that it seems insoluble. Use logical, persuasive arguments. *Example: If you are requesting funds so your center can add an after-school component for elementary school children, state the problem in terms of the hardship for families, employers, and communities caused by lack of such care. Then show how your program will alleviate those hardships.*

Project Description. Three pages detailing what you hope to accomplish and how, what personnel are needed, how you will measure success, and whether the project will continue after the grant period. Include:

1. **Objectives.** Concrete and measurable outcomes. *Example: Rather than "increase the supply of high-quality infant care in X community," say "to increase the licensed capacity of XYZ center by providing six additional infant spaces, maintaining a rating of at least 6.0 on the Infant–Toddler Environmental Rating Scale."*
2. **Methods.** Tell *how* and *when* you will carry out objectives. *Example: Give a timeline for acquiring the space you hope to use, ordering equipment and supplies, hiring and training staff, and enrolling children.*
3. **Personnel.** How many staff members will be needed? What qualifications are required and why? How will they be selected? *Example: Because you propose to maintain high standards of quality, you will probably want to specify certain levels of education and experience for your teachers. You will need to explain this because the persons reading your application may hold the misconception that "anyone" can take care of children.* Remember to include details about who will administer the program—most likely, you—and documentation of your credentials to do so.
4. **Evaluation.** How will you determine whether you have met your objectives and to whom you will report these findings?
5. **Potential.** How will your project impact extend beyond the grant period? *Example: How will you continue after-school care when the grant ends?*

Budget. May be limited to an outline of proposed expenses, or may need an additional section detailing proposed revenue and a narrative explaining each line item. Group categories of expenses: for example, personnel costs include subcategories for salaries and benefits as well as outside services; nonpersonnel costs include all materials, space, and equipment.

(Continued)

FIGURE 6.3 *Continued*

> **Organization Profile.** Two-page summary giving more details about your program's history, mission, and make-up; include information about the qualifications of staff, board members, and volunteers as well as the role that each plays.
>
> **Wrap-Up.** In one or two paragraphs, make your best case for why your proposal should be funded.
>
> ---
>
> *Source*: Based on information provided in The Foundation Center's online *Proposal Writing Short Course* (Retrieved July 6, 2005, from http://fdncenter.org/learn/shortcourse/propl.html

The procedure of applying for grants takes time and energy, and the wait for an answer may be long, but the rewards are worth it. A funded proposal not only extends the resources of your center, but it also may bring recognition of your center and staff in the local, state, or national child development center arena. Even the process of writing a proposal that does not get funded can stimulate you, your advisory board, and your staff members to work harder or in new directions.

Budget Planning

Now that you have a rough idea of how much money is available, where it is coming from, and where it has to go, it is time to begin putting the details on paper—part of the manager's planning process. A **budget** is a plan, expressed in dollar amounts, for how your program will use its resources to meet its goals. Thus, creating a budget is part of the planning process discussed in chapter 5. Following a budget and making adjustments when needed is part of another process, monitoring and controlling.

Establishing Priorities

The first important thing to remember is that *the budget is a tool for achieving goals, not an end in itself*. Start with your strategic plan, determine what you need in order to achieve it, and then allocate dollars accordingly. For example, if your strategic plan is to provide high-quality care and you know that staff education and stability are key components of that quality, you want a salary and benefit package that attracts highly qualified candidates, as well as a system of promotions and raises that encourages them to stay with your program. With this in mind, you may, for example, choose to add money to your salary budget rather than purchasing an expensive packaged curriculum.

No program enjoys unlimited income, however, and the available dollars may not stretch to cover all of your goals at the level you would like. Thus, you have to prioritize those goals or establish a time frame for accomplishing them gradually. In the previous example, we suggested that salaries were given a much higher priority than purchasing a packaged curriculum. You may even give salaries a higher priority than something as worthy as new, high-quality playground equipment. But even after prioritizing, you might discover you cannot immediately pay the salaries you would like. Instead, you have to establish a long-term plan for reaching that goal over a number of years, perhaps by raising fees for the next budget cycle or initiating an ongoing fund-raising activity.

Types of Budgets

Different types of budgets are needed at different points in the organization's life cycle. A start-up budget is just what the name implies: a plan for starting a new program from scratch, for translating a concept into reality. Operational budgets plan for the upcoming year. Some organizations might budget for longer cycles. A narrative budget (often required as part of grant proposals) is a written explanation of what is included in each category and why.

Flexibility

A budget is a plan, not a straitjacket. It is based on predictions of what the program's income and expenses will be, and it is subject to change when those predictions do not develop. Of course, the more complete the information is that supports your predictions, the more accurate they are likely to be, so it is essential to do your homework.

In our hypothetical small center, Rainbow Place, the manager is likely to be the person responsible for gathering the information and preparing the budget. Should you manage a larger organization, you may have help from a financial manager or assistant director. In corporate franchises or public school programs, your job may be to carry out budget decisions made by a central office.

Constructing a Budget

Keeping these important points in mind, you can use a spreadsheet computer program to begin constructing an actual budget for Rainbow Place. (You can do the same thing with pencil, paper, and a handheld calculator, but you cannot make changes as easily as with the computer.)

Income

First, under the heading "Income," list all sources of expected revenue for the period your budget covers. (Figure 6.4 demonstrates one way to organize and display your calculations.) Some budgets, such as those you might submit with a grant application, include in-kind resources and list those in a separate column from cash income. For the sake of simplicity, we will consider only cash income for this example. For Rainbow Place, income sources include tuition fees, enrollment fees, government subsidies, interest on bank accounts, grant awards, and money gotten through fund-raising activities.

Start-up costs for a new child development program will include major investments in equipment, such as large hollow blocks.

Importance of Accurate Projections

Recalling that the accuracy of our budget predictions depends on the degree to which it reflects complete information, we must also include an item in our income category to reflect a potential loss of income. It is highly unlikely that Rainbow Place will operate at its capacity of 100 children for 12 months a year. Families move or withdraw their children for other reasons, and even with an extensive waiting list, it may be impossible to fill the vacancies immediately. The center may suffer some losses when families fall behind in payments and leave owing money. Insert a row in your spreadsheet and enter a formula to total each type

FIGURE 6.4 *Sample budget for Rainbow Place*

INCOME				
Tuition	Number	Month	Annual	
Infants ($600/mo)	12	$ 7,200.00	$ 86,400.00	
Toddlers ($550/mo)	16	$ 8,800.00	$ 105,600.00	
3–5-Year-Olds ($430/mo)	72	$ 30,960.00	$ 371,520.00	
Total Tuition Income				$ 563,520.00
Other Income				
Initial Enrollment Fees ($100)	25*	$ 2,500.00		
USDA Food Subsidy		$ 5,000.00		
Interest		$ 600.00		
Grants		$ 1,200.00		
Fund-raising Activities		$ 4,000.00		
Total Other Income			$ 13,300.00	
Estimated 1 percent Vacancy Rate			$ (5,635.20)	
TOTAL INCOME				$ 571,184.80
EXPENSES				
Salaries				
Director			$ 28,000.00	
Lead Teachers (8 @ $22,000)			$ 176,000.00	
Assistant Teachers (12 @ $16,000)			$ 192,000.00	
Substitutes			$ 2,000.00	
Cook (Half-time)			$ 6,000.00	
Total Salaries			$ 404,000.00	
Benefits			$ 80,800.00	
Total Personnel Cost			$ 484,800.00	
Other Expenses				
Rent			$ 42,000.00	
Utilities			$ 16,000.00	
Food			$ 15,000.00	
Equipment			$ 4,000.00	
Supplies			$ 4,584.80	
Insurance			$ 3,000.00	
Custodial Service			$ 1,800.00	
Total Other Expenses			$ 86,384.80	
TOTAL EXPENSES				$ 571,184.80

*Example assumes 25 new enrollees per year as current children leave program.

of income, as well as another row and formula that totals all of the income. Be sure to enter the dollar amount for expected vacancies as a negative number.

Expenses

Next, create a category for expenses and enter all of the expense types that your program will incur. Personnel costs include salaries for each staffing category, as well as an amount for Social Security, workers' compensation, unemployment compensation, and any benefits (e.g., health insurance) that you will provide. Other expenses include occupancy costs (rent or mortgage, utilities, telephone), food, equipment, supplies, insurance, and fees for services such as cleaning or bookkeeping.

Again, insert a row on your spreadsheet and enter a formula to total each sub-category of these two categories (Personnel and Other Expenses), and another to add those two totals together and compare that number to the sum total of your projected income. If the two numbers match, you have a "balanced budget." If, as is more likely, your anticipated expenses exceed your anticipated income, revise the budget, finding ways either to raise revenue or to lower expenses.

Take a moment to study the sample budget for Rainbow Place in Figure 6.4 and consider the factors that went into the projections. The vision guiding our planning is, of course, a commitment to the highest possible quality of care. In keeping with this overall goal, our group sizes and staff ratios meet or exceed NAEYC standards, as discussed earlier. We also made the decision to pay salaries in excess of the averages found by the Cost, Quality, and Outcomes Study Team. We added 20 percent to our salary costs to cover FICA, workers' compensation, unemployment compensation, and an amount for health insurance.

Balancing Act

When balancing our budget, however, we had to face the fact that we cannot offer our teachers salaries that are competitive with what they might earn in public schools, for example. We also had to raise our fees, bringing them closer to the full cost of care discussed earlier. In determining other income, we made conservative assumptions about the number of new children we would enroll each year as other children leave the program. On the other hand, we also assumed that we would be able to fill vacancies rapidly (as a consequence of our high-quality services). If we were drafting a start-up budget for a new facility, we would have based our calculations on a much higher vacancy rate, with a corresponding reduction in anticipated staffing costs until the program reached full enrollment. Our projected equipment expenses would also have been considerably higher.

We had to make several other sacrifices to balance our budget. We decided that we could not afford even a part-time secretary or custodian, and opted instead to contract with a cleaning service for a few hours a week. This means that the director must handle the secretarial duties and the teachers have to pitch in with day-to-day cleaning. You will note that the budgeted amounts for supplies and equipment are minimal—again assuming that the director and teachers will take up the slack by locating and using free or inexpensive materials and holding fund-raisers or applying for grants to cover major purchases. Finally, although you earn a salary as director of Rainbow Place, you will not earn a profit on any money you invested to start the program.

Decisions, Decisions . . .

Discuss the budget in Figure 6.4 with your classmates. What changes would you suggest? For each change, note what other changes are required in order to balance the budget. If possible, enter the budget in a computer spreadsheet so you can see the way your proposed changes alter other aspects of the budget.

Starting a New Business

Writing about the prospects for new businesses, Sylvia Porter, a noted business analyst, stated that the odds of surviving in a new business for 2 years are less than 50–50. In "9 out of 10 cases the reasons underlying the failure will be the manager's incompetence, inexperience, ineptitude, or a combination of all three," she said (Porter, 1982). Porter presented a quiz for people contemplating a new business. We have adapted her questions, shown in Figure 6.5, to fit the particular business of operating a child development program. If a potential manager must answer no to any of the questions, he or she is probably wise to rethink the idea of starting a new child development program.

Decisions, Decisions . . .

Take the quiz in Figure 6.5. Do you think you would be a good candidate for opening your own child development program. Why or why not?

Help Is Available

Small Business Administration. The U.S. government's Small Business Administration (SBA) in Washington, DC, offers a variety of information on many aspects of operating a business, including loans, management and technical assistance, business classes, publications, and procurement assistance. Even if you don't live in a city that has a branch of this organization, you can tap its resources by logging on to the website www.sba.gov or by visiting your library. You can also check with your chamber of commerce for information and assistance as you plan your business.

Child-Care Resource and Referral Agencies. Although these resources address the needs of small business operators in general, a local child-care resource and referral agency can provide advice and guidance more specifically tailored to your needs as an entrepreneur in the child development field. CCR&R specialists have a wealth of information about what child care is available and what is needed in your community, and one of their goals is to increase the supply. They can help you with a needs assessment and provide technical assistance in several aspects of financial management. You also should take a few courses in business management, perhaps at your community college, and consult some of the "Resources for Further Study" listed at the end of this chapter.

FIGURE 6.5 *Quiz for a potential owner-operator of a new child development center*

Your Knowledge of the Field

_____ Have you had experience in a program like the one you envision?

_____ Have you managed a center or closely observed a manager at work?

_____ Do you know the characteristics of a high-quality child development center?

_____ Do you know the local zoning rules related to child development centers?

_____ Do you know the licensing rules for child development centers in your city or state?

Your Personal Characteristics

_____ Do you have a real interest in children, parents, and staff?

_____ Are you a careful and sensible planner?

_____ Can you delegate authority and responsibility to staff?

_____ Can you fire friends or others who do not perform well and don't improve with training?

_____ Are you willing to work long hours without the assurance of extra pay or even a regular paycheck?

Have You Done Your Homework?

_____ Are families in your area interested in putting their children in your center when it opens?

_____ Are centers like the one you plan doing well locally and nationally?

_____ Have you checked with both a lawyer and a banker about the various legal and financial aspects of operating a business?

_____ Do you know the advantages and disadvantages of single proprietorship, partnership, or incorporation?

_____ Do you know how much start-up money is required?

_____ Do you know how much a bank will lend you or how much credit you can tap from various sources and suppliers?

_____ Can you personally put up a large share of the capital required to establish your center?

_____ Have you estimated carefully the yearly income you can expect to cover your salary and provide a return on your investment?

_____ Can you live on less than your net income and invest additional dollars to help your center grow and improve?

_____ Are other businesspeople optimistic about the success of your center plans?

Business Plan

You learned about various types of planning in chapter 5, and common sense tells you that careful planning is essential to success in any enterprise. Creating a business plan consists of putting your organization's strategic and operational plans into writing. This is something every business operator should do; it is something you have to do if you must seek financial backing for your proposed venture. A formal business plan consists of several parts (see, e.g., Covello & Hazelgren, 1998; Pinson & Jinnett, 1999):

- A **cover sheet** with the names, addresses, and telephone numbers for your company, a list of corporate officers with their titles, the author(s) of the plan, and the date created. If your organization has a logo, it can be included here.

- An **executive summary** (written after you have completed the entire plan) presenting the main points of the plan in capsule format. If your plan is part of a loan application, the executive summary must explain why you need the money and how you will repay it.

- An **organizational plan** describes your business, its services, its management structure and personnel, its legal structure (e.g., partnership or corporation), its financial management system, its physical facility, and the provisions for safeguarding an investor's funds (e.g., insurance, security measures).

- A **marketing plan** describes the potential pool of customers, competitors who offer similar services, and the strategies for attracting potential customers.

- **Financial documents** show the organization's past performance (profits and losses, loan history); its current status (budget and cash-flow statement); and its projected income and expenses over the next several years.

- **Appendices** include the documents that support or prove the statements made in other parts of your plan. They can include letters of recommendation, a glossary of any specialized terms, your center's brochure or copies of any advertising, newspaper clippings about the need for child care in your community, complete data from the needs assessment that were summarized in the market analysis, and so on.

Loans

Most businesses operate with some borrowed money. Loans may be available from various sources. Frequently, friends and relatives invest in the dreams of small entrepreneurs. Before deciding whether or how much to borrow, you should consider interest rates—both the rate you would pay for the loan and the rate you might earn by investing your own savings elsewhere.

The **Rule of 72** is a quick method for calculating how many years it will take for the interest costs (or interest earned if you lend the money) to equal the principal. If you divide the number 72 by the interest rate, you will find the doubling time—the time required for the accumulated compounded interest to equal the principal. For example, if you borrow $1,000 and pay 10 percent interest, it will take 7.2 years (72 ÷ 10 = 7.2) for the compounded accumulated interest to equal the loan principal.

Control of Funds and Expenses

Once you have the budget in place, you then move from the planning process to organizing its implementation. The monitoring and controlling process involves comparing actual performance with projections and making necessary adjustments. You also are expected to report to the board periodically—quarterly or yearly.

Financial Decisions. Each process requires you to make decisions. Financial decisions can be either **programmed** or **nonprogrammed,** as discussed in chapter 4. Recall that a programmed decision is one that is routine, handled the same way from one time to the next. For example, the formula for calculating an employee's withholding tax is the same and does not require new procedures each time it is done. On the other hand, when a parent cannot pay the tuition and asks for an extension, this may be a nonprogrammed decision that necessitates procedures for weighing various considerations and arriving at the best decision for that individual and your center.

Written Policies and Procedures.   In financial matters, as in other areas, written policies and procedures simplify your decision making and help maintain consistency and fairness within the operation. Will your center offer different rates for full- or part-time enrollment? What about discounts for families with more than one child enrolled, or a sliding fee scale based on family income? Under what circumstances will you make tuition refunds? Will your program pay for employee health insurance? If so, will you cover all of the cost or only a portion? Will part-time employees be eligible? How much sick leave will an employee earn each month? What circumstances qualify for the use of sick leave?

Once the policies are determined, procedures must be established to facilitate speedy and consistent decision making. For example, once the amount per child is decided, you must decide whether tuition payments are to be collected weekly, monthly, or quarterly. This decision may depend on whether many of the parents are paid weekly, biweekly, or monthly. As you and your policy board formulate the policies regarding fees, you also must consider the following questions:

1. Will payment be required in advance or after services are rendered? Payment in advance, obviously, lessens the chance that the center will be "stuck" with a large outstanding balance if a family withdraws their child. However, for many families, this is not a realistic expectation. Furthermore, government agencies do not usually allow centers to bill for services until after they are rendered.

2. Will parents be required to pay only for the actual days their child is in the center's care? Or will they be expected to pay for an agreed-on number of hours per week, whether or not the child actually attends those hours? On the one hand, parents usually balk at paying for a service they feel they have not received; but on the other hand, centers must schedule and pay staff regardless of whether a particular child is out ill or a family goes on vacation one week. Some centers handle these fluctuations in attendance by sending employees home when few children are present, but this approach hardly seems fair to employees who must be able to count on at least their minimum salaries each week.

3. Will families be required to pay additional fees if they arrive late to pick up their child? Certainly, this occurrence is a problem for staff members who are eager to get home to their own children, but sometimes the costs in public relations exceeds the gain to be had by charging the extra few dollars. Is there a way to offer a "grace period" or to consider the number of times a parent has been late before imposing the penalty?

The Efficiency Rule.   When making financial decisions, you can apply the efficiency rule, which simply requires that the greatest possible good be achieved for a given resource expenditure. There are always competing demands for your limited supply of resources. Purchasing sturdy, high-quality equipment rather than less expensive items that must be replaced more frequently is an example of the efficiency rule in action.

Record Keeping

Keeping business records, like teaching, is a professional skill. Whether your program is for-profit or nonprofit, you or the person to whom you delegate this task will need special training to do an adequate job of keeping the books. Consulting an accountant or tax adviser is essential. Many centers contract with a regular accounting service to prepare records that are clear and accurate each month. These records are used to prepare quarterly and annual reports for the policy board and for reporting income taxes.

Cash-Flow Analysis

While your budget is your plan for the year, a **cash-flow analysis** is a tool that tracks the rate at which money is coming in and going out. It shows how much cash your program has on hand and compares your expected receipts and expenses with the actual figures for each month. Using a computer spreadsheet program simplifies the preparation of this document. Figure 6.6 is a sample cash-flow analysis.

Begin by looking at the totals for items in your annual budget and break those numbers down into the amounts you expect to receive or spend each month. For example, Rainbow Place's $42,000 annual rent is recorded as $3,500 under Projected Expenses for each month, and the same amount is listed under Actual Expenses each month because rent typically does not vary from month to month. Should the landlord raise the rent midyear, the new figure is recorded under Actual Expenses, indicating a variation from the projected figure. Because some other expenses, such as insurance or bulk orders for classroom supplies, occur only once or twice a year, they do not appear every month. Receipts can be expected to vary as well. For example, Rainbow Place's Expected Receipts from tuition payments are listed in

FIGURE 6.6 *Sample cash-flow analysis for Rainbow Place*

	January Projected	January Actual	February Projected	February Actual
Opening Cash Balance	$ 950.00	$ 1,100.00	$ (1,293.00)	$ (282.00)
RECEIPTS				
Tuition	$ 46,490.00	$ 46,960.00	$ 46,490.00	$ 46,960.00
Enrollment Fees	$ 100.00	$ 300.00	$ 100.00	$ —
USDA Food Subsidy	$ 416.00	$ 424.00	$ 416.00	$ 424.00
Interest	$ 50.00	$ 58.00	$5 0.00	$ 58.00
Grants	$ —	$ —	$ —	$ —
Fund-raising Activities	$ —	$ —	$ 500.00	$ 750.00
TOTAL RECEIPTS	$ 47,056.00	$ 47,742.00	$ 47,556.00	$ 48,192.00
EXPENDITURES				
Salaries	$ 33,666.00	$ 33,666.00	$ 33,666.00	$ 33,666.00
Benefits	$ 6,733.00	$ 6,733.00	$ 6,733.00	$ 6,733.00
Rent	$ 3,500.00	$ 3,500.00	$ 3,500.00	$ 3,500.00
Utilities	$ 2,000.00	$ 1,800.00	$ 2,000.00	$ 1,950.00
Food	$ 1,250.00	$ 1,300.00	$ 1,250.00	$ 1,100.00
Equipment	$ —	$ —	$ —	$ —
Supplies	$ 500.00	$ 475.00	$ —	$ 200.00
Insurance	$ 1,500.00	$ 1,500.00	$ —	$ —
Custodial Service	$ 150.00	$ 150.00	$ 150.00	$ 150.00
TOTAL EXPENDITURES	$ 49,299.00	$ 49,124.00	$ 47,299.00	$ 47,299.00
Closing Cash Balance	$ (1,293.00)	$ (282.00)	$ (1,036.00)	$ 611.00

the budget as $563,520 per year, or $46,960 per month. If the center receives state subsidized payments for any of the children enrolled, however, the payment for the care of those children in any given month is actually received sometime during the following month. In our example, we projected tuition receipts based on our anticipated 1 percent vacancy rate. During months when Rainbow Place enjoys full enrollment, actual receipts will exceed projections.

In both the Expected and Actual columns, the total expenses for a given month are subtracted from the total receipts, yielding a cash balance for that month. This is a negative number in those months that the expenses exceed income. The cash balance for the month is added to the opening cash balance (the amount on hand at the beginning of the month) to arrive at the new cash balance to be carried forward to the following month.

Decisions, Decisions . . .

Figure 6.6 shows a projected negative cash balance for January. Should the manager be worried about this? Why or why not?

Day-to-day record keeping includes written receipts for tuition payment, with one copy going to the parent and the second kept for posting in the ledger or account of each child. Individual expenditures must be carefully recorded. Salaries as well as benefit and tax withholdings must be properly paid and reported. You may choose to contract with an accountant to prepare the payroll checks and deliver them to employees on a regular schedule.

Technology and Financial Management

Business supply stores carry a variety of appropriate record-keeping forms, but a computer can facilitate your financial record keeping, just as it helps with writing and printing letters, proposals, and newsletters. A recent survey found that, while many early childhood program managers felt proficient with word-processing applications, they are much less familiar with spreadsheet applications and fewer than half use database management programs (Center for Early Childhood Leadership, 2004). Like the directors surveyed, you may lack confidence in your ability to use technology, but learning to do so would be a wise investment in your own human capital—one likely to return your investment of time and energy many times in the future.

Using a spreadsheet, you can quickly and easily perform calculations to see what effect a 2 percent pay increase for all your teachers would have on your bottom line and what adjustments in your fee schedule would be necessary to cover it. A database could record things like child immunization records and generate periodic reports showing you which children are due for boosters. You (perhaps with the help of someone with more expertise) could use generic software to set up your own databases and spreadsheets or you can invest in software programs specifically designed for child-care center record keeping. According to a recent review of center management software, you should consider these key questions when making your selection:

1. What do you want or need the software package to do—to generate specific reports or to bill in the unit that you have established, whether hourly or weekly?
2. Is it so user-friendly that you can install and run the program with minimal outside help? Can you try out a demonstration copy? Does the company offer technical support?

Using a computer spreadsheet to create a budget makes it easy to calculate the effect of changes (such as raising fees or staff salaries) on the bottom line.

3. Does it fit your budget? What features come with the package? Are extras available? At what cost? Does it work with your current hardware and operating system, or will you need to upgrade?
4. Does the company stand by its product? Do you know others who use the product and can recommend it? (Walker & Donohue, 2005).

Internal Controls

Any cash income, including parents' checks, should be deposited promptly. Some centers keep a petty cash fund for small items and give staff members specific guidelines for its use. A specific record must be kept when petty cash payments are made. Drawbacks to petty cash include the potential for pilfering as well as the danger of impulsive spending rather than planning ahead for more economical bulk purchases.

Inventory Records

New purchases must be added to the inventory. Packages should be checked immediately on delivery to verify the condition of the contents. You should develop or purchase a system that adds and deletes items from the inventory. Having such procedures helps protect the inventory and keeps you from running out of supplies. Again, a computer is an excellent tool for keeping track of the inventory. Several flexible and efficient inventory control software programs are available for all brands of computers.

Avoiding Waste

Judicious use of all resources (money, food, supplies, and time) is another aspect of the control process, requiring the help of your entire staff. For example, monitoring leftover foods lets you know that some recipes are too big for your needs. Recipes can be adjusted to eliminate leftovers and avoid contamination, waste, or improper use by employees. (Be sure you and the center's cook know the rules governing the use of leftover foods.)

Comparison Shopping

It is important to ensure that you are getting a fair price for the resources you purchase. For large items, ask several companies to make bids. For smaller items, check vendors' websites or call for prices and make comparisons. Unit pricing in large supermarkets is very useful in cost calculations. Insurance and other employee benefits may be available at different prices from different carriers, and professional groups such as NAEYC often offer opportunities to purchase various kinds of insurance through a group plan for members. Always double-check the prices and benefits before making an agreement. Sometimes savings accrue if one carrier handles all of a center's insurance, rather than having several policies with separate carriers.

Consider Hidden Costs

Determine, for example, whether disposable tableware, which must be continually replenished, is actually less expensive than a one-time investment in multiuse tableware and a commercial dishwasher. Remember to include any costs incurred for trash disposal with the former alternative and the cost of staff time to load, operate, and empty the dishwasher in the latter.

Quantity Buying

Bulk purchasing often generates a substantial discount. Paper goods, for example, can be purchased in quantity at considerable savings. Of course, you must have secure, fireproof storage places for items purchased in quantity. Buying groceries in quantity when the supermarkets have specials also saves money, if you have a place to store the purchases. Large cans of vegetables are not always the best buys and may lead the cook to open too much on a given day. Therefore, purchasing small cans may be the least expensive in the long run.

Cycle Menus

Plan 3 or 4 weeks of menus and repeat the cycle to make purchasing more efficient and reduce the likelihood of packaged foods being stored for too long. Cycle menus also help to manage the labor costs because cooks develop time-saving techniques with repeated preparation of the recipes. Of course, money spent on food is wasted if high standards for the nutritional quality of the foods are not maintained.

Cooperative Purchases

Centers in some communities band together to purchase supplies in greater quantities than would be possible for any single center. Their combined buying power makes it possible to bargain with vendors for deeper discounts, thus increasing their savings. Investigate one of these cooperatives or organize one yourself.

Money-Saving Tips

Other measures to stretch your dollars include:

- Monitoring and reducing energy use by using energy-efficient light fixtures and setting thermostats at reasonable levels.
- Using homemade materials such as play dough, fingerpaint, and paint extenders.
- Using "found" or recycled materials that cost only the time of the adults—parents, teachers, and custodians—to collect and store them. Orderly fireproof storage is a must for any combustible materials.
- Rationing the amount of materials put out at one time. Paper products, such as napkins, towels, and tissues, last longer if dispensers are not overfilled and the children are enlisted in an effort to conserve resources and protect the environment. Partially filled cups of paint produce less waste should the children muddy them by mixing the colors.
- Allocating a given quantity of supplies to each classroom teacher, even when supplies are ordered in bulk, can help motivate the classroom teachers to avoid waste without hindering their creation of a high-quality program.
- Returning the savings to teachers to buy "extras" for their classrooms. Teachers often complain that they use their own money to buy supplies. Managers should see to it that all nondurable supplies are purchased by center funds. If teachers have money of their own they wish to spend, it should go into something that lasts—for example, books that they can take with them if they leave or use at home with their own

Some of the best materials cost little or nothing. "Beautiful stuff" collected by the children and displayed in organized, attractive ways encourages creativity while stretching budget dollars.

children. A center that is so short-funded that teachers must purchase paper is in bad shape financially; it may not be a good place for children and perhaps should be closed.

Conclusion

It takes a tough head to plan the budget, organize its implementation, and monitor and control the balance sheet—all the while maintaining a tender heart for giving the children the loving care and education a high-quality program requires. Your assertive leadership and vision are essential to marshal the funds needed to operate such a program. You must spend a great deal of your time securing funding and then actively monitoring and controlling so that those funds yield the best possible program for children.

NAEYC accreditation standards require that centers maintain a sound fiscal policy in order to meet their obligations to children and families. Written policies and procedures are required to keep decision making consistent and fair. Managers must "MESH," or coordinate all materials, equipment, space, and human energy, to achieve program goals. They must develop a careful procedure for budgeting, purchasing, record keeping, and controlling expenditures.

This chapter can provide only an overview of the financial aspects of an early childhood administrator's job. You should enlist the advice and assistance of business and accounting experts when you assume the manager's role. You also should continue your own study of this topic. You can begin by consulting some of the Resources for Further Study listed at the end of this chapter, and you can take courses in business management at your university or community college.

QUESTIONS FOR REVIEW

1. Define a request for proposal (RFP) and explain what information is generally required.
2. Give the definitions for each part of the MESH formula.
3. When budgeting, what are the percentages of the total expenses typically used for the personnel, space, equipment, and materials needed to operate a center?
4. Discuss programmed and nonprogrammed decisions in relation to monetary decisions.
5. Explain the Rule of 72. Apply the rule to a major purchase you might make (e.g., a new car or home entertainment system). Label all of the parts.
6. Discuss how a budget differs from a cash-flow analysis.
7. List at least five ways of controlling waste, expenses, and funds.

APPLICATIONS

1. Arrange an interview with the manager of a child development program in your community. Ask the following questions:
   - What is your biggest financial problem as manager?
   - What have you done to solve this financial problem?

- What type of assistance do you have with financial matters? An accountant? A bookkeeper? A clerk?
- Do you plan using a monthly budget?
- Do you keep a petty cash fund?
- What happens if your spending goes over the budget?

Add other questions that occur to you, but be concise and respectful of the busy manager's time. Report your findings in class. Compare and discuss with classmates.

2. If you do not already know how to use spreadsheet software, invite someone who does (a classmate, your instructor, a member of the technology support staff at your college or university) to visit your class and demonstrate. Construct a sample budget for a new child-care program following the example in Figure 6.4.
3. Study equipment catalogs or visit an equipment store to compare tables and chairs needed for a center. Discuss the pros and cons of the various types. This approach can be repeated with many types of toys and furnishings.

PROFESSIONAL PORTFOLIO

1. Begin constructing a business plan for a program you hope to manage some day. At this point, you should be able to write the mission and goals statement, as well as the financial plan. As you complete subsequent chapters, you can add the organizational and marketing sections. Write the executive summary after you have completed the entire plan.
2. Develop an annual budget for your hypothetical program. Add a narrative component explaining how your budget reflects your program goals and objectives.
3. Develop short- and long-range fund-raising options to support your goals; evaluate the cost-effectiveness and appropriateness of each.
4. At your public library, your local child-care resource and referred agency, or on the Internet, locate an actual RFP that applies to child development programs. Write a grant proposal for your hypothetical center—or for a real center in your community.

RESOURCES FOR FURTHER STUDY

Print

Burton, E., James, & Bragg, Steven M. (2001). *Accounting and finance for your small business*. New York: John Wiley & Sons.

Greenman, Jim (1998). *Places for childhoods: Making quality happen in the real world*. Redmond, WA: Exchange Press.

Jack, Gail (2005). *The business of child care: Management and financial strategies*. Clifton Park, NY: Delmar.

Internet

Budgeting the True Cost of Quality Toolkit

www.ci.seattle.wa.us/humanservices/fys/TrueCostQualityCare

Budgeting the True Cost of Quality Toolkit, an online resource developed by a community collaboration in Seattle and written by Julie Bisson; provides step-by-step instructions (including a sample spreadsheet) for developing a budget, with the goal of identifying and beginning to close gaps between "actual" and "true" costs of providing high-quality care.

Provider Resources

http://www.acf.hhs.gov/programs/ccb/providers/index.htm#funding

Provider Resources from the Administration for Children and Families, U.S. Department of Health and Human Services. Includes documents such as "What Providers Should Know about Child Care Assistance for Families" (English and Spanish versions) and links to several resources for funding to start or improve a child-care program.

The Foundation Center

http://fdncenter.org

Website of The Foundation Center, based in New York City, which publishes the *Philanthropy News Digest* and maintains a clearinghouse of information for both grant seekers and funders. A "learning lab" tab on the menu bar accesses an array of resources for beginning grant seekers, including a glossary of philanthropy-related terms and a short course in proposal writing. The site provides a link to the center's *RFP Bulletin*, which describes current requests for proposals in various categories (e.g., Children and Youth, Education), and provides direct links to the grantmakers' websites.

7

CHAPTER SEVEN

Personnel Management

You've done the planning and have the program's broad goals outlined, along with ideas about how to implement those goals. You have created a budget—a plan, expressed in dollar amounts, that governs how your program will use its resources to meet its goals. It's time to begin the tasks of organizing and staffing and come one step closer to bringing those plans on paper to life. Thus, we turn our attention to **personnel management,** an administrative competency that taps into both the organizing and staffing processes. *Organizing* involves deciding what jobs must be done, what skills or training are required, and how those jobs relate to one another. Once those decisions are made, *staffing* consists of developing procedures for recruiting, selecting, and retaining employees to do the various jobs. After those employees are hired, your human relations competency is necessary to fully use and enhance the resources they bring. Chapter 8 explores the human relations competency.

Organizing

Organizing is defined as arranging elements (e.g., people, supplies, and equipment) and coordinating joint activities so that all of the interdependent parts contribute effectively to the desired goal. Organizing is the second component of the managerial process; that is, materials, equipment, space, and human energy must be assembled and integrated through organizing to get the program under way. An infinite number of details must be woven together to make a coherent whole. A good organizer can create mental images of activities, their parts, and sequences easily. Organizational arrangements are the means to an end. The end is the goal of providing high-quality care and education for young children.

Consider the following example: A child development specialist was given the task of organizing services at a camp for orphans in the war-ravaged African country of Rwanda. Jacqueline Hayden arrived at the camp with no supplies, no assistance, and no office space. Within 12 weeks, she had organized children into mixed-age, family-style groups, with an adult refugee assigned as "tent-mother"; found "foster families" for the youngest and most traumatized orphaned children; and enlisted groups of children and adults to take care of cooking, laundry, foraging for supplies, making storybooks, and making culottes to clothe the other children (Hayden, 1995).

Job Design

You may never work in a refugee camp, but wherever you start a new program, your first organizational task is to determine what jobs must be done. If you are taking over the manager's responsibilities in an existing program, you should familiarize yourself with each job description, making changes as appropriate. Job design is "the process of laying out job responsibilities and duties and describing how they are to be performed" (DuBrin, 2000, p. 162). In a small dress-making factory, for example, some employees cut out the patterns, others stitch the pieces together, and others add the buttons or other trimmings. Other jobs include creating the designs, buying the fabric and other supplies, distributing the materials to the work stations, checking the finished product, selling the dresses, shipping them to buyers, and so on. If the factory is large enough, the jobs might be even more specialized, with different workers assigned to sew each part of the garment. The factory owner may strive to make each job as automated as possible in order to meet the goal of maximum production at minimum cost.

Decisions, Decisions . . .

With your classmates, create a list of all of the jobs required in a child development program. Discuss how much specialization or automation is possible or desirable in each.

Job Analysis

You may be hired to manage an existing program, perhaps one that grew from a very small operation where everyone "just knew" what had to be done and did it without much planning or discussion. In order to put this program on a more businesslike footing, you should complete a job analysis for each individual. You can do this by observing the person who is doing the job or by having that person help analyze the job using a worksheet such as that shown in Figure 7.1. After careful analysis, you might decide to reallocate some of the tasks assigned to that staff member. Figure 7.2 is an example of a completed job analysis for the position of cook in a child development program.

Job Description

The job description should be available when you hire an individual. It should be written in terms that allow it to serve as the basis for periodically monitoring or evaluating the staff member's work. Figure 7.3 is an example of a job description for a teacher. Notice that the description includes a space for both the manager and the employee to sign and date it. The staff member should read this document carefully and agree to the tasks. Later, the manager and staff member should confer before reassigning or adding tasks. This document serves as an agreement and acknowledgment that the job description will be used as the basis for periodic evaluations of the individual's performance. (See chapter 8.)

Job descriptions should be available to all employees and kept on file in their personnel folder. The manager should discuss the job description with each employee so that she feels

FIGURE 7.1 *Model Civil Service worksheet for obtaining job analysis data*

Identifying Information

Name of incumbent

Organization/unit

Title and series

Date

Interviewer

Brief Summary of Job

This statement includes the primary duties of the job. It may be prepared in advance from class specifications, job descriptions, or other sources, however, it should be checked for accuracy using the task statements that result from the analysis.

Job Tasks

What does the worker do? How does he do it? Why? What output is produced? What tools, procedures, aids are involved? How much time does it take to do the task? How often does the worker perform the task in a day, week, month, or year?

Skills, Knowledge, and Abilities Required

What does it take to perform each task in terms of the following.

1. Knowledge required:
   a. What subject-matter areas are covered by the task?
   b. What facts or principles must the worker have an acquaintance with or understand in these subject-matter areas?
   c. Describe the level, degree, and breadth of knowledge required in these areas or subjects.
2. Skills required:
   a. What activities must the worker perform with ease and precision?
   b. What are the manual skills that are required to operate machines, vehicles, equipment, or to use tools?
3. Abilities required:
   a. What is the nature and level of the language ability, written or oral, required of the worker on the job? Are there complex oral or written ideas involved in performing the task or merely simple instructional materials?
   b. What mathematical ability must the worker have? Will he use simple arithmetic, complex algebra?
   c. What reasoning or problem-solving ability must the worker have?
   d. What instructions must the worker follow? Are they simple, detailed, involved, abstract?
   e. What interpersonal abilities are required? What supervisory or managing abilities are required?
   f. What physical abilities, such as strength, coordination, or visual acuity, must the worker have?

(Continued)

FIGURE 7.1 *Continued*

Physical Activities

Describe the frequency and degree to which the incumbent is engaged in such activities as pulling, pushing, throwing, carrying, kneeling, sitting, running, crawling, reaching, and climbing.

Environmental Conditions

Describe the frequency and degree to which the incumbent is working under conditions such as cramped quarters, moving objects, vibration, and inadequate ventilation.

Typical Work Incidents

1. Situations involving the interpretation of feelings, ideas, or facts in terms of personal viewpoint.
2. Influencing people in their opinions, attitudes, or judgments about ideas or things.
3. Working with people beyond giving and receiving instructions.
4. Performing repetitive work.
5. Performing under stress when confronted with emergency, critical, unusual, or dangerous situations; or in situations in which work speed and sustained attention are make-and-break aspects of the job.
6. Performing a variety of duties, often changing from one task to another of a different nature without a loss of efficiency or composure.
7. Working under hazardous conditions that may result in violence, loss of bodily members, burns, bruises, cuts, impairment of senses, collapse, fractures, or electric shock.

Work Interest Areas

Identify from the list the preferences for work activities suggested by each task.

A preference for activities:

1. Dealing with things and objects
2. Concerning the communication of data
3. Involving business contact with people
4. Involving work of a scientific and technical nature
5. Involving work of a routine, concrete, organized nature
6. Involving work of an abstract and creative nature
7. Involving work for the presumed good of people
8. Relating to process, machine, and technique
9. Resulting in prestige or the esteem of others
10. Resulting in tangible, productive satisfaction

Source: U.S. Civil Service Commission.

FIGURE 7.2 *Job analysis (based on U.S. Civil Service Guidelines)*

Identifying Information

Name of Incumbent: Mary Jones

Organization: XYZ Child Development Center

Title: Food Service Employee: Cook

Date: [Today's date]

Interviewer: Janie Bolls

Brief Summary of Job

The cook prepares breakfast, lunch, and midmorning and midafternoon snacks for children and staff in the center; assists with serving breakfast and lunch; prepares market orders; and keeps kitchen, dining areas, and food storage areas clean and sanitary.

Job Tasks

Cook's Duties: Daily (8 hours, 5 days weekly; 6:30 a.m. to 3:00 p.m.)

1. Prepares breakfast and helps serve to center's young children and staff.
2. Prepares lunch and helps serve to center's young children and staff.
3. Prepares snacks for children and break beverages for staff.
4. Supervises assistant who sets up tables, chairs, etc., for meals.
5. Washes dishes and pans using dishwasher.
6. Cleans countertops, appliance tops, floors.
7. Directs assistant's work and gives training as needed.

Occasional Duties

1. Cares for kitchen appliances, keeping alert for problems.
2. Orders food for classroom projects as directed by manager.
3. Prepares play dough, fingerpaint, cookie dough as directed by manager.
4. Keeps food and paper inventory up to date.
5. Makes market orders from menus supplied.
6. Confers with manager regarding menus, food on hand, etc.
7. Attends inservice workshops or meetings.
8. Makes year-end inventory of food and supplies in June.
9. Recommends maintenance or replacement of appliances or painting of surfaces in the unit.
10. Attends staff meetings as applicable.
11. Prepares (with help) food for special occasions such as parents' meeting, directors' meeting, staff meeting.

Knowledge, Skills, and Abilities Required

1. Knowledge required:
   a. Knowledge of appropriate cooking techniques for the typical foods served in the center
   b. Knowledge of the nutritional requirements for children
   c. Knowledge of the characteristic food habits of children
   d. Knowledge of sanitation principles related to food and food service

(Continued)

FIGURE 7.2 *Continued*

2. Skills required:
   a. Skill to prepare foods
   b. Skill to organize materials for and prepare several foods to meet the serving schedules of the center
   c. Skill to operate and maintain kitchen appliances

3. Abilities required:
   a. Ability to read recipes, regulations, written memos
   b. Ability to write shopping lists, memos, etc.
   c. Ability to calculate quantities for recipes and food costs using simple arithmetic
   d. Ability to explain or demonstrate to an aide or assistant how to do an activity such as prepare a food or set up the dining room
   e. Ability and willingness to be friendly to children, parents, staff members, and vendors
   f. Ability and stamina to be on your feet, to lift or move 25–50 pounds of food or equipment

Physical Activities

Include walking around the kitchen, storeroom, and dining room for most of the 8 hours and lifting up to 50 pounds.

Environmental Conditions

Environment is kitchen, storerooms, and dining room. Generally pleasant, may be extra warm when ovens are used. A variety of interpersonal relationships with staff, children, and parents. Generally a moderately quiet place except for happy sounds of children playing.

Typical Work Incidents

1. Conferring with manager regarding menus, inventories, purchase orders (generally Fridays).
2. Cooking is routine activity, not repetitive because different menus are used daily in 3-week cycles. Considerable challenge to get a large number of meals on the table at a set time.
3. Routine cleaning tasks are generally minimal because they are done daily.
4. Emergencies may arise if orders do not arrive or appliances do not work; thus, ingenuity is required to keep the service at a high-quality level.
5. Assistants in the kitchen, other staff, children, and parents are an unusually pleasant group to work with, generally caring about individuals and their interests.

Work Interest Areas

1. Involves work for the good of others
2. Involves work satisfaction when meals are served on time, taste good, are attractive and nutritious, and are enjoyed
3. Involves variety, yet some routine
4. Involves activity relating to home activity

FIGURE 7.3 *Sample job description*

Job Title: Child development center teacher

Description: The teacher plans, implements, and documents a developmentally appropriate program for children (in collaboration with assistant or coteacher and curriculum coordinator) and works in partnership with parents to promote each child's development.

Hours: 7:30 to 4:30 or 8:30 to 5:30, with one-hour lunch break, Monday through Friday.

Responsibilities

- Plan, implement, and document curriculum.
- Organize and maintain environment to support program goals.
- Establish and maintain relationships with families through group meetings, home visits, and conferences.
- Maintain records and write reports.
- Participate in professional development activities.

Signed _____   Date _____
       Employee

       _____   Date _____
       Manager, XYZ Child Development Center

a commitment to the responsibilities specified. Child development centers are dynamic rather than static, meaning that they must grow and develop to meet changing community needs. Job descriptions must be current and reflect any changes that occur when staff are reassigned or given additional duties as a result of this growth.

Job Specification

After preparing the job description, you are ready to devise a job specification to be used in advertising the open position. This document specifies the type and level of education and previous experience required. It lists essential personal characteristics such as judgment, initiative, physical effort, physical skills, communication skills, emotional characteristics, and the necessary sensory demand such as seeing, hearing, and smelling. The position's responsibilities are clearly stated. Figure 7.4 is an example of the job specification for a child development center teacher.

The job specification is the basis for a newspaper advertisement. You can duplicate it and hand it out to possible candidates at a meeting or post a flyer, with tear-off tags listing the program's phone number, where potential employees might see it. You can reach a broader audience by asking your local Child Care Resource and Referral agency to post the announcement on their website or by posting your announcement on the websites that reach a national audience such as the National Association for the Education of Young Children (http://www.naeyc.org/careerforum/) or the Child Care Information Exchange (http://www.ccie.com/). Be sure all essential information is included. To screen the telephone calls from applicants, you may wish to use an answering machine. Your printed job specifications and ads should reflect this arrangement. State, for example, "Please leave a message stating your name, phone number, and previous experience by calling 555-4444 or e-mailing childslifecdc@aol.com."

FIGURE 7.4 *Sample job specification*

Job Title

Child development center teacher

Position Available: September 1, 2006

Qualifications

BA or BS degree in early childhood education or child development; state teaching license in early childhood education.

Experience

Minimal experience required is one semester supervised student teaching with young children (ages birth through 5).

Responsibilities

- Plan and implement a developmentally appropriate program for children (in collaboration with assistant or coteacher and curriculum coordinator).
- Organize and maintain environment to support program goals.
- Establish and maintain relationships with families through group meetings, home visits, and conferences.
- Participate in professional development activities.
- Maintain records and write reports.

Hours: 7:30 to 4:30 or 8:30 to 5:30, with one-hour lunch break, Monday through Friday.

Compensation: Commensurate with public school salaries for comparable preparation and experience. Benefits include health insurance, paid holidays, and vacation days.

Contact

Mary Right, Manager
Child's Life Child Development Center
444 Adams Street
Baker, TX 67777
214-555-4567

Procedure

Send resume and three letters of recommendation to address above.

Closing Date

July 1, 2006

An equal opportunity employer

Job Classification

Classifying a job in your center relative to other jobs requires considering the level of difficulty, responsibility, and preparation required for that job, as well as the amount of supervision necessary. Salary can then be based on the level of the job in the classification. Figure 7.5 illustrates one such classification scheme.

FIGURE 7.5 *Job classification scheme*

Level	Food Service	Teacher	Office	Maintenance
Level 7			Center manager	
Level 6				
Level 5	Dietitian	Experienced teacher	Accountant	
Level 4		Second-year teacher		
Level 3	Cook	First-year teacher	Bookkeeper	
Level 2				Maintenance supervisor
Level 1	Assistant cook	Teacher's aide	Clerk/typist	Housekeeper

Source: Adapted from *Day Care Personnel Management* (Atlanta: Atlanta Southern Education Board, 1979), p. 19.

Job Coordination

Now that you have analyzed, or carved into specific jobs, the work necessary to accomplish your goals, you have to figure out how to put all of those parts together. This requires decisions about organizational structure, authority and responsibility, and span of control. Your job is to keep the broad picture in mind. Given an organization where most responsibility is delegated to the classroom teachers, the organizational chart might be similar to one of the plans represented in Figure 7.6.

Authority and Responsibility

A clear definition of responsibility is essential when assigning teachers or coteachers the authority to manage their classrooms. For example, although you might expect teachers to arrange space, organize storage, set up learning centers, and make appropriate adaptations for individuals and situations in their classrooms, you might not expect them to handle business matters such as collecting and recording fee payments.

Giving teachers the authority to manage their classrooms is an example of **decentralizing authority.** This decentralization generally makes for a responsive, creative, and adaptive organization, highly desirable qualities in any people-centered operation. Recall from the discussion in chapter 3 that a central tenet of quality management is the empowerment of all staff members so that each one has the maximum feasible authority to carry out the assigned responsibilities. Teachers who have the authority to manage their classrooms invest more creativity and energy than those who simply have the responsibility to carry out the manager's plans.

Compensation and Time for Additional Responsibility. Delegating managerial functions to teachers requires an organizational system that allows paid time for their accomplishment. The Center for the Child Care Workforce (1998) recommends a minimum of two hours paid planning time per week plus closing the program at least one day per year for long-range planning and renewing the physical environment. To achieve high quality, the standards are five hours per week and two days per year.

FIGURE 7.6   *Examples of organizational charts*

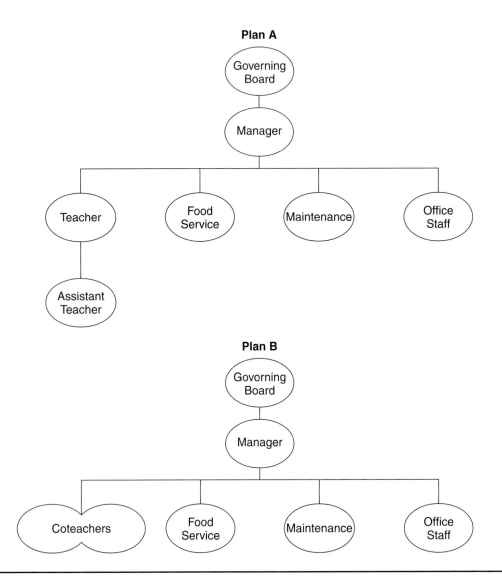

Plan A

Governing Board — Manager — Teacher, Food Service, Maintenance, Office Staff; Teacher — Assistant Teacher

Plan B

Govorning Board — Manager — Coteachers, Food Service, Maintenance, Office Staff

Links Between Classrooms and Other Units.   Links between the classrooms and the program's maintenance, food service, and business units are essential. In a decentralized plan, a system for obtaining materials, supplies, and equipment is especially critical for preventing duplication and waste. Each teacher might be assigned a budget for classroom use. Teachers could make appropriate inventories and place requests for supplies, which can then be ordered collectively. In a centralized plan, the manager assumes more responsibility for ordering, allocating, and distributing supplies.

Decisions, Decisions . . .

A local club has just raised $1,000 for your center to purchase some new play equipment. Because your philosophy is to delegate as much authority as possible to the teachers, you ask them to decide how to spend the money. How can you do this, yet ensure that the money is spent wisely—that is, on materials of high quality? How will you organize the task to accomplish both goals?

Some employees might be granted the authority to direct the work of other employees. The program's organizational chart is a visual representation of these lines of authority. In the Plan A organization (see Figure 7.6), the teacher directs the assistant teacher, reflecting the difference in training and experience required for each job. In the Plan B organization, coteachers share authority. This type of organization is used when job specifications call for teachers of equal training and experience. It symbolizes the expectation that the work and the responsibilities are shared equally.

Some lines of authority are necessary because they help employees know where to turn for solutions to their problems. They also let the parents and even the children know who can make a final decision. Unless your center is very small, it is a good idea to put these lines of authority down on paper in the form of a flowchart or graph that clearly shows the chain of command. This visual representation can be supplemented with written policies that inform parents and staff where to go with particular concerns.

Span of Control

Span of control generally refers to the number of subordinates reporting to a manager. In child development centers, the span of control refers to the number of children and families within the group assigned to a particular teacher. Thus, span of control incorporates concepts of teacher–child ratio as well as group size. These concepts are of particular significance when close supervision is required to provide the individual attention and analysis that are the hallmarks of high-quality service. How many people can one or two teachers comfortably and effectively influence through their caring and teaching?

Organizing Classrooms or Groups

While many consider low adult:child ratios to be indicators of quality, even a one-to-one adult–child ratio does not ensure a high-quality experience for children if the manager does not also consider the number of children to be cared for in one group or classroom. Imagine a room full of 20 crying babies! Nearly a quarter century ago, the National Day Care Study made a distinction between human ratio and mathematical ratio:

> In a group of 14 children with two caregivers the *mathematical* ratio is 1:7, just as the mathematical ratio for 28 children and four caregivers is 1:7. The *human* ratio is, for the caregivers involved, twice as much in the second case as the first. *Each* caregiver has 28, not 14, children's names and needs to know. (Ruopp et al., 1979, pp. xxvi–xxvii)

Managers who want to achieve the highest quality when organizing classrooms must look beyond their state's licensing regulations. Although the minimum standards for adult–child ratios are included in each state's licensing regulations, they vary widely from state to state.

A manageable group size means that each child is able to get the teacher's attention at least some of the time.

In spite of its importance, group size is addressed by licensing regulations in only 32 of the 50 states (Children's Defense Fund, 2001, p. 138).

At least two other sets of standards do address this issue. Accreditation guidelines of the National Association for the Education of Young Children (2005) emphasize that small group sizes and fewer children per staff member are associated with a higher quality of care. Although the recommendations of the American Public Health Association and the American Academy of Pediatrics (2002) support those of the NAEYC, they are more stringent because they do not allow staff with higher levels of training to care for more children. Table 7.1 shows the adult–child ratios and maximum group sizes recommended by each organization for children of various ages.

Public school policy makers are also paying attention to group size, with several states establishing goals for reduced class sizes. Full-day kindergartens can also have a positive impact. Recall the concept of human ratio (as distinct from mathematical ratio) discussed earlier. Although a kindergarten teacher with 20 children in the morning and another 20 in the afternoon is dealing with a **mathematical ratio** of 1:20, the **human ratio** for the teacher is 1:40 because that is the number of names, personalities, and families to know. With only one group of 20 and the extended time period, a teacher can get to know each child and each family far better than with two groups of 20.

TABLE 7.1   *Adult–child ratios and maximum group sizes recommended by the National Association for the Education of Young Children, the American Public Health Association, and the American Academy of Pediatrics*

Age of Child	Maximum Number of Children per Caregiver		Maximum Group Size	
	NAEYC	**APHA/AAP**	**NAEYC**	**APHA/AAP**
Under 12 months	4	3	8	6
13–24 months	5	4	12	8
25–30 months	6	4	12	8
31–35 months	7	5	14	10
3 years	10	7	20	14
4 and 5 years	10	8	20	16
6–8 years	12	10	24	20
9–12 years	14	12	28	24

Source: Research into action: The effects of group size, ratios, and staff training on child care quality (1993, January). *Young Children, 48*(2):65; *Caring for our children: National health and safety performance standards: Guidelines for out-of-home child care programs* (2nd ed.) (2002). Elk Grove Village, IL: American Academy of Pediatrics; Washington, DC: American Public Health Association; and Aurora, CO: National Resource Center for Health and Safety in Child Care, p. 4.

Age Ranges

Organizing also applies to the group composition within classrooms. There are many arguments for single-age groups and for multiage groups, with strengths and weaknesses on each side. Some teachers believe they are more effective with one age group than with another. Multiage groups are thought to be more familylike, providing older children opportunities to be helpful to younger ones. On the other hand, some argue that activities in a single-age group can be more challenging. Teachers in multiage groups might avoid difficult or complex projects because they think the younger children will be frustrated—either by trying to do things beyond their capacity or by being excluded from an activity that might be too hard or dangerous for them. The concept of human ratio provides another argument in support of mixed-age groups. When groups include 5-, 6-, and 7-year-olds, and each child stays with the same teacher over a 3-year period, the teacher deals with fewer new families in any given year. The teacher, child, and family are spared learning about each other anew every year and are able to develop deeper relationships.

Decisions, Decisions . . .

Divide your class into two teams. Let one team brainstorm a list of arguments in favor of mixed-age groupings, and let the other team brainstorm a list of the arguments against this practice. Discuss your lists. Which set of arguments do you personally find most persuasive?

Organizational Structure

In addition to determining the number of children and staff members in a given classroom, the manager must decide on an organizational structure. In Plan A in Figure 7.6, the teacher is clearly the top authority figure, with the assistant teacher responsible to the teacher and the aide responsible to both the teacher and the assistant teacher. Some center managers prefer Plan B in Figure 7.6—that is, to hire teachers of equal qualifications and give them coteaching responsibilities. In either case, the aide is responsible to both teachers. Particularly in child-care operations exceeding an 8-hour day, having coteachers with staggered times of arrival and departure makes considerable sense.

Supervisory Staff

An employee called a **curriculum coordinator,** or assistant to the manager, may be assigned to help plan the children's programs and advise the teachers about curriculum choices and children's behaviors. This position may be staffed when a manager has several building sites and cannot be available to oversee the details of each classroom.

In centers where less than highly qualified teachers are hired to operate the classrooms, a qualified early childhood teacher or specialist is generally assigned to coordinate the programming or planning of specific activities. This supervision may be required by licensing regulations. In this case, joint planning is required, which means that the supervisor and teachers need a time and place to go over the plans and get their ideas coordinated before the teachers carry them out. Plans must be understood, match each teacher's ability, and fit the characteristics of the children in the group. The details of this coordination effort should be included in the job description of each teacher and the supervisor.

Another way to look at this position has been developed in the world-renowned early childhood programs of Reggio Emilia, Italy. There, a ***pedagogista*** works collaboratively with teachers from several centers "to analyze and interpret the rights and needs of each child and family, and then use this knowledge in [their] work with children" (Filippini, 1994, p. 116). The *pedagogista* also facilitates parent–teacher relations and organizes meetings where they can discuss and extend the children's curriculum projects. There is no exact translation for the job title in English, but some programs in the United States are finding it useful to have such a facilitator to help the teachers reflect on their observations and interactions with children and families as they plan where to go next in their curricula.

Volunteers

Volunteers are valuable assets, giving considerable amounts of their human capital to child development centers each year. Their presence is in addition to the required minimum for child–staff ratios. To make the best use of this valuable resource, you should attend to the same types of tasks with volunteers as you do with paid staff. That is, you have to find people with the skills and attitudes that make them suitable for work in a child development center; acquaint them with the center's organization and policies; provide necessary training; assign them worthwhile tasks; and monitor and guide them in the performance of those tasks. Finally, if you want volunteers to keep coming back, let them know how they are doing and give appropriate recognition for a job well done.

Organizing Support Services

The work in a child development program includes much more than the day-to-day interactions between children and teachers. There are several behind-the-scenes jobs that support those interactions.

Office Services.   Child development centers are businesses and require systems for record keeping, as well as for interacting and communicating with parents and the public. Records are essential to document compliance with regulations and track financial matters such as fees, bills, rents, and taxes. Centers must have up-to-date lists of family names with home addresses and phone numbers, work addresses and phone numbers, and other pertinent data, as well as contact information for vendors, health, fire, social services, and professional organizations. Someone must collect the fees from the parents, write receipts, pay bills, and deposit money in the bank. The office support unit is responsible for the timely and accurate payments of salaries, benefits, withholding and Social Security taxes, bills, and rents.

Efficiently organizing and storing the center's various forms (e.g., admission, health, and financial) and office supplies from the outset facilitates handling routine matters. A larger center usually hires an office assistant or secretary at least part-time. An accounting system must be established with the aid of a qualified accountant. Routine accounting services may be obtained through a contract if the center cannot afford to hire one. Smaller centers may attempt to handle day-to-day secretarial chores with volunteer help, perhaps from a parent. It is shortsighted for qualified managers to spend much of their time typing, sorting mail, filing, and answering the phone when someone to do these tasks can usually be hired at a relatively small cost to the center. The manager's time should be spent more productively, writing grant applications, for example, or conferring with teachers or parents.

The center's office is the "window to the world." People receive their first impressions of your center from a phone call or visit to the center. Therefore, the careful training of office staff is essential to ensure that information is given accurately and professionally.

People who call the center will be favorably impressed by a pleasant voice inquiring, "This is the XYZ Center. How may I help you?"

If your program does not have secretarial support, you might want to use a telephone answering machine or voice-mail system to take incoming messages. You must weigh the relative advantages and disadvantages carefully. On the negative side, callers who reach a machine when they want an immediate response are likely to be frustrated. You might lose potential customers. It may soften the irritation if the message explains that staff cannot come to the phone because they are busy with the children, that messages are checked regularly (perhaps every hour), and that calls are returned at a specific time. On the plus side, you and your staff gain control of your time and energy. Instead of being interrupted throughout the day, you can plan to return calls at particular times. Of course, the system works only if you do check messages at regular intervals and return calls promptly.

Food Services.   Both licensing regulations and accreditation criteria follow the food service standards of the U.S. Department of Agriculture. A qualified cook is capable of planning the meals and all of the activities of the kitchen and dining room. As manager, you may have to plan the meals for a less qualified cook or you may contract with a registered dietitian for this service. Procuring the food and other supplies may be the responsibility of the manager, the cook, or an employee assigned to handle all purchases. The person assigned this task must purchase and organize the supplies and control the inventory carefully to minimize expense and avoid the risks of loss, waste, theft, and food spoilage. The Department of Agriculture food reimbursement program is discussed in chapter 11, along with other details regarding food services.

Planning for links between the classrooms and the food service unit saves time and dollars. Foods used as part of various learning experiences can readily be purchased in large lots with other foods and then incorporated into the regular menus. For example, a teacher might plan to make fresh-squeezed orange juice with the children as a science activity exploring simple machines. The juice can be served as a snack beverage. This requires that the cook purchase an orange for each child and make a corresponding adjustment in the total quantity of snack beverages purchased that week. A number of food items used in learning activities are not eaten; for example, play dough requires flour and salt.

Because the organization chart does not show all of the tasks included in the list of the cook's duties, a job analysis and a job description are needed. It is important, for example, to indicate who asks the cook to provide oranges for the science activity or the flour and salt for play dough. Do teachers ask directly, or go through the manager's office? If such purchases are specified in the cook's job description, they can become a simple routine activity. If not, the cook may feel burdened by the request.

As you organize the various functions and tasks associated with food service for your center, keep human factors clearly in mind. One of the hallmarks of excellence in many high-quality programs is the family atmosphere that is engendered when the support staff interact with the children regularly, becoming rich resources along with the teachers. Even though your management techniques must be professional and businesslike, your center provides high-quality care to the extent that it resembles a home more than a business. In addition to the obvious skills required of a cook or secretary, it is wise to include the ability

Support staff can be teachers too, so managers should look for candidates with some of the same qualities they seek in teachers. Here the cook is helping children identify and label plants in their vegetable garden.

to relate well to children as part of the job description. Programs are enriched immeasurably when children get to know these important people in their lives. One center, for example, has the tradition of a weekly "food lab," in which the cook invites two or three preschoolers into the kitchen to help prepare some part of that day's lunch. The cook prepares a child-size workspace, borrowing a small table from a classroom and positioning a stepstool so that the children can reach the sinks. The children eagerly anticipate their turn to help and learn a lot in the process.

Maintenance and Cleaning Services.   These services apply to the entire center, covering the classrooms, service areas, and outdoor play areas. Cleanliness and safety are essential and very dependent on adequate attention to maintenance details on a daily, even hourly, basis. A custodial-maintenance person may provide the most effective arrangement, with the center manager helping with overall goals and timetables. In small centers, one individual may have complete responsibility. The job specifications should be carefully drawn because a person who can relate well to children is highly desirable. Women can be efficient in this position; limiting a search to men is shortsighted. In the organization's plan, the procedures to acquire maintenance tools, cleaning tools and supplies, and services are needed. Duties include light and heavy cleaning; trash and garbage removal; storage and repair of equipment; painting and general upkeep; disinfecting the kitchen, food service areas, and rest rooms; and maintaining the outdoor play area.

Each unit's staff should be delegated some responsibility for preparing the unit for cleaning. The children enjoy helping in the classrooms. Food and waste paper should be removed from lockers. Objects that may appear unsightly should be picked up. Children can be taught to be helpful in beautifying the yard. Parents may enjoy offering assistance or advice.

Transportation Services.   Transportation services are important benefits to some center customers. Clearly, licensing standards for the qualification of drivers, seat belts for children, and extra adults are all essential. Although having a center bus or van makes field trips easy, transportation is a costly item, and finances must be calculated carefully, including adequate insurance coverage.

Staffing

Merely defining the jobs necessary to accomplish your program's goals is, of course, not enough. You have to find the right people to do those jobs. A child development center is a labor-intensive operation. That is, lots of human energy or labor is essential for the center to reach its goals. No mechanical robots can perform the services. People's knowledge, skills, abilities, stamina, enthusiasm, and love are aspects of their human energy. Such attributes are called **human capital.** The importance of human capital is underscored by the statistic that the salaries for a center's personnel often consume over 70 percent of the operating budget. **Staffing** is the process of recruiting and dealing with the human resources (human capital) required to perform the center's functions.

Staffing Decisions

When a teacher resigns or retires, you have an opportunity to reanalyze that position and consider various alternative organizational structures. You can move a particular teacher up to the next age group, keeping the children and teacher together another year. You might reorganize your groups or promote a staff member. Or you may want to hire an individual with more experience with the hope that hiring will not have to be done so often. Depending on the size of your operation, you might hire a person to work as a part-time teacher and a part-time librarian or as a part-time parent educator. Or two people might be hired to share one position. In other words, the vacancy gives you an opportunity to think about new ways to structure the work assignments.

As you sort through these possibilities, you may consult your policy and advisory boards. Your center may already have established policies concerning promotion from within or the qualifications for specific jobs. If these options seem unworkable, you have to work with your board to change them before proceeding.

Organizing the Search

Once a decision is made to hire, a committee should be formed to conduct the search. Unless your board is very small, it is wise to include only selected representatives on the hiring committee. Other potential members of the hiring committee include parents of children enrolled in the center and staff members who will be working with the new teacher. Each of these groups can bring a valuable perspective to your deliberations. Parents consider whether they feel comfortable leaving their child with a particular candidate or sharing their own concerns with that person. Staff members are likely to wonder whether the candidate will pitch in and do a fair share of the work or be fun to work with.

Make it clear at the beginning who has the authority for the final decision. Will it be a democratic process? Or will the committee provide recommendations, with the final authority resting with the manager? Each method has advantages, so you want to weigh your decision carefully.

Decisions, Decisions . . .

As the director of ABC Child Development Center, you are committed to a democratic style of leadership. You include two staff members along with two parents and two board members on the hiring committee for a teacher vacancy. You and the board members favor candidate A, whose background includes extensive experience serving children with disabilities. The parents and teachers on the committee favor candidate B, who has limited experience but whose personality seems friendlier to them. How will you decide? What are the potential outcomes of your decision in either case?

Educational Preparation of Teachers

Numerous studies have demonstrated the connection between staff training and program quality (e.g., Cost, Quality, and Outcomes Study Team, 1995). As a manager committed to providing a high-quality program for young children, one of your major policy decisions is the level of education required of your teaching and caregiving staff. The NAEYC has established a timeline for centers to comply with new accreditation standards for teacher education. The standards become effective in 2006 and become successively more stringent in 2010, 2015, and 2020. (Details are available at the NAEYC website: http://www.naeyc.org/accreditation/performance_criteria/teacher_qualification_timeline.html)

A wide range of formal and informal preparation is possible. Some employees may enter as aides with no formal training or experience and develop the skills necessary to work with

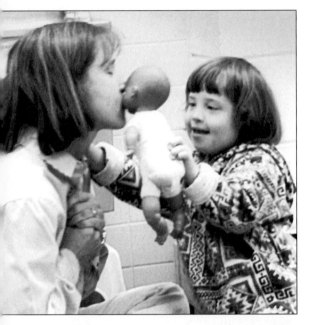

Wise managers seek to hire the most well-qualified teachers—those whose education, experience, and disposition enable them to respond to children with a playful spirit.

young children on the job. Others may come with formal training acquired in a variety of ways. Secondary vocational schools, community colleges, as well as 4-year institutions offer several programs that prepare caregivers and assistant teachers. Such programs generally include child development and practicum courses that give the student experience working with children in a center.

Child Development Associate Credential. The Child Development Associate Credential (CDA) can be viewed as a blend of on-the-job training and formal study. The program was initiated by the U.S. Office of Child Development to provide a system for assessing and recognizing the competence of individuals who work with young children. The CDA is led by a private nonprofit corporation, the Child Development Associate Consortium, and is financed with federal funds. Assessments are conducted in the center where the individual works and candidates work individually or with other candidates to enhance and document their skills in specified competency areas.

Associates and Baccalaureate Degrees. Early childhood education programs offered by 2- and 4-year colleges prepare individuals to work with young children. When finished, graduates hold either an associate or a bachelor's degree. Many individuals, inspired by their success in completing the 1-year program, decide to pursue further education. Articulation agreements between 2- and 4-year institutions facilitate this progression by spelling out exactly what coursework will apply toward the higher degree and reducing duplication of content. Four-year degrees often include state certification to teach in public schools. In some states, the certificate is in early childhood education; in others, it is in elementary education with an endorsement in early childhood education. Programs have varied across the country as to the nature of the courses and experiences provided. Given the recent movement toward the inclusion of children with disabilities in all programs for young children, several states, such as North Carolina and Kentucky, offer an early childhood certificate that combines course work and practical experience in child development, early childhood education, and early childhood special education.

State Licensure or Certification. Preprimary programs within the public school systems typically require the state certification of all teaching personnel. Many centers expect to hire certified teachers to lead each group of children and hire somewhat less-educated people to serve as aides or assistants. Other centers expect to hire one certified program director who works with all caregivers to plan the center's educational program. In a public school, the early childhood education specialist may report to the school superintendent and be responsible for coordinating all kindergartens, prekindergartens, and before- and after-school programs. The No Child Left Behind Act, which mandates highly qualified teachers in K–12 classrooms, does not specifically address requirements for early childhood or preschool teachers unless a state considers them a part of its elementary and secondary system. Individual states, however, may choose to extend the NCLB standards and require that teachers in state-funded early childhood programs hold appropriate degrees as well as meet other qualifications, such as passing particular standardized tests (Kauertz & McMaken, 2004).

Level of Experience

As you plan to hire a person to fill a position, you want to consider the level of experience that best fits your needs and budget. A highly experienced candidate may be able to step into the job more easily and assume a leadership role more quickly, while the new graduate is likely to need training and time to adjust to the job. On the other hand, the seasoned candidate is likely to require a higher salary than the neophyte. In a tight job market, these considerations might be academic, but if there is a choice, you and your board should weigh the various options as part of the decision-making process.

Legal Aspects of Staffing

A number of laws and regulations govern the operation of a child development program, including those specifically related to staffing. It is important for managers to be familiar with these requirements, but it is equally important to seek the advice of legal experts because interpretations, as well as the laws themselves, can change over time and vary with locale. Recall that the Civil Rights Act of 1964 prohibits all discrimination on the basis of race, sex, religion, color, or national origin. This is the law that addresses the issue of sexual harassment. An earlier law, the Equal Pay Act of 1963, mandates that employers give women and men equal pay for equal work. The Civil Rights Act of 1991 gives victims of discrimination the right to sue for compensatory and punitive damages, in amounts up to $300,000, depending on the size of the employer. Because some laws protecting workers' rights apply only to employers above a certain size, a small child development program may be legally (if not morally or ethically) exempt.

- The Americans with Disabilities Act of 1990 prohibits employers of 15 or more employees from discriminating against individuals on the basis of disability or chronic illness, unless their condition prevents them from performing the job functions or the employer would suffer "undue hardship" by accommodating them.
- The Age Discrimination in Employment Act of 1967 applies only to organizations with 25 or more employees and prohibits discrimination (including mandatory retirement based on age) against individuals 40 and older.
- Employers with more than 21 employees may not discriminate against pregnant women as long as they are able to do their jobs, according to the Pregnancy Discrimination Act of 1978.
- Under the Family and Medical Leave Act of 1993, employers of 50 or more must provide up to 12 weeks of unpaid, job-protected leave for employees during any 12-month period to care for newborn, newly adopted, or seriously ill children or a spouse or parent (DuBrin, 2000, p. 210).

Staffing Procedures

Listing the Job. After your job specification is prepared, you must use a number of avenues to put it before the public so possible candidates can see it. You may be in a recruiting mode more than in a screening mode; that is, you are trying to get the best person in as much as keeping the unqualified out. Certain positions should be advertised widely—even nationwide.

Managers must ensure that advertising methods do not inadvertently exclude any particular group. Men, for example, are underrepresented in early childhood programs.

The Internet is one way to publicize openings to the widest possible audience. You can also list your job opening with the U.S. Department of Labor and state employment offices serving your community, and advertise in a local newspaper. Child-care resource and referral agencies as well as placement services operated by unions, professional organizations, and colleges are other possibilities. Personal contacts in agencies or among your professional colleagues across the country can be excellent sources of referrals. Finally, you may encourage particular individuals to apply for positions rather than simply waiting to see who responds to a published job specification.

Your goal is to give your job specifications as much visibility as possible so as to attract a number of qualified applicants. In addition to meeting applicable affirmative action regulations, you should enrich the diversity of your applicant pool as much as possible by ensuring that your advertising methods do not inadvertently exclude any particular group, especially groups that are underrepresented in your center's staff. This step is easily neglected. While the majority of directors in a recent survey asserted the importance of having both male and female staff, only 39 percent had geared their recruitment efforts toward men (Center for Early Childhood Leadership, 2004b).

The Job Application.   You should develop a standard job application form that provides the information your screening committee needs (see Figure 7.7). For professional jobs, a curriculum vitae or résumé and a letter of application may be preferred. Some managers ask for a letter from applicants to help gauge the quality of the candidate's writing and language usage. The job specification announcement should state where applications are available and, if desired, where letters and résumés should be sent. An application form should include name, address, phone, educational background with credits or degrees, work experience, most recent position and a reference from that position, a list of previous employers and references, and general character references. In accordance with antidiscrimination laws, you may not ask applicants questions regarding race, religion, gender, pregnancy, number or ages of children, marital status, child-care plans, height or weight, disabilities, age, criminal record, union affiliation, medical problems, or workers' compensation claims on previous jobs, *unless the area in question is job related* (DuBrin, 2000, p. 216). Thus, child development programs may ask—and are usually required to do so by state licensing regulations—for information about a candidate's health and criminal history. Some centers require the potential employee to sign a declaration similar to that in Figure 7.8.

Most states now require that all child-care workers be screened for serious criminal convictions and histories of the abuse or neglect of children or adults. The two types of screening should not be confused: screening for criminal convictions does not reveal a history of child abuse unless the person has been convicted in criminal court. In many states, instances of child abuse are handled in family or probate court and do not result in criminal convictions. Some states require this screening for the director only, while others require it for each employee. Some states require it at initial licensure only, and some require it annually. Some states allow employees a provisional period during which they may work until clearances are obtained; others require clearances to be on file before an employee starts work. Ask your licensing consultant for the correct procedure in your particular state.

FIGURE 7.7 *Sample application form*

Name _____

Address _____   Telephone _____

_____

EDUCATION

School or College   Dates Attended   Degree or Certificate

_____   _____   _____

_____   _____   _____

_____   _____   _____

WORK EXPERIENCE

Employer   Position   Dates   Supervisor Name/Phone

_____   _____   _____   _____

_____   _____   _____   _____

_____   _____   _____   _____

_____   _____   _____   _____

_____   _____   _____   _____

_____   _____   _____   _____

REFERENCES

Name   Address   Phone

_____   _____   _____

_____   _____   _____

_____   _____   _____

I certify that the information above is accurate and complete.

Signature _____   Date _____

FIGURE 7.8 *Sample employee statement*

I hereby certify in good faith that a case of abuse or neglect has not been substantiated against me nor have I been named in any proceeding for abuse or neglect that is pending in any court. I also certify that I have not been convicted of any crime (excluding minor traffic offenses) nor are there felony charges pending against me. I understand that the falsification of this or any part of my application is grounds for my discharge from employment.

_____   _____

Date   Signature

Having completed the necessary screenings, however, does not mean that you have, in fact, eliminated all applicants with such histories. Police records are incomplete in some instances, and perpetrators of abuse can assume false identities to conceal their records. Experts on child sexual abuse contacted during a federal study of child-care employee screening practices concluded that the best safeguards were "(a) education and alertness of parents, staff, and children; (b) careful listening and observation by parents and staff; (c) child care participation and monitoring by parents; and (d) parent networks within programs" (Staley, Ranck, Perrault, & Neugebauer, 1986, p. 23). Figure 7.9 is an example of one organization's written procedure for screening applicants.

References. Before the interview, you should check the references provided by the applicant. Contact each reference by telephone rather than relying on written statements an applicant might submit. In addition to verifying the authenticity of the written statements, you can follow up on areas where you have questions and you can listen for subtle cues or hesitations that suggest the person's recommendation for a particular candidate is less than wholehearted. References are not foolproof, however. First, these are names provided by the applicant, and they probably can be expected to give a positive view. One way to surmount this difficulty is to ask whether the reference can give you the name of another person or two who is acquainted with the applicant's job performance. By calling those people, you may be able to get a more balanced picture. A second problem is that many employers, out of a fear of lawsuits, are reluctant to provide any information except to confirm an individual's dates of employment. Thus, you have to rely on the information you can glean during your contacts with the candidate.

The Interview. After the closing date for receiving applications is passed, the applications are organized in individual folders with all relevant attachments—letters of reference, transcripts, personal letters from the candidate, and any notes you may have made during contacts. The next steps are to rank the applicants in order of apparent desirability based on how well they meet requirements listed in the job specification; to schedule appointments with the most promising candidates; and to conduct interviews. These tasks are carried out by the selection committee.

The primary objective during the interview is to get the applicant to talk about experiences, knowledge of the job, and, for teachers, knowledge of the philosophy of disciplining children and organizing classrooms. Of course, knowledge is one thing and attitudes are

FIGURE 7.9 *Sample screening procedures for employees and volunteers*

XYZ CHILD DEVELOPMENT CENTERS, INC.

All employees and volunteers having contact with children in care must have on file a signed copy of the Abuse, Neglect, and Criminal History Statement. Signed statements are maintained on file at each center.

In the event that the statement reveals a conviction for a misdemeanor or felony or substantiated involvement in the abuse or neglect of children or adults, the following information will be reviewed to determine acceptability:

1. A criminal history file search
2. The nature and seriousness of the offense
3. The date of the offense
4. Relationship of the offense to the job assignment

If the candidate is determined to be satisfactory after these reviews, the applicant is referred to the Department of Social Services for final review and approval.

quite another. Some people believe that they can teach appropriate methods to a person who has an open and caring attitude toward children and a genuine enthusiasm for learning much more easily than they can change a negative attitude in a person who knows all of the theories and "right answers." You can gauge a candidate's initiative and leadership potential by asking questions about new ideas they have introduced or helped implement in their previous jobs (Carter, 1995, pp. 60–62).

If your program has a clearly stated philosophy and a complete job description, you can use that description to help formulate the kinds of questions you want to ask. The interviewing committee may use a structured form, as shown in Figure 7.10, for reporting impressions. Using a system like this helps ensure that each candidate is treated equally and fairly. Retain these forms to document the objective basis for your decision.

FIGURE 7.10 *Applicant interviewing form*

Position Open: _____

Applicant Name: _____

Education: (Meets minimal specifications? Comment.)

_____

_____

Experience: (Meets minimal specifications? Comment.)

_____

_____

_____

References:

_____

_____

Interview:

_____

_____

_____

_____

_____

Recommendation:

_____

_____

_____

Signed _____

Title _____ Date _____

(Retain in applicant's folder for affirmative action reports.)

FIGURE 7.11 *Hypothetical situations for teacher candidates*

> *Four-year-old Johnny comes to school with a holster holding a toy gun attached to his belt. What would you do?*
>
> > How do the candidate's ideas about toy weapons fit with center policy on this controversial issue? Can the candidate enforce policy, yet respect the feelings of the children and parents?
>
> *Three-year-old Jennie picks a dandelion in the yard and shows it to you. What would you do?*
>
> > Does the candidate's response reflect a sensitivity toward the child and an awareness of the curriculum possibilities contained within this simple encounter?
>
> *A business offers your center a thousand multicolored handbills printed on one side but unusable because they contain the wrong information. Your center is short of funds for supplies, and you appreciate the donation. What would you do with the handbills?*
>
> > Is the candidate able to think creatively and generate several possible uses for this potential resource?

As part of the interview, you may wish to pose hypothetical questions about situations appropriate to the job the person is seeking. See Figure 7.11 for examples related to a teaching position. Using this interviewing technique requires planning to avoid "leading" or giving the applicants your answers. Rather than simply posing hypothetical situations, some programs ask teacher candidates to spend time in a classroom in order to observe their interactions with children and other staff.

Of course, you want to avoid unlawful or unfair questions that serve only to discriminate against certain groups and are not relevant to the person's ability to do the job. For example, you may ask what languages an applicant speaks fluently because that has a direct bearing on the job of a teacher in a center where children come from several ethnic backgrounds. However, you may not ask about an applicant's ancestry or nationality. Because most states regulate the minimum age at which a staff member can be counted in the adult–child ratio, you may ask a question such as, "Are you 18 years old or older?" You should not ask, "How old are you?" or "What is your date of birth?" (Michigan Department of Civil Rights, 1986). Contact your state's Department of Civil Rights for further guidance.

Keep in mind that all of the parts must fit together: Your job description reflects your center's basic philosophy, and performance evaluations are based on the job description. Therefore, your interview questions should tap the qualities that you will be evaluating later.

From the Candidate's View. Wise candidates do their homework and know a lot about your center before arriving for the interview. They want to check out information they have heard or read, so allow ample time for them to ask you questions. A tour of the facility and an opportunity to meet the staff will help applicants get a feel for the working conditions and be more ready to respond should you make an offer.

Highly qualified professionals may interview for several positions simultaneously and have several offers from which to choose. Thus, your screening process must be short enough to encourage candidates to stay with you throughout. If your application process is too slow, they may select another position. Continued communication with them and prompt action are essential. Although you want to be very careful and hire just the right individual, you must also realize that the applicant also has criteria for selecting a position. If another organization fulfills most of those criteria, the applicant may decide in that direction, leaving you back where you started.

The Offer.   Hiring staff is a lengthy, costly process that you do not want to repeat frequently. Your goal is to hire excellent people and keep them, making openings infrequent. After reflecting on what was learned through the interview process, the committee ranks the applicants and decides which one(s) should receive an offer of employment. The manager may ask the committee for permission to proceed down the prioritized listing should the first-choice candidate drop out of the running. Generally, an offer can be made by phone, with a follow-up letter sent immediately after. The salary, working hours, and assignment should be provided by phone and in the letter. The benefits that the job carries should also be stated. Presumably the applicant has received a job description (see Figure 7.3); but a copy should be attached to the letter and reflect any modifications that may have been negotiated. For example, if the applicant's child received admission to the center as part of the offer, then that agreement should be put in writing. You and the candidate also have to agree on the starting date for the position. Generally, there is a probationary period for new employees, and this point should be stated clearly, both orally and in writing.

In some instances, a physical examination is required and thus the job offer is tentative until that is completed. If the applicant is to bear the expense of this exam, this requirement should be clearly stated from the beginning.

Some centers prefer a contract that is signed by the candidate, manager, and head of the policy board. Whether a contract or letter is used, copies of all hiring documents should be sent to all parties and filed. Once you have signed documents from a candidate, communicate that information to your staff.

Informing Unsuccessful Candidates.   Common courtesy requires that you inform the other applicants that a decision has been reached as soon as possible after your offer of employment is accepted and the papers are finalized.

Orientation.   Finally, the new employee arrives. There are payroll, Social Security, and income tax withholding documents to sign. Keys are issued at this time, and any printed information prepared for new employees is provided (see Figure 7.12).

The manager or a designee should take responsibility for orienting the new employee. Working with a more experienced employee, or mentor, can alleviate early anxiety for new employees. The concept of mentoring is discussed in further detail in the next chapter. A warm welcome from all employees sets a positive tone from the outset and is especially important when a new employee is somewhat different from the current staff. "Different" may mean a male in an all-female staff, a person of color in an all-white staff, a younger person in an older staff, and so on. The focus should be on the skills and talents the person brings to the job, rather than any differences.

Establishing Expectations.   During the orientation with a new employee, clearly state how you evaluate on-the-job performance and other activities. State how often you monitor the performance—monthly, quarterly, yearly—with the proviso that you will make efforts to become familiar with their work by dropping in frequently and getting

FIGURE 7.12 *New employee orientation checklist*

Employee Name _____

Position _____ Date of Hire _____

Note: The purpose of this checklist is to ensure that you have been adequately oriented to the XYZ Child Development Center and to the policies for which you will be responsible. Please initial and date the items listed below as they are accomplished. When all are completed, please sign the form and return it to the office for the manager's signature and date.

■ **Explanation of orientation process**

Hiring conference

■ Discussed and signed job description

■ Signed contract

■ Provided center policy handbook and state licensing rules

■ Provided timetable for introductory phase

■ Discussed probationary period

■ Set date for first day of work

Routine procedures and policies

■ Set daily schedule

■ Completed paperwork (payroll_____, W-4_____, health certificate_____, child abuse form_____)

■ Clarified call-in procedures

■ Discussed pay dates

Professional responsibilities (see handbook)

■ Dress and appearance

■ Code of conduct

■ Discipline policies

■ Supplies

Orientation to the school

■ Received tour of facilities and designated personal space

■ Issued keys and supplies

■ Introduced to staff members

■ Introduced to children and parents

■ Explained coworker relationship

■ Explained emergency procedures

Probationary conference

■ Discussed center policy handbook and licensing rules

■ Results of initial observation of skills shared

■ Clarified inservice expectation

■ Had opportunity for your questions

Comments:

_____

_____

_____

_____

Employee's Signature _____ Date _____

Manager's Signature _____ Date _____

acquainted. Strategies for conducting a performance appraisal and providing feedback are discussed in the following chapter.

You and the staff should remember that during the candidate's probationary period, the candidate is not the only one being evaluated. The center is also being evaluated by the candidate. After devoting so much time to the hiring process, you should make every effort to make the new employee comfortable and successful.

Conclusion

Details about organizing and staffing your program flow from the goals developed during the planning process. You must determine the specific jobs necessary to achieve those goals and define an organizational structure that coordinates all of the individual jobs into a coherent whole. Human capital (knowledge, skills, and abilities) and nonhuman resources are required to produce the center's services. Many steps are required for hiring staff, orienting them to their new job, and setting the stage for evaluating their performance. This chapter has addressed the mechanics of organizing and staffing your program. In the next chapter, we turn our attention to the human relations involved in retaining staff and developing their potential.

QUESTIONS FOR REVIEW

1. Define organizing. Give an example from your own experience in child development programs or elsewhere.
2. Define job analysis. Observe a staff member at a child development program and write a job analysis of that person's function.
3. Diagram the organizational plan for a center known to you. List what you think are the pros and cons of this plan.
4. Define centralized and decentralized authority. Discuss the difference.
5. Define span of control. Explain how it relates to operating a child development center.
6. Describe how the job description is used when hiring and evaluating an employee.

PROFESSIONAL PORTFOLIO

1. Write a job description, job specification, and job classification for a position in a child development center.
2. Create (or locate and copy) a staff evaluation instrument that reflects the qualities addressed in your job description and classification. Describe how you would use it.
3. Develop a career ladder and salary scale for your program that takes into account the individual's education, experience, and job performance.

RESOURCES FOR FURTHER STUDY

Print

Anthony, M. A. (2001, January/February). *Designing a job classification and wage scale system.* Child Care Information Exchange, 137, 74–78.

Center for Child Care Workforce & Worker Options Resource Center (1997). *Rights in the workplace: A guide for child care teachers.* Washington, DC: Author.

Internet

National Association for the Education of Young Children

http://www.naeyc.org/ece/critical/compensation.asp

A list of resources compiled by the National Association for the Education of Young Children to aid efforts to improve compensation for members of the early childhood workforce; includes descriptions of initiatives by several states as well as the U.S. military and links to related NAEYC position papers.

U.S. Small Business Administration

http://www.sba.gov/starting_business/employees/law.html

Information from the U.S. Small Business Administration. Lists applicable laws based on number of employees in an organization and provides links to details outlining specific provisions.

MenTeach

http://www.menteach.org

MenTeach, a national nonprofit organization that serves as a clearinghouse for research, education, and advocacy with a commitment to increase the number of men teaching young children in early and elementary education.

8

Human Relations

The Importance of Human Relations

People are the resources that hold the key to meeting the goals of a service organization such as a child development center. Of course, many nonhuman resources (e.g., facilities, equipment, and supplies) are needed, but these resources stand idle or are ineffectively used without skilled people to put them into appropriate operation.

A child development center is a labor-intensive operation. That is, lots of human energy or labor is essential for the center to reach its goals. No mechanical robot can perform the staff functions. As you learned in the previous chapter, people's knowledge, skills, abilities, stamina, enthusiasm, and love are all aspects of their human energy. Such attributes are called **human capital.** Your job as manager is to invest that capital wisely—put it to its best use—so that it grows. Your ability to do that depends on your human relations competency. No matter how much you know about finances and the legal aspects of staffing your program, achieving the center's goals is possible only if you understand people and cultivate strong relationships.

Coping with a Staffing Shortage

Of course, you cannot build relationships until you have a staff. More importantly, because relationships take time, you must have staff who stay with your program over the long haul. It is common knowledge that a large number of workers either change jobs or leave the child development field entirely every year. Attracting and retaining qualified staff is one of your most important challenges as a director. How can you accomplish this?

Establish Salaries and Benefits That Reflect a Respect for the Individual's Worth. We noted in chapter 6 that one of the most obvious reasons people leave the early childhood profession is poor pay. Even those who love their work with young children must face the reality of supporting their own families. They need health insurance and the right to take time off when they are sick or want to take a well-earned vacation. Centers must strive to provide compensation that is comparable to what an individual with similar education and experience could earn in other fields.

Treat Employees Fairly.

Inadequate pay is a serious concern, but teachers report that many other factors contribute to their job dissatisfaction, including unrealistic or ill-defined workloads, unfair or disrespectful treatment, and lack of basic support (e.g., having pay for supplies out-of-pocket or arrange one's own substitute when sick) (Whitebook & Bellm, 1999, p. 40). New employees want to start the job with a clear understanding of what is expected of them and how they will be evaluated. They want to know that if they perform well they will have fair chances for promotion and that if their performance does not live up to expectations they will be given a chance to improve rather than summarily fired. They want to know what to expect from one day to the next and to have a voice, or at least a warning, when changes in work assignment or center policies are needed.

Provide a Supportive Environment.

This concept pertains to both the physical and psychological environments. Staff have a basic right to a safe, healthy work environment, where their needs as adults are addressed along with those of the children. For example, centers should offer a place away from the children where staff can relax or work on planning using adult-size chairs and provide child-size steps up to the diapering area to save employees' backs from the stress of lifting heavy toddlers. A program that supports its staff avoids stress-inducing demands, such as responsibility for too many children at a time or juggling cleaning and clerical tasks on top of caring for children. It helps staff deal with stress by ensuring that they have someone to turn to when they have questions or concerns.

Respect and Value Diversity.

Early childhood professionals vary widely, as all people do, in their modes of interacting and preferred learning styles. Recall from our discussion of personality type in chapter 4 that some people are naturally more extroverted than others; they enjoy dealing with the public and feel comfortable speaking up about their ideas and feelings. Others are more reserved and prefer to watch from the sidelines, think things over, and interact with one or few people at a time. Some people find it easiest to gain new ideas and information by reading or listening to lectures. Others have to try things out for themselves and learn best by doing. Having a set of detailed rules for every operation makes some people feel secure, while it might be stifling for someone with a very playful disposition and a high tolerance for risk taking. Some of these characteristics and preferences are related to cultural background; however, there is likely as much difference between individuals within a given culture as there is between cultures.

Respecting and valuing diversity means going beyond basic requirements of nondiscriminatory hiring and promoting. It means being proactive and setting a tone that encourages employees to reflect on their own and others' heritage, and to think about ways that their differences complement one another.

Staff members who feel supported and encouraged will be more likely to support and encourage children.

Expect, Encourage, and Reward Professional Development.

Staff members bring a wealth of human capital to their positions. They have knowledge, skills, and abilities acquired through education as well as individual qualities of love, warmth, and empathy. Recognizing these assets and offering opportunities to enhance them can build employee loyalty. Feelings of stagnation on the job can lead to dissatisfaction and turnover as employees look for more interesting challenges elsewhere. You will find a more detailed discussion of professional development, including suggestions for activities, later in this chapter.

Win Professional Recognition for Your Program and Staff by Earning NAEYC Accreditation. Another reason that child development professionals leave the field is the low status that comes from a public perception that they are "just babysitting." NAEYC center accreditation is a nationally recognized hallmark of excellence, and the self-study process that it entails can help raise staff members' consciousness about the value of their work. Consequently, employees in accredited centers feel an increased pride in their work, and this feeling can spread to potential employees as well. University students, searching for a center in which to complete their senior internships, often limit the search to accredited centers in their region. They reason that they want the best possible experience, and that strategy is one way to increase chances of getting it. Of course, this approach means that the accredited centers have been given the first opportunity to recruit these enterprising and well-qualified young people upon their graduation. In a tight labor market, the accredited center has an advantage.

A characteristic of a good place to work is a center that seldom has a vacancy unless someone retires or has to move away because of a spouse's job transfer. A stable staff is the dream of every manager. Its opposite—rampant turnover—is the reason most frequently cited by directors for thinking about quitting themselves (Whitebook & Bellm, 1999, pp. 41–42). When the conditions discussed in this section are met, staff stability is possible. The Center for the Child Care Workforce (1998) has developed model work standards that spell out the working conditions that will help programs attract and retain staff. Acknowledging the challenges involved in meeting the standards, the center established benchmarks to recognize progress or striving toward high quality and suggests that programs set reasonable goals, working toward achieving a few standards at a time.

The Manager's Role

As a manager, you may have a voice, but not the final say, in establishing salaries and benefits or pursuing accreditation. The day-to-day work of creating a supportive environment and helping staff members enhance their skills is your primary responsibility. Although the responsibility for these tasks rests with you, you have help from a variety of sources, including your staff members, if you are wise enough to tap that resource. Accomplishing these tasks hinges on the relationships you are able to cultivate with and among the staff members. Relationships do not happen overnight; they grow from the countless interactions that occur minute-by-minute and day-by-day in any human enterprise. As manager, you have to create some opportunities for interactions. Most interactions are informal, almost automatic, but even these informal interactions can be made more productive if you make a conscious effort to improve your communication skills. Both the formal and informal interactions with staff members are enhanced if you have a basic understanding of human motivation.

Understanding Staff Members' Needs and Desires

Why would people want to work in your child development center? Why do people work at all? The research of psychologist Abraham H. Maslow (1954) has had a major impact on management education and practice. To help explain people's motivation, Maslow proposed a "hierarchy of needs," symbolized by a ladder or pyramid representing the different levels of needs that people have (see Figure 8.1).

FIGURE 8.1   *Maslow's hierarchy of human needs*

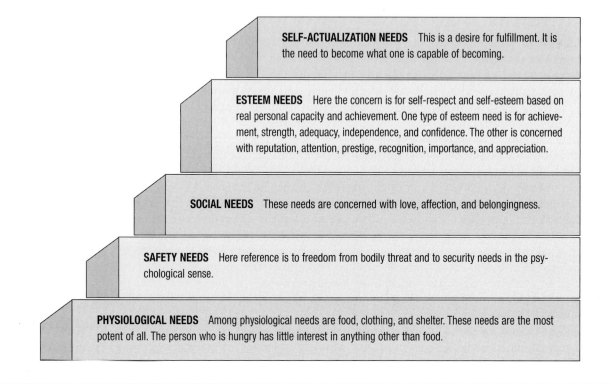

SELF-ACTUALIZATION NEEDS   This is a desire for fulfillment. It is the need to become what one is capable of becoming.

ESTEEM NEEDS   Here the concern is for self-respect and self-esteem based on real personal capacity and achievement. One type of esteem need is for achievement, strength, adequacy, independence, and confidence. The other is concerned with reputation, attention, prestige, recognition, importance, and appreciation.

SOCIAL NEEDS   These needs are concerned with love, affection, and belongingness.

SAFETY NEEDS   Here reference is to freedom from bodily threat and to security needs in the psychological sense.

PHYSIOLOGICAL NEEDS   Among physiological needs are food, clothing, and shelter. These needs are the most potent of all. The person who is hungry has little interest in anything other than food.

Source: A. H. Maslow. *Motivation and personality* (New York: Harper & Row, 1954).

Physiological needs—food, clothing, and shelter—form the foundation of the pyramid because they are the most basic. Maslow's theory is that once the basic needs are reasonably satisfied, a person becomes concerned about the needs at the next level—safety and security. Once the first two levels are met, the next level comes into prominence, and so on.

Maslow also suggested that people have two basic desires: the desire to know (i.e., to be aware of reality, get the facts, and satisfy curiosity), and the desire to understand (i.e., to systematize and look for relations and meanings). Taken together, Maslow's concepts of needs and desires explain the diversity of human motives present in work environments.

At the most basic level, the theory suggests that staff members with salaries too low to provide their families with adequate food, clothing, and shelter are unlikely to get much out of a staff training session. The same is true of those staff members who suffer from spousal abuse or live and work in violent neighborhoods. Unless their physiological and safety needs are met, staff members are unlikely to benefit from efforts to address the higher level needs.

A manager's role in relation to these basic needs is to strive to adhere to the model work standards regarding wages, benefits, health and safety, and physical setting. You might also advocate for adequate salaries, offer resources for counseling, or take part with your staff in neighborhood committees to combat violence. You can help staff meet esteem needs by providing constructive feedback about their performance and calling attention to their successes when appropriate. You can encourage your staff to become all that they are capable of becoming by guiding them toward formal and informal opportunities for professional development and by challenging them with tasks that tap their new skills.

It is important to remember that the progression through Maslow's hierarchy is not a simple one-way process. People functioning at the highest level, self-actualization, might revert to an earlier level in the face of a personal or family crisis. An effective manager has the ability to recognize where on the hierarchy a particular staff member might be at any given time.

Decisions, Decisions . . .

Think about your own development in relation to Maslow's hierarchy of human needs. At which level are you functioning in relation to various aspects of your life—school, work, family, friendships? Have you noticed any changes over the past few years? What factors do you think account for those changes? If you feel comfortable sharing personal examples, discuss them with your classmates.

Employee Motivation

An important consideration for the manager concerned with staff members' needs and desires is the distinction between intrinsic and extrinsic motivation. **Intrinsic motivation** has to do with satisfaction in accomplishment or doing something for its own sake, while **extrinsic motivation** implies doing something simply for the sake of getting something else. Research has shown that "rewards cause people to lose interest in whatever they were rewarded for doing" (Kohn, 1994). Other research has suggested that teachers who enter the profession for extrinsic motives (e.g., using it as a stopgap until they get the job they really want) are most likely to leave the profession (Curtis, 1995). These findings did not imply that extrinsic rewards, such as adequate salaries, are not important; rather, they suggested that rewards are necessary but not sufficient. Satisfying work and a living wage are both necessary to keep our best professionals in the field.

Decisions, Decisions . . .

You have noticed that the bulletin board displays in your center's classrooms are becoming yellow and frayed with age. Someone suggests that you offer coupons for free pizza to the teachers as an incentive for changing the displays more often. Is this an intrinsic or extrinsic reward? What are the likely results? What happens when you run out of coupons? What alternatives can you imagine?

Increasing responsibility can be a motivating force and result in greater satisfaction for employees. The concept of **job enrichment** is applicable here. According to DuBrin (2000, p. 185), job enrichment is "an approach to making jobs involve more challenge and responsibility, so they will be more appealing to most employees." Dubrin identifies eight characteristics of an enriched job (pp. 165–166). Applied to the early childhood teacher's position, these characteristics are:

1. *Direct feedback*—either from a supervisor or from the successful completion of a particular task (e.g., helping an anxious child settle down for nap without tears for the first time).
2. *Client relationships*—involves interacting with and serving children and families instead of just working for a boss.
3. *New learning*—either on the job or through more formal staff development opportunities.
4. *Control over scheduling*—being able to decide when to do which tasks (e.g., schedule snack or group time) or even setting working hours to the extent possible within the framework of the program's goals and resources.
5. *Unique experience*—certainly a strong feature of working with young children whose ideas and behavior are a continual source of delight and challenge for teachers.
6. *Control over resources*—includes the opportunity to decide how to spend the classroom's equipment budget, how to use particular materials, or how to allocate the duties of classroom aides or volunteers.
7. *Direct communication authority*—being able to speak directly with the children and families who benefit from or use one's services, a feature usually built into client relationships.
8. *Personal accountability*—responsibility for outcomes whether positive (e.g., when a group of children and parents return from a field trip excited and happy) or negative (e.g., when a poorly planned field trip leads to tearful children and cranky parents).

The concept of job enrichment as a motivating factor corresponds with the earlier discussion of Maslow's theory of basic needs and desires: after meeting their basic needs, people seek achievement and self-fulfillment.

Communication

Some managers are so aloof and unapproachable that employees quake at the thought of entering their offices. Other managers try the "pal" approach and downplay their authority. Which style works best for a child development center? Probably, some position in the middle is best. Managers, like all other people, have unique qualities that must be used advantageously. They should be approachable; yet, they must also be authoritative.

Communication Between Staff Members.   Teachers see many children and parents each day—they must have time to share their own lives and concerns with colleagues. Ironically, some early education and care programs profess a belief in person-to-person communication, yet they set little time aside for personal communication between staff members. Staff members are often scheduled to arrive at staggered times to cover the entire time the children are present and to limit each person's workday to 8 hours. When teachers are on duty, they must pay close attention to the children and not be chatting with one another about personal matters. Usually, teachers are also responsible for the children during lunch and at break time; one teacher takes charge of the children with the support of an aide and the other teacher is out of the room. Thus the teachers have no time together to learn about one another. This example is typical of the situations that interfere with personal communication.

If it is not planned, you may find staff talking about personal concerns when they should be listening to and talking to the children, gathering in a corner of the playroom or yard conversing and largely ignoring the children. Other symptoms that staff members have too little time to talk with one another include instances when a staff member has an emergency at home with a child, spouse, or aged parent, and other staff members do not even know, or when misunderstandings arise over little things that might have been worked out in a friendly fashion if people had been talking together.

What can you, as manager, do? You can plan evening or weekend events that bring the teachers together to socialize freely. Arranging these opportunities helps ensure that the caregivers are focused on the children when they are on duty. Apart from time for socializing, paid planning time outside the center's usual hours of operation can help promote communication because even though the focus is on professional matters, the atmosphere is likely to be more relaxed. You might consider paying the teachers for a few hours one evening or one Saturday each month to do planning. Joint planning sessions boost the esprit de corps, and the money invested in providing this time pays off in high-quality programs.

You can also facilitate communication among staff members more directly. When a staff member comes to you with a concern, determine whether the concern is a personal matter or whether it involves several people. Sometimes the most effective approach is to bring all parties involved to the table together. In one center, for example, teachers had frequent complaints about the cook not preparing sufficient food, not having it set out on time, or not making modified meals available for a child with cerebral palsy who had difficulty swallowing. The director believed that simply repeating these criticisms to the cook would engender defensiveness and resentment, so instead she invited teachers and cook to sit down together and discuss the problems. It turned out that there had been several misunderstandings about the expectations that the teachers and cook had for one another. Each walked away from the meeting with a new understanding of the challenges faced by the others and a concrete plan for correcting the problem.

Communication Between Manager and Staff.   Just as you devise strategies for facilitating communication and collaboration among staff members, you need to plan consciously for effective communication between you and your staff. An informal technique for opening channels of communication with your staff is termed **managing by walking around** (Albrecht, 1998). Applied to a child development center, this approach involves the manager walking around, dropping into classrooms, playgrounds, and lounges and mingling with staff and children as they are involved in their activities. The manager becomes familiar and is seen as relaxed and approachable, giving staff members a feeling that their work is known and appreciated. Using this style, a manager personally and quietly can give a word of encouragement here and a suggestion there or make note of material shortages or needed repairs that had not been reported. More structured opportunities for communication with staff members include regularly scheduled evaluation reviews, meetings (with the entire staff or with particular subgroups), and individual appointments when concerns arise. Whatever the context for your communication, active listening and conflict resolution skills will help.

Active Listening

Active listening as an approach to communicating among individuals is a concept recommended by parenting educator Thomas Gordon (1970, pp. 41–94). Gordon adapted the method for use by teachers and managers as well (1974). Active listening means more than just keeping quiet while the person talks; it means showing with your body language that you are giving the speaker your full attention and letting that person know that you have heard and understood what was said by restating it in your own words. Active listening focuses on the feeling expressed, not on the content of a person's complaint. The listener's reflected response is nonjudgmental. If it is in error, the sender can correct the impression immediately. The sender takes responsibility for the feeling expressed and finds a solution to the problem. Consider the following examples of how you might respond when Sherri, a teacher in the 2-year-old classroom, storms into your office one morning with a complaint:

Scenario I

Sherri: I've had it. Either Deanna (her coteacher) goes or I do! I just can't work with her any more.

Manager: There, there, now. Try to simmer down. I'm sure you can work things out.

Sherri: Believe me, I've tried. But she is constantly undermining me with the children. When I try to ignore Molly's temper tantrums, Deanna rushes over and picks her up.

Manager: It can't be that bad. You two just have different styles.

Sherri: That's not the point. All that attention is just making the problem with Molly worse.

Manager: Well, I don't know what you expect me to do about it. You're just going to have to work something out.

Scenario II

Sherri: I've had it. Either Deanna (her coteacher) goes or I do! I just can't work with her any more.

Manager: I can hear that you are frustrated. Can you tell me more about what the problem is?

Sherri: Well, for one thing, she constantly undermines me with the children.

Manager: You feel as though you are working at cross-purposes.

Sherri: Yes. Yesterday, Molly had another one of her temper tantrums. I tried to let her cry it out, but Deanna ran right over to pick her up and made a big fuss. I think that makes Molly think tantrums are a good way to get attention.

Manager: You feel that your coteacher is making matters worse instead of supporting you.

Sherri: Yes. I'm afraid some of the other children might get the idea that they should have tantrums too.

Manager: You're worried that the problem will spread if you and Deanna can't agree about how to deal with tantrums. What would you think about the three of us sitting down during nap to see if we can generate some solutions together?

How would you feel as the teacher in each of these situations? Which response from a manager would make you feel that your concerns had been taken seriously? Which would make you more willing to think about constructive solutions to the problem?

Conflict Resolution Techniques

While constant conflict is probably a sign of deeper problems, occasional conflict is a part of life and it occurs in the most well-managed organizations. Conflict resolution techniques are essential skills for you, the manager.

Kostelnik and her colleagues (2001) have outlined a seven-step conflict mediation process. Although the process was developed to provide teachers with a method to help children resolve a dispute, the steps are equally applicable to adult conflict resolution:

1. *Step 1:* Name the problem and decide to address it. In the situation described above, the manager might say to Sherri and Deanna, "I understand that you disagree on the best way to handle Molly's temper tantrums. The inconsistency is not helping her with the problem, and I'm sure it is frustrating to both of you. Let's sit down together during nap and see if we can come to some understanding."

2. *Step 2:* Listen to both sides. Sherri believes that tantrums are typical behavior for a 2-year-old, so the tantrums should be ignored as long as Molly is not in danger of hurting herself or the other children. Deanna is concerned about the other children being frightened by Molly's screams and thrashing about, so she thinks Molly should be picked up and soothed. Each teacher feels resentful that the other does not seem to respect her point of view.

3. *Step 3:* Recap. Summarize each person's point of view. "Both of you are feeling stressed because of this issue. Sherri thinks the tantrums will go away if the behavior is not reinforced with attention. Deanna finds it hard to ignore behavior that is so disruptive to the group. The problem is that Molly is confused by the different responses she gets and, in fact, that may prolong the problem. Each of you feels irritated when your teaching partner seems unsupportive, and this is damaging your ability to function as a team. We need to find a solution you can both live with."

4. *Step 4:* Brainstorm several possible alternatives. As one party offers a suggestion, the other should be given a chance to react frankly and constructively. If neither can develop potential solutions, the manager might make some tentative suggestions or suggest some resources that the teachers could consult for ideas.

5. *Step 5:* Agree on a workable solution and plan methods to carry it out. No one should leave the conversation feeling coerced into an unacceptable solution. In this situation, the teachers might agree that they will neither ignore nor fuss over Molly's tantrums. Instead one of them will move her to a safe part of the room away from other children and stay nearby, calmly reassuring Molly that she is safe and that the strong feelings will pass.

6. *Step 6:* Acknowledge the work that each individual contributed to the problem-solving process. The manager thanks both Sherri and Deanna for listening to each other and for persevering to map out a solution.

7. *Step 7:* Follow up by checking in with the teachers a few days later to see if they have implemented their plan and ask how they think it is working. Be prepared to go back to the planning table in the event that the solution has proven unworkable Some programs have found it useful to underscore the value they place on openly addressing and resolving inevitable conflicts by putting procedures similar to these in writing and asking staff members to sign a statement indicating that they will follow them (Carter & Curtis, 1998, pp. 243–245).

Fostering Teamwork and Collaboration

One of the most effective means of motivating staff is to build a sense of belonging to a team, of contributing to something larger than oneself. If you accomplish this, you have enlisted the help of all staff members in motivating each other. Neugebauer (1998a, pp. 250–254) developed a list of five steps to effective team building. Note that his steps correspond closely to the planning, organizing, staffing, leading, and monitoring management functions:

1. Set goals acceptable to all team members—neither too ambitious to be realistic nor too modest to inspire commitment and effort. Translate goals into measurable objectives and establish time frames for their achievement.

Sharing observations and questions after visiting one another's classrooms is an effective means of professional development for teachers.

2. Break each goal down into the tasks necessary to reach it, and then assign specific team members to each task. Make sure that people performing the behind-the-scenes tasks get attention—this encourages group spirit and draws out the less assertive members.

3. Foster supportive relationships between team members by identifying the strengths of individual members that can be tapped by the others, as well as teaching the art of giving constructive feedback to each other. Provide opportunities for the open communication of each member's perceptions and feelings.

4. Ensure that the group reaps the full benefit of what each member has to offer. Encourage everyone to contribute: Raise interesting problems to solve, provide opportunities for learning new ideas and approaches, and allow individuals to pursue their own interests. Show your interest in each team's progress and hold off criticism of creative ideas that may seem unworkable at first. When a team gets stuck, offer help but be judicious about how much and how soon.

5. The manager and the team members monitor the team's effectiveness. Are the goals being accomplished or is there at least some measurable progress in that direction? More importantly, is the group functioning more smoothly as a team?

Staff Meetings

Staff meetings are an important avenue of communication. Managers should be sure that staff meetings serve three communication goals: manager to staff, staff to manager, and staff to staff.

Paid Staff Meetings

The Model Work Standards (Center for Child Care Workforce, 1998) require at least one paid staff meeting per month. Although it is a challenge to carve out the time, it is simply not fair to expect teachers, whose salaries are already too low, to put in extra unpaid hours at meetings. Some centers solve this problem by scheduling meetings during nap times. Others either pay teachers for attending evening meetings or give them equivalent amounts of compensatory time off during the regular school day. Of course, providing compensatory time off has a price tag: either paying for a substitute teacher or using your time to fill in for the absent teacher.

Full-Staff versus Team Meetings

Meetings with the entire staff are desirable for some purposes. At the beginning of a new school year, or at any time when there has been an influx of new staff members, full-staff meetings help build solidarity—everyone has a chance to get to know one another. Or you may want to boost staff morale and commitment by scheduling a full-staff meeting to reflect on and perhaps revise the program's mission statement. For other purposes, such as accomplishing a specific task, meetings involving only a small team are more productive. Issues that concern only a single staff member should be dealt with individually.

Make the most of your precious meeting time by establishing clear goals in advance. Meeting for the fun of it is fine, but even then, individuals should know the purpose of the meeting in advance.

Agenda

Except in dire emergencies, announce meetings and distribute an agenda at least a week in advance. Identify which items on the agenda will require action, which are for discussion, and which are merely for information and allocate the relevant amount of time for each. Participants will need to be familiar with past discussions to deal with action items; they may need to read or consult some outside sources to contribute to discussion items; and particular individuals should be assigned responsibility for preparing reports or other items of information. Start the meeting with a few moments of announcements and give staff members who wish to speak time to do so. Items of special interest raised by the speakers can become agenda items for future meetings, if desired. Keep the meeting moving along by sticking to the agenda topics. If you have set time limits for each item, the discussion of one topic should not consume all of the time allotted for the meeting. On the other hand, it is not necessary to continue with a discussion merely because there is still time available. Ending a staff meeting a few minutes early is refreshing, and staff members can do needed individual work.

Minutes

Record meeting minutes or the agreements reached at the meeting, and circulate them within the next few days. Minutes provide a record for future reference. They make it clear that the work accomplished is important and that you plan to follow up on the decisions made at the meeting and expect others to do the same.

Group Dynamics

You may find it challenging to manage the complex interactions that occur when your staff comes together as a group. It is up to you to ensure that everyone's voice is heard and that everyone participates actively. Employees may become cynical and disengage themselves from discussions if they get the idea that meetings are just a formality—you listen to their opinions and then go ahead with your own plans. For that reason, it is important to make it clear from the outset which decisions belong to the group and which rest with you or the board of directors. For example, do not let the employees think that it is their decision whether or not to pursue NAEYC accreditation if the board has already mandated that course of action. They can, however, decide how to go about the process—which components to tackle first, which individuals are responsible for particular tasks.

Personal characteristics also influence group dynamics. Shy staff members may be tempted to sit quietly while the discussion whirls around them. Those who are more assertive might dominate the discussion, causing others to feel left out. Your job is to find ways to engage the former and rein in the latter without embarrassing either. One technique is to ask participants to discuss an issue in pairs or threes and have each small group report their opinion to the whole group. Tactfully arrange the groups so that dominant personalities are together with others who can hold their own in the conversation. This gives your quieter individuals a chance to blossom in a group of their counterparts.

An employee with a personal grudge can derail your best-laid plans by picking at everything. If you allow yourself to be drawn into a verbal duel with such an individual, the rest of the participants might withdraw in embarrassment. Try to remain calm and acknowledge the validity of the person's opinion to the extent possible. Ask the others for their opinions about the statements, and put the ball back in the complainer's court by asking her to suggest possible solutions to the problem—preferably in the form of a written memo. This strategy conveys the seriousness you accord the issue, while encouraging constructive thinking on the part of the complainer.

Some negative attitudes and behaviors displayed by staff members may have nothing to do with you; rather, they grow out of childhood experiences. Consistently practicing the conflict mediation strategy discussed earlier can help build your staff's trust and perhaps reduce negative feelings (Swain, 1994). Sometimes what you experience as resistance to your ideas stems from different life experiences and cultural perspectives. Shareef and Gonzalez-Mena (1997) shared the inner thoughts of a hypothetical trainee about a lesson on diapering:

> I don't want to be told how to change diapers. I feel like I've been cleaning up poop all my life, and now somebody wants me to pretend I like doing it. As a woman of color, I feel like I have to clean up the poop of the world and I'm really sick of it. (pp. 7–8)

Be careful not to see every disagreement as a problem or a challenge to your authority. If all of your meetings run smoothly with everyone agreeing on every issue, you may be experiencing "groupthink"—conformity for conformity's sake. Honest disagreements, openly discussed, can stimulate creative new solutions.

Time is precious, and it is important to follow an agenda to keep meetings at a reasonable length. You may be tempted to force closure on issues by calling for a vote and letting the majority rule. This may save time, but it could be a false economy. People who do not feel ownership of a decision are not likely to support it wholeheartedly. It may be more efficient in the long run to keep talking until a solution that reflects everyone's priorities is devised. If that is not possible within the time allowed for a meeting, table the issue until the next meeting. Even if the issue is one that cannot wait, you can accept a temporary decision that reflects the group's best effort at reaching a consensus, and make it clear that the topic will be revisited at another staff meeting.

Decisions, Decisions . . .

Your program has a tradition of celebrating holidays with fairly elaborate parties. Families seem to enjoy and expect the parties and always participate in large numbers. At a staff meeting the week before Valentine's Day, you ask for volunteers to organize the celebration. Several staff members raise objections—the preparation and the cleanup afterward are too much work. Others chime in that they have been reading articles that suggest that such parties are culturally insensitive and developmentally inappropriate. As manager, what are your options?

The Staff's Professional Development

As a center manager, your ability to understand the complexity of human needs, desires, and motives is essential. That each staff member is expected to participate in ongoing professional development must be explicitly stated in the job analysis, job specification, and job description documents. Professional development keeps every staff member—including you—alive and growing year by year. Clearly stating this expectation during the hiring process avoids later complaints. Stated more positively, professional development is a "right of each individual teacher *and* of all teachers within the school" (emphasis in original) (Rinaldi, 1994, p. 55).

Stages of Professional Development

Lilian Katz, a prominent teacher educator, has suggested that there are four developmental stages for early childhood teachers (see Figure 8.2) (Katz, 1984).

FIGURE 8.2 *Teacher's development stages and inservice needs*

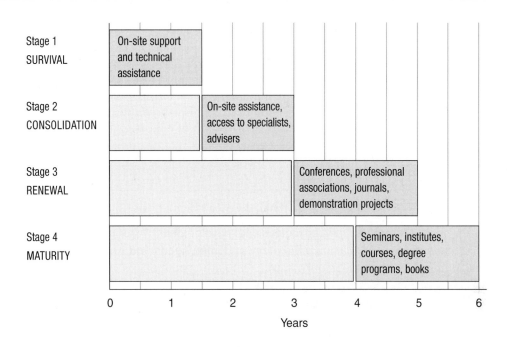

Source: Based on Katz, L. G. Developmental stages of preschool teachers. In *Exploring early childhood,* by M. Kaplan-Sanoff & R. Yablans-Magid (Upper Saddle River, NJ: Prentice Hall, 1984), pp. 478–482.

1. Stage 1: *Survival* lasts for about the first 2 years. Teachers at the survival stage may, at times, feel overwhelmed at having the full responsibility for a group of immature and vigorous young children. These are the teachers you see at a conference eagerly harvesting ideas to take back to their classrooms on Monday morning. Katz said, "During this period the teacher needs support, understanding, encouragement, reassurance, comfort, and guidance."

2. Stage 2: *Consolidation* covers the period from approximately 18 months to 3 years. By this stage, the teacher has decided she can survive and is ready to consolidate her gains. According to Katz, this teacher requires on-site assistance, access to specialists, colleague advice, consultants, and advisers.

3. Stage 3: *Renewal* comes between the 3rd and 5th years. Now, the teacher has become tired of the routine and wants to learn about new developments. The teacher finds it rewarding to meet colleagues from various programs at conferences and to compare notes with them. At this time, teachers become objective about looking at their classrooms, said Katz.

4. Stage 4: *Maturity* is reached between the 4th and 5th years. The person has come to terms with being a teacher and is ready to look at deeper and more abstract questions. Conferences, institutes, or advanced-degree programs are needed to stimulate this person.

The Early Childhood Career Lattice

Professional development implies professional advancement—moving up a "career ladder." NAEYC uses a **lattice** (rather than ladder) as a symbol representing the interrelatedness of the many strands that make up the early childhood profession (Bredekamp & Willer, 1992).

Imagine a lattice of woven wooden slats in a rose garden. The vertical strands of the lattice represent the various settings in which early childhood professionals work: child development programs, family day-care homes, resource and referral agencies, and so on. The horizontal strands represent the increases in knowledge, responsibility, authority, and compensation within each of those settings. Professionals can move upward within the same setting (e.g., by being promoted), they can move across settings (e.g., the caregiver who leaves your center to become a classroom aide in a Head Start center), or they can move diagonally (e.g., completing a community college training program that qualifies them to take a higher level position in another setting). Furthermore, as professionals increase their core knowledge, they acquire a greater breadth of opportunities at increasingly higher levels on the career lattice.

Decisions, Decisions . . .

Where are you in your professional development? What connections do you see between Maslow's hierarchy of human needs and Katz's stages of professional development? Again, if you are comfortable sharing any examples, discuss them with your classmates.

Supporting Professional Development at All Stages

We deliberately use the term *professional development* instead of *staff training* because we believe it more accurately conveys the complexity of the process as well as the participation of staff members in their own growth and learning. In our view, staff training implies a more passive role for the individuals being trained and suggests that providing high-quality care and education is simply a matter of mastering the "right" techniques and applying them across the board.

Centers support professional development when they provide paid registration and time off for staff to attend workshops and conferences. They also promote professional development when they provide ongoing, knowledgeable feedback and arrange paid time for teachers to collaborate on projects, to observe each other's classrooms and reflect on their teaching practices (Rous, 2004). Professional development can be viewed as an ongoing process that is fostered whenever teachers observe children closely, reflect on those observations, and share their ideas with parents or other staff. Margie Carter (1993), who has worked extensively in the area of professional development in early childhood programs, found that by focusing on their observations of children's play, early childhood professionals are able to gain insight and develop new knowledge without the stress and defensive feelings usually incurred when focusing on staff behaviors.

Professional development can be stimulated through interactions with individuals or small groups from the same job category or the entire staff. As noted earlier, such interactions can occur at the center or in conferences elsewhere. Depending on the topic and your knowledge of the staff members' individual learning styles, you might distribute a handout for all staff to read and discuss. Or you might, with permission, visit a classroom to observe, reflect, or model some technique; suggest that teachers visit one another's classrooms; or bring in an outside consultant. Whatever mode or location is selected, professional development activities cost time and money and must become a budget item.

Sometimes what seems like just another responsibility can become a vehicle for rewarding professional growth. For example, the teacher at stage 3 or 4 who is asked to take responsibility for helping a new employee can be challenged to rethink his or her own practice in the process, with the result that both teachers learn and grow. Similarly, employees who participate in discussions about the center's mission and policies are engaging in the type of reflection that fosters their professional growth.

Professional Development Activities

Professional development for your staff is much like curriculum planning for children; that is, start where individuals are and use their interests as guides. This procedure assumes that the individuals have some interest in their work and in improving themselves. You might let small groups take turns making suggestions.

Hines has suggested 10 guides for professional development activities (1983, pp. 186–187):

1. ***Focus on positive traits and behaviors of the staff member rather than dwelling on the negatives.*** For example, say, "It was really effective when you stooped down to Pete's level and looked him in the eye when you wanted him to stop hitting Jacob."

2. ***Whenever possible, offer a variety of choices when critiquing any behavior or action.*** For example, you might say, "You could place fewer chairs at the art table, or you could ask for help from the aide, or you could plan a less complicated project. Which one do you think would help solve the problem of children pushing each other out of the way at the art table?"

3. ***Avoid using judgmental comparisons to motivate individuals to improve.*** For example, say, "I see that you are working on using positive forms of guidance," rather than "Why can't you quit saying 'don't' and begin using positive guidance like Doris does?" Such comparisons may create a dislike of Doris.

4. ***Be sure the individual knows what to expect from you.*** Will you be observing, taking notes, and sharing these with the staff member? Or will you be coming into the classroom to demonstrate and then observe while he or she practices? Timing of feedback in either case is crucial: People are more likely to cooperate if they know they will hear what you think right away rather than waiting and worrying about it.

5. ***Avoid setting yourself up as "the expert" who knows "the one way" things are done.*** Acknowledging personality differences and a variety of ways in which tasks can be accomplished helps people feel they can experiment to discover what works best for them and find their own style.

6. ***Use a variety of teaching techniques to help meet individual learning styles of staff members.*** One person may learn well from demonstrations, another may learn best from reading a book or article, and another might like a discussion.

7. ***Help staff members appreciate how improving their skills helps children.*** For example, point out how children have been more cooperative since the teacher began moving close and speaking to them at eye level rather than calling across the room.

8. ***Practice what you preach.*** If you expect staff members to see the positives in children, then you must try to see the positives in the staff members. If you want staffers to be consistent with children, then you should model consistent behavior with them.

9. ***Solicit—and follow-up on—suggestions from staff for inservice education.***

10. ***Share examples of things you have learned in your own professional development.***

Resources for Planning for Professional Development

Figure 8.3 lists several suggestions for professional development activities. You can get additional ideas from publications such as *Child Care Information Exchange*, a bimonthly journal tailored to child development program directors, which features a section called

FIGURE 8.3 *Suggestions for professional development activities*

1. Invite teachers to complete a self-assessment and create a plan for their own professional development. Set an example by doing the same thing yourself. Examples of self-assessment and planning tools can be found at http://www.ncchildcare.org.

2. Set up a teacher resource area equipped with books, journals, videotapes, VCR, and a computer with Internet access. Give teachers time to search for information about topics of interest to them, with the stipulation that they share their findings with others. Let the teachers know when you add books related to their interests.

3. Encourage teachers to visit one another's classrooms and share their observations and questions afterward. When a particularly significant project takes place in one class, be sure other teachers, and sometimes the children, get a chance to visit that classroom and see the results (e.g., children's block structures, dramatic play props, paintings).

4. Suggest that teachers subscribe to an electronic discussion group on the Internet. The Early Childhood and Parenting Collaborative (http://ecap.crc.uiuc.edu/), affiliated with the University of Illinois, hosts several on a number of topics of interest to early childhood professionals (e.g., the Reggio Emilia Approach and the Project Approach).

5. Show (or learn along with) teachers how to use documentation panels to capture the excitement and insights that characterize each stage of a project undertaken with the children. Documentation panels, an idea drawn from the renowned early childhood programs of Reggio Emilia, are visual displays that include photographs, drawings and diagrams by the children and teachers, printed transcripts of recorded conversations, and teachers' reflections on what the children are thinking and learning.

6. With the teacher's permission, observe, or better yet, videotape a teacher–child interaction in each classroom. Review your observation notes or the video clip with the individual teacher. Again with permission, select positive examples and show them at a staff meeting to stimulate a discussion on a particular topic (e.g., supporting children's play or helping them resolve conflict).

7. Encourage teachers to make presentations at local, state, or national conferences and to practice giving their presentations to center staff beforehand so they can get suggestions for improvement and build confidence.

8. Invite a local college faculty member to bring students to do a hands-on workshop of science or art ideas for your teachers.

9. Trade workshops with another center. For example, invite a couple of teachers to your center to show art activities. Then, send two of your teachers to the other center to show science.

10. Tap into the expertise within your pool of families and ask them to share it with an individual staff member, a small group, or a meeting of the entire staff. Parents, grandparents, aunts, uncles, and even older brothers or sisters may have skills to share. A nurse, doctor, or emergency medical technician may be able to offer first-aid or CPR training. An artist or craftsperson might provide information about the possibilities inherent in fibers or clay. Members of various cultural groups can share information, stories, songs, and customs that can become part of the curriculum, as well as sensitize everyone to individual differences.

"Beginnings Workshop" in every issue. It focuses on a particular topic, such as environments, and is chock full of information, as well as ideas for sparking staff discussions. *Texas Child Care*, a quarterly journal for early childhood personnel, includes a self-study guide in each issue that challenges readers to ponder and apply the ideas contained in the articles. Some publishers and organizations offer materials—videos with discussion guides or slide presentations that can be downloaded from the Internet. Other resources are listed at the end of this chapter.

Another possibility is to collaborate with schools and centers in your locality for inservice events. In some communities, several child development organizations (e.g., a Head Start agency, the school district, and corporate child-care chains) have pooled their resources to establish a consortium for professional development. This approach enables them to bring in several outside speakers throughout the year, and they all benefit from a wider array of activities than any one of them could afford.

The Manager's Relationships with Individual Staff Members

We now turn our attention to the more structured, formal elements of your one-to-one relationship with each employee. You lay the groundwork for that relationship before the employee's first day on the job by providing a clear job description. Recalling Maslow's concept that people need a sense of belonging and contributing to a higher purpose, you want to ensure that the new employee knows the program's mission and overall goals, as well as the way his job fits into that plan. This can be part of the orientation process discussed in chapter 7. The beginning of any relationship is full of potential—for positive or negative outcomes. The time and energy you devote to getting off on the right foot with a new employee is an investment that will be repaid many times over.

Mentoring

A mentor is someone who provides information, guidance, and emotional support for a person with less experience. With the help of a mentor, new staff members learn how to fit in with your organization's "culture," its particular way of doing things based on shared beliefs (Hatch, 1997, pp. 202–206).

Mentors can be an important professional development component at any stage of one's career. You may have enjoyed the support of several mentors in your life's journey thus far. Perhaps, a teacher helped you think about career options and decide which college program to enter. A supervisor may have encouraged you to apply for a promotion and suggested the skills you needed to hone in order to qualify for it. Now, as manager, it is your job to mentor your staff members.

As noted earlier, assigning an experienced staff member to take a new employee under her wing is one way to multiply the benefits of mentoring. The new employee may feel more at home and less anxious working alongside another employee. Staff members assigned to mentor newcomers take pride and satisfaction in this recognition of their talents, and they are less likely to feel they are in competition with new staff members for your approval. More importantly, mentoring another individual stimulates one to think a little more deeply—to reflect—about the reasons for the procedures being demonstrated or explained—a surefire strategy for professional growth. In other words, you mentor the experienced employee when you ask him to mentor someone else.

The value of mentoring extends beyond the new employee. Assigning a mentor can help a long-term employee move to the next level of competence. Taking on the mentoring role can rejuvenate a staff member's enthusiasm and prevent burnout. Although people

A mentor is someone who provides information, guidance, and emotional support for a person with less experience.

routinely and informally seek advice from those with more experience, the concept of mentoring implies a particular, more formal, type of relationship. The key ingredients of the mentoring relationship, according to Fenichel (1992, p. 9), are reflection, collaboration, and regularity. Mentor and protégé must both think about the reasons for their actions and decisions. They should view themselves as partners, respecting the valuable resources and life experiences that each brings to their task, and they must be clear about what they hope to accomplish. Lastly, they must have regularly scheduled, protected periods of time to meet with each other.

Another way to provide mentoring relationships for your staff is to partner with other programs in the community. Each teacher visits the other's classroom on alternating weeks, and the teacher pairs meet with a facilitator once every two weeks to process what they have learned. An important part of this facilitator meeting is to help participants discuss and resolve conflicts and disagreements openly so that everyone grows from the experience (Poelle, 1993).

Performance Appraisal System

During the orientation with a new employee, clearly state how you evaluate on-the-job performance and other activities. Indicate how often you monitor performance—monthly, quarterly, yearly—and that you will become familiar with their work by dropping in frequently and getting acquainted.

One purpose of these regular appraisals is to provide an early indication that an employee has trouble meeting the expectations for the job. An opportunity to discuss progress should be provided every week or two at first; then, less frequently as the employee adjusts. Supportive and positive feedback are always essential, but especially during the early weeks. Remember that the job description is your agreement between you and the employee about what is expected, so your appraisal instrument should reflect those expectations and spell out components of each. Figure 8.4 is an example of a performance appraisal for a child development teacher based on the job description provided in the previous chapter.

After the probationary period, continue to use the appraisal instrument as a basis for evaluation conferences with each staff member at least once each year. Invite staff members to give their own appraisal of their performance in each area. The discussion should focus on an evaluation of past performance, as well as projections for the future, including specific suggestions or plans for growth and improvement. If you are considering changes in the job description, this is a good time to discuss those proposed changes. The new job description then applies to the coming year. Your task is to acknowledge success and discuss problems in a straightforward manner, seeking the employee's input about reasons for the difficulties, as well as possible solutions. A written summary of the points discussed, with space for the employee's comments, should be signed by the manager and the employee, with copies provided to each. It is important to date your observations and evaluation forms and to keep copies of each in the employee's personnel file.

FIGURE 8.4   *Sample performance appraisal for a child development center teacher*

Name _____   Period Covered _____ to _____

Circle response that most accurately describes performance during current evaluation period.
(Key: **N** = Never or Seldom; **O** = Occasionally; **F** = Frequently; **C** = Consistently)

**Plan, implement and document developmentally appropriate
curriculum (in collaboration with colleagues)**

• Bases plans on observations of children's interests	N	O	F	C
• Fosters emotional, social, physical, and intellectual growth	N	O	F	C
• Incorporates children's prior knowledge, skills, etc.	N	O	F	C
• Promotes growth and development for ALL children	N	O	F	C
• Assesses each child's needs and progress regularly	N	O	F	C
• Materials and activities reflect and respect diversity	N	O	F	C
• Balances small/large group; teacher/child initiated	N	O	F	C
• Supports children effectively as they play and learn	N	O	F	C
• Uses effective communication techniques with children	N	O	F	C
• Documents children's experiences with variety of tools/techniques	N	O	F	C

Comments:

Organize and maintain environment to support program goals

• Arranges room to support children's play and self-regulation	N	O	F	C
• Prepares and maintains organized display of materials	N	O	F	C
• Engages children in maintaining orderly environment	N	O	F	C
• Adheres to all health and safety requirements	N	O	F	C

Comments:

**Establish and maintain relationships with families through group
meetings, home visits, and conferences**

• Treats families with respect and warmth	N	O	F	C
• Shares information about child or program informally	N	O	F	C
• Shares results of formal assessments appropriately	N	O	F	C
• Uses planned contacts (home visits, progress notes, telephone calls, conferences) effectively	N	O	F	C
• Contributes meaningful material for center newsletter	N	O	F	C
• Contributes to documentation panels and displays	N	O	F	C
• Encourages family participation in program in variety of ways	N	O	F	C
• Helps plan and participates in meetings or other family events	N	O	F	C

Comments:

Maintain records and write reports

• Maintains required records accurately (e.g., attendance)	N	O	F	C
• Records observations of children and compiles progress reports	N	O	F	C

(Continued)

FIGURE 8.4 *Continued*

• Keeps records of contacts regarding individual children (e.g., parent concerns, therapists' suggestions, etc.)	N	O	F	C
• Respects and maintains confidentiality	N	O	F	C

Comments:

Participate in professional development activities

• Works with a mentor to develop and implement individual plan	N	O	F	C
• Helps to plan and attends staff meetings and retreats	N	O	F	C
• Attends workshops and/or professional conferences	N	O	F	C
• Maintains membership in professional organization(s)	N	O	F	C
• Reads professional journals, books, etc.	N	O	F	C

Comments:

Signature of Employee	Date	Signature of Evaluator	Date

Dismissing Staff Members

Sometimes, an employee simply does not work out satisfactorily and has to be dismissed. This step should not be taken lightly. Full regard must be given to the individual's right to due process. Due process involves giving prompt feedback as part of your evaluation process—clearly stating both your expectations for improvement and the consequences for the failure to do so. You might bring in an objective outside observer if you wonder whether a personality conflict, rather than the quality of the work, is the cause of the problem. If, after efforts are made to get the performance on track, the employee has not responded, you have no choice but to terminate employment. Copies of evaluation forms, dated observation notes, and a written record of any conferences, including dates and actions taken, are necessary to support your decision to dismiss the individual.

You, as manager, may have to say, "We have a problem. Somehow this job is not right for you." A humane attitude lets the person know that you care about her as an individual, but that you must act when performance is not up to par because so much depends on each staff member doing his or her job well. Generally, an employee is surprised to find warmth and is grateful for the opportunity to depart gracefully and will leave in a short time. In the meantime, you have an obligation to limit the person's duties to those where children would not be harmed in any way. Such a humanistic procedure does less harm to the morale of the remaining staff members than outright firing. Obviously, such an approach cannot be used in cases of suspected abuse of the children because your obligation to protect the children takes precedence over other concerns. In these cases, licensing and law enforcement authorities become involved, and, if the abuse is substantiated, immediate dismissal is warranted.

Of course, not every staff member who leaves your program has been fired. People quit for a variety of reasons. By conducting an exit interview with employees who resign, you gain valuable information that can be used to improve aspects of the program such as staff turnover, morale, and training procedures. Exit interviews can take place face-to-face before an employee leaves, or you can follow up a few weeks later via a telephone interview or a mailed questionnaire with a self-addressed, stamped envelope (Olsen, 1993).

Volunteers

Volunteers are valuable assets, contributing considerable amounts of human capital to child development centers each year. Some volunteer for an hour or two a month; others volunteer many hours each week. As noted in the previous chapter, you should follow the same steps with volunteers as you do with paid staff if you are to make the best use of this valuable resource. That is, you have to locate people whose skills and attitudes make them suitable for work in a child development center, acquaint them with your center's organization and policies, provide any neces-

In addition to providing valuable service, volunteers receive satisfaction from the positive and professional relationships they build with children.

sary training, assign them worthwhile tasks, monitor and guide them in the performance of those tasks, let them know how they are doing, and give appropriate recognition for a job well done.

Many family members enjoy volunteering in their child's classroom, and centers should make specific plans to extend such opportunities. Many mothers and fathers willingly take time from their job to help, although some fathers complain that when they have volunteered, they were treated in a sexist manner, as though men could not do the tasks properly. Of course, such treatment, in addition to being contrary to the respect for differences that we advocated at the beginning of this chapter, is shortsighted and very likely to dampen the enthusiasm that families feel for volunteering.

Churches, civic clubs, high schools, and colleges are other potential sources of volunteers. For example, every community has high school and elementary students who could participate for a period each day. Managers should explore this resource with school boards, principals, and teachers. Many people believe that older children who participate in activities with young children are learning responsible parenting attitudes in a natural way. Contacting schools and youth clubs is a way for managers to begin. In addition, some high schools and colleges offer organized courses in child development or early childhood education and child development centers can serve as laboratories for those students. Naturally, such centers are screened by the educators to ensure that the students learn appropriate techniques. If you operate a high-quality center, it might qualify for this important teaching function. Such students bring fresh ideas, excellent energy, and stamina. They are often enthusiastic and appeal to staff members who may be nearly burned out from the day-in, day-out commitment. In exchange for serving as a laboratory for these students, your staff could be invited to attend seminars and special programs that stimulate professional growth.

Senior citizens are often available to volunteer regularly in schools and centers, providing warm laps, skillful storytelling, and one-to-one attention. You may be more successful recruiting from the older people that you know than from senior citizen groups. After a few older men and women start and enjoy helping, others are likely to follow suit.

Volunteers can be very well educated and experienced or they may lack much of both traits. Untrained volunteers must be trained, supported, and rewarded if they are really to be of help and to stay on over a period of time. Guiding volunteers takes time—both the manager's time and the classroom teachers' time—but the efforts have many payoffs. The more you treat your volunteers like professionals, the more professionally they will behave. Remember to include volunteers in the professional development opportunities made available for the staff. Guard against always giving them the dirty work or the cold side of the play yard while paid staff take the more pleasant tasks or stay indoors where it is warm.

In addition to giving from their storehouse of human capital, volunteers receive satisfaction from the positive and pleasurable relationships they build with the children and staff. The work experience added to the volunteer's résumé is potentially a more tangible benefit; all volunteers should be encouraged to keep records of their volunteer time. Perhaps most important, volunteers usually become more knowledgeable and more committed to serving children and their families. They are marvelous allies to have in a community. Having connections with many groups, they can rally political support should that become necessary.

Conclusion

Human relations are the heart and soul of any human service organization and child development programs are no exception—particularly in view of the acute staffing shortage in this field. Successful managers understand human needs and motivation and communicate effectively with individuals and groups during their day-to-day interactions, as well as in more formally structured encounters. The manager's relationship with staff members begins prior to hiring and continues until (and often after) an employee leaves the program. In between, the manager's job is to make the best use of each employee's store of human capital and to help each employee develop that capital to the fullest extent possible. Encouraging mentoring, fostering teamwork, and providing clear feedback are all part of the human relations aspects of the manager's role.

QUESTIONS FOR REVIEW

1. Describe Maslow's hierarchy of needs and explain how his theory applies to management, staffing, and employee relations in a child development center.
2. Describe each developmental stage of a teacher as identified by Katz. Explain how knowing these steps is useful to a manager.
3. List the 10 guidelines for planning professional development activities developed by Hines. Give either a negative or positive example of each from your own experience.
4. Define the following terms: active listening, mentor, job enrichment, intrinsic motivation.
5. Describe three strategies that directors can use to manage group dynamics during meetings.
6. List the seven steps of the conflict mediation process. Apply the steps to a real or imagined conflict between child development staff.
7. Think of a team project you have experienced or witnessed. Discuss how well the group did (or did not) follow the five steps for effective teamwork.

PROFESSIONAL PORTFOLIO

1. Locate an instrument used to evaluate staff members at a child development program in your community, or develop one that you might use in a center that you manage. Describe how you would use the instrument: Who is evaluated? Who completes the

instrument? When and how often are staff evaluated? When and how is the staff member informed of the results? What happens afterward?

2. Access the website sponsored by the National Early Childhood Technical Assistance System (NEC*TAS) at http://www.nectas.unc.edu/inclusion/. Describe the information provided and explain how you could use this Internet resource as part of a staff development plan in a program that you manage.

3. Outline a professional development plan for staff in a child development program, addressing the following components: the goals for each individual or staff level, the resources available for meeting each goal, and the strategies a program might use to facilitate or support the pursuit of the goals, as well as reward completion.

RESOURCES FOR FURTHER STUDY

Print

Bloom, Paula Jorde. (1997). *A great place to work: Improving conditions for staff in young children's programs* (rev. ed.). Washington, DC: National Association for the Education of Young Children.

Bloom, Paula Jorde (2000). *Workshop essentials: Planning and presenting dynamic workshops.* Lake Forest, IL: New Horizons.

Carter, M., & Curtis, D. (1994). Training teachers: A harvest of theory and practice. St. Paul, MN: Redleaf.

Center for the Child Care Workforce (1998). *Creating better child care jobs: Model work standards for teaching staff in center-based care.* Washington, DC: Author.

Internet

North Carolina Institute for Early Childhood Professional Development
http://www.ncchildcare.org/
Website for the North Carolina Institute for Early Childhood Professional Development: Just one example of a state initiative to support professional development, the North Carolina site provides online workbooks for teachers and administrators to develop a personal and professional plan of action, as well as a planning checklist for communities wishing to support professional development as a means of increasing child care quality.

North Carolina Institute for Early Childhood Professional Development
http://www.nncc.org/Who/orgs/options-prof.html#anchor223726
A list of resources for professional development and training; includes descriptions and links to more than 15 national organizations, many of which contain further links to publications or online training opportunities.

Beyond the Journal
http://www.journal.naeyc.org/btj/200405/innovations.asp
"Innovations in E-learning: New Promise for Professional Development." This article by Chip Donohue and Roger Neugebauer appeared in the May 2004 issue of *Beyond the Journal,* an online supplement to *Young Children,* the journal of the National Association for the Education of Young Children, It lists and provides links to a wide variety of online resources for professional development.

Natural Resources Listserv
listserv@unc.edu
Provides weekly email announcements of free or low-cost professional development resources in a variety of formats, on topics related to early childhood and early intervention, along with "tips for trainers." Send an e-mail to listserv@unc.edu. Leave the subject line blank, and type the following in the body of the message: subscribe natural_resources

9

Facilities Management

The physical facility that houses a child development program supports (or impedes) all of the human interactions therein. Managers must consider the activities and needs of both children and adults and exercise all management functions as they procure, renovate, arrange, decorate or redecorate, allocate, furnish, and maintain living space for their programs. We call the competency required to create and maintain space that supports the human interactions **facilities management.**

Managing Space: An Ecosystems Perspective

A center's physical facilities are part of the human-built environment of the human ecological system. In other words, like schools, shopping centers, and office buildings, they are physical structures constructed to serve human needs. As part of the human-built environment, the center exists within and has many connections with the natural, physical-biological environment discussed in chapter 3. The land on which the building rests, the surrounding terrain, the play yard's size and landscaping, the fresh air and sunshine, and the drainage and wind protection all impact the program's quality of life. The sun, which gives the center light and heat inside and makes playgrounds usable even on cold days, is part of the natural environment, as are the fuels used for heating and cooling the building. Within the natural, physical–biological environment, the center comprises a complex social–cultural environment where humans interact for the purpose of nurturing and educating young children.

These interactions reflect the social and cultural context of the center, as well as the moment-to-moment personal contacts of the individuals involved. For example, child development centers in the United States place a higher priority on teaching children to talk through their conflicts than do centers in Japan (Tobin, Wu, & Davidson, 1989). Furthermore, individual children and adults bring different temperaments, learning styles, abilities, cultures, and experiences to their relationships with one another, as well as with the tangible environment. Some people feel constricted by an overly neat environment, while others crave visual order and symmetry. What seems like a pleasant hive, humming with activity, to one person can seem like noisy chaos to another. Ideally, the physical environment (both natural and human-built) supports relationships between the center's children, staff, and families, as well as connections between the center and the world surrounding it (Ceppi & Zini, 1998).

Regulations and Professional Standards

Local building codes and state licensing regulations set minimum standards for the location and configuration of child-care facilities. Some cities, for example, prohibit the location of infant or toddler classrooms on a second floor. Fire codes mandate the number of required exits and specify that they must be easily pushed open from the inside even when locked to entry from the outside. Lighting, fresh air circulation, hot water temperature, and the number and location of sinks and toilets are the province of sanitation codes. It may seem confusing to coordinate the requirements of so many sets of regulations, but your state licensing representative can help you sort things out. If you are involved in planning a new facility or in renovating an existing one, it is a good idea (and usually a requirement) to draw up plans and submit them to the various authorities for review before beginning construction. Correcting the direction of a door swing or the location of a handwashing sink is much easier, and less costly, on paper than after it is set in bricks and mortar.

The National Association for the Education of Young Children (NAEYC) accreditation criteria call for 35 square feet of indoor space per child and 75 square feet of outdoor space. The latter can be calculated on the basis of the number of children using the play yard at a given time (National Association for the Education of Young Children, 2005). Some argue that 40 or 50 square feet of indoor space per child comes closer to ideal (Olds, 2001). Licensing regulations, on the other hand, specify the minimum amount of space required for each child. If you are fortunate enough to be involved in the planning and building of a facility, you may have an opportunity to argue for the ideal space allowance. Most managers, however, must work with existing facilities, and they are usually pressed to stretch available space as far as licensing regulations allow.

Even then, additional considerations must go into calculating the capacity of a given space. Imagine an empty warehouse with 35,000 square feet. Using the standard of 35 square feet per child, some might conclude that this space could accommodate 1,000 children. But licensing regulations regarding the number of toilets and washbasins, the amount of equipment, and the number of required staff add constraints to your total capacity. And, if you are striving for a quality above and beyond the minimum regulations, you must, of course, be concerned with maximum group sizes. When all of these things are taken into consideration, your 35,000-square-foot warehouse—with the addition of toilets and washbasins—will house no more than 20 children, and those 20 children will be too overwhelmed by the openness of the space to have a high-quality experience. Adding walls and additional bathrooms can increase the capacity, but you have to plan carefully so that all of the new rooms have proper exits and ventilation. In short, managing spatial resources is a complex matter and deserves careful thought.

Children's Basic Environmental Needs

Anita Olds was a visionary leader in the design of child-care facilities based on principles of human development and psychology. She founded and directed the Child Care Institute, an annual seminar cosponsored by Tufts University and the Harvard Graduate School of Design, where she guided child development and design professionals to explore the ways the human-built environment supports and enhances life. Olds believed that every child is a "miracle" and that a child development program designed with that in mind differs radically from one designed simply to meet minimum standards. According to Olds, children have four basic environmental needs:

1. ***An environment that encourages movement.*** The first function of any physical environment is to meet physical needs, and children's first physical need is to move. Asking them to sit or stand still for long periods, in addition to being an impossible task, inhibits their healthy growth and leads to inevitable frustration for both children and teachers. If the environment does not provide legitimate and safe opportunities to run, climb, jump, and crawl, children create their own—sometimes dangerous—challenges. Planning to accommodate these natural drives with safe opportunities for movement in the classroom supports the children's growth and makes life easier for teachers.

2. ***An environment that supports comfort.*** Comfort, in the psychological sense, requires an environment with just the right amount of stimulation or variety. Too much stimulation is overwhelming, while too little is deadening. Olds suggested that designers take inspiration from nature's rhythmic fluctuations to counter the sterile sameness of many institutional settings. She contrasted babbling brooks, soft breezes, and the play of light and shadow when sunlight is filtered through leaves with echoes bouncing off hard tile floors in long corridors and rectangular classrooms flooded with harsh fluorescent light. Comfortable settings provide "difference in sameness" by introducing variations in scale, floor and ceiling height, and the texture of interior finishes and furnishings. Such settings carve out spaces for being alone or with companions, for quiet or active pursuits.

This comfortable entry area provides a cozy place for parents and children to sit for a few minutes at the beginning or end of the day.

3. ***An environment that fosters competence.*** Well-designed spaces are adapted to the children's size and abilities so that they can move about freely and accomplish their aims without constant adult help. Any group of children displays a wide range of abilities and tastes, and any child's preferences vary from day to day. Offering a wide variety of things to do ensures that each child is able to find something to do that is just challenging enough to be interesting. When the room arrangement creates several defined spaces, children are less overwhelmed and can see the choices available to them. When the materials within those spaces are organized and accessible, children can concentrate and carry out their plans. Low chairs and tables, child-height bulletin boards and easels, and accessible equipment stored on open shelves invite children to get their own learning materials and to put them away when finished.

4. ***An environment that encourages a sense of control.*** Spaces designed to meet this need allow children to experience the sensation of privacy without foregoing the need for adult supervision. Child-height barriers, cubbyholes, and small alcoves offer possibilities for retreat and momentary solitude. Child-sized equipment and low door latches facilitate the child's control of the environment. Child-high lavatories, toilets, and drinking fountains help children gain control of their own personal care sooner. Handrails on stairs make it easier to go up and down independently. Children also benefit from predictability in their environment, from knowing how to get in and out of a room, as well as what is on the other side of the door or wall. A loft, or similar structure, that affords an overview of the entire space helps meet this need. Finally,

children (like adults) feel more control in protected spaces, with walls at their backs, than exposed in the middle of large open spaces.

Olds believed that planners must take all four needs into account, adjusting the emphasis on each to achieve a balance. If, for example, you are going to ask children to sit still for group time or meals, you will be more successful if you provide interesting things to do or look at, comfortable places to sit, and a view that imparts a sense of control over the space (Olds, 2001, pp. 8–12).

The concepts of personal space and territoriality are relevant to the sense of control.

Personal Space. All individuals, including young children, need some personal space that is theirs to claim and defend, according to Pastalan (1971). In the child development center, this is usually the locker or cubby holding the children's personal belongings—their coats, boots, and items they accumulate at school such as paintings. It may also be important that each be given a specific place at the lunch or snack table or a cot in a certain spot as her personal space. According to Pastalan, it should be arranged so that it is very difficult for others to infringe on the individual's personal space. He suggested that "possession of a tangible piece of space seems almost essential for one's identity." With this point in mind, the center that has no lockers for the children's belongings must be violating the children's sense of personal space and contributing to their insecurity. The teacher who removes a 5-year-old's toy from his locker and places it on a high shelf is also violating the child's personal space.

Territoriality. In a center, territoriality means a child's specific claim to a place in the learning environment—the place at the easel, in the sandbox, or on the carpet in the block room. Teachers often say to young children, when a conflict arises over a piece of equipment or a space on the floor or in the sandbox, that it is "yours while you are using it." This rule may be a source of confusion for some children—those who have had no claim to equipment or space in their prior experience or those who come from small families in large homes where almost all of the territory is theirs most of the time. Parents teach children to use their own tricycle and to keep it in their own yard, so the communal use of tricycles at school may be confusing.

Territoriality also refers to how close you like to have others come to you in a social interaction. Variations have been observed in adults and in different cultures. Some North Americans, for example, have experienced discomfort traveling in other countries where people stand much closer together when commuting on crowded buses or push against one another to get served at train stations or post offices. If they judge these behaviors by their own cultural standards, they might become offended at what they perceive as rudeness when, in fact, their distancing behavior might seem insulting to members of the other culture.

Further complicating these cultural differences are the differences that exist between individuals because of temperament or other personality factors. Some people simply do not like to be touched as much as others. All of these factors influence the behavior of even very young children, as well as the adults in the center.

Decisions, Decisions . . .

During your observations of child development centers, have you witnessed any conflicts that seemed to be caused by territoriality? Describe what you saw and provide suggestions on how a director might manage the space to alleviate the problem.

Density

Density, or the number and size of the people who use a space, will affect all aspects of the environment. Clearly an overcrowded classroom impedes opportunities for movement either because children bump into one another or because teachers find ways to limit movement in order to prevent such bumps. Increased density relates to comfort because more people produce more noise and movement, with the possible result that children (and adults) suffer from sensory overload. Feelings of competence and control are also impacted. Pastalan (1971) suggested that density is related to an individual's feeling of mastery. As sensory acuities develop, individuals can cope with a larger number of people and larger spaces. He warned that high density and overcrowding produce negative effects on behavior.

The National Day Care Study compared groups of 12 children and groups of 24 children and found that the small groups fostered positive behaviors, such as cooperation, reflection, and innovation, in the children. The children in the small groups were more verbal, giving opinions and making spontaneous comments. They also were more involved in tasks and were less frequently seen wandering aimlessly than the children in the large groups (Ruopp et al., 1979).

NAEYC accreditation criteria stipulate a group size of 6 or 8 for infants, 6 to 12 for toddlers and 2-year-olds, 12 to 18 for 3-year-olds, and 16 to 20 for 4- and 5-year-olds (National Association for the Education of Young Children, 2005). Of course, each of these groups must have a minimum of two adults present at all times.

Density applies not only to the total space for the whole group, but also to the ways children use that space. Dividing the room into learning or interest centers so that children work and play in small groups facilitates positive behaviors. There must be a sufficient number of centers, however, and they must be interesting and appealing to children. Typically, children flow from one area to another as they finish a project and decide to move to a new activity. Because independent decision making is important, children are not required to march in lockstep from learning center to learning center.

Managing Density. The number of children in each area can be flexible and still be limited for safety reasons. Older children in particular can take part in deciding how to control the traffic flow. To avoid overcrowding and prevent conflict, some teachers post "tickets" or signs with stick figures that show the number of children the area can accommodate, for example, four in the painting area or six building with blocks. The children are expected to learn to read the numbers or count the stick figures, count the children already in the space, and wait their turn if there is no space available. Teachers who use this method argue that it teaches children one-to-one correspondence, counting skills, and the ability to delay gratification. The system has drawbacks, however. For it to work, it must be enforced consistently. Children who have difficulty remembering to count themselves in the total or waiting their turn are often evicted from an area only to slip back in when teachers are not looking, undermining all prior "learning" of the rule. In some centers, the teachers seem to give as many reminders at the end of the school year as they did at the beginning—a good sign that the rule is not being learned, and perhaps that it is inappropriate.

Some teachers question whether they should invest so much time and energy in the role of enforcer and whether children should be taught blind obedience to arbitrary rules. They prefer to manage spatial density more subtly, and more efficiently, through the use of **indirect guidance techniques** (Hearron & Hildebrand, 2005). That is, they arrange the environment to give concrete cues that tell the children something about how many can play in a given area, as well as something about why that is so. For example, two pairs of safety goggles are in the woodworking area, and there is a rule that safety goggles must be worn in order to protect the eyes.

Besides ensuring that enough interesting activities are available at any one time it is important to offer popular activities often enough for the children to get their fill. A sign with four stick figures does not limit the number of children crowded around the play dough table if the dough is rarely available and all of the other materials in the room have been there since the center opened. When there is an especially popular center, children are often content to wait if they can put their names on a sign-up sheet and be assured that they will get a turn. Rather than imposing their own arbitrary time limits on play in a particular area (e.g., with a cooking timer), teachers can ask the children in the area to tell the next child on the sign-up sheet when they are finished. When given the right to decide for themselves, children often surprise us by relinquishing the spot much sooner than the arbitrary timer would have dictated, and while in the learning center, they focus more on their play and less on their impending eviction.

Whether teachers choose the direct or indirect way of limiting group size, there are at least two good reasons for doing so. First, children in groups of four or fewer are more likely to participate fully in the group's activity. Second, because group unity decreases as the size of a group increases, larger groups require more outside control. Thus, the freedom and self-control desired in a high-quality child development center is facilitated by small groups.

Organizing Space

Building Layout

When designing the overall layout of a child development center, it is important to consider several factors. The children's safety from fire, tornado, and other disasters must be of paramount concern. Heat sources, such as furnaces and water heaters, must be separated from children's areas by fire-retardant walls. Pathways to exits must be clear and although doors may be locked to entry from the outside, they have to be unlocked and easily opened from the inside. All rooms should be equipped with smoke detectors and fire extinguishers. Neither staff nor visitors should smoke in the center. Sufficient security to prevent theft and vandalism requires locks on windows, doors, storage sheds, and gates, as well as careful control over the center's keys. It is essential, for example, that employees return any keys after they have resigned or been terminated.

What activities or functions are planned? What separate spaces for infants, toddlers, and older children are necessary? What spaces will staff members need for planning or rest breaks? Will the program offer hot meals and need a kitchen? Where can parents linger with the children or meet with teachers? Which activities should be located near each other, and which should be apart? Which activities or functions will be assigned to the most convenient or attractive spaces? When you have to make a choice, who gets the sunniest room? Who gets the rooms with easiest access to the outdoor play area? It seems logical to give infants and toddlers priority on these spaces because older children can usually get outside easier and stay longer periods once they are out there (Olds, 2001, pp. 110–113).

Considering the traffic flow between the separate spaces influences decisions about where to locate doors and windows and where to establish inside common areas. Olds called the

Low dividers with rounded edges provide a safe place for toddlers to pull up and meet each other face-to-face over an interesting toy.

common area the "center of gravity of social life" in a children's center and recommended that it be placed at the heart of the building, centrally located, but protected from through traffic. The *piazza* of the Diana School in Reggio Emilia, Italy, is a prime example of such a space, echoing both the form and function of the town's central plaza. Olds distinguished this public space from the more private spaces such as children's classrooms, bathrooms, offices, or kitchen. She recommended that public spaces be located near the building's entrance, allowing traffic patterns to flow from there to progressively more private spaces, much as they would in a private home (Olds, 2001, pp. 116–121).

Room Layout

When designing the layout of an individual room, begin once again by considering the activities planned for that room—the space's functional requirements. Every age group requires, in varying degrees, space for four activity types: (1) caregiving, (2) movement and active play, (3) quiet play, and (4) messy play. Programs with infants also need space for the babies to sleep. The first activity type, caregiving, takes place throughout the room, while the other three (movement and active play, quiet play, messy play) require separate zones. The decision about where to place each of these zones is influenced by the room's fixed features, the parts that are built in and cannot be changed. Door locations determine the entry and exit points and convey a feeling of exposure, while corners lend a sense of protection. The room arrangement must respect these qualities in order to work.

Regions and Zones.   The room's fixed features help divide it into two regions: a wet region comprising the entry zone and the messy zone, and a dry region comprising the quiet and active play zones (Olds, 2001, pp. 137–141). The room's water source dictates the location of the wet region, which should have waterproof, easily cleaned flooring. Carpeting can demarcate the dry region.

Well-defined zones within each of these regions and arrangements that reduce or control traffic through the zones make it possible for children to play without undue interference and conflicts. Children begin to know what the appropriate behavior or activity is in each area. For example, furniture arrangements that eliminate long open pathways make it less likely that children will run about and collide with each other or the furniture. Painting takes place in the wet region/messy zone because the washable floor surface means that spills do not matter. Blocks are located in the dry region/active zone on carpeted areas where sounds are deadened, and out of traffic lanes, so that cherished buildings are less likely to be knocked down accidentally.

Other activities appropriate for the messy zone include water and sand play, woodworking, arts and crafts, cooking, eating, and science and nature study. This is also the place to locate bathrooms, changing tables, water fountains, and separate sinks for handwashing and for the children's activities, as well as the cupboards and closets needed to store all of the necessary materials for these activities.

In addition to the blocks, the active zone supports climbing and other types of large muscle play, dramatic play, music and movement, and fantasy play with puppets or other

Decisions, Decisions . . .

Sketch the floor plan of a child development classroom you have visited or worked in. Think about the considerations discussed in this section and decide what, if any, changes, you would recommend. Discuss with your classmates.

FIGURE 9.1   *Sample layout for an infant–toddler room*

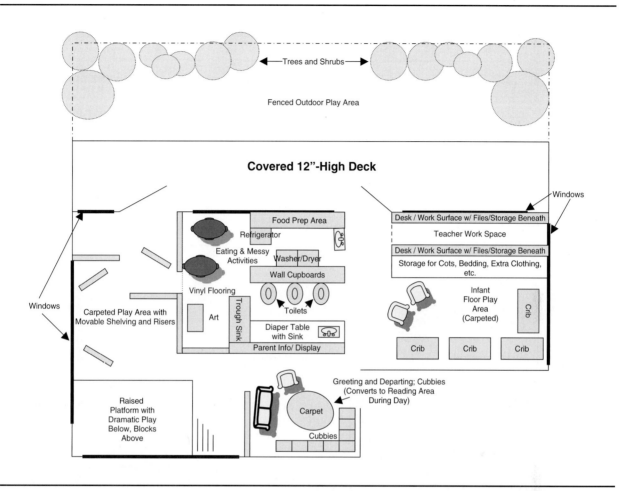

miniature figures. The quiet zone provides space for reading, writing, listening, playing with manipulatives (e.g., puzzles or small construction materials), resting or relaxing, and group meetings. The line between the carpet and the washable floor surface marks the boundary between wet and dry regions. This boundary, as well as the boundaries between the various zones, can be emphasized by lighting variations or by ceiling and floor height. A strategically placed tall structure, such as a loft, helps create a buffer between zones (Olds, 2001, pp. 144–152). Figures 9.1 and 9.2 provide examples of classroom design for different age groups.

Organizing Space to Meet Children's Basic Environmental Needs

Movement.   Children's need for movement is supported by the provision of an active zone, as described above, where movement is permitted and encouraged. Creating spaces where children are challenged to use their large muscles reduces the likelihood that they will seek such opportunities elsewhere in the classroom, injuring themselves or disturbing other children's play in the process. Texture and sound can help convey the possibilities within a given space. The same room can signal when it's time for active play or napping simply by adjusting

FIGURE 9.2 *Typical classroom with learning areas*

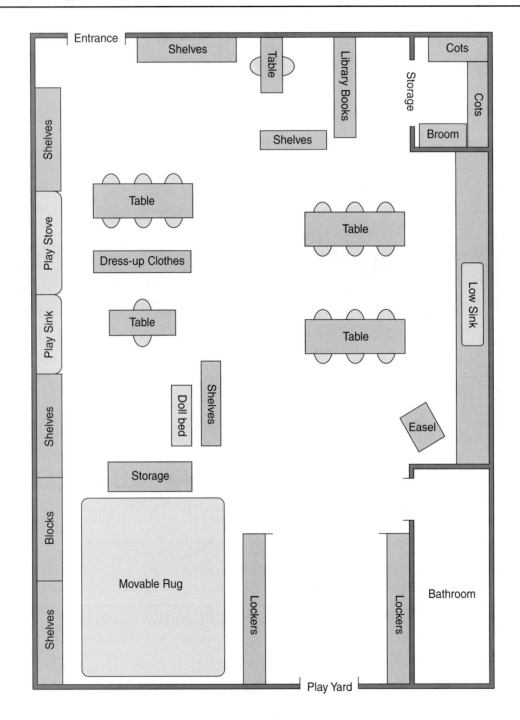

the light and adding or removing soft background music. A low-pile area rug on a hardwood or vinyl floor creates a well-defined boundary for block building, and the exposed perimeter floor suggests a "road" that steers riding toys away from block structures. Given boundaries and cues such as these, the children easily learn the appropriate behavior for each space.

Comfort.   The typical child development center is full of sensory stimulation for children. It might be the sound of their playmates laughing in the block corner, the sight of a piñata being constructed in the art area, or the smell of cookies baking in the kitchen. Stimulation for its own sake is not necessarily desirable, however. Constant bombardment with visual or auditory stimulation can lead to children—and adults—tuning out their environments. Too many early childhood classrooms are visually chaotic—walls are crammed from floor to ceiling with dozens of commercial "decorations" and multiple versions of every craft project from the beginning of the year. Many people in such an environment simply shut out the excess stimulation and stop seeing their surroundings. Because some children may not be able to exclude the excess stimulation, they are unable to focus on any one aspect of the environment. If you intend that children take in information, provide some blank space around the pictures and symbols displayed on the walls. The same principle applies to sound. Some teachers feel that they are creating an appreciation for music by using it as a "background" for play. Does the Muzak in the shopping mall or elevator stimulate an appreciation in adults, or do they simply tune it out? Other teachers use music as a "white noise" to deaden the sound of voices and footsteps in a room with poor acoustic qualities.

Children must feel secure in their environment if they are to function fully and attain their potential. Parents must feel that everything possible is being done to ensure their child's safety and security within the center, or they will be unable to leave their child with confidence.

The personal space discussed earlier helps assure the child that he will not be left out when it is lunchtime or naptime. A personal locker provides a child with a place for treasures. Having easy access to the play yard, lunchroom, library, or indoor large-motor area without having to traverse long halls reduces children's anxiety. Adequate lighting can also reduce anxiety. A sturdy 4-foot fence around the play yard helps the adult supervisors keep the children safely inside and unwanted intruders outside.

Competence.   While it is important to provide novelty by introducing new materials or rearranging a space, it is also important for the room arrangement to remain stable, especially for younger children or children with disabilities, to promote feelings of security and competence that come from knowing where things are. Any major changes should be introduced one at a time, perhaps after consulting the children. Indoors, a few lightweight room dividers or hollow blocks often encourage the children's spatial creativity—they might build an office, a hideout, or an airport. For the older children, who have been in school for a period of time and feel very secure, a reorganization of space often stimulates new ways to play. For example, if the music area is moved near the blocks, the sight of blocks may stimulate the children to build a stage for an impromptu performance. Moving the blocks near the housekeeping corner may stimulate them to combine the blocks and the dolls or to add to the housekeeping area by using the blocks to build a room. Older children can participate in the decisions about the changes and learn a great deal in the process as they discuss the merits of various possibilities or draw proposed floor plans.

Control.   A principle called *prepared environment*, applied in the Montessori schools, requires that each material be limited to its own special space for use. The child is taught where to use the material and to return it to its rightful place on the shelf when finished. The items to be used in a particular activity are often color coded to help with organization: two small blue pitchers with a blue sponge on a small blue tray, for example, comprise a pouring activity complete with the tool needed for clean up. Additionally, the materials are arranged on the shelves in a sequential order of difficulty so a child knows that something from the top left, for example, is easier than something from the bottom right. Small mats are provided for children to spread on the floor and demarcate their work space. These aspects of Montessori's approach to managing spatial resources have been adapted by many teachers in other types of centers to help children work independently and without interference from others.

Aesthetic Quality of Space.   The impact of the environment's aesthetic quality on human interactions and perceptions is illustrated by a study that Abraham Maslow and Norbett Mintz conducted in the 1950s. They arranged three separate rooms: a "beautiful" room with comfortable furnishings, natural lighting, and tasteful decorations; an "ugly" room with "bare light bulbs, grey walls, and torn shades," and an "average" room that was clean and neat but nondescript. Then, they asked volunteers to sit in each room, examine photographs of people, and decide which showed evidence of "energy" and "well-being." The volunteers, as well as two of the three research assistants who interviewed them, were unaware of the actual purpose of the study, which was to see whether people reacted differently while in the three environments.

The findings were striking. Not only did the volunteers find the same pictures more full of "energy" and "well-being" when they viewed them while in the "beautiful" room, but the research assistants also spent less time on the interviews in the "ugly" room and had more negative feelings toward their work there, including "monotony, fatigue, headache, sleepiness, discontent, irritability, hostility, and avoidance." The findings for the "average" room were more like those for the "ugly" room than for the "beautiful" room (Hiss, 1987).

Care is needed, however, to ensure that all of the colors harmonize and create an aesthetically pleasing environment. Many centers today are using more muted and subtle tones rather than the garish mixture of primary colors so often associated with children's spaces. Think of what you would like in your own home instead of limiting yourself to stereotyped images of what children are thought to like.

Space Arranged for Ease of Supervision

Children must be supervised at all times by a reliable adult. Learning centers set off by child-high shelves or dividers not only encourage children to select an activity and settle down to concentrate on that activity, but they also enable adults to observe the entire room at a glance. A clear view of all equipment and the space's corners enables the adult to notice behavior that might become dangerous and move quickly to provide closer supervision or take care of an emergency. Adequate supervision contributes to the children's safety and to the protection of the center's reputation. More than one center has found itself mired in an investigation of possible sexual abuse because staff failed to notice curious children exploring each other's bodies in a hidden corner of a classroom or playground.

Based on a study of sexual abuse in child-care centers, experts recommended that doors and stalls in bathrooms be eliminated along with any other place where a young child could be isolated (Finkelhor, Williams, Kalinowski, & Burns, 1988). This precaution serves to protect staff from unwarranted accusations, as well as to protect the children from harm. A wise manager ensures that staff are not put in the position of being alone with the children.

Space Organized to Meet Special Needs

Organizing space to meet the needs of children with disabilities may seem challenging to some managers and caregivers. It may help put the challenge into perspective if we consider that child development centers have been accommodating special needs as long as they have been in existence. After all, what are child-size toilets, or "sippy cups," or wooden puzzles with large knobs on the pieces if not adaptations to the special needs of individuals who are smaller in stature or less physically coordinated than others.

The essence of developmentally appropriate practice is that programs and services for children be individually appropriate, as well as age appropriate—they begin with a general knowledge of what children are like at various ages but tailor this knowledge to the unique needs of each individual. Accommodating the needs of children with disabilities may take a little extra effort, but it is really a matter of extending the concept of developmental appropriateness to all children.

Center managers can take comfort in the fact that they are not alone as they try to meet the special needs of a particular child with a disability. Recall from the discussion of legislation in chapter 2 that children with disabilities must be provided with an Individualized Education Plan (IEP) or an Individualized Family Service Plan (IFSP), depending on whether they are over or under 3 years of age.

These plans are the product of collaboration on the part of parents, teachers, therapists, or other specialists. If the child is enrolled in the center as part of a previously formulated plan, the manager and caregivers will certainly want to study the plan and perhaps have a role in subsequent revisions. Sometimes, the planning process results when center staff observe signs of developmental delays and make an appropriate referral for screening. In that case, child development staff may be included in the team from the beginning. The challenge is not for any one member of this team to meet all the child's needs but rather for the team to develop the communication and cooperation needed to make the best use of each individual member's expertise.

The plan might include providing special types of equipment for the child with a disability. Standers or other positioning devices can help a child stand or sit to play with peers. Electronic switches allow a child with limited use of hand muscles to control movement or sound in electronic toys. Some types of communication devices can be programmed to play brief statements when tapped, so that a child with language impairment can communicate a message such as "I want to play" or "I'm all done." Many communities have resource centers where such adaptive equipment can be borrowed. Usually the specialists on the child's IFSP or IEP team can help locate these resources as well as funding if needed. All adaptive equipment need not be high tech, however. Everyday items can often be modified relatively easily to meet special needs. One inventive teacher found that by simply twisting the handle on an ordinary teaspoon, she made it possible for a child with cerebral palsy to maneuver food into his mouth. Haugen (n.d.) suggests seven strategies for adapting materials so that all children can use them:

1. Add something to make the item easier to use (e.g., foam wrap on paint brush handles or "fluffers" between book pages).

2. Hold the item steady so the child can use it (Velcro on blocks, a dab of clay on the bottom of a toy pan to keep it from sliding while the child stirs).

3. Make things easier (fewer materials to choose from; puzzles with fewer pieces; lower basketball hoop).

4. Provide boundaries (raised edges on tables to prevent spills, enclosed space for reading alone).

5. Appeal to many senses (colored blocks, textured or musical balls, scented play dough).

6. Expand the choices (stack beanbags instead of blocks, provide stories on tape as well as in books).

7. Involve other children (to catch and retrieve balls or follow a parade led by child in a wheelchair).

Decisions, Decisions. . .

Think about a child development facility you have visited or worked in. What modifications to the environment might be necessary in order to accommodate a child with severe vision impairment? What about a child who uses a wheelchair or walker? Discuss with your classmates.

One major concern when considering space for meeting special needs is accessibility. The center itself and all of the activities in the center must be accessible to all children. If you are planning a new center or renovating an old one, local building codes may require that you install ramps, wider doorways, larger restrooms, and handrails. Advocates for universal design hold that "products and environments should be usable by all people, to the greatest extent possible without the need for adaptation or specialized design" (Center for Universal Design, 1997). Child development centers adhere to this principle in that they already have materials on low shelves, handwashing sinks at child height, and several other features that make things more accessible to all children. Are these same shelves and drinking fountains accessible to children using wheelchairs or walkers? What about the blocks—are they accessible to children who cannot get down on the floor? Or can an elevated platform be installed that allows everyone to build?

Another important concern is safety. For the sake of all of the children, you will eliminate sharp corners on furniture and obstacles that might trip people; these precautions become doubly important when you enroll a child with vision impairment. The fire drill signal you have always used may not alert a child with a hearing impairment. Is there room on your bus for wheelchairs? Do you have a place to store adaptive equipment? Hearing aids, for example, often need replacement batteries, and these must be stored and disposed of safely. Children with severe physical disabilities might have a variety of "standers" for different positions, and those that are not in use must be stored out of the way so that classrooms are not cluttered.

Space must be managed to provide the additional services that children with disabilities might need. Sometimes, this means providing a separate, quiet room where speech therapy can take place away from distractions. Many therapists, however, are moving toward more integrated ways of delivering services to children. Instead of singling out the child with a disability, they might stay right in the classroom and work individually with the child or with a small group that includes children who are developing in typical, as well as atypical, patterns. Some therapists adopt a consultative model—they discuss the child's needs with the teacher or caregiver and offer suggestions of ways to modify everyday classroom routines and activities to accomplish therapeutic aims. Typical center classrooms and offices can probably meet the spatial needs of these approaches without much alteration.

Some types of disabilities require that children wear diapers or receive more help with toilet functions than their age-mates. Thus, diapering areas may have to be enlarged to accommodate the larger bodies. The diapering surface may have to be lowered to reduce the strain on the caregivers' backs, or it may have to be relocated to provide privacy for those older children whose mental and emotional maturity exceeds their physical capability.

Whatever the challenge, the center manager can find help from a number of sources. For example, the child's family has already found ways to make an ordinary house meet new and changing needs. Ask what they have done to make it possible for the child to get up close to the table.

Outdoor Play Areas

Outdoor play areas have the potential to support children's development in all domains—emotional, social, and intellectual as well as physical (Frost, Brown, Sutterby, & Thornton, 2004). To achieve this potential, however, the outdoor play area requires the same level of planning and thought as indoor spaces. In too many child-care facilities, the outdoor play area seems tacked on as an afterthought, a place where children are expected to run around and let off steam while staff members relax on the sidelines.

Safety

Safety is, of course, the primary concern, starting from the ground up:

- Tripping hazards, such as exposed tree roots, should be removed.
- An area extending at least 6 feet from all sides of any item of playground equipment where children climb or swing should be filled with cushioning material (either an approved commercial product or wood chips, mulch, sand or pea gravel). The amount or depth of cushioning required depends on the maximum height from which a child might fall.
- Minimize the likelihood of falls by ensuring that any elevated surface is enclosed by a guardrail at least 29 inches high (38 inches for school-age children).
- Make sure that any opening large enough for a child's body to slip through is also large enough for his or her head (i.e., smaller than 3.5 inches or larger than 9 inches).
- Remove or otherwise correct hardware where children might pinch their fingers in moving parts. Close S-hooks and shorten or cap protruding bolts that can snag clothing and perhaps cause strangulation (U.S. Consumer Products Safety Commission, 1997).

The U.S. Consumer Products Safety Commission publishes the *Handbook for Public Playground Safety* (1997), which provides detailed guidelines for these and all other aspects of planning, equipping, and maintaining safe outdoor play areas.

Developmental Needs

The equipment must be suited to the children's sizes and level of development. That is, it should not be too small or too large, too easy or too difficult. This is important from the point of view of safety as well as overall development of children. Equipment that is too easy or too small often inspires children to increase the challenge by using it in unsafe ways, while equipment that is too large or too difficult poses risks that children lack the skills to manage.

The outdoor play area must be tailored to the needs of each age group. Infants benefit from a variety of textures to crawl over, shady areas to protect them from harsh sun, and ground surfaces that do not scrape their tender knees—all in a space where they are not trampled by more mobile children. Toddlers need the addition of more things to walk in or on, to climb over or crawl under, to carry about. Still more challenging opportunities should be added for 3- and 4-year-old children: pedal toys, swings, skates, ropes, climbing structures, balance beams, and seesaws. Children of all ages enjoy digging in sand or dirt, though care must be taken to prevent the youngest from putting it in their mouths.

The outdoor play area must also consider the needs of children with disabilities, providing multiple ways to access and ways to use various areas. Paths must be smooth enough and wide enough to accommodate wheelchairs or other devices for physical support. All children, not only those with visual impairments, benefit when the outdoor play area is rich

A garden adds a rich dimension to the outdoor play area.

with sensory appeal: varied textures underfoot, the scent of herbs or new-mown grass, the sounds of wind in trees or home-made chimes and percussion instruments. Some children, such as those with autism, may need protected areas where they can play alone sometimes.

The Outdoor Landscape

A covered deck creates a transition between the indoor and outdoor play areas and allows children to play outdoors when rain or muddy ground might have made that impractical. Wide-open spaces where children can run with abandon and develop locomotion skills should be arranged outdoors, but there should also be outdoor places for quiet play, such as the sandbox tables for snacks or games, and easels (perhaps attached to fences) for painting. Children soon learn to play where their energy needs dictate when there are choices of quiet or active play.

Carefully selected shrubs and trees provide shade and give a variety of foliage and blooms. Bushes can serve the same purpose as low dividers inside the classroom—that is, they break up the space into smaller, more intimate areas and help control density. Some shrubs can serve as windbreaks, making the yard usable for much of the year even in colder climates. Knolls and hills make the yard more interesting and help children gain experience running over uneven surfaces. To make tricycle riding safer and more organized, a strip of concrete going around a segment of the yard is useful.

It is desirable to leave a small area without grass so children can plant a garden when spring comes. A few flowers and vegetables with short growing seasons provide opportunities to learn about plants, dig in the soil, and find earthworms. Grass must be mowed when children are indoors or not at the center because of the danger that objects may be sent flying by lawn mowers.

Water is an essential ingredient of the outdoor learning environment. In addition to gardening, children use it for moistening the sandbox, playing in mud, and washing the sidewalk or the tricycles. Both children and teachers need plenty of fresh water to drink, especially in hot weather. To avoid expensive plumbing repairs, keep the drinking fountains separate from the water sources used in the children's play so that there is no temptation to fill the drain with sand or leaves (McGinnis, 2000, pp. 60–61).

Equipment

The requirement of sufficient individual play spaces for the number of children using the playground applies outdoors as well as indoors. These spaces can be easily calculated: for example, two for a wagon and its puller, two for a push–pull swing, one for a tricycle or two if the tricycle has room for a rider on the back. If there are more than enough places, one can anticipate more harmony on the playground than if there is a shortage of equipment and related play spaces.

It is not always necessary to spend a lot of money to provide an adequate number of play spaces. Children sometimes have the most fun and spend the most time with "found" or homemade items. An empty refrigerator carton can serve as a house, a hideout for the "bad guys," or a ship at sea from one day to the next and be sent off to the recycling center when it finally falls apart. A more permanent alternative would be to enlist the help of a carpenter (perhaps a parent volunteer) to construct sturdy wooden boxes. Make sure the wood is sanded, smooth and coated with paint or varnish to prevent splinters. Some movable equipment stimulates children to create their own spaces—they may enclose an area with packing boxes or use long planks to wall off an area. Remember, too, that many of the activities that you plan for indoors can be carried on outside as well, meaning that equipment and materials can serve double duty. Children can help to choose which dress-up clothing, dramatic play props, art supplies, books, and games to take outside, and they can help gather them up when it's time to come inside.

It is important to study all options carefully before investing in large expensive items for the playground. Items designed for backyard use by one or two children can become unstable and dangerous when subjected to the heavy use of a large group of children. Even sturdy, commercial equipment can take up too much space and quickly become boring. Children need open spaces to run, skip, and pull their wagons.

Maintaining the Facility

Space that is easily kept clean contributes to the child's sense of mastery. The creation of wet and dry zones discussed earlier eliminates problem areas where children might be admonished to "be careful" or be reprimanded if they spill something. Carpeting presents special cleaning problems that must be considered before it is installed. Some centers require staff and children to wear slippers or designated "indoor" shoes when entering the classroom in order to cut down on tracked-in dirt. Professional cleaning at regular intervals, in addition to daily vacuuming and regular steam cleaning, must be scheduled at least occasionally to keep carpeting sanitary and odor-free.

Sufficient storage is closely related to the tidiness of a center. Storage should be planned for each area to ensure a place for everything and everything in its place. If you notice a large number of items lying around, it may indicate that the storage is inadequate. Children can be taught to put items away if storage is accessible to them. When the storage for equipment or materials is inadequate or inconveniently located, the staff might be tempted not to bother getting things out and the children cannot help put things away—a task that helps them learn to care for equipment. When planning for storage, a wise manager considers the children's freedom to use the equipment and the staff members' time and energy used to store it. The center's investment in equipment is at stake.

Space for Staff

Space should also be designed and furnished to meet adult needs, supporting them as they meet children's needs. Comfortable, adult-size seating makes it easier for staff members to relax and cuddle children, promoting attachment and a sense of security. Retractable stairs leading up to the diapering table reduce the risk of back injury at the same time that they support children's motor skill development and drive for independence.

In addition to the spaces they share with children, adults must have a secure place for their personal items such as handbags or wallets and clothing and a quiet, comfortable place with appropriate furniture and adequate storage, where they can attend to paperwork tasks.

The manager should have a closed-off office space for working alone and holding one-to-one conferences with parents or staff. Because this space is often the place where parents come to enroll their child, it provides them with their first impression of your center. Will that impression be one of sterility with no sign that children live and work here? Will it be cluttered and chaotic? Or will it be peaceful and businesslike with displays of the children's art and photographs of center events to convey a sense of the program's spirit? Some centers display photographs of each staff member in this space so that the parents can recognize the

Retractable stairs leading up to the diapering table support staff needs by reducing risk of back injury at the same time that they support children's drive for independence.

people with whom they leave their child each day. A conference room for larger meetings, such as staff meetings and parent meetings, is desirable. Adult restrooms should be available nearby.

A teachers' workroom with storage for classroom supplies is necessary. A washable counter with a sink where the children's paints can be mixed is highly desirable—the teachers should not have to mix paints in the children's bathroom. These materials must be kept orderly—paper supplies are a fire hazard, as are the collections of fabric and paper scrap used for art projects. Any bulk quantities of these materials should be kept in the center's storage room. As noted earlier, fire safety regulations require that storage rooms have fire-retardant walls and that the doors remain closed. You can further reduce the fire hazard by keeping these materials well organized and sorted into noncombustible containers. Only the amounts actually in use daily should be brought into the areas used by the children. Building and equipment maintenance requires a separate workroom and an array of supplies. Dangerous cleaning solvents and the like must always be kept locked away from the children.

The kitchen and food service areas must meet state requirements. Work surfaces should be easy to keep spotless. Storage should be adequate for the required supplies and kept locked to prevent the children and others from entering. Of course, art and cleaning supplies are not stored in areas designated for food.

A washer and dryer are considered a must by many managers for laundering clothing and bedding, as well as dress-up clothes, aprons, and soft toys.

A sanitary and safe place for garbage and waste disposal must be provided, along with frequent garbage removal. Employees are expected to keep the area clean and free of odors, insects, and rodents.

Smoking is prohibited everywhere in the center at all times. This prohibition applies particularly to bathrooms, conference rooms, and play areas. Prompt all visitors to deposit smoking materials in a receptacle at the door.

Managers should encourage adults to be as creative and flexible as the children as they try new ways to organize the available space. If teachers often find themselves carrying certain equipment from place to place, they might question why this is necessary. Could new storage for that equipment be planned nearer to its usual use area? Could carts or dollies be used to save the teacher's energy and give the children an experience with energy-saving equipment? Could duplicate items be purchased if the item is frequently needed in two locations? Creative solutions to spatial problems can often be found by questioning the customary usage and then developing alternatives to test. Children can help with this problem solving.

Furnishing Space

Furnishing the center's various units follows the acquisition and preparation of suitable space. Many commercial companies have booths at most professional meetings where they exhibit and demonstrate equipment and supplies for child development centers. Consequently, managers should attend professional meetings not only to hear important workshops and lectures, but also to visit the exhibits. Some of the major equipment companies are listed at the end of this chapter. Consulting other managers about their experience using particular equipment and dealing with vendors is usually helpful.

Managers might want to exercise their creativity and have some items custom built. This approach may save money and usually adds individuality to the center. Of course, care must be taken to ensure high-quality workmanship—there should be no wobbly joints or protruding bolts.

Equipping the manager's space deserves high priority because the work accomplished there makes it possible for the entire facility to function smoothly. Here the manager attends to many details related to licensing and reporting requirements, confers with parents and staff, and does the planning and organizing required so that all staff members can function effectively.

Every day it seems that a virtual blitz of paper comes into the center, and it must be filed carefully to facilitate the retrieval of the proper materials when needed. An adequate computer system is essential. A comfortable place must be arranged for conversations with visitors. A convenient space to conduct business is essential for both the manager and the secretary. To plan for furnishings, equipment, and supplies, carefully consider the tasks to be performed in each room.

Decisions, Decisions . . .

Consider the tasks to be performed by each of the following staff members: center manager, secretary, cook, and custodian. List the furnishings and supplies that should be made available in a work space for each of them. Visit a child development center and compare your lists to the items you observe.

Room Arrangement

Figure 9.1 (see p. 181) is a sample floor plan for a room intended to accommodate a mixed-age group of 8 infants and toddlers. It has direct access to the outdoor play area via a low covered deck. The room is carpeted except for the section in the middle, which houses all water-related functions and has vinyl flooring. A food preparation area opens toward the children's eating area. The bathroom is separated from the kitchen by a full-length wall and surrounded on the three other sides by half-walls so that teachers can easily keep an eye on the entire room while diapering children or helping them with toileting. Teachers can also see over the shelf that defines their work space, where two long work surfaces with room for files and storage beneath. Adult-size seating in the infant area and in the greeting and departing area provides a comfortable place for teachers to hold and read to children and encourages family members to linger with their children. A low shelf nearby contains parent information, and the wall below provides a place to display images of the children or their artwork. A large open, carpeted area is easily reconfigured with movable shelves and risers.

The sample classroom for 3- to 5-year-olds in Figure 9.2 (see p. 182) shows the use of shelves, furnishings, or dividers to help define the activity expected to take place and provide nearby storage for necessary equipment and supplies. For example, the learning center marked "Library Books" with its small table, two chairs, and two pillows sets the stage for a few children to have a quiet time looking at books. The dramatic play area has a child-sized stove, sink, and other props, which suggest a housekeeping theme for play. Blocks located in an out-of-traffic area near a rug allow a few children to build with a minimum of interference from other children. When the blocks are put away, this area serves double duty as a place to hold large-group activities. Placing tables and chairs close to a low sink allows for activities requiring water. Snacks or meals are served in this area too so that inevitable spills are easily cleaned. Adequate shelving enables the teachers to rearrange most areas in numerous ways to stimulate interest in the various activities. Lockers are conveniently close to the door to the outside play area.

As discussed in chapter 3, the theory that you choose as your program's foundation provides guidance in the selection of materials to include in the various areas. Additional ideas are available in most early childhood curriculum books, as well as in some of the resources for further study at the end of this chapter. Following are suggestions to start your own brainstorming process.

Learning Areas

Writing/Communications Area

- Table with seats for about four children
- Working typewriter or computer and printer
- Paper in a variety of sizes, weights, and colors
- Envelopes
- Pencils, markers, and pens
- Receptacles labeled with each child's name for receiving messages
- Stick-on letters
- Divided trays for sorting letters cut from newspapers
- Old greeting cards
- Stamps, stickers, and reply envelopes from junk mail
- Old checkbooks or check registers
- Blank books

Library Area

- Book display rack
- Appropriate books (including some made by the teachers and children) representing diverse ages, cultures, abilities.
- Comfortable seating (e.g., cushions, soft chairs)
- Adequate lighting
- Tape cassette player and headphones
- Tape recordings of familiar stories (commercial or teacher made)
- Storybook props (e.g., puppets, flannel boards, and figures)

Science Area

- Table or cupboard with a working surface
- Magnets and objects to pick up
- Magnifying glasses
- Prisms
- Scales
- Thermometer
- Dry-cell batteries with hookups for lights and bells

- Bulletin board and display area with interesting items (e.g., photos, insects, acorns, bones, and rocks) arranged to encourage the children to look at them on their own
- Cages, food, and water for animals if the appropriate facilities and care are available
- Field guides to birds, minerals, plants, and so forth
- Notebooks and pencils for recording observations
- Various containers for sorting and organizing collections

Block Area

- Unit blocks
- Other blocks of interest
- Block accessories—plastic or rubber figures of people and animals, small vehicles, markers and tagboard for signs, pipe cleaners and other materials for child-made accessories
- Hollow wooden blocks

Some teachers prefer reinforced cardboard blocks instead of the hollow wooden blocks for younger children because they are easier to stack and less likely to cause injury if they fall on a child. Others simply consider them more economical and are disappointed to find that they deteriorate rapidly when older children stand or walk on them.

Art Area

- Table and chairs sufficient for about six children
- Two easels
- Supplies—18-inch × 24-inch easel paper (newsprint roll ends often obtainable from newspaper shops), manila drawing paper, construction paper, pastel mimeograph paper, fingerpainting paper, wrapping paper, powdered tempera in many colors including white, wheat paste for mixing fingerpaint, liquid soap for extender, pastel chalk, large size crayons, felt markers, scissors for both left and right hand, white glue (buy a dozen small bottles and fill them from a gallon jug of glue using a plastic squeeze bottle with a pointed tip like a mustard bottle), paste brushes, easel brushes, collage materials (usually "found" materials), stapler, masking tape, and paper punch

Table Games

- Table and chairs sufficient for about six children
- Shelves and puzzle racks
- Wooden puzzles from simple to complex designs
- Lotto games
- Sorting games of various shapes, sizes, and colors
- Perceptual matching toys
- Parquetry block set
- Dominoes with both numbers and pictures
- Nested toys
- Tinkertoys and other connector toys
- Beads and strings
- Candy Land and other commercial, teacher-made, or child-made games (See Kamii, 1982).

Carpentry Area

- Work table
- Hammers (adult quality; light weight)
- Saws (variety of types)
- Vises
- Nails (variety of sizes and types)
- White glue
- Soft wood scraps (usually available at cabinet shops)
- Safety goggles
- Peg board with space delineated for hanging each tool

Music/Rhythm Area

- Simple compact disk player that children can operate
- Variety of recorded music (folk, classical, jazz, etc. in addition to "children's" music)
- Illustrated music books
- Rhythm instruments (e.g., drums, maracas)
- Xylophone

Water Play/Sand Play Table

- Child-height table with waterproof liners, permitting water or sand play for about six children; ideally separate tables for sand and water
- Unbreakable containers for pouring, measuring, or comparing amounts of water or sand
- Pipes, pulleys, and pendulums
- Sifters and waterwheels
- Small animal figures and vehicles

Dramatic Play Area
(Ideally two areas: one for representing home life and another that children can modify to recreate other types of settings)

- Child-size stove, sink, and refrigerator
- Table and two chairs
- Doll high chair
- Bed, sturdy enough for a child to lie in
- Blankets, tablecloth
- Cooking utensils, tableware, and dishes
- Grocery items stored in cupboards and refrigerator
- Dolls, male and female, with various ethnic characteristics
- Dress-up clothing representing both genders and variety of adult roles
- Several phones
- Full-length mirrors
- Literacy items typically found in homes (e.g., newspapers, magazines, telephone books, paper and pencils for grocery lists)
- Letters, stamps, and so forth to play post office

- Menus, trays, and pizza pan to play restaurant
- Rollers, play razor, and combs to play beauty/barber shop
- Tent and suitcases for camping out
- Keyboard, paper, and phones for office play

Play Yard

- Sandbox with containers for filling and shovels
- Jumping boards and sawhorses
- Packing boxes of various sizes
- Wheel toys—tricycles and wagons
- Swings, preferably the two-person cooperative type
- Ribbon of cement for tricycles to follow
- Water fountain
- Water faucet and hose
- Balls of various sizes
- Plastic bats
- Acrobat's bar
- Outdoor wooden blocks (large size)
- Garden tools—shovel, rake, and hoe
- Climbing structure with various ladders, slide, and hideouts

In addition to these activity areas, the center should provide the following spaces:

Nap Facilities

- Either in a separate room where the cots can remain set out or in a safe storage area away from the children's play
- Enough cots for each child to have one labeled with her name, or cots equal to the number of children who will be napping on any given day, which can be sanitized between uses
- A blanket for each child, labeled with the owner's name and stored apart from all of the others to avoid cross-contamination. Some centers find that bath towels serve the purpose well and are less bulky to store. If the cots are used by the same children each day, the blankets can simply be stored on the individual cots, unless they will come in contact with any part of another cot.

Isolation Space

A small space equipped to make an ill child comfortable while waiting for a parent to come is necessary. Usually, a room close to the center office enables the manager or office staff to look in on the child while attending to other duties. This space should include the following items:

- Child's cot, sheet, blanket, and pillow
- Child's chair near the cot
- Adult chair, perhaps a rocker
- A child's book or two; soft, washable, cuddly toy

Parents' Area

The objective is to provide an inviting place for a parent to wait for a child, visit another parent, or select reading material. This room could also serve as a conference room or the policy board room. If the table is large, it can accommodate the staff when assembling booklets, advertising, and so on. The following features should be part of this space:

- Table and chairs
- Bookcase with books to lend
- Bulletin board with educational exhibits
- Wastebasket
- Coffee-making supplies

Classrooms

Each teacher needs some office supplies to handle the business portions of the job. Lined tablets, scratch pads, memo pads with the center's letterhead and telephone number for notes to parents, stapler, staples, ruler, yardstick, masking tape, adhesive tape, glue, rubber cement, paper clips, scissors, pens, and pencils are necessary. Although the teachers usually do not have desks, they do need a cupboard where all of these materials can be organized and readily available. A workroom with adult tables is desirable for planning and preparation.

Conclusion

Because a carefully planned environment supports growing children and their development and learning, managers and teachers must use space well. Four basic needs should guide the planning:

1. An environment to encourage movement
2. An environment to support comfort
3. An environment to foster competence
4. An environment to encourage a sense of control

When planning the use of spatial resources, managers must consider the needs of all children, including those with disabilities, and plan for accessibility, safety, special services, and privacy of older children. Suggestions were offered for organizing space to facilitate supervision and promote positive behavior as well as to meet adults' needs and support their work. All are part of the desired balance within the center's ecosystem.

STUDY QUESTIONS

1. Given a class of 18 children, ages 3 through 5 years, calculate the required total square feet of indoor space and outdoor space using the NAEYC accreditation standards.
2. List the four basic environmental needs of young children. Give an example of how a child development center can meet each need.
3. Define and give examples of territoriality.
4. How does the concept of density apply in a child development center?
5. Define a learning center and give examples of how they are used in child development centers.

PROFESSIONAL PORTFOLIO

1. Observe and record the way children use one or more of the existing interest centers in a program where you work or where you have been assigned as a practicum student. With permission of your supervising teacher, make any changes necessary to increase the level of the children's participation and engagement. Be sure to take "before" and "after" photographs. Observe and record the children's behavior for several days after the changes are made. Write a description of what you did, including the rationale for your changes, and what happened afterward. Evaluate the effectiveness of your changes.

2. Draw up a floor plan for a staff resource center in a child development program. List the furnishings and other items (including specific books, journals, videotapes, etc.) you would include and explain your rationale. If you have access and proficiency, use a software program such as AutoCad to create your design. Calculate the cost of creating such a center and list possible suggestions for obtaining the necessary funds.

RESOURCES FOR FURTHER STUDY

Print

Curtis, D., & Carter, M. (2003). *Designs for living and learning: Transforming early childhood environments.* St. Paul, MN: Redleaf Press.

Frost, J. L. (2004). *Playground checklist.* In J. L. Frost, et al. (Eds.), *The developmental benefits of playgrounds.* Olney, MD: Association for Childhood Education International, pp. 227–231.

Isbell, R., & Exelby, B. (2001). *Early learning environments that work.* Beltsville, MD: Gryphon House.

Moyer, J. (Ed.). (1995). *Selecting educational equipment and materials for school and home.* Wheaton, MD: Association for Childhood Education International.

Internet

Program for Infant/Toddler Caregivers

http://www.pitc.org

Website of California's WestEd Program for Infant Toddler Caregivers featuring "virtual tours" of five community college child-care centers selected to serve as demonstration sites for the program's model of responsive, respectful, relationship-based care.

Spaces for Children

http://www.spacesforchildren.com

Spaces for Children is an enterprise involving collaboration of an architect (Charles Durrett) and an educational consultant (Louis Torelli) to design furnishings, classrooms, buildings, and outdoor areas that support both children and adults in child-care programs. The website includes floor plans and images of several spaces designed by the team.

Planet Earth Playscapes

http://www.planetearthplayscapes.com

Website for Rusty Keeler, a designer and consultant promoting creation of beautiful, meaningful outdoor environments for young children. Includes images depicting examples of Keeler's work on outdoor play areas for infants, toddlers, and preschool children in the United States and China; also provides a link to "The Natural Play Environment Group," an international online discussion group of designers, child care professionals and others.

FPG Child Development Institute

http://www.fpg.unc.edu/~pfi/pdfs/diversity_booklist.pdf

Diversity in Children's Lives: Children's Books & Classroom Helps. A comprehensive, annotated listing of books that feature children and adults with diverse abilities, languages, and culture.

CHAPTER TEN

Managing Health and Safety Issues

People were comforted by dozens of stories of individual courage and human compassion after the attacks on the World Trade Center and Pentagon on September 11, 2001. Along with firefighters, police, and emergency personnel, several early childhood professionals emerged as heroes on that dark day. Sue Shellenbarger (2001) reported in the *New York Times* that 14 teachers at the Children's Discovery Center (located in a building that later collapsed) evacuated 42 children safely. They followed the procedures they had practiced every month, even though they had to improvise once outside because their planned destination was inaccessible. The teachers, some barefoot as their paper booties shredded, commandeered shopping carts to transport their charges more than a mile, and passersby donated their own shirts to protect the babies from flying debris. The children were resting peacefully in a hospital and a preschool by the time their parents arrived to get them. Meanwhile, at the Pentagon, 36 child-care staffers evacuated 136 children and kept them calm through five relocations, even as the director worried about her husband, a naval officer working in the path of Flight 77. He was safe, as it turned out, but three children in the program lost a parent that day.

Planning for a Healthy Environment

These stories of heroic efforts in the face of disaster underscore the crucial importance of planning for health and safety. Above all else, parents and society trust you to keep the children safe while they are in your care. It is a trust that you and your staff members must assume with a deep sense of responsibility. As we emphasized in previous chapters, plans for a child-care facility's structure, decor, layout, equipment, finishes, and furnishings must all begin with attention to the children's safety and include provisions for maintenance and upkeep. You have seen that plans for staffing must also begin with safety and health in mind as you establish the number of staff you will need to supervise children and the skills you will expect them to have. In this chapter we will examine more closely the strategies you will need to keep your center a safe and healthy place as well as to deal with accidents or illness when they occur.

Licensing Regulations and Professional Standards

Licensing regulations are designed to ensure that child development facilities maintain children's health, prevent exposure to unhealthful conditions, and protect children from harm. They establish minimum standards for record keeping and reporting in cooperation with public health officials. Since parents usually are not knowledgeable about such details, they must depend on regulatory agencies to monitor the center. Each state establishes its own set of standards to address areas such as those listed below:

1. Certification that all staff members are free of tuberculosis
2. Permission from parents for the center to seek emergency medical care for their child
3. Requirements for immunizations, medical checkups, and a physician's statement of good health for each child
4. Prior written permission from each parent to give prescription medication to a child
5. A policy requiring that a doctor's prescription for a child's special diet be on file
6. A plan for health-care services provided by the center
7. Individual records on children's health indicators
8. A plan for reporting child abuse, protections from abuse occurring within the center, and compliance with regulations prohibiting the hiring of staff with records of child abuse
9. A plan for medical and safety emergencies
10. A plan for training staff and communicating with parents on health and safety matters

Specific requirements vary from state to state, so it is imperative that you refer to the regulations for your own state. You can find your state's current regulations at the website for National Resource Center for Health and Safety in Child Care, http://nrc.uchsc.edu.

The American Public Health Association and American Academy of Pediatrics have developed national health and safety guidelines for child-care programs (American Public Health Association & American Academy of Pediatrics, 2002). Some states model their licensing regulations on the guidelines' recommendations regarding such things as adult–child ratio. It is useful to have staff members read and discuss the guidelines as a group to completely understand what licensing requires and the necessity for the center to comply with the requirements.

The health and safety of children are significant aspects of the accreditation criteria established by the National Association for the Education of Young Children (2005). A careful reading of this chapter and a familiarity with the national guidelines will prepare you to meet the health and safety standards of the accreditation process.

Policies and Practices

A society's health-care system is part of the human-built environment. As a center manager, you contribute to the well-being of the families you serve, as well as to the survival of the program when you plan ahead and think through all of the ways that your facility can protect the children from harm and keep them healthy.

Medical Advice and Referral.   When planning the center's health-care services, the manager works closely with health professionals. The American Academy of Pediatrics recommends that every child-care facility have access to a child-care health consultant. This medical professional with specialized knowledge of pediatrics and developmentally appropriate practices for child care settings can help:

- Review and develop your policies and practices regarding health, safety, and nutrition practices
- Provide information on nutrition, feeding, and communicable diseases
- Train staff
- Develop and implement plans to care for children with special health needs
- Create connections with community resources such as health screening or mental health programs

The staff must be aware of the closest source of emergency medical treatment and the procedures for calling for help. Some centers establish contacts with the nearest hospital in anticipation of emergencies. In this way, they can be sure that the records they keep on file meet the hospital's requirements should a child require emergency treatment when a parent cannot be reached. Some hospitals require specific wording on permission forms, for example, or they might expect the center to provide health insurance information for the injured child. A manager who keeps these links open can serve the children better. Phone numbers for emergency medical service should be posted at each phone.

A Medical Home for Every Child.   The American Academy of Pediatrics asserts that every child should have a *medical home,* a term that refers not to a place, but to a concept of an approach to providing health-care services that are "accessible, continuous, comprehensive, family centered, coordinated, compassionate, and culturally effective" (American Academy of Pediatrics, 2002, p. 9). Child-care providers are in a unique position to partner with families and medical professionals to ensure that every child has a medical home. In the process of obtaining required records of physical examination and immunization upon each child's enrollment, providers quickly learn whether families have access to health care. They can help families who do not by providing information and referrals to community resources.

As teachers come to know a particular child over time, they become sensitized to changes in appearance or behavior that signal illness or potential problems. Because of their knowledge of child development and direct experience with many children, child-care providers are often able to notice cues that parents might miss. They can bring these to the parents' attention and suggest a medical evaluation. For example, teachers might be the first to notice subtle signs of unexplained hyperactivity or lethargy, either of which can be a symptom of elevated blood lead levels, a condition estimated to affect 1.6 percent of U.S. children ages 1 to 5 years (Centers for Disease Control, 2005). Observant, sensitive caregivers who keep careful records become valuable components of the child's medical home, cooperating with parents and medical professionals to safeguard health.

Primary Caregiver.   It is clear from the above discussion that one reason child-care providers can play this important role in the child's medical home is because they get to know the child over time. Thus, consistency of care is an essential component of any health plan. This consistency of care is important for all young children, but doubly so for infants and toddlers who are unable to tell you when they do not feel well. Assigning a primary caregiver responsibility for no more than four infants or toddlers provides a real opportunity for that caregiver to know those children well. This approach not only helps meet the mental health needs associated with emotional attachment, but also gives the caregiver plenty of opportunity to become familiar with the way a particular child looks and acts when she is healthy. Then, any change in activity level or appearance can be investigated as possible signs of illness. Another advantage to assigning primary caregivers is that the number of children any one caregiver contacts is reduced, thereby limiting the potential of spreading contagious diseases to all of the other children in the center.

Confidentiality. You and your staff must use the families' personal information as is expected of any professional—in confidence and only for the benefit of the parent or child. You should not permit staff members to gossip about any confidential information. Right-to-privacy laws should be kept in mind as you make any records. Expect that the parents will eventually read your notes and records and refrain from writing down anything you do not want them to see. Direct, dated observational notes are acceptable. These notes should remain without interpretation unless you are an expert. Any information about the child should be available to the parents, especially if the parents ask.

During each family's orientation, ask that any family happening, event, or crisis that could cause a change in the child's behavior be reported to the teacher. It can be a happy occurrence, such as a visit from grandparents, or a sad situation, such as a divorce or death in the family. Whoever receives the information must relay it to the appropriate teachers or caregivers to help them determine the best way to interact with the child. All such information received from the child's parents must remain confidential.

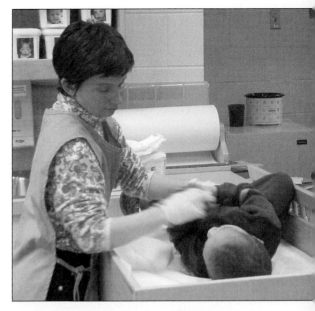

Assigning a primary caregiver to each child, and limiting the number of children each primary caregiver is responsible for, helps reduce risk of transmitting infection. Other precautions include having all supplies conveniently located near the diapering table and using disposable gloves.

Decisions, Decisions . . .

Samantha is the lead teacher in a toddler room, and primary caregiver for Brandon, a 30-month-old boy whose speech is barely intelligible. Samantha is working with Brandon's mother to arrange for an evaluation at a speech clinic. One day, the mother of another child joins the group for lunch and starts asking Samantha a lot of pointed questions about Brandon: "How old *is* he? Does he always talk like that?" What should Samantha say or do? Why? Have two members of your class role play this situation.

Risk Management

When you accept responsibility for other people's children, you inevitably incur a certain degree of risk. Accidents happen and risk cannot be eliminated; it can be reduced by adhering to good health and safety practices. Liability insurance does not protect the children's health and safety—only staff members following sound procedures can do that. Insurance simply protects the center's owners and operators from financial devastation. Most allegations of negligence come as a result of problems in the health and safety arena.

Perhaps the most important factor in protecting children's safety is adequate supervision. Children must be supervised at all times. Adult–child ratios are set by licensing authorities to ensure the children's safety. The level of supervision required depends on the children's ages. Infants and toddlers require close supervision; older children may do some things alone, although adults must still be completely aware of where they are and what they are doing.

Safe Arrival and Departure

Parents are usually responsible for the children as they are transported to and from the center. You can help protect the children by encouraging families to use seat belts and child restraint devices whenever they transport their children. The next step is to organize a safe procedure for parking. Children should not have to walk in parking lots. They are so short in stature that drivers may not see them. If there is no room to park immediately adjacent to a safe sidewalk, establish a one-way traffic circle approaching the building's entrance in a counterclockwise direction so that the car's passenger side is closest to the door.

Your records must contain the names of any people to whom the center is authorized to release a child, and staff members should require photo identification if they do not know an individual on sight. Young children cannot be expected to know who is or is not allowed to pick them up, especially if the person is a familiar and now estranged parent or grandparent. Staff members should refuse to release a child without written authorization, and families must be informed of this policy upon enrollment. It is better to cope with the momentary anger of the person you turn away than to risk releasing a child to the wrong person.

Decisions, Decisions . . .

One afternoon at your center a woman you have never seen comes in, asking to pick up her niece. She shows you her driver's license, which indicates that she has the same last name as the 1-year-old girl. Her name does not appear on the list of people authorized to pick up the child, however. What should you do?

Transporting Children

Safety precautions are essential whenever your center is responsible for transporting children. Some centers transport children to and from school each day. Others transport children only occasionally, on field trips for example. In every case, transporting children requires special preparations and precautions:

- Vehicles must be in safe operating condition and properly insured.
- Drivers must be well qualified and hold the license required for the type of vehicle used.
- There should never be more passengers (adult or children) than the vehicle is designed and equipped to hold.
- A sufficient number of adult assistants must be present to ensure that the children are under control and the driver can concentrate on driving.
- The driver as well as all passengers (children or adults) must use an approved restraint device, properly installed and used in accordance with manufacturer's specifications. For young children, up to and including most 4-year-olds, this means a special car seat when riding in a private vehicle. The U.S. Department of Transportation's National Highway Traffic Safety Administration provides specific

guidelines for use of restraint devices, which are available online at
http://www.nhtsa.dot.gov/people/injury/childps/newtips/.

- The driver should be provided with a list of children as well as emergency
information for each child.

When children are taken home, drivers must be certain that they are received by authorized people and not left on a corner or allowed to walk unaccompanied into an empty house or other potentially unsafe situation. Careful accounting procedures are necessary to ensure that no child is left in an unattended vehicle. This is especially crucial when transporting infants or children with disabilities because they may not be able to make their presence known. More than one tragic news story has reported the death of a child left all day in a parked vehicle in stifling heat.

The same type of accounting is used to ensure that no child is left behind on field trips. When parent volunteers drive, make sure that each small group stays with the same car and driver going and returning. Licensing regulations (and common sense!) require that centers secure a parental release before taking children on supervised field trips. Before each trip, parents must be informed specifically when and where the children are going.

Child Abuse

Child-care providers are legally required to report any evidence of a child's having been abused. Therefore, one of your responsibilities as a manager will be to educate your staff about the signs of abuse. Figure 10.1 gives a list of signs and symptoms that might indicate a child is being abused or neglected. Most child abuse occurs in the home. Not every bump or bruise is caused by abuse, but a pattern of recurring bumps and bruises, without plausible explanations for their sources, may be sufficient to suspect abuse. Keeping a dated record each time you observe such marks on a child, as well as any explanation you are given, is the only way you will be aware if such a pattern develops. Some centers keep such a record in a spiral-bound notebook (pages cannot be inserted or rearranged) that serves as evidence should staff be falsely accused of injuring a child.

Reporting Suspected Abuse.   Your staff will also need to know what procedures to follow should they suspect a child has been abused. If you are unsure of whom to contact, call the Childhelp USA National Child Abuse Hotline (1-800-4-A-CHILD) and make careful note of where and how to file a report in your community so you will have the information readily available should the need arise. The person who suspects the abuse should make the report to the appropriate agency. This is generally the child's caregiver; however, as manager you need to be kept informed when caregivers have reason to suspect a child is abused or neglected. Your responsibility would be to support the caregiver in making the decision to report and to document the fact that he or she did so. Although the identity of the individual making the report is confidential, families are very likely to suspect the center and may become very angry and take it out on the child's caregiver. You can help a caregiver prepare to remain calm in the event of confrontation, but you may also have to step in to defuse it. A family may even withdraw the child from care, and the staff needs to be prepared for the feelings that will evoke.

Children who have been abused may have a greater need for a relationship with a consistent caregiver and extra patience to help them reestablish their trust in adults. They may have trouble controlling their impulses and require continued, firm reminders of the center's limits. They may make caregivers uncomfortable as they work through their concerns in dramatic play. You may wish to secure the advice of mental health center personnel or other professionals if a child in your center has been abused. Some drop-in centers are specifically established to take in children whose parents are prone to child abuse and are in treatment. The parent may secure counseling nearby while the child plays in the center.

Preventing Abuse. Your first responsibility in preventing abuse from occurring in your child-care program is to hire staff who are capable of proper conduct toward children. A few recent, highly publicized cases of child abuse in child-care facilities have horrified the child-care community; however, a recent review of research in this area indicates that fewer instances of abuse occur in child-care programs than in homes or residential facilities (Fiene, 2002). Nevertheless, managers must take every precaution to ensure that such acts never occur in their centers. States have instituted clearance procedures for teachers, caregivers of young children, and family child-care operators in an effort to prevent convicted

FIGURE 10.1 *Recognizing signs of abuse or neglect*

Consider the possibility of **physical abuse**	
When the **child:**	When the **parent or other adult caregiver:**
■ Has unexplained burns, bites, bruises, broken bones, or black eyes. ■ Has fading bruises or other marks noticeable after an absence from school. ■ Seems frightened of the parents and protests or cries when it is time to go home. ■ Shrinks at the approach of adults. ■ Reports injury by a parent or another adult caregiver.	■ Offers conflicting, unconvincing, or no explanation for the child's injury. ■ Describes the child as "evil" or in some other very negative way. ■ Uses harsh physical discipline with the child. ■ Has a history of abuse as a child.
Consider the possibility of **neglect**	
When the **child:**	When the **parent or other adult caregiver:**
■ Is frequently absent from school or child care. ■ Begs or steals food or money. ■ Lacks needed medical or dental care, immunizations, or glasses. ■ Is consistently dirty and has severe body odor. ■ Lacks sufficient clothing for the weather. ■ Abuses alcohol or other drugs. ■ States that there is no one at home to provide care.	■ Appears to be indifferent to the child. ■ Seems apathetic or depressed. ■ Behaves irrationally or in a bizarre manner. ■ Is abusing alcohol or other drugs.
Note that these types of abuse are more typically found in combination than alone. A physically abused child, for example, is often emotionally abused as well, and a sexually abused child also may be neglected.	

FIGURE 10.1   *Continued*

Consider the possibility of **sexual abuse**	
When the **child:**	When the **parent or other adult caregiver:**
■ Has difficulty walking or sitting. ■ Suddenly refuses to change for gym or to participate in physical activities. ■ Reports nightmares or bedwetting. ■ Experiences a sudden change in appetite. ■ Demonstrates bizarre, sophisticated, or unusual sexual knowledge or behavior. ■ Contracts a venereal disease. ■ Runs away. ■ Reports sexual abuse by a parent or another adult caregiver.	■ Is unduly protective of the child or severely limits the child's contact with other children, especially of the opposite sex. ■ Is secretive and isolated. ■ Is jealous or controlling with family members.
Consider the possibility of **emotional maltreatment**	
When the **child:**	When the **parent or other adult caregiver:**
■ Is overly compliant or has demanding behavior, extreme passivity, or aggression. ■ Is either inappropriately adult (parenting other children, for example) or inappropriately infantile (frequently rocking or head-banging, for example). ■ Is delayed in physical or emotional development. ■ Has attempted suicide. ■ Reports or exhibits a lack of attachment to the parent.	■ Constantly blames, belittles, or berates the child. ■ Is unconcerned about the child and refuses to consider offers of help for the child's problems. ■ Overtly rejects the child.
Source: National Clearinghouse on Child Abuse and Neglect Information, U.S. Department of Health and Human Services.	

child abusers from entering child-care work. Your role is to know and follow the law carefully in this regard. Ask your licensing office for information if you do not know.

Abuse can be physical, mental, or sexual. Research indicates that the most likely form of physical abuse is excessive discipline, which may be related to a caregiver's conflict with a particular child or a family's encouragement of the use of corporal punishment (Schumacher & Carlson, 1999). Of course, no high-quality center uses corporal punishment as a form of discipline. Nor should a center tolerate mental punishment in the form of teasing, scolding, or shaming a child as a means of controlling behavior. Any teacher or caregiver who cannot handle a group of children without resorting to physical or emotional punishment should be immediately discharged. You can prevent the likelihood of having to discharge an employee by minimizing stress levels for staff: for example, provide appropriate staff–child ratios, frequent breaks, and effective staff development, focusing on developmentally appropriate practices and expectations (Daly & Dowd, 1992, cited in Fiene, 2002). You must also monitor your staff to ensure that they interact appropriately with children. One advantage to having a probation period for a new employee is that it gives you an opportunity to determine whether the employee's temperament and methods of dealing with children are compatible with high standards. Many managers require that all interior doors remain open so that staff can monitor one another. This policy also protects staff members from false accusations.

With regard to sex abuse, research indicates 60 percent of the sexual abuse in child care is done by men even though men represent only an estimated 5 percent of the staff. Perpetrators were caregivers, volunteers, janitors, bus drivers, staff family members, and outsiders. In two-thirds of all cases, the sexual abuse occurred in the facility's bathroom. Removing bathroom partitions and stalls that create private areas where children can be isolated and establishing control over who takes children into the toilet areas are two ways you can lower the risk of such abuse occurring in your center (Finkelhor, Williams, Kalinowski, & Burns, 1988, pp. 1–16).

Emergency Procedures

Risk management is not limited to accident prevention—it also includes being prepared to deal with emergencies when they occur. A legible, up-to-date list with telephone numbers for fire, police, ambulance, poison control, licensing representative, and child abuse authority should be prominently posted near each telephone. Include your home or cell telephone number as well, because emergencies may occur in your absence. It is also a good idea to display the center's name, address, and telephone number prominently on the list because the stress of an emergency could cause even well-prepared staff to experience a momentary memory block and thereby delay the arrival of help.

In any emergency, it is useful to know where the electricity breakers, water valve, and gas valve are located so these can be turned off. Keep a flashlight handy to use in case the electricity goes off, and test it regularly to be sure the batteries work.

Fire, Tornado, or Other Disasters.
Smoke alarms, tested regularly and located in each room and the exit corridor, provide an early warning in case of fire. Post a fire emergency plan in each classroom showing the quickest route from the classroom to a designated meeting area outdoors. The plan should also indicate which staff member is responsible for certain duties: leading the children out, checking to make sure no child is left behind, bringing attendance records to the meeting place. Frequent drills help ensure that each staff member and child knows what to do and can remain calm.

If a fire occurs, the children must be removed from the building immediately. Their safety is your number one priority. Adults must remain calm because the children's lives are depending on them. The children should be counted several times by different people and checked against attendance records to be sure no one is missing. Reporting the fire is second in importance. Each adult in the center should be aware of the location of the nearest fire alarm box.

Reporting a Serious Accident or Fire.
Whenever a child is injured, an accident report must be completed immediately, indicating the time, place, and people present. In addition to the manager's office, the center's insurance company and the licensing agency require the reports. Fires resulting in the loss of life or property must be reported immediately to the appropriate state official—usually the fire marshal. Check your state's licensing regulations for the fire reporting procedures.

Decisions, Decisions . . .

You have been told that monthly fire drills are recommended to ensure that all staff and children become thoroughly familiar with the routine. Four weeks have passed since your last drill and you want to have another, but it has been cold and snowing. What should you do and why?

A plan similar to the fire evacuation should be in place in case of a tornado or severe weather warning. You can get advice for your specific situation from local civil defense authorities. Generally, the rule is to go to a basement and get near inside walls, such as halls, and away from windows. Remember that if a tornado or other weather emergency occurs, the children's parents are likely miles away. They have to seek shelter where they are and depend on the center staff to give their child the best possible protection. Parents should be aware of the emergency plans so that they know where to expect to find the children and teachers. Provide this information to the parents during their orientation.

Accident or Injury.   Bumps and scrapes are an inevitable part of childhood, and their occurrence multiplies in settings where a large number of children spend their days. A special form for reporting minor blows and abrasions to parents should be devised. The report, dated and signed, should include the day and time the mishap occurred. Keep a copy for your file. At an office supply outlet, you can purchase a ledger containing perforated, self-carboned forms sometimes used to record telephone messages. The teacher tears off the top sheet (about a quarter page in size) and sends it home; the second carbon sheet remains in the ledger. Making written reports and keeping copies are essential procedures. Without them, staff members find it difficult to accurately recall the particulars of a minor incident after a long, busy day. Family members who are notified at pickup time that their child had some mishap may become upset, but their reaction is likely to be far stronger should they encounter an unexplained bruise or scrape when bathing their child later that night.

Medical Emergencies.   Some injuries require more than simply writing a note to the family. Part of your procedure for handling more serious accidents or injuries begins at enrollment when you secure the parents' permission to obtain medical treatment in the event of an emergency. State licensing regulations often prescribe specific forms for obtaining this permission as well as other emergency information. (Figure 10.2 is an example.) Handling emergencies involving children with disabilities requires more detailed information. The American Academy of Pediatrics has developed a sample form, which can be downloaded at http://www.aap.org/advocacy/blankform.pdf. Obtaining the information is important, but it is just as crucial for teachers to know what is on the emergency forms, to know where they are kept, and to have access to them at all times.

Basic First Aid Training.   All staff members should know how to treat minor injuries and to recognize when outside help is needed. This training is generally available from public health services or the Red Cross.

Cardiopulmonary Resuscitation (CPR).   It is essential to have at least one individual in the center at all times who can administer CPR. The most practical way to meet this standard is to routinely give staff members the initial training and refresher classes in CPR and first aid. Training for CPR is obtained from the American Heart Association and the American Red Cross.

FIGURE 10.2 *Emergency medical treatment consent for minors*

Dear Parent or Guardian:

This form is provided for you to leave with those responsible for your child in your absence. If your child needs emergency medical treatment during your absence, the completed form will be presented to the attending physician. Individual hospitals and medical personnel may require additional authorization. Please return this form to the XYZ Child Development Center. Report any changes to the center office.

Child's name _____ Birth date _____

Address _____

Father's name _____ Place of employment _____

Home phone _____ Work phone _____

Mother's name _____ Place of employment _____

Home phone _____ Work phone _____

Child's physician _____

Office phone _____ Home phone _____

Preferred surgeon (if any) _____

Office phone _____ Home phone _____

List any respiratory illnesses or medication allergies the child has _____

_____

List any medications the child is now taking _____

_____

List any other special illnesses (epilepsy, diabetes, etc.) _____

_____

Date of last tetanus shot _____ / _____ /   Blood type _____

Number at which parent can be reached _____

Friend or relative who can be contacted _____ Phone _____

Insurance company _____ Policy number _____

AUTHORIZATION

I hereby authorize the treatment of my minor child _____ in the event of an emergency occurring in my absence. This authorization extends to any hospital and both physician and nursing personnel within the hospital. I authorize the hospital medical authorities and physicians to perform those medical procedures deemed necessary for my minor child. If I cannot be reached in case of an emergency, please allow _____ to act in my behalf.   Name of Center

_____   _____

Signature of Parent or Legal Guardian   Date

_____   _____

Witness   Date

Employees' Health

Most states require an up-to-date tuberculosis test for all center employees. The employee should otherwise be in good health and have the physical strength to do the necessary lifting and other required physical activities. A model health assessment form for child-care staff has been developed by the American Academy of Pediatrics and American Public Health Association and can be accessed online at http://nrc.uchsc.edu/CFOC/PDFVersion/ Appendix%20E.pdf. It is desirable to provide an employee health insurance plan to enable them to consult a physician regarding their health. Paid sick leave reduces the chance that an ill staff member will expose others because she cannot afford to miss a day's pay.

Meeting Ongoing Health Needs

Once policies and procedures are established, the manager must organize a system to ensure that they are implemented consistently. A number of routine health forms may be developed and signed by the parents when a child is enrolled. Often, state licensing regulations mandate the completion of specific forms (e.g., permission to obtain emergency medical care or to administer medication to children). You will also need a system to ensure that children have the required immunizations for their age at the time of enrollment and that their immunizations are kept up to date in accordance with the recommendations of the American Academy of Pediatrics (APHA/AAP, 2002b, p. 415). Forms to help you monitor this may be provided by your state or local health department as part of its monitoring system.

In addition to securing the necessary documents, meeting ongoing health needs requires routine application of standard (or universal precautions) outlined by the Centers for Disease Control and Prevention. All bodily fluids (such as blood, vomit, urine, or feces) should be thoroughly cleaned up with soap and water and then the surface sanitized with a solution of one-quarter cup of chlorine bleach per gallon of water or one tablespoon of bleach per quart of water. The solution should be mixed fresh daily, stored in a labeled container, and kept out of the children's reach. Ideally, the surface should then be allowed to air dry.

This procedure also applies to toys that have been mouthed by children and thereby contaminated with saliva. This precaution is of special concern in infant and toddler groups where mouthing is an expected behavior. One center has colorful plastic buckets suspended out of children's reach where a staff member can quickly put a toy that has been mouthed until it is put through the dishwasher and disinfected. Such procedures reduce the spread of germs and increase the staff's awareness of health conditions. Centers can further reduce the transmission of germs by using the same solution to sanitize faucet handles, toys, and table surfaces frequently.

Probably the greatest line of defense against germs is proper handwashing (by children and adults) upon entering the classroom, after using the toilet, before eating or preparing food, and after coughing, sneezing, or using a tissue. (Staff should also wash their hands after helping children with diapering, toileting, or nose-blowing.) Proper handwashing means using soap and warm running water, lathering for at least 10 seconds, rinsing thoroughly, and drying with a disposable towel.

Meeting Children's Physiological Needs

It is the center's responsibility to ensure that each child's basic physiological needs regarding nutrition, digestion, elimination, respiration, and circulation are met daily. All of these systems are interrelated and require an equilibrium or balance. For example, the body needs adequate and appropriate food to be well nourished. Chapter 11 will examine the topic of

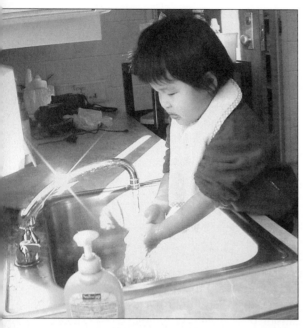

Teaching children to wash their hands frequently, especially after toileting and before meals, is part of a developmentally appropriate curriculum.

nutrition in detail. The timing, amount, and type of food, intake of fresh water or other beverages, and exercise all influence digestion and elimination. Exercise, fresh air, and rest are related to respiration and circulation.

Consistent routines for eating, resting, eliminating, and exercising help children develop habits that contribute to their overall physiological health and well-being. Research has demonstrated a positive correlation between healthy lifestyles in early childhood and higher quality of life in adolescence (Chen, Sekine, Hamanishi, Yamagami, & Kagamimorig, 2005). Teachers quickly become aware of the individual differences in the children's physiological functioning and set the stage so that the children can independently take care of their own needs as soon as they are ready.

In addition to meeting children's needs, the staff should provide the parents with the details of how that was accomplished throughout the day via a written record that indicates feeding times, bowel movement (s), and naps. This is especially helpful with infants and young toddlers, for whom the daily note also might report special milestones the child has reached (e.g., stood alone, spoke a new word, walked 10 feet). In some states, these and other written records are required by licensing regulations.

Activity and Rest

As discussed in the previous chapter, equipment, both indoors and outdoors, must be developmentally appropriate and challenging enough to encourage children to take healthy risks; the children should not be permitted to use inappropriate equipment in unsafe ways. If you find yourself constantly reminding the 4-year-olds to "go down the slide on your bottom," it could be that they are bored with the available toddler-sized climber and are simply trying to create a more interesting challenge for themselves.

Allow plenty of time for outdoor play every day so that the children can breathe fresh air and exercise their lungs and muscles. Typically, programs remind the families to provide appropriate clothing for such play and set reasonable guidelines (e.g., wind-chill factor, not staff preference) for determining when to stay inside. A nutritious snack replenishes energy needs after a busy hour or two of play. To help children rest and recuperate after a period of active play, teachers might plan a restful activity such as story time. A high-quality program balances active, less active, and quiet play. However, because energy levels differ among children or even within a single child from day to day, teachers' expectations should be flexible, allowing one child to engage in a restful activity, such as listening to records, while others enjoy more vigorous play. With such a plan, the children can choose the activity most suited to their current need.

In a short-day program, the need for rest is usually met by having a quiet snack, story time, or singing time. Making children lie down on mats is not recommended because the time spent getting them to comply is often less than restful. However, in a full-day program, a planned resting period is needed and most children will sleep during this time. Many full-day children arrive early and are ready for a nap after lunch. To be refreshed and restored for another round of play and interaction, they need an hour or so of sleep about midday. Some centers put children who actually sleep in rooms apart from those children who only rest quietly. This practice applies particularly when older children are in attendance.

Although all children need a quiet period to rest and recuperate from a busy morning, the amount of actual sleep required varies with the individual and often depends on how much sleep the child gets at home.

Usually, nap time follows immediately after lunch and toileting. Keeping a low-key atmosphere in a darkened room helps the children sense that quiet behavior is expected. By receiving quiet personal attention, each child is encouraged to get ready for a nap without dawdling. Teaching children to breathe deeply with their eyes closed and to think about what they will do after resting is usually all that is needed to get them to relax and fall asleep. Some caregivers sing a personalized song to the child as soon as she arrives on the cot—a positive reward for getting ready quickly. In other centers, caregivers gently rub the children's backs or softly stroke their heads to help them relax. Nap time should never become a battle of wills; rather, it should be a pleasant respite for children and staff alike. If problems occur, the manager should make suggestions to help the situation. Bed-wetting should be handled tactfully without scolding or shaming the child.

The nap room must be equipped with a washable cot or crib and appropriate sheets and blankets for the exclusive use of each child. Sheets should be laundered each week or whenever they become wet or soiled. The opening between crib railings must be narrow enough to prevent entrapment of babies' heads, and they should be high enough that children cannot climb over them. To reduce the risk of sudden infant death syndrome (SIDS), infants should always be put to sleep on their backs, on a firm mattress that fits snugly against all sides of the crib.

Managers must give special attention to providing adequate supervision for napping children. There should be sufficient staff on duty to safely evacuate the sleeping children in case of a fire or tornado. All cribs and cots and other furnishings must be placed so that the fire exits are free. Rooms must be equipped with smoke detectors. At least one crib should be small and sturdy enough to be pushed out a door in case of an evacuation. Several sleeping infants can be easily moved this way.

A cot with clean bedding, a cuddly toy, and a chance to wind down with a favorite book make nap time pleasant for children and their teachers. Cots nestled against a wall or a piece of furniture, rather than in the middle of an open space, enhance feelings of security.

Diapering Infants

When centers enroll infants, diapering procedures must be carefully planned and executed to prevent the spread of contamination by feces. The type of diapers to use in child development centers has come into question. Some argue that disposable diapers are costly and that depositing untreated feces in landfills is problematic. National health and safety guidelines state that either disposable diapers with an absorbent filling or cloth diapers with a waterproof covering are acceptable—if the cloth diaper and waterproof covering are removed together and neither part is used again before being sanitized. In other words, caregivers should not put the same pair of plastic pants back on the child after they change the diaper underneath (APHA/AAP, 2002b, pp. 91–92). Therefore, center managers can take factors, such as cost or environmental concerns, into consideration when they decide between these two alternatives.

Always use a diapering table, not the carpet or any other surface, for changing babies. The table surface must be cleaned and disinfected after each use, whether or not a disposable paper cover was used. After changing the diaper, the caregiver's hands as well as the child's must be washed thoroughly and a paper towel used to turn the faucet off to avoid recontamination. Better yet, install a faucet that is operated by a pedal. Soiled diapers must be placed in a sealed container (for laundry pickup or for disposal) immediately. Disposable gloves are not a substitute for handwashing and, if improperly used, may actually be a source of contamination. Furthermore, some adults and children suffer serious allergic reactions to latex.

Ensure that staff members realize how important it is for primary caregivers to diaper their own children and to talk to the infants and respond to communication cues from the babies while they are doing so. This eye-to-eye contact provides an opportunity for the infant to develop a trust in the caregivers. It helps babies feel important to those caring for them and to practice communicating with others. Children are not machines, and assembly-line techniques, such as having one person diaper all the children, may seem efficient on the surface while they are actually be counterproductive. How much more efficient it is to meet a child's needs for intimacy, attachment, language stimulation, and cleanliness—all through the simple act of diapering. How inefficient it is to have to close a center because one child's shigella diarrhea has been spread to everyone, staff and children alike!

Toilet Training

For toddlers, the manager and staff must confer with the parents to reach agreement on when the child is ready to be toilet trained and the techniques to be used. This coordination with the parents is absolutely essential so that the children face similar expectations and routines at home and at school. Even the words to be used for urinating and defecating have to be discussed.

Most professionals feel that if toilet training is started only after the muscle and nervous systems are sufficiently mature, a child can become responsible for independent toileting faster and more easily. Parents may push for toilet training before you feel it is develop mentally appropriate. They may believe that it is an adult's responsibility to anticipate a child's need to urinate or defecate and to get the child on a potty chair in time. They may not realize that what is possible when caring for one child whom you have known since birth is more difficult when caring for four (or more) children with whom you are less familiar. You must be sensitive to their concerns as you try to reach a consensus about what is appropriate for their child.

Helping children accept and adjust to their changing bodies is a basic developmental task that continues from birth through life. Children are very interested in learning about their bodies and how to take care of themselves. Good health habits relating to urinating, defecating, washing hands, and eating must be established during the early years. During the course of teaching these routines, questions about the genitalia may arise. These questions should be accepted and answered at the child's level of understanding. No shame should be attached to a child's questions or explorations. Self-manipulation of genitalia is a common behavior among young children. It is also harmless; thus, the child should not be admonished for doing it. At times, there may be chapping or a rash in the genital area that needs a simple cleaning and baby lotion to heal. Staff members might require help understanding these issues because old myths and practices may have been part of their upbringing. Be sure they are not shaming the children.

Decisions, Decisions . . .

A 4-year-old boy in your center has toilet accidents several times each week. The lead teacher in his room has started confining him to a time-out chair after each incident. What would you say to this teacher as the program manager? Discuss with your classmates.

Parental Responsibility for Children's Health

Because children are generally exposed to many groups and public places in addition to attending a center, the center cannot be held responsible for all of the children's illnesses. But the center is responsible for establishing and enforcing policies to eliminate as much as possible children's exposure to communicable illness. Parents are more likely to cooperate with you in this effort if you communicate clearly the reasons behind your policies and emphasize that you are trying to protect their child as well as all the others.

National health and safety guidelines specify that children should not be at the center when they are too sick to join in the activities; when caring for them makes it impossible to care for the other children adequately; or when any of the following conditions exist: fever over 101°F, indications of severe illness such as lethargy or wheezing, uncontrolled diarrhea, repeated vomiting, mouth sores with drooling, rash with fever or behavior change, conjunctivitis with discharge, scabies or head lice, tuberculosis, impetigo, strep infections, chicken pox, mumps, pertussis, or hepatitis A. Once the child has received treatment or the infectious period has passed, as confirmed by medical personnel, the child may be readmitted.

Even parents who want to cooperate with these prohibitions may be tempted, if their job hangs in the balance, to claim that a fever is caused by teething, for instance, or that the diarrhea is the result of too many blueberries the night before. You can help prevent these occurrences by making your exclusion policies clear at the time of enrollment and by providing ongoing opportunities for parents to learn more about health issues. Your center health consultant can help you, perhaps by giving talks to groups of parents or by providing information you can pass on to them. A publication, *Caring for Our Children* (APHA/AAP, 2002), gives a detailed rationale for each of the recommended standards. Becoming familiar with this information will help you explain your policies to parents and bolster your confidence that you are acting in the best interest of children.

You can also work with families to devise a plan for what they will do in case of the child's illness. In two-career families, the plan may involve sharing the responsibility of picking up their ill child. In other cases, the parent may be able to enroll the child in a service such as the network of family child-care providers or a hospital-based center. The Community Coordinated Child Care Association or a similar agency in your locale may be able to provide a variety of resources that you can share with parents.

When Children Become Ill

In spite of your best efforts, you will eventually be faced with a child who becomes ill at the center. Although traditional nursery schools, and the public schools of yesteryear, often had a nurse on staff to conduct daily health inspections, few of today's centers have that luxury. Therefore, your staff must be trained to recognize the signs and symptoms of illness—fever, unexplained rashes, or lethargy. A 3-year-old might be able to tell you that she vomited last night, but an infant must rely on your power of perception. Ongoing training in these skills is required by the national health and safety guidelines.

A child who becomes sick during the day must be isolated from the other children until a parent arrives. Children must be supervised while isolated, and they often need special attention from a staff member to help them feel secure at this time. In addition to a quiet, secluded place where the child can wait to be picked up, the center needs accurate information to reach a parent or another emergency contact person. It is important that parents understand the need to inform you of any changes in the location, schedule, or telephone number of their place of employment, as well as any changes in the emergency contact information. Obsolete information is as good as no information at all, as is information locked in an office file cabinet and inaccessible to staff who might be faced with a sick child when you are not there.

Some health professionals argue that mildly ill children who are no longer contagious should be cared for in their regular center. They reason that the sick child has already infected others during the disease's incubation period and that excluding the child from the regular center only increases the chance that a desperate parent will simply take the child to another (unsuspecting) center and infect more children.

Readmission After Illness

NAEYC accreditation criteria require that a written policy specifying the limitations on admitting sick children be established. This policy should be clearly stated in your handbook for families and discussed along with all your other policies upon enrollment. Many centers find it useful to have families sign a statement of understanding and agreement with the center's policies.

The NAEYC criteria indicate that children with a fever of 101°F, diarrhea, contagious illness, or head lice should be excluded. However, the criteria also indicate that the children may no longer be contagious once symptoms appear. Thus, if a center has appropriate staff to care for such children, they could be admitted (Bredekamp, 1991, p. 49). Some conditions require a medical evaluation. Although some centers routinely require a physician's statement before they will readmit a child, this practice could place an undue burden on the time and finances of working parents. Your health consultant can help you decide exactly what is needed to readmit a child after various illnesses. Such discretionary decision making requires consultation with local health authorities, as well as your licensing agency. More detailed guidelines on the reasons for exclusion and the readmission conditions can be found in *Caring for Our Children* (APHA/AAP, 2002, pp. 124–130).

With some conditions, such as head lice, a child may be readmitted once appropriate treatment has been administered. Treatment includes thoroughly washing all linens, clothing, or toys that have come in contact with the infected child(ren)—at home and at the center. Items that cannot be washed can be sealed in airtight plastic bags for two weeks. As with an infectious disease, parents should be informed so that they can watch for symptoms in their own child. Center staff should also monitor all children for signs of infestation and be especially vigilant about cleaning dress-up clothing.

Whether or not you allow mildly ill children to remain at your facility, if the illness becomes serious or a child is injured, you must have a plan to get the child to the nearest hospital or emergency facility. The plan must provide for a staff member to stay with the child until the parents arrive and provide for backup care for the children who remain at the center. Figure 10.2 (see p. 208), the emergency medical care permission form, has space for emergency contact information.

In some communities centers have been established specifically to care for sick children—a response to working parents' needs. Because this type of care is beyond many teachers' professional expertise, it may require specialized personnel. Caring for sick children is an expensive service because of the special facilities and personnel required. Other communities are experimenting with a system in which family child-care providers are paid to reserve a certain number of spaces for sick children. Parents pay to enroll their children in the network, and families meet with providers in advance. Then, when an illness arises, parents have the peace of mind that comes with knowing that there is a place for their child, and the children are not placed with a total stranger while feeling sick and vulnerable. Another option might be for a center manager to maintain a list of caregivers (perhaps a substitute list or applicants waiting for full-time openings at the center) who could be sent into the sick child's home to provide care.

Children with Disabilities and Chronic Medical Problems

As a center manager, you are not only concerned with protecting the health and safety of the children in general, but you must also be prepared for the special health needs of children with disabilities or chronic medical problems. The key to your successful response to this challenge is your ability to form a partnership with the parents and health professionals. You must educate yourself and your staff and establish procedures to make the center a safe and healthy place for all children. Your greatest asset is knowing and trusting that others will help. The burden is not yours alone.

The national health and safety guidelines (APHA/AAP, 2002) provide assistance with developing a service plan for children with special needs and coordinating services between the various components of the health, education, and social services systems involved. Some considerations for special equipment and space needs were discussed in chapter 9.

Once the plan, the space, and the equipment are in place, your staff must acquire the knowledge and skills necessary to accommodate special feeding, toileting, or respiratory needs. Some disabilities involve difficulty swallowing, and staff have to be alert for choking. Other conditions might involve catheterization or suctioning, and the staff must be trained to carry out these procedures. Depending on the nature of the disabilities involved, staff may have to know how to handle seizures (remaining calm and removing hazards from the child's vicinity) and when to call for medical help if the seizures become uncontrollable.

Although estimates vary regarding the number of children in the United States afflicted with chronic medical problems, the likelihood of your center having such children is very high (Frieman & Settel, 1994). As manager, therefore, you must ensure that your staff can recognize the signs of an asthma attack and that they know how to help a child calm down and regain control of her breathing. With a diabetic child, staff must be alert for the symptoms of low blood sugar and be prepared to assist with sugar cubes, fruit juice, or hard candies and to call for medical help if the child does not respond to these interventions. Children with sickle cell anemia are subject to painful episodes triggered by exertion. When an attack occurs, teachers should comfort and quiet a child until parents can be summoned.

The key to handling all of these situations lies in planning. Decide ahead of time who will be responsible for helping the child in crisis, who will go or call for help, and who will attend to the other children.

Because more than 1 in 10 newborn babies have been exposed to drugs or alcohol during pregnancy (California Department of Education, 1994, p. 1), it is likely that such a child will be in your center. Like all children, they exhibit individual differences and do not conform to stereotyped preconceptions. Some infants have to be swaddled and held or rocked in special ways; some young children have a greater need for stability and predictability in their environment. Careful consultation with the families and medical professionals will help you and your staff learn the most effective ways of assisting each child.

Acquired immune deficiency syndrome (AIDS) is another health problem that early childhood professionals confront, although intervention efforts nationwide have succeeded in dramatically reducing the incidence of AIDS in babies (Santora, 2005). Even if no child in your center is infected, however, you may encounter the disease in one of your caregivers or a child's family member.

Hepatitis B is another virus, transmitted via blood or infected bodily fluid, that is of growing concern to public health officials because of the increasing number of carriers—particularly children adopted from parts of the world where the virus is widespread.

Your role as manager is to seek out accurate, up-to-date information to combat the fear and ignorance that surround these diseases. Train your staff to practice universal precautions described earlier in this chapter.

Staff and families may worry about the risk that ill children pose to others at the center. Although the child with hepatitis B who bites other children does pose a health risk, it is actually the adults or children with HIV who require extra protection from exposure to normal childhood illnesses because of their depressed immune systems. If they are exposed to measles or chicken pox, for example, they should be immediately referred to their health-care provider for follow-up (APHA & AAP, 2002, pp. 304–305).

A large part of your program's responsibility involves helping all of the children and families understand and respond appropriately to children with disabilities or chronic medical problems. Of course, confidentiality must be protected. If you are not able to ensure confidentiality, families may not share needed information with you. Sometimes, when a disability or medical problem is visibly obvious, caregivers prohibit the other children from mentioning it in a misguided attempt to spare someone's feelings or (more likely) to avoid dealing with their own discomfort. For the same reasons, adults sometimes ignore or gloss over a child's comments about his disability, illness, or fears. It is more helpful for all concerned to acknowledge these comments openly and to discuss the various conditions matter-of-factly with all of the children. Parents might also benefit from such a discussion at parent meetings.

Sooner or later, all early childhood professionals are called on to respond to the children's feelings and questions about the death of a pet or the classroom guinea pig. Someone may lose a grandparent while enrolled in your center. Somehow, these losses seem part of the natural scheme of things. Helping children and families confront the death of a child or family member is likely to be much more challenging for you and your staff. Just as with disabilities or illnesses, you have to confront your own feelings first. Then, you can provide the necessary factual information, reassurance, and comfort. You may wish to tell the parents what you are saying to the children so that they can give the same information at home if the child asks.

Consult the agencies and suggested readings listed at the end of this chapter for additional information about disabilities and chronic medical problems. As a center manager, you are in a unique position to provide needed education and model compassion and common sense for the entire community in the face of these challenges.

Prescription Medications

Ideally, all medication would be administered to children by their own family members while the child is at home. Sometimes, however, a condition requires medication during the time the child is in your care. For the protection of the child as well as that of your staff members, you will need a written policy stating clearly when, and under what conditions, your staff will undertake this task. Because regulations vary from one state to another, you should work closely with your health consultant to develop your policy for administering medication. The following are basic considerations:

- Will you administer only prescription medication, or will you also administer over-the-counter treatments, such as diaper creams or cough syrups? (Note that sunscreen is also treated as a medication.) If the latter, how will you ensure that the medication is, in fact, appropriate for the child in question?

- What written information and instructions will you require from parents? Again, states vary in the precise wording required, but certainly the parental permission must specify the name of the child, the name of the medication, the amount, and the method and time(s) for administering it.

- Does your state require special training for any individual administering medication? Identifying one person, with a back-up in case of absence, to administer all medication can help prevent the possibility that a child will either miss a dose or be given too much medicine. What steps will you take to ensure that the parents' instructions are appropriate for the child (i.e., that they comply with a physician's orders and match the instructions on the label)?

- Do you have a plan for storing medication safely (e.g., out of reach of children, under refrigeration if needed, and where it cannot accidentally contaminate food)?
- How will you document each dose, including the time and person administering it? How long will you keep this documentation on file?

The same precautions (written permission, careful labeling, etc.) apply to sunscreen and diaper ointments.

Health Education for Children and Their Families

In addition to protecting children's health while they are in care, a high-quality child development program teaches children good health habits that last a lifetime. These include:

- Washing hands after going to the toilet or covering a cough and before eating
- Using a sleeve-covered arm or shoulder instead of a hand to cover a cough
- Brushing teeth after meals
- Eating a variety of nutritious foods
- Becoming comfortable with the idea of visits to doctor and dentist through dramatic play

Supporting the parents and guiding them as they teach their children good health habits is part of the center's responsibility. Literature on health-related topics is widely available through your local health department or organizations such as the American Academy of Pediatrics. Health-care workers in your community may also be willing to come and speak at a parent meeting.

Meeting Children's Mental Health Needs

A discussion of children's health needs is not complete without mentioning their mental health needs. Child-care professionals support children's mental health when they:

- Promote the development of relationships that foster security and attachment by arranging for children to stay with a consistent caregiver over time
- Develop strong connections with families so children know that the important adults in their lives respect and care about each other
- Provide warm, loving interactions that promote development of a positive self-concept
- Provide plenty of time for children to do what they do best—that is, to play—and provide appropriate challenges so that children develop strong feelings of self-efficacy
- Recognize the importance of eating, toileting, and dressing as opportunities to meet both physical and mental health goals

When children learn to clean up their own spills, they help maintain a safe, healthy environment and develop their own feelings of self-efficacy.

- Use positive guidance with the goal of promoting self-discipline and never punishment to control children's behavior
- Help families see their children in a positive light by pointing out increasing abilities or sharing important accomplishments
- Provide opportunities for families to learn more about child development behavior, from "experts" as well as from other families

Helping Children Cope with Catastrophic Events

As illustrated by the anecdote at the beginning of this chapter, well-planned emergency procedures that are practiced regularly can save lives and help both staff and children remain calm during a disaster. Moreover, early childhood professionals have a responsibility for the children's psychological and emotional safety, not just their physical safety. Sometimes, as in the aftermath of the terrorist attacks of September 11, 2001, even children who have not directly experienced the traumatic event are deeply affected. Symptoms can include increased anxiety, exaggerated fears, acting-out behaviors such as tantrums or aggression, crying, clinging, whining, and physical aches and pains (Hogan & Graham, 2001, p. 3). Children with none of these obvious symptoms might reveal their fears or confusion during their play.

Adults who believe that children are unaware of frightening events may avoid the topic or try to distract children who ask questions. Most experts, however, agree that these efforts to protect children are misguided (Council for Professional Recognition, 2001, October; Hogan & Graham, 2001). Children are comforted by the knowledge that they can talk about their fears with at least one important person in their lives. Without overemphasizing the issue, adults can invite children to say or draw what they understand. They can listen without judging, and provide clarification and reassurance later. Adults must ensure that the children experience the stability of a predictable schedule at their child-care center and that they know the teachers will keep them safe. Perhaps, most importantly, adults can help put some fun back into the children's lives with a few special projects or activities.

Monitoring Health and Safety Conditions

Monitoring and controlling for quality is a vital aspect of managing health and safety issues. Ongoing vigilance is necessary to ensure that all policies and procedures are being implemented as planned and to determine when those policies and procedures should be changed. To assess the health and safety performance of your center, make a list such as that shown in Figure 10.3 and review it at least once a month. That way you can catch small problems before they turn into large ones. If you notice a pattern of problems in the same areas from month to month, you can bring it up at a staff meeting or perhaps enlist the assistance of your health consultant to achieve a more long-lasting correction.

Conclusion

Both parents and society trust you to keep children safe from harm. This chapter discussed the health of teachers and caregivers, the ways that centers can protect the health and safety of all children, and the ways they can work with the families and other professionals to meet the needs of children with disabilities or chronic health problems. Policies and practices relating to immunizations, medical examinations, medications, observations and record keeping, and the exclusion and readmission of ill children have been suggested.

FIGURE 10.3   *Monitoring health and safety conditions*

✓	Check Each Item Observed	Comments or Corrections Needed
	Written health and safety policies reviewed with all staff upon hiring and at least annually thereafter	
	Health and safety policies included in handbook for families; reviewed before enrollment	
	Emergency procedures for fire, tornado, and accident or injury posted; parents informed	
	Emergency telephone numbers posted (fire, police, ambulance, poison control, child abuse, director)	
	Permission to seek emergency medical treatment on file for each child; current contact information	
	Medication administered only with written permission of parents; physician's instructions; documented	
	Written health and emergency plans in place for each child with disability or chronic illness	
	Compliance with fire regulations maintained (date inspected _____; corrections made)	
	Smoke detectors and fire extinguishers in place and maintained	
	Fire drills conducted monthly; staff trained in evacuation plans for tornado; chemical spill; other	
	Compliance with sanitation regulations maintained (date inspected _____; corrections made)	
	No indoor hazards (e.g., water temperature at outlets accessible to children 120° or less; electrical outlets covered)	
	Cleaning supplies, medications, staff belongings, other hazardous materials stored away from children	
	Cribs meet safety standards (slats at least $2\frac{3}{8}$ inches apart; fitted mattress; no protruding corner posts	
	No choking hazards (e.g., toys less than 1 inch diameter; popcorn, peanuts, hotdogs, whole grapes)	
	Separate sinks for food preparation, handwashing, and other activities; sanitized regularly	
	Handwashing procedures posted; followed by staff and children before handling food, after contamination	
	Sanitation solution proper strength, mixed daily; used regularly on tables, counters, toys, etc.	
	Outdoor play area free of hazards: sharp edges, protrusions more than 1 inch, entrapment (openings smaller than $3\frac{1}{2}$ inches or larger than 9 inches)	
	Railings in place to prevent falls from climbing equipment; adequate cushioning in fall zone	

Safety precautions during the transportation of the children were outlined, as well as measures for preventing and reporting child abuse.

QUESTIONS FOR REVIEW

1. Where do health and safety fit in the human ecological system of a community?
2. What safety and emergency preparations are required for licensing a child development center?
3. What plans must the manager have in place to protect children's health?
4. Name and describe the special forms parents must sign that give center staff permission to serve the children's medical needs.
5. Describe the steps for proper handwashing to prevent spread of germs.
6. List the child's physiological needs that staff must meet. List any necessary precautions related to serving these needs.
7. Discuss child abuse and the recommendations for protecting children that must be followed.
8. Discuss the necessary precautions and requirements related to transporting children.
9. In what ways may the children's mental health be protected in a center?

PROFESSIONAL PORTFOLIO

1. Find out what requirements your state has for administering medication to children while in child care. Write a sample policy that meets those requirements and could be included in a parent handbook.
2. Use database software to create a checklist of the health forms a center must collect for each child enrolled. (Some community health departments furnish providers with such forms on disk, or you could write to commercial vendors of child-care data management programs and request a preview.) Print out a sample report and add a cover sheet explaining how you would monitor the health records in a program that you manage. For example, in addition to recording immunizations at the initial enrollment, how would you document that children had received subsequent immunizations according to the recommended schedule?

RESOURCES FOR FURTHER STUDY

Print

Coleman, J. G. (1993). *The early intervention dictionary.* Rockville, MD: Woodbine House.

Health and safety topics for early childhood educators (2004, March) *Young Children 59* (2), entire issue.

Internet

National Resource Center for Health and Safety in Child Care
http://nrc.uchsc.edu
National Resource Center for Health and Safety in Child Care (NRC), a project of the University of Colorado Health Science Center and the Maternal and Child Health Bureau of the U.S. Department of Health and Human Services. Provides links to online version of latest edition of *Caring for Our Children* and the companion document, *Stepping Stones to Using Caring for Our Children;* current licensing and regulation information for each state; and other health and safety-related resources for child-care providers.

National Dissemination Center for Children with Disabilities

http://www.nichcy.org

National Dissemination Center for Children with Disabilities, operated by the Academy for Professional Development and funded by U.S. Department of Education's Office of Special Education Programs; provides information on specific disabilities, related legislation, and research-based practices; available in English and Spanish as well as via a BrowseAloud text reader.

National Clearinghouse on Child Abuse and Neglect Information

http://nccanch.acf.hhs.gov/pubs/reslist/rl_dsp.cfm?rs_id=5&ratechno=11-11172

National Clearinghouse on Child Abuse and Neglect Information, part of the Administration for Children and Families, U.S. Department of Health and Human Services; lists toll-free and local telephone numbers as well as websites for reporting suspected child abuse in each state.

Healthy Child Care America

http://www.healthychildcare.org

Website for the Healthy Child Care America campaign of the American Academy of Pediatrics. Includes sections for families, child-care providers and health professionals and links to free materials on child health issues as well as contact information for the Healthy Child Care American representative in each state.

It Pays to Prepare

http://nrc.uchsc.edu/RESOURCES/VAEmergencyPreparBro.pdf

It Pays to Prepare! An Emergency Preparedness Guide for Child Care Providers. Developed by the Virginia Department of Health; includes guidelines for evacuation plans, emergency kits and supplies, handling medical emergencies and communicable diseases, and staff responsibilities.

Managing Food Service

ronically, in a country where millions of children live in poverty and go to bed hungry at least part of the time, millions of others are either obese or somewhat overweight. Whether you are dealing with homeless and hungry children or with children at risk for health problems because of obesity, as a center manager, you must devote considerable attention to providing the food that the children must have today and fostering the healthy eating habits that they need for a lifetime.

Planning Meal Service

The number of meals children consume at a child-care facility varies with the length of time they spend there: Those in short-day programs generally have a snack, while those in full-day programs have breakfast, lunch, and snacks in the morning and afternoon. Some centers require parents to send sack lunches or snacks with their children, some provide all the meals, and others fall somewhere in between, perhaps providing snacks and milk but requiring families to provide the lunch.

Regardless of who furnishes the food, providing young children with adequate nutrition for growth and body maintenance requires a great deal of planning. Proper nutrition is necessary for all areas of a child's development—physical, mental, social, and emotional. And proper sanitation is necessary to prevent illness. This chapter outlines the ways that centers meet nutrition and sanitation requirements when they provide the food. The same considerations apply when centers serve food that parents provide: It remains a center responsibility to ensure that the snacks or lunches are safely stored (refrigerated if necessary) and, when they are nutritionally inadequate, to provide supplemental foods.

Parents and teachers generally have a number of goals for each child:

1. To eat a well-balanced nutritious meal
2. To enjoy mealtime with friendly people
3. To taste, and ultimately enjoy, a wide variety of foods

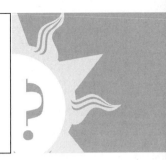

Decisions, Decisions . . .

Suppose you are a manager of a child development program struggling to make ends meet financially. One of your board members suggests that you discontinue providing snacks and lunches for the children as a way of balancing the budget without raising fees for families. Discuss the pros and cons of this decision with your classmates.

4. To learn to eat independently
5. To sit at the table and develop acceptable table manners
6. To develop an understanding that good food is related to growing and being strong and healthy
7. To see a connection between the foods eaten at home and those eaten at school

Of course, serving a highly nutritious menu does not guarantee that each child will eat a nutritious meal. Careful guidance helps children learn to eat, and eventually enjoy, a variety of foods. Eating a wide range of foods is considered an important factor in being well nourished throughout life.

Meeting Regulations and Professional Standards

Because many factors must be considered when developing a good food service program, it is essential that adequate time be devoted to planning. The national health and safety guidelines (APHA/AAP, 2002), National Association for the Education of Young Children (NAEYC) accreditation criteria, and state licensing regulations all require that child-care facilities adhere to recommended standards regarding the types and amounts of foods to be served, the conditions under which food is prepared and stored, involvement of families, and plans for handling emergencies or special dietary requirements. Specific requirements for nutritional content of meals have been established by the U.S. Department of Agriculture (USDA) and the Child and Adult Care Food Program (CACFP).

Federal Subsidies for Food Programs

Child development centers and family child-care homes may qualify for federal reimbursement of the meal and snack costs if 25 percent of the children are needy. Although the USDA manages the food program, it is administered locally by state or regional agencies. In some states, for example, the Department of Education administers the Child Care Food Program. You can find out who administers the program in your state by checking the CACFP website: http://www.fns.usda.gov/cnd/Contacts/StateDirectory.htm.

For each child, the center must document the parents' income level and the family's size and report this information on the application. The center is reimbursed at a higher rate for the costs associated with feeding the lower-income children than the rate reimbursed for the moderate- and higher-income children. A center serving 30 children could receive reimbursements ranging from $200 to $2,500. The federal funds do not completely pay for the food service program, but they are of a sufficient amount that most centers participate in spite of the extra effort required.

The calculations for receiving the reimbursements are somewhat complex, and detailed records must be kept for each meal. Also available is some reimbursement of the costs associated with paying personnel to take the training, do the bookkeeping, and file the reports. Computer software companies that have developed child-care center record-keeping programs have created a program specifically designed to keep the records for USDA food reimbursements.

The USDA has established guidelines, adopted by the APHA/AAP, that specify the amounts and types of foods that must be included in each meal or snack for each age group.

Organizing Food Service Facilities

As manager, you may have the opportunity to plan an ideal kitchen and serving area. Or you may have to use the space and equipment that someone else planned or spend some time planning a renovation. Adequate equipment and space for food preparation and storage, dishwashing, and serving meals are essential for high-quality meal service.

Your state's minimum child-care licensing standards must be applied from the very beginning—you may be able to obtain technical assistance and consultation from your licensing agency as you make your plans. Institutional dishwashers and other equipment may be required by the licensing standards. Applying the proper finishes to cabinets and floors makes complying with the sanitation standards rather simple. A manager should visit a number of centers and food service programs and question the dietians, cooks, and managers about the latest and best arrangements or the best equipment to buy. Getting advice from people who have recently made similar decisions or who are involved with a food service program daily may eliminate some costly mistakes.

Always compare the information obtained informally from colleagues with the specific written standards for food service equipment. The National Sanitation Foundation (NSF International) is an independent, not-for-profit organization that certifies the safety of products and equipment to protect public health. You can search for manufacturers of NSF certified food equipment at http://www.nsf.org/Certified/Food/.

Even the most modern facilities for preparing and serving food are of little use if appropriate storage and the equipment and supplies necessary to keep the facilities clean are not available:

- Floor and counter surfaces in food preparation area must be easily cleaned.
- Shelves where food items are stored should have hard-gloss finishes that are easily cleaned. (Crates or cans of food should never be stored on the floor.)
- Refrigerators and freezers should be equipped with thermometers so that the temperatures can be monitored.
- The kitchen (as well as the entire center) should be well-ventilated, with screens on any windows or doors that open.
- A separate sink for handwashing must be stocked with soap and paper towels.
- Disposable gloves must be worn when handling food.
- Food preparation surfaces must be cleaned and sanitized after each use; floor should be mopped at least daily, more often if soiled.
- Trash cans must have covers and disposable liners and be emptied at least daily.
- Outside the center, garbage should be stored in a covered Dumpster or can and removed at least weekly.

Food Service Personnel

When initially planning the food service program, the manager and the board determine the staff that they can afford to hire. A large child-care corporation or agency with many centers may hire a dietitian or nutritionist, while individual or small centers may use a dietician on a consultative basis one or two days per month to help plan menus and give advice when problems arise. Or the manager may be able to fulfill the nutritionist's role, so only a cook is needed. Carefully writing a job analysis, job specification, and job description is necessary (see chapter 7 for more information on hiring staff). Food service personnel are usually responsible for the following tasks:

1. Planning menus with proper nutritional content
2. Buying foods
3. Checking in food ordered and keeping track of inventories
4. Operating and maintaining the kitchen and dining rooms
5. Maintaining high sanitation standards for all food handling and preparation, dishwashing, and garbage disposal
6. Monitoring costs, reporting to the manager, and assisting with the USDA reports
7. Cooperating with the teaching staff to provide any food product learning material, such as play dough, or foods used in learning projects in the classrooms
8. Preparing foods using methods that maintain its nutritional quality
9. Getting to know the children, their individual needs, and the appropriate guidance methods for interacting with them—especially related to eating
10. Appreciating the families' needs and cultural differences that may affect meal service

The food service personnel who work in the kitchen are responsible for following the menus and organizing the food, equipment, and labor needed to get the meals on the table on time. Each task requires the ability to think through the steps to completion. Once items appear on the menus, the organizing begins. The food service director must consider the feasibility of each menu in terms of equipment, utensils, and available help. For example, a main dish and a dessert that both require the oven may not be feasible on the same day unless the dessert is cooked ahead of time.

Food service workers must know, or be willing to learn quickly, the proper methods of cooking to preserve nutrient qualities. A reputable quantity-cooking recipe book is essential. If staff members follow the suggested methods and temperatures, the products should remain nutritious. Vegetables, for example, generally cook quickly; prolonged cooking destroys the very vitamins the vegetables are expected to provide the children.

The food service staff must understand children—their development, nutritional needs, and typical behaviors related to food. Ideally, food service staff are included in all professional development activities, and nutrition education for the entire staff should include information about how children develop healthy eating habits and appropriate guidance techniques. Staff should not admonish a child for not eating, cajole a child to entice him to eat, or talk across the child as though she were not present. For help with nutritional questions, managers might recruit a board member with a dietetic or family and consumer science background. Together, the manager and board member can help the teachers plan and integrate nutrition education within regular play activities.

Food Poisoning Prevention

All staff members who handle food must be fully aware of their responsibility to prevent food poisoning. In addition to the harm done to the individuals involved, a food poisoning outbreak among the children or staff can severely damage a center's reputation. According to the USDA's Food Safety and Inspection Service (USDA FSIS, 1998), salmonella is the most frequently reported cause of food-borne illness, affecting up to 3.8 million people each year. It is most associated with meat, poultry, seafood, eggs, and dairy products, but it can also grow on fruits, vegetables, and sprouts and in orange juice if the right conditions exist. You cannot see, taste, or smell it. Symptoms, including diarrhea, cramps, fever, and sometimes chills, headache, and vomiting, appear between 8 and 72 hours after eating the contaminated food and last up to 7 days. Most victims recover without medical intervention, but effects can be severe or life-threatening in the very young or elderly.

Other food poisoning bacteria cause similar symptoms; however, botulism can be fatal in very small doses. Therefore, home-canned foods or foods from damaged or unlabeled cans should never be used.

Safe food handling practices prevent illness by keeping the bacteria from growing to high levels and to destroying the bacteria through thorough cooking. The USDA's Food Safety and Inspection Service (FSIS, 1998) recommends four basic strategies to accomplish this:

1. *Cleanliness.* Wash hands thoroughly before handling food and after toileting, diapering, or touching pets; wash and sanitize dishes, cooking utensils, and work surfaces after each use; use nonporous cutting boards and disposable towels.
2. *Separation.* Keep raw meat, poultry, and seafood apart from other foods; use a different cutting board for each; don't put cooked food on a plate that had held raw meat, poultry, or seafood.
3. *Cooking.* Use a clean thermometer to make sure meats are cooked to at least 145°F for roasts and steaks, 160°F for ground beef, 170°F for poultry parts, and 180°F for whole poultry. Cook eggs until firm and fish until it is opaque and flakes easily. Cover, stir, and rotate food to avoid uneven cooking when using a microwave oven.
4. *Cooling.* Refrigerate all perishable food; always defrost frozen food in a refrigerator, under cold running water, or in a microwave; make sure air circulates in refrigerator.

As a center manager, you are responsible for ensuring that the staff understands the importance of good hygiene practices. Posting signs over sinks and in lavatories may help remind some to wash their hands. Simple training exercises can be conducted at staff meetings to emphasize the importance of thorough handwashing practices.

Staff should never work with food if they have symptoms of an illness, such as diarrhea or vomiting, or cuts or sores on their skin that cannot be covered with disposable gloves. Using disposable gloves must not lull the staff into a laxness about washing their hands. Ideally, staff responsible for changing diapers should not be responsible for preparing food. In smaller facilities, where such double duty might be unavoidable, staff members must be even more scrupulous about washing their hands with soap and running water each time they move from caregiving to food preparation.

One way to help you and your staff conceptualize the sanitation aspects of your center's food service is to ask yourselves whether you would feel comfortable eating in a restaurant with a kitchen that resembled yours. Sometimes, in their effort to create a homelike atmosphere, child-care providers forget that they are feeding a public clientele and must exercise every precaution to protect the health and safety of their "customers."

Considerations When Feeding Babies

The food requirements for infants are noted in Figure 11.1. Licensing standards also provide important details. Each baby's needs are likely to be very different from those of the baby in the next crib. The proper amount and kind of formula is essential to the infant's health and well-being. Some centers provide infant formula and some rely on the parents to bring it. In either case, it must be handled properly. That means that each bottle must contain only enough for one feeding, be labeled with the child's name and date, and stored in the refrigerator. Formula left in a bottle after a feeding must be discarded.

FIGURE 11.1 *Meal requirements for infants in child care*

	Birth through 3 Months	4 through 7 Months	8 through 11 Months
Breakfast	4–6 fluid ounces of formula[1] or breast milk[2,3]	4–8 fluid ounces of formula[1] or breast milk[2,3];	6–8 fluid ounces of formula[1] or breast milk[2,3], and 2–4 tablespoons of infant cereal[1]; and 1–4 tablespoons of fruit or vegetable or both
		0–3 tablespoons of infant cereal[1,4]	
Lunch or Supper	4–6 fluid ounces of formula[1] or breast milk[2,3]	4–8 fluid ounces of formula[1] or breast milk[2,3];	6–8 fluid ounces of formula[1] or breast milk[2,3]; 2–4 tablespoons of infant cereal[1]; and/or 1–4 tablespoons of meat, fish, poultry, egg yolk, cooked dry beans or peas; or $\frac{1}{2}$–2 ounces of cheese; or 1–4 ounces (volume) of cottage cheese; or 1–4 ounces (weight) of cheese food or cheese spread; and 1–4 tablespoons of fruit or vegetable or both
		0–3 tablespoons of infant cereal[1,4], and 0–3 tablespoons of fruit or vegetable or both[4]	
Snack	4–6 fluid ounces of formula[1] or breast milk[2,3]	4–6 fluid ounces of formula[1] or breast milk[2,3]	2–4 fluid ounces of formula[1] or breast milk[2,3], or fruit juice[5]; and 0–$\frac{1}{2}$ bread[4,6]; or 0–2 crackers[4,6]

[1]Infant formula and dry infant cereal must be iron fortified.

[2]Breast milk or formula, or portions of both, may be served; however, it is recommended that breast milk be served in place of formula from birth through 11 months.

[3]For some breast-fed infants who regularly consume less than the minimum amount of breast milk per feeding, a serving of less than the minimum amount of breast milk may be offered, with additional breast milk offered if the infant is still hungry.

[4]A serving of this component is required when the infant is developmentally ready to accept it.

[5]Fruit juice must be full strength.

[6]A serving of this component must be made from whole-grain or enriched meal or flour.

Source: USDA Child Care Nutrition Resource System. Retrieved July 25, 2005, from http://www.nal.usda.gov/childcare/Cacfp/index.html.

Babies who cannot hold their own bottle should be held while feeding.

Infant caregivers should hold the baby warmly while giving the bottle. One reason for the recommended 3- or 4-to-1 infant–adult ratio is the babies' need to have 1-to-1 contact with the same caregiver. Security and trust are fostered in both infants and parents by this arrangement. In addition to meeting psychological needs, holding babies while feeding them avoids choking and ear infections. It also prevents dental caries that can result when babies are put to bed with bottles in their mouths.

Because of the special benefits that breast-fed infants receive, even for a few months, the center should assist mothers who desire to feed their infants this way. Encourage breast-feeding mothers to return to the center to feed their infants and provide a comfortable rocking chair in a quiet, private room or corner so mother and baby can enjoy a relaxing time together. Mothers who cannot come to the center during their workday can leave expressed breast milk in a bottle. If a mother is planning to do this, you might recommend that she try using the bottle at home a few times before you try it at the center. That way, the baby does not have to adapt to too many changes all at once.

Of course, refrigerate breast milk as you do any milk. It can be stored in the refrigerator for up to 48 hours, in the freezer for 2 weeks. Frozen breast milk should be thawed in the refrigerator. Warm all baby bottles by putting them in pans of hot (not boiling) water for 5 minutes. Never use the microwave because it heats foods unevenly, and bottle contents that feel only lukewarm to the skin on your adult wrist can scald a baby's tender mouth.

Solid foods are started around the sixth month, always in consultation with the child's parents. Introduce foods one at a time and carefully observe the child for possible allergic reactions before introducing another food. Because babies have grown accustomed to using a different type of tongue movement for sucking, they may require some time to learn the finer points of taking and swallowing food from a spoon. Pushing food out of the mouth with the tongue may be part of this effort and not necessarily a sign of dislike. Be alert for possible choking.

All foods should be of high quality, unsalted, and kept covered and fresh. Never feed a child directly from a jar of baby food. The saliva on the spoon can carry bacteria back to the jar where it can multiply and cause illness the next time you use it. For each feeding (and for each baby if you are feeding more than one at a time), use a clean spoon to place a small amount of food in a clean dish. Replace the cover on the jar and refrigerate it immediately. Discard any food left in the dish at the end of the feeding.

At about 6 months of age, the infant begins self-feeding and will enjoy a graham cracker while sitting at the feeding table. It is the beginning of independence! Be careful that you do not provide foods that can cause choking: avoid grapes, pretzels, or popcorn. If you serve hotdogs, make sure the skin is not tough—slice them in half lengthwise and cut the strips into small chunks.

Your center is usually required to keep records on the individual infants showing food intake, sleeping patterns, bowel movements, and developmental milestones. A copy of the report should be sent home with the parents daily. Parents must also be encouraged to report to the center staff any unusual changes in their baby's food intake, sleeping patterns, or bowel movements. A sample report form is shown in Figure 11.2.

FIGURE 11.2 *Sample report to parents*

XYZ Child Development Center

Caregiver _____

Baby's Name _____ Date _____

Food: Times for bottle _____

         New foods _____

         Unusual _____

Sleeping: A.M. _____ P.M. _____

         Unusual _____

Bowel Movements _____

         Unusual _____

New Motor Skills _____

New Words _____

Other   _____

Note: Parents, please feel free to discuss any item with your baby's caregiver.

Menu Planning

Figure 11.3 shows the nutritional standards for children ages 1 to 12 years. Although you may remember "the four basic food groups" from your elementary school days, the USDA and the Department of Health and Human Services have recently updated the way we conceptualize a balanced diet (see Figure 11.4). The old "Food Guide Pyramid" has been renamed "MyPyramid: Steps to a Healthier You" to emphasize a more personalized approach to gradual improvement in healthy eating and physical activity. It takes into account the proportion, as well as the variety, of foods required for a healthy diet, but it recognizes that exact amounts will vary among individuals depending on many factors, including physical activity level. Each food group (grains, vegetables, fruits, oils, milk, and meat or beans) is represented by a band on the pyramid that gradually narrows from the bottom toward the top, indicating the declining proportion that those foods which contain solid fats and added sugars should occupy in one's daily diet. Individuals are encouraged to log onto the website www.mypyramid.gov to calculate suggested daily amounts of each food group based on age, gender, and daily activity level.

Several considerations can guide food choices. In addition to meeting standards for nutrition and safety, meal and snack menus should include foods that are colorful and interesting in texture and flavor. As mentioned earlier, the combination of foods must fit the quantity and type of equipment available.

The children's likes should also guide menu planning. Though it is highly desirable to introduce children to new foods, it helps their transition from home to school to be served some familiar foods. Foods from various ethnic groups are often desirable for this reason (Endres & Rockwell, 1990). All children can learn to enjoy foods from a variety of ethnic groups.

Cycle menus provide a shortcut to menu planning. The cycles are often a 15- or 20-day sequence of menus repeated throughout a season with minimal changes. New cycles can be planned for a new season. Once checked by the dietitian, the combinations should not be

FIGURE 11.3 *Meal requirements for children ages 1 through 12 in child-care programs*

Breakfast (3 components)

Food Components	Ages 1–2	Ages 3–5	Ages 6–12[1]
1 milk			
fluid milk	$\frac{1}{2}$ cup	$\frac{3}{4}$ cup	1 cup
1 fruit/vegetable			
juice[2], fruit and/or vegetable	$\frac{1}{4}$ cup	$\frac{1}{2}$ cup	$\frac{1}{2}$ cup
1 grain/bread[3]			
bread or	$\frac{1}{2}$ slice	$\frac{1}{2}$ slice	1 slice
cornbread or biscuit or roll or muffin or	$\frac{1}{2}$ serving	$\frac{1}{2}$ serving	1 serving
cold dry cereal or	$\frac{1}{4}$ cup	$\frac{1}{3}$ cup	$\frac{3}{4}$ cup
hot cooked cereal or	$\frac{1}{4}$ cup	$\frac{1}{4}$ cup	$\frac{1}{2}$ cup
pasta or noodles or grains	$\frac{1}{4}$ cup	$\frac{1}{4}$ cup	$\frac{1}{2}$ cup

Lunch or Supper (4 components)

Food Components	Ages 1–2	Ages 3–5	Ages 6–12[1]
1 milk			
fluid milk	$\frac{1}{2}$ cup	$\frac{3}{4}$ cup	1 cup
2 fruits/vegetables			
juice[2], fruit and/or vegetable	$\frac{1}{4}$ cup	$\frac{1}{2}$ cup	$\frac{3}{4}$ cup
1 grains/bread[3]			
bread or	$\frac{1}{2}$ slice	$\frac{1}{2}$ slice	1 slice
cornbread or biscuit or roll or muffin or	$\frac{1}{2}$ serving	$\frac{1}{2}$ serving	1 serving
cold dry cereal or	$\frac{1}{4}$ cup	$\frac{1}{3}$ cup	$\frac{3}{4}$ cup
hot cooked cereal or	$\frac{1}{4}$ cup	$\frac{1}{4}$ cup	$\frac{1}{2}$ cup
pasta or noodles or grains	$\frac{1}{4}$ cup	$\frac{1}{4}$ cup	$\frac{1}{2}$ cup
1 meat/meat alternate			
meat or poultry or fish[4] or	1 oz.	$1\frac{1}{2}$ oz.	2 oz.
alternate protein product or	1 oz.	$1\frac{1}{2}$ oz.	2 oz.
cheese or	1 oz.	$1\frac{1}{2}$ oz.	2 oz.
egg or	$\frac{1}{2}$	$\frac{3}{4}$	1
cooked dry beans or peas or	$\frac{1}{4}$ cup	$\frac{3}{8}$ cup	$\frac{1}{2}$ cup
peanut or other nut or seed butters or	2 tbsp.	3 tbsp.	4 tbsp.
nuts and/or seeds[5] or	$\frac{1}{2}$ oz.	$\frac{3}{4}$ oz.	1 oz.
yogurt[6]	4 oz.	6 oz.	8 oz.

changed without checking the nutritional content of the substitute food. To keep a balanced diet, it may be better to substitute an entire day's menu if you have a shortage of some crucial item. (Sample menus for four weeks are available online at http://www.cdasandiego.com/nutrition/cacfp/cacfpmenus.htm.)

Figure 11.5 is a sample worksheet that you can use to plan a week's menu. The USDA publishes nutritional standards and other helpful meal planning information for centers and for families. These materials are available online from the Child Care Food Program, U.S.

FIGURE 11.3   *Continued*

Snack (2 Components)			
Food Components	**Ages 1–2**	**Ages 3–5**	**Ages 6–12[1]**
1 milk			
fluid milk	$\frac{1}{2}$ cup	$\frac{1}{2}$ cup	1 cup
1 fruit/vegetable			
juice[2], fruit and/or vegetable	$\frac{1}{2}$ cup	$\frac{1}{2}$ cup	$\frac{3}{4}$ cup
1 grains/bread[3]			
bread or	$\frac{1}{2}$ slice	$\frac{1}{2}$ slice	1 slice
cornbread or biscuit or roll or muffin or	$\frac{1}{2}$ serving	$\frac{1}{2}$ serving	1 serving
cold dry cereal or	$\frac{1}{4}$ cup	$\frac{1}{3}$ cup	$\frac{3}{4}$ cup
hot cooked cereal or	$\frac{1}{4}$ cup	$\frac{1}{4}$ cup	$\frac{1}{2}$ cup
pasta or noodles or grains	$\frac{1}{4}$ cup	$\frac{1}{4}$ cup	$\frac{1}{2}$ cup
1 meat/meat alternate			
meat or poultry or fish[4] or	$\frac{1}{2}$ oz.	$\frac{1}{2}$ oz.	1 oz.
alternate protein product or	$\frac{1}{2}$ oz.	$\frac{1}{2}$ oz.	1 oz.
cheese or	$\frac{1}{2}$ oz.	$\frac{1}{2}$ oz.	1 oz.
egg[5] or	$\frac{1}{2}$	$\frac{1}{2}$	$\frac{1}{2}$
cooked dry beans or peas or	$\frac{1}{8}$ cup	$\frac{1}{8}$ cup	$\frac{1}{4}$ cup
peanut or other nut or seed butters or	1 tbsp.	1 tbsp.	2 tbsp.
nuts and/or seeds or	$\frac{1}{2}$ oz.	$\frac{1}{2}$ oz.	1 oz.
yogurt[6]	2 oz.	2 oz.	4 oz.

[1]Children age 12 and older may be served larger portions based on their greater food needs. They may not be served less than the minimum quantities listed in this column.

[2]Fruit or vegetable juice must be full strength. Juice cannot be served when milk is the only other snack component.

[3]Breads and grains must be made from whole-grain or enriched meal or flour. Cereal must be whole grain or enriched or fortified.

[4]A serving consists of the edible portion of cooked lean meat or poultry or fish.

[5]One-half egg meets the required minimum amount (1 ounce or less) of meat alternate.

[6]Yogurt may be plain or flavored, unsweetened or sweetened.

Source: USDA Child Care Nutrition Resource System. Retrieved July 25, 2005 from http://www.nal.usda.gov/childcare/Cacfp/index.html.

Department of Agriculture, at http://www.nal.usda.gov/childcare/, from your local Cooperative Extension Service, or from the nutrition department of many universities.

Snacks

Snacks should be considered a nutrition break that restores the children's energy after a busy period of play. Sitting at the table for a short time also provides active children with a needed rest. Snack time is usually a social time of day with conversations about activities and

FIGURE 11.4   *Food guide pyramid: A guide to daily food choices*

Source: U.S. Department of Agriculture and the U.S. Department of Health and Human Services.

events at school or home. Only highly nutritious foods should be served. The emphasis should be on vegetables, fruits, cereal, and protein foods. Foods with a high sugar content should be avoided. As you may note in Figure 11.3, the snack requirement calls for any two of four food categories: milk, juice or fruit or vegetable, meat or meat alternate, or bread or cereal. For example, milk and apples, juice and sandwiches, or carrots and meat sticks all are adequate snacks. Excellent arguments can be made for using milk as a beverage a large portion of the time. Seeing their friends drink milk often helps some children learn to drink this highly nutritious and essential food.

Children need plenty of drinking water throughout the day. A small cup of water is preferred by younger children, and older children can usually manage a drinking fountain. Many do not like ice water.

Special Diets

Centers must cooperate with families and medical personnel when children have allergies or other special dietary needs. Managers should develop a written policy defining the responsibilities of parents and center staff in regard to special diets. Requiring parents to bring a physician's statement when special diets are requested protects the center as well as the child. Some parents who are highly conscious about dieting themselves are minimally informed about nutrition and could jeopardize their child's health with diet restrictions. Diet restrictions that may make sense for sedentary or weight-conscious adults do not generally make sense for active, growing children.

The physician's statement should identify the child's condition and specify foods to be avoided as well as acceptable substitutes. It should also indicate the symptoms associated with exposure to the allergen and instructions for what center staff should do in the event of an allergic reaction. Posting a list of children's names and specific allergies in each area where food is prepared or served will help staff make sure that children never receive food that could be harmful for them.

FIGURE 11.5 *Menu planning worksheet*

		Monday	Tuesday	Wednesday	Thursday	Friday
Breakfast	Week of:					
	Fluid milk					
	Fruit, veg., or juice					
	Cereal or					
	Cereal / bread / alt.					
A.M. Snack	*Choose 2 (of 4)*					
	Fluid milk					
	Fruit, veg., or juice					
	Cereal / bread / alt.					
	Meat or alternative					
Lunch	Fluid milk					
	Meat or alternative					
	Vegetable or fruit					
	Vegetable or fruit					
	Bread or alternative					
	Other (e.g., condiments)					
P.M. Snack	*Choose 2 (of 4)*					
	Fluid milk					
	Fruit, veg., or juice					
	Cereal / bread / alt.					
	Meat or alternative					

Some families request special diets for their children because of religious or other personal preferences. Child-care facilities are challenged to balance their goal of being family friendly with their responsibility to ensure that children's needs are met. For example, some nutritionists are concerned about vegetarian diets because giving young children enough complete and tasty protein without using meat, poultry, or fish requires concerted attention. Centers enrolling children whose families espouse vegetarianism must give special attention to the children's need for protein to support their growth—building a mass of muscle tissue composed largely of protein. Milk, cheese, egg, whole-grain cereals, dry beans, soy products, and peanut butter are the protein foods that appear in vegetarian diets. A young child who is growing and highly active requires calories and nutrients for these activities that an unknowing parent may attempt to deny. This is another instance where your health consultant may be able to help you work with families so that you can be sensitive to their preferences while still upholding your professional obligation to protect children's health.

Some centers provide the special foods (e.g., soy milk for children who are lactose intolerant or graham crackers made with vegetable shortening rather than lard for children whose culture prohibits consumption of pork). Others ask that families provide the necessary substitutions. Even in those cases, however, it is a center responsibility to ensure that every child receives all required food components and to supplement those that families may fail to provide.

Seating and Serving Children

Large lunchrooms are overwhelming for young children and frustrating for the adults who accompany them. Small-table settings with an adult and four or five other children are much more conducive to a pleasant dining experience. Planning the children's places at the meal tables means that children who need help can be located where an adult can reach them. Seating independent eaters among the less experienced allows children to learn from peer role models. Having a name card or a regular seat at the table assures each child that he has a place to sit.

Child-size pitchers make it possible for children to pour their own beverages.

Choosing where and with whom to sit can be an interesting social activity for young children. Some programs, inspired by the preschools of Reggio Emilia, Italy, have developed the practice of forming small "committees" of children to help with table setting and seating assignments each day, providing rich opportunities for discussion, negotiation, and learning to consider other people's preferences and feelings.

An adult should sit and eat with each small group of children so that the program can meet socialization goals without sacrificing sanitation. The teacher sitting with a small group serves the children family-style and grows accustomed to each child's likes and dislikes. Volunteers, school-age children, and high school students can serve as helpers at meal times. Make the serving bowls small enough for the children to manipulate to reduce the risk of contaminating large quantities of food should a child lick a serving spoon, for example, or handle all the toast on the plate. The adult gives each child a serving to get things started and then children can serve themselves seconds. They often eat more when they can serve themselves. Keep servings child-size so that children who are unfamiliar with a food, or think they don't like it, are not overwhelmed by an unappetizing mound on their plates. A small pitcher, holding just a cup of milk so that the children can pour it by themselves, will entice many of them to drink "seconds." Adults should remember that children like lukewarm food—not very hot or cold—so they should not be bothered when the soup gets cold and the ice cream gets mushy. That is the way most children like soup and ice cream!

If your goal is to support children's independent eating, remember that bite-size pieces of meat or other foods are easier for small fingers to grasp. As the children get a little older, they can manage small spoons and forks. Often the spoon is held in one hand while the child happily carries food to her mouth with the other. Once children have mastered eating utensils, they may be ready to use a stick of toast rather than their fingers to push food onto the spoon. Children should be taught to keep the food on their plate rather than strewing it around the table.

Observing other children independently serving themselves and eating encourages a more dependent child to assume the same responsibility. Parents who visit at lunchtime are often amazed at the maturity of their child who, they say, "acts like a baby at home!" Teachers and caregivers should never cajole or bribe a child to eat. If the child is too tired to eat, it may be helpful to schedule a resting time just before mealtime or to eat a little bit earlier.

Young children have quite a bit of concentrating to do as they eat, and after a busy morning they are usually hungry. However, as they become more adept at quelling their hunger pangs, their attention turns to conversations during meals. Children should never be told to "be quiet and eat" if a pleasant mealtime atmosphere is desired. They can talk about how they helped prepare the food, how milk makes their teeth strong, or the origins of the food they are eating. Caregivers can provide a good example by speaking quietly and only to the children at their table rather than to adults or children at another table. They should take care not to detract from the pleasure of the occasion in their zeal to make it a learning experience.

Children should be encouraged to sit at the table until they have finished eating, to carry their plate to a serving cart for their dessert, and to remove their dishes when finished. If a child wants to get up and down frequently, she may not be hungry and, with adult assistance, should be excused to go to the toilet and get ready for nap time. Because the teacher eating with the children should not leave them to tend to a child who is ready to leave early, another adult must be available to help.

It can be tiring for teachers and aides who have worked all morning with the children to eat their lunch with them; however, the children really do better at eating and feeding themselves if these familiar people guide their mealtime. Managers and food service staff must be aware of the teachers' needs and ensure that they get adequate food as they supervise mealtimes. Having adequate support people in the dining room eliminates the need for the teacher to jump up and get items or tend to emergencies—interruptions that interfere with the teacher's resting and eating an adequate meal.

Influencing Children's Eating Behaviors

Adults have probably always worried about, and tried to influence, what and how much children eat, and this concern is exacerbated by recent dramatic increases in childhood obesity rates in the United States. Between 1990 and 2000 the percentage of overweight children nearly doubled to almost 12 percent of 6- to 23-month-old children and more than 10 percent of 2- to 5-year-old children (Lumeng, 2005). This trend is alarming because obesity is associated with serious health problems, including diabetes, hypertension, and elevated cholesterol

Children ages 3 to 5 enjoy the challenge of using child-size table knives and forks.

Growing a vegetable garden may encourage children to try a new food.

levels in children just as in adults. Furthermore, children who are overweight or obese are more likely to suffer low self-esteem, depression, and social withdrawal. How can child-care providers help counteract this trend? The answers may not be as simple as we would like.

First of all, obesity in children and adults is heavily influenced by our human-built and social–cultural environments, which include highly processed foods, hectic family schedules promoting dependence on fast foods, sedentary lifestyles, and the pervasive influence of advertising. Parents and other adults may try mightily to influence children's eating behaviors, but research shows that peers and advertising are much stronger influences (Lumeng, 2005).

Some research suggests that the more adult control exerted over a child's eating habits at age 5, the greater the likelihood of that child eating while not hungry at age 9 (Lumeng, 2005). Children who are allowed to follow their body's signals are able to adjust their intake of food to meet their caloric needs. Because energy needs vary from day to day and because adult interference reduces the children's capacity to recognize their body's signals, adults should not be concerned or call attention to the fact that a child does or does not eat very much at any given meal. Research has shown that when children are given a wide variety of appropriate foods from which to choose, they eat a balanced diet. They may taste a new food as many as 10 times (without being forced or coaxed) before deciding they like it (Birch, Johnson, & Fisher, 1995, pp. 71–78).

One good reason for serving meals family-style is that children can ask for—or better still, help themselves to—second portions. This approach helps the children learn to make their own decisions. Research has demonstrated that children who receive a food as a reward for eating another food increase their preference for the "reward" food and learn to dislike the food they were supposedly being encouraged to eat (Birch, Johnson, & Fisher, 1995, p. 74). Accordingly, child-care providers should never use food (including dessert) as a reward for a clean plate, withhold it as punishment, or use it as reinforcement in any way.

While child-care programs might not be able to control what children eat at home, or even what they choose to eat at the center, they can make sure that while at the center the child has a healthy selection from which to choose. In addition to adhering to the USDA guidelines, centers can incorporate the following strategies, suggested by Carol Huettig and her colleagues (2004, p. 51):

- Use low-fat milk for children over 2
- Limit fruit juice consumption to 6 ounces per day (use fresh fruits instead of juices to meet that meal component and let children have water instead of second helpings of juice)
- Encourage children to drink plenty of water throughout the day, outdoors as well as indoors
- Make healthy foods more attractive by involving children in their preparation (e.g., fruit smoothies; vegetable kabobs)

Food and Curriculum

Food provides more than just nourishment for the body. Because food involves so many sensory modalities and offers such immediate gratification, it is engaging for young children. It provides a rich source of topics to investigate because it is so much a part of daily life, culture, and commerce. Projects and investigations about food production, distribution, and preparation help the children become aware of all aspects of the human ecological system, providing what Katz and Chard called "horizontal relevance"—connections between school life and life in the everyday world outside (Katz & Chard, 2000).

Food is integrally bound up with culture, making it an excellent means of cultivating an appreciation for diversity. Breads and noodles, for example, are used in many forms by the various cultures of the world, and the forms these items take are often associated with particular stories or beliefs. Young children could begin by thinking about all of the bread types they have eaten and eventually branch out into tasting the breads eaten by other cultures (Mitchell & David, 1992). Such a study has the additional advantage of avoiding a "tourist" approach—exposure only to the exotic aspects of other cultures.

Decisions, Decisions . . .

List the pros and cons of fingerpainting with chocolate pudding as an art activity for 2-year-olds. Is the list the same if you considered the activity for 4-year-olds?

When thinking about learning goals for young children in connection with food, teachers might consider the four categories suggested by Katz and Chard:

1. Knowledge (factual information, content)
2. Skills (actions that can be taught and practiced)
3. Dispositions (mental habits or tendencies such as curiosity and creativity)
4. Feelings (emotional states such as feeling of belonging or competence) (2000, pp. 25–26)

In the realm of knowledge, you might want the children to know things about various foods—their names, sources, or value for growing healthy bodies. Or you might want them to know general things—colors, shapes, size comparisons, or the meaning of printed labels. With regard to skills, as they become progressively more mature, children are expected to drink from a cup; eat finger foods; use napkins, spoons, forks, and simple food preparation tools; chew with their mouths closed; and observe the table manners appropriate to their culture. With assistance, the children eventually develop a disposition to eat healthy foods and to eat only as much as they need to satisfy their hunger. Finally, feelings of belonging to a culture, of competence at being able to meet one's own needs, and of friendliness toward meal companions should be nourished.

If you keep these goals in mind, together with what you know about the development of the children's cognitive abilities and food acceptance patterns, you can avoid using guidance techniques that work at cross purposes to your goals. For example, the lessons about "the four food groups," favored by so many teachers, are probably ineffective for two reasons. First, the concept of which foods go together is too abstract for young children to comprehend. They are much more likely to categorize food in ways that are personally meaningful: liked and disliked foods, for example, or foods at home and foods at restaurants. One classification scheme to be avoided is "good" and "bad" foods. Most nutritionists counsel that there are no bad foods and that the important thing is a balance between all of the foods eaten. Second, the ultimate goal of such lessons lies more in the realm of disposition than of knowledge. After all, how many adults do you know who can recite all of the food pyramid's components but subsist on a diet of fast-food sandwiches and soft drinks?

Decisions, Decisions . . .

Keep a record of everything you eat for 1 week. Compare your findings with your own Pyramid Plan, calculated at www.mypyramid.gov. Do you consume more or less than the recommended amounts of any food category?

As we noted earlier, research suggests that the best way to cultivate a disposition toward healthy eating habits and an openness to new food experiences is by providing "children with a variety of healthful foods in a positive social environment and then allowing children the freedom to eat what they wish" (Birch et al., 1995, p. 78). Children also seem more disposed to eat foods that they have helped prepare, so wise managers include frequent opportunities for the children to help peel carrots for a snack or slice and assemble fruit kabobs. Children's participation in food preparation is even greater when they plant, tend, and harvest vegetables in their own garden.

Modeling is another factor: Children who think they do not like a food are often persuaded to try it when they see another child enjoying it. On the other hand, these adults who encourage children to take a bite of green beans, when they do not eat any themselves, usually meet with little success.

Decisions, Decisions . . .

Is there a particular food that you eat too often? Is there one that you dislike intensely? Think about your childhood experiences with that food. Can you see any connection between those experiences and your attitude toward that food today? Discuss your conclusions with your classmates.

Field trips to the dairy, orchard, or grocery store are all concrete ways for children to learn about the food they eat. Teachers should prepare the children for such visits by encouraging them to think of questions they want to have answered and once there, give them plenty of time at the site to explore. It helps to prepare the people you are visiting so that they have an idea of what to tell the children. One group of 4-year-olds paid little attention as the orchard owner told their teacher and parents all about his modern farming methods, but they became very excited when a teacher asked about the age of a particular row of young trees and was told they were 4 years old. "Just like us!" they exclaimed. The conversations at the snack table, as they enjoyed their apple slices the next day, contained many references to the 4-year-old trees.

Volunteers and visitors can help you meet many nutrition-related goals. Parents might make family or ethnic specialties for the children or, better yet, come in and make them with a small group of children. Older children can come in to help with meal service and to eat with the children so that more of them can have individual attention. Boy or Girl Scout groups, 4-H Clubs, and home economics classes are all potential sources of volunteers to share information or conduct food-related activities. A dentist or hygienist could demonstrate toothbrushing techniques. The possibilities are limited only by your own creativity.

Collaborating with Families About Food Matters

Centers collaborate with families regarding food in a number of ways. We have already noted that even when families provide the child's meals, it is a center's responsibility to ensure that meals meet nutritional requirements. The expectation for adequate nutrition must be clearly spelled out in the center's nutrition policy and included in the handbook families receive when they enroll their children. In the short term, the simple correction for occasional lapses is for the center to provide the missing food component when the meal from home falls short. When the meals from home are consistently inadequate, a more comprehensive approach is needed. Begin by discussing the issue with the family. They may need a reminder of your policy or they may simply be unaware of what constitutes adequate nutrition and you can provide information. They may be experiencing financial hardship, in which case you can guide them to community resources for help. If the situation persists in spite of your efforts, you may need to report the family to the appropriate authorities as possibly neglecting the child.

When the center provides the meals, parents like to know what their children are eating at school so that they do not duplicate the menu at home in the evening. Accreditation criteria, as well as national health and safety guidelines, require that parents be informed of the type of food served at the center. Menus can be posted where the parents can see them as they drop off or pick up their child. Observing and recording what a child eats helps parents as well as nutritionists plan wisely. Some schools report to the parents exactly what their child ate by using a daily checksheet. The USDA publication, *Tips for Using the Food Guide Pyramid with Young Children 2 to 6 Years Old*, listed among the resources for further study at the end of this chapter, includes a 7-day menu plan with a grid displaying the recommended number of daily servings in each food group. A family can record what a child eats at each meal and check off the corresponding food group for each item. The visual record provides an easy way to see whether the child is getting too little or too much of any particular food group(s). A child-care program could adopt this 7-day format for its printed menu, fill in the meals served at the center and the corresponding checks on the grid, and thus help families see the total picture of their child's nutritional intake.

The center should encourage families to report any special problems their child has or might have as a result of some home experience. The report could include such events as a digestive upset during the night or having a relative in for a big supper the night before, which kept the child eating fancy food at all hours. Either episode may significantly impact the child's food intake the next day.

Another way to involve families in regard to food is to invite parents to eat with the children when convenient. For those children whose parents cannot come at lunchtime, extend the invitation to breakfast or snack time as well. Adults learn to appreciate their child's eating habits when they see him functioning with other children. They also gain additional respect for the teaching staff as they realize how much effort and organization a simple meal requires. If you are encouraging the children to invite their parents for meals, remember that children with divorced parents may want to invite each parent on a different day. The child might also be encouraged to invite a grandparent, aunt, or special family friend. A child should be helped to feel included in a special event even if a parent cannot come.

Many families enjoy joining their children for lunch on birthdays, and they often want to bring a treat. Some local sanitarians take a strict interpretation of the AAP/AAPH guidelines on food from home (e.g., being labeled for the individual child and not shared) and prohibit the use of homemade birthday treats. If you do allow them, you should do so only for children age 3 and over. Encourage parents to consider healthy alternatives prepared in individual servings, such as frozen yogurt "popsicles" or oatmeal cookies. An alternative would be to invite the birthday child's family to come in on the big day and help make cupcakes using the center's ingredients (which you know come from approved sources and have been safely stored).

Accreditation guidelines also recommend a nutrition education program for parents. Telling parents about the nutritional quality of a food (perhaps in a special "cook's corner" in your newsletter) may help them understand why you include it on the menu. If a child particularly likes a food, you might share the recipe with the parents. You can let families know what you are doing at the center to encourage healthy eating and exercise and share ideas for doing the same things at home. Be careful about preaching, however, because you don't want parents to feel pressured or blamed. Recall our earlier discussion about the limits of adult influence on children's eating behaviors and the fact that coaxing a child to eat or refrain from certain foods can actually have the opposite effect. As Lumeng (2005) points out, some advice that seems sensible may be based on scanty research and, in fact, run counter to families' cultural preferences.

Culture and Food

It is necessary for managers to consider the cultural diversity of their families because culture influences people's beliefs about what foods are to be eaten and what behaviors regarding food are acceptable. Some groups have strong prohibitions against eating certain foods. For example, many Hindus do not eat beef, many Muslims and Jews do not eat pork, and some groups are vegetarian; substitutes for meats must be available.

Some groups that do not typically serve a particular food in their homes do not object if their children learn to like that food at the center. For instance, Chinese typically do not serve raw vegetables, but their children can eat raw carrots, broccoli, or cauliflower at school if they like. People from Germany may consider corn a food only for pigs, but they often learn to enjoy corn when they come to the United States. Some groups use a lot of seasoning or eat fried foods, yet they can learn to taste foods that are bland or cooked without much fat. Such differences should be kept in mind as menus are planned and meals served. Guiding children to try foods they have never seen at home takes patience and will likely be more successful if you start with small servings.

Western middle-class culture places a high value on independence, and many adults believe that, except for infants, who are not yet ready to feed themselves, a child should be encouraged to become self-sufficient. Other cultures place a higher priority on interdependence, however, and believe that children learn to be tender caregivers when they are helped with things that they could actually do for themselves (Gonzalez-Mena, 1997). If the conservation of precious food resources is a concern, adults might find it wasteful to let children smear food around their high-chair trays. It is important to recognize and respect cultural differences and arrive at mutually satisfying arrangements through open-minded discussions with the families.

Monitoring and Controlling Food Programs

Monitoring the menus, food shopping lists, supermarket specials, and the center's storage systems helps managers get the most food service for their food dollars. To prevent food service personnel from intentionally mixing up too much food, it is essential to have a policy prohibiting anyone from taking leftover food home. Keeping freezers and storerooms locked is advisable. A large inventory is costly when interest rates are high; thus, keeping an inventory larger than reasonable amounts for emergencies is a questionable practice. Managers have learned that it is essential to count the cans in cases of delivered foods, after some boxes were found to be short.

Check on the hygiene habits of staff members who handle or serve food to ensure that they are washing their hands with soap frequently to help prevent the transmission of bacteria.

In addition to tracking food costs, the nutritional content of the meals must be monitored regularly by the dietitian. This measure is essential for federally funded programs.

Staff should note the amount of food left on the plates after the children have finished their meal. Occasionally, the waste can be explained by its being a new food or a different recipe, but it is still wasted food. Plan to serve new food or a new recipe in smaller quantities until the children develop a taste for it through repeated exposure.

Parents may give you helpful feedback through the questions they ask and the recipes they request after their children report to them about the foods they are eating at school. Managers may use an evaluation form similar to that shown in Figure 11.6 to check the food system.

FIGURE 11.6   *Food service monitoring guide*

Rating Scale: 4—Very Satisfactory   2—Unsatisfactory
                 3—Satisfactory   1—Very Unsatisfactory

Personnel

____ 1. Dietitian or home economist plans menus with adequate nutritional quality?

____ 2. Food service director takes adequate leadership to ensure high-quality service?

____ 3. Food service assistants are trained to do their jobs adequately?

____ 4. Food service personnel are appropriately clean, with hair nets and clean aprons, and hands washed with soap?

____ 5. Food service personnel are at work on time?

____ 6. Food service personnel have required health checks?

Facilities

____ 7. Is the food service space adequate in size?

____ 8. Is the food service equipment operating properly?

____ 9. Is the storage space adequate in the food service area?

____ 10. Is the refrigeration space adequate?

____ 11. Personnel keep the kitchen, appliances, and counter spotless?

____ 12. Children's chairs and tables are adequate in number and size?

____ 13. Dishes, utensils, and glasses are safe and adequate in number?

____ 14. Appropriate dishwashing procedures are used?

Menu Planning

____ 15. Menus for meals meet minimum USDA standards?

____ 16. Menus for snacks meet minimum USDA standards?

____ 17. Records for federal funding are kept daily (if applicable)?

____ 18. Are cycle menus being used appropriately?

____ 19. Are menus posted for parents and others to read?

____ 20. Are copies of menus made available to parents?

____ 21. Are records of the children's intake maintained?

____ 22. Are children's prescriptions for special diets posted where a substitute cook could easily find them?

(Continued)

FIGURE 11.6 *Continued*

Preparation and Service

____ 23. Do food service personnel know appropriate cooking methods for each type of food?

____ 24. Is food served in a very sanitary manner?

____ 25. Is food served on time?

____ 26. Is food service well organized with each worker knowing the required tasks and doing them well?

____ 27. Is food regularly served family-style?

____ 28. Is adequate attention given to individual children's needs?

____ 29. Does each teacher who sits with children have good rapport with the group of children?

____ 30. Does each teacher get enough to eat?

____ 31. Is a worker ready to take care of emergencies so the teacher does not have to leave the table?

____ 32. Are procedures known to children who have been in attendance for a while?

Interpersonal Climate

____ 33. Do children seem to be happy and enjoying the meals?

____ 34. Are voices quiet and pleasant?

____ 35. Do children seem adequately rested to facilitate eating?

____ 36. Are children regularly given a quiet restful period just before mealtime?

____ 37. Are parents invited to attend a meal periodically?

Nutrition Education

____ 38. Do teachers tell children about foods that are good for them?

____ 39. Do children demonstrate an interest in foods?

____ 40. Are food projects offered in the curriculum?

____ 41. Are parents informed about food projects?

Budgetary Matters

____ 42. Is cost consciousness adequate among food service staff?

____ 43. Is the amount of wasted food reasonable?

____ 44. Is leftover food appropriately stored and used?

____ 45. Does the food service staff plan adequately to avoid running out of commodities, calling for quick trips for supplies?

____ 46. Are orders placed and deliveries made on time?

____ 47. Are deliveries checked for correct quantities?

____ 48. Is petty cash disbursement monitored?

Conclusion

Meeting the children's food needs requires all of the steps in the managerial process—planning, organizing, staffing, leading, and controlling. Meal service may consist of breakfast, lunch and snack, or snack only. Meals may be provided by the center, by the families, or by some combination thereof. Licensing and accreditation standards apply to food service regardless the source. Because of the integrated, holistic nature of young children's thinking and learning, food is viewed as part of the curriculum. Whether they are making a special snack as a science experience or enjoying a healthy lunch with their friends, the children are acquiring knowledge, skills, dispositions, and feelings related to healthy nutrition. The careful monitoring of expense, waste, and leftovers is essential to get the most nutrition from the food dollar. Federal subsidies help centers meet food expenses if they meet the requirements regarding the income eligibility of the families, provide the right kinds and amounts of food at each meal, and complete the required records and reports.

QUESTIONS FOR REVIEW

1. State the goals for the food service program in a developmentally appropriate child development facility.
2. What are the sources of the standards for meal service in a children's center?
3. What criteria are used for a child-care center to receive federal funds for meals and snacks?
4. List the recommendations for:
   a. feeding infants
   b. feeding 2- to 5-year-olds
   c. seating children at meals

5. Why is it recommended that you have a doctor's prescription if parents want to put their children on a diet?
6. Explain the concept of cycle menus. Prepare a sample cycle menu.
7. Explain the role of employees' personal hygiene in preventing the spread of harmful bacteria through food.
8. List 10 tasks that food service personnel are responsible for in a full-day children's center.
9. List ways the center can:
   a. inform parents about their child's eating habits
   b. enlist the parents' help with their child's nutrition education

PROFESSIONAL PORTFOLIO

1. Write a job description for a food service manager in a child development facility. (See chapter 7 for an example.)
2. Write 15-day cycle menus for breakfast, lunch, and an afternoon snack.
3. Using a desktop publishing program, create a brochure to distribute to families that provides information about children's nutritional needs and suggestions for making mealtimes at home pleasant for the entire family.

RESOURCES FOR FURTHER STUDY

Print

Climbing onto the pyramid: Food and fitness with children (2005, Summer). *Texas Child Care*, 38–42.

U.S. Department of Agriculture (2000). *Building blocks for fun and healthy meals: A menu planner for the child and adult care food program*. Washington, DC: Author. Available online or in hard copy by request at http://www.fns.usda.gov/tn/Resources/buildingblocks.html.

Internet

Food Safety and Inspection Service

http://www.fsis.usda.gov

Food Safety and Inspection Service of the U.S. Department of Agriculture; provides fact sheets on safe food handling, appliances, and food-borne illnesses, and links to other resources.

Food and Nutrition Service

http://www.fns.usda.gov/cnd/Care/ProgramBasics/basics.htm

FNS online, the U.S. Department of Agriculture's Food and Nutrition Service website, with information about eligibility, reimbursement, and meal pattern requirements for the Child and Adult Care Food Program.

Edible Schoolyard

http://www.edibleschoolyard.org

Website of an organic gardening project spearheaded by food writer Alice Waters for middle school children in California with the goal of fostering environmental stewardship by helping children learn about connections between what they eat and where it comes from. Includes links to resources for starting a school garden and revamping school lunches.

CHAPTER TWELVE

Educational Programming

In this chapter we focus on *what happens* in the facility's classrooms and outdoor spaces—what some call the curriculum. As you will learn, curriculum is much more than a sequence of prescribed activities for the children, and the manager's role requires more than merely purchasing a book of activities for the staff to follow. In our view, the manager is responsible for guiding the staff and stakeholders (e.g., corporate sponsors, policy boards, parents) as they select—or invent—the desired curriculum. Then, the manager's role is to do what is necessary to make it possible for the staff members to do *their* work—implement the chosen curriculum so that it supports the children's growth and development as fully as possible.

Preliminary Organization

Your mission statement provides a starting point for developing an educational program. The decisions you make about the educational program will both dictate and reflect the facility's design, the staff selection, and the implementation of systems to support the staff. In general terms, if the goals of your educational program are for children to explore, to challenge themselves, to form relationships with others, and to experience joy, you need indoor and outdoor playspaces designed and equipped to invite those behaviors. You also need staff with the knowledge and disposition to recognize and appreciate them when they occur. Specific types of educational programs often imply more precise requirements. For example, adopting a Montessori approach calls for specially designed materials and room arrangements, and staff with particular qualifications. All of these aspects are discussed in detail in chapters dealing with organizational, personnel, and facilities management.

As with all of the other aspects of your managerial role, educational programming requires planning, organizing, staffing, leading, and monitoring and controlling. As the educational leader of your center, you will take an active part in planning the overall shape of the educational program. Once your staff is in place, you may delegate the responsibility for organizing individual classrooms and planning the daily activities to the teachers. Then, your management skills will be used to support and facilitate their work and to troubleshoot problems. You must monitor all aspects of the program to be certain that the goals and standards established during your planning sessions become realities.

Regulations and Professional Standards

Planning and implementing an educational program requires familiarity with multiple levels of regulation and professional standards. Some are mandatory (e.g., licensing) while some are voluntary (e.g., accreditation). Others may be either mandatory or voluntary depending upon the program's funding or organizational context. Head Start programs, for example, are required to document 100 specific growth and learning outcomes for children as a condition of their federal funding (Head Start Bureau, 2001). A governing board might establish a policy that its program will attain accreditation (through the National Association for the Education of Young Children or the American Montessori Society, for example). Keeping your program's mission and goals clearly in mind will help you work your way through what can seem like an overwhelming array of requirements.

Licensing

Because state licensing regulations are designed to set minimum standards to protect the health and safety of children in out-of-home care, they typically address educational programming only in general terms. For example, they usually require that centers provide certain types of activities (e.g., construction, dramatic play, art, outdoor play) in order to promote development in all domains and that there be a sufficient number of each type of material to accommodate the number of children in care. Knowing and complying with these requirements is essential but only the first step toward creating a high-quality educational program.

Decisions, Decisions . . .

What aspects of the educational program are addressed by licensing regulations in your state? (If you have not already done so, you can access the relevant documents and the responsible agency at the website for the National Resource Center for Health and Safety in Child Care, http://nrc.uchsc.edu/STATES/states.htm.) Discuss with your classmates how a manager of a child development program would go about meeting these requirements.

Accreditation

Accreditation gives early childhood professionals a goal to work toward after meeting the minimum licensing standards. It also gives parents some assurance that their child is receiving appropriate opportunities to develop cognitively, physically, socially, and emotionally. High-quality children's programs were largely unrecognized until 1984, when the NAEYC launched its center accreditation program. In April 2005, the NAEYC governing board approved new Early Childhood Program Standards and Accreditation Performance Criteria. The new standards focus on four areas: children, teaching staff, partnerships with family and community, and leadership and administration. In the first focus area (children), educational programming is addressed in standards for relationships, curriculum, teaching and assessment:

- The program promotes positive relationships among all children and adults to encourage each child's sense of individual worth and belonging as part of a community, and to foster each child's ability to contribute as a responsible community member.
- The program implements a curriculum that is consistent with its goals for children and promotes learning and development in each of the following domains: aesthetic, cognitive, emotional, language, physical, and social.
- The program uses developmentally, culturally, and linguistically appropriate and effective teaching approaches that enhance each child's learning and development in the context of the program's curriculum goals.
- The program is informed by ongoing systematic, formal, and informal assessment approaches to provide information on children's learning and development. These assessments occur within the context of reciprocal communications with families and with sensitivity to the cultural contexts in which children develop. Assessment results are used to benefit children by informing sound decisions about children, teaching, and program improvement (National Association for the Education of Young Children, 2005).

Detailed performance criteria have been developed for each standard, and criteria are identified as applying to all early childhood programs ("universal") or to programs serving particular age groups (infant, toddler, preschool, or kindergarten). For example, in the category of relationships, one group of criteria pertains to "creating a predictable, consistent, and harmonious classroom." Criterion 1.29 states, "When children's behavior exceeds group limits, teachers respond by keeping all children safe, and then provide feedback that builds children's competence," and applies to all programs. Criteria 1.31 and 1.32, requiring teachers to promote prosocial behavior and counter potential bias and discrimination, apply only to toddler, preschool, and kindergarten programs.

The standards define curriculum as including "the goals for the content that children are learning, the planned activities linked to these goals, the daily schedule and routines, and the availability and use of materials for children." To become accredited, programs must foster children's development and learning in seven domains:

1. social–emotional
2. early literacy
3. early mathematics
4. technology, scientific inquiry, and knowledge
5. understanding ourselves, our communities, and our world
6. creative expression and appreciation for the arts
7. physical development and skills

Criteria for teaching approaches address scheduling, environments, handling routines, and interacting with children in ways that build on their strengths and support their intellectual development. Criteria for assessment specify areas to be addressed in the program's plan for assessment; characteristics of appropriate procedures; communicating with families. They also delineate appropriate uses of assessment to identify children's interests and abilities, determine their progress toward program goals, and make needed adaptations.

Tiered or Rated Licensing

As mentioned in chapter 5, some states have instituted a tiered licensing system to recognize and reward providers who exceed minimum standards, thus encouraging others to do the same. Several states have adopted the **Early Childhood Environmental Rating Scale** (Harms, Clifford, & Cryer, 2005) and companion scales for infant and toddler, school-age, or family home child care as a component of their rating system. Managers who strive to attain a higher-level license will need to become familiar with indicators of quality defined by these instruments. In addition to requirements for space and furnishings, personal care routines, and provisions for parents and staff, the scales address several aspects of educational programming:

1. The "language and reasoning" subscale contains four items pertaining to number and types of books and pictures, and the ways adults support children's communication and thinking skills throughout the day.
2. The "activities" subscale identifies types of activities to be included (e.g., fine motor, art) as well as materials to support those activities and amount of time children should (or in the case of electronic media, should not) have access to those materials. The program's attention to diversity is also considered here.
3. The "interactions subscale" assesses the general tone of interactions among children and between staff and children as well as the ways staff supervise play and guide behavior.
4. The "program structure" subscale assess the balance and flow of the daily schedule with specific attention to provisions for freeplay, group time, and children with disabilities.

Each item in each subscale is rated on a scale from 1 to 7, with 1 being inadequate and 7 being excellent. For example, in the "activities" subscale, a program would score a 1 if art activities were rarely available or never involved individual expression. It would score a 7 if, in addition to meeting criteria for the amount and accessibility of materials and providing plentiful opportunities for free expression, some art activities reflected other classroom experiences, children could occasionally carry a project over several days, and the program provided opportunities for using materials like clay or wood (Harms et al., 2005, p. 28).

State Early Learning Standards

In response to the federal government's Good Start, Grow Smart initiative and requirements of the Child Care and Development Fund, your state may have established standards for children's learning and development before kindergarten in addition to requirements for licensing. While licensing and accreditation focus on what goes into the educational program, early learning standards focus on outcomes—on what young children should know or be able to do by the end of their participation in those programs.

As of 2005, 36 states had published such standards and more were in the process of doing so. Most of these standards address five domains defined by the National Education Goals Panel (physical–motor, social–emotional, approaches to learning, language, and cognition), although they vary in the degree to which particular domains are emphasized as well as in the overall level of specificity. Academic areas (language and cognition) are represented in state standards at about three times the rate for developmental areas (social–emotional, physical–motor, and approaches toward learning) (Scott-Little, Kagan, & Frelow, 2005).

Managers of child development programs that use state standards can help raise the level of quality of their educational programs, but only if those standards adhere to principles established by the National Association for the Education of Young Children and National

Association of Early Childhood Specialists in State Departments of Education. They must address all domains of development and establish expectations that are meaningful, developmentally appropriate, and sensitive to cultural, linguistic, and ability differences among children (NAEYC & NAECS/SDE, 2002). Ideally, state standards will not replace or drive educational programming, but simply provide a gauge of whether your curriculum does, in fact, address what your state expects of young children. Given the fact that many states' standards place disproportionate emphasis on the domains of language and cognition, you may establish much broader and more comprehensive expectations for what children will gain from your educational program. Unfortunately, there is a danger that, in their zeal to focus on areas covered in the standards, some programs will scale back their efforts to support development in all domains. NAEYC accreditation criteria (which affirm the importance of all domains) can help you safeguard against this pitfall if you happen to work in a state with narrowly defined standards. The goal should be a program that is *both* developmentally appropriate *and* meets state standards, not either/or.

The Early Childhood Education Assessment Consortium of the Council of Chief State School Officers has conducted a survey to determine which states had developed standards and how the standards were being implemented. You can access findings from the survey at http://www.ccsso.org/content/PDFs/ECstandards.pdf to learn more about the status of early learning standards in your state.

Decisions, Decisions . . .

Find out whether your state has established early learning standards and, if so, whether they are mandatory or voluntary. If they are mandatory, which child development programs or types of programs must comply? Compare those standards with your state's licensing regulations and with NAEYC accreditation standards for educational programming. Discuss your findings with your classmates.

Selecting a Curriculum Model or Approach

You will have no shortage of options when choosing a curriculum model or approach for your educational program. Some models prescribe particular practices based on a particular individual's beliefs about how children grow and develop rather than formal theory. Maria Montessori, for example, was an Italian physician who began her career as an educator working with children with mental retardation. The methods and materials she designed proved successful, and in 1907 she established a school for poor children in a Roman tenement, where she continued to refine her ideas. She was ahead of her time, however, and did not receive wide recognition among educators in the United States until the 1960s. Of the thousands of schools that currently identify themselves as "Montessori," only about 1 in 5 are formally recognized by either the American Montessori Society or the Association Montessori Internationale (Edwards, 2002). Montessori schools are characterized by the concept of the "prepared environment," in which furnishings are child sized and self-correcting materials, such as cylinders or blocks in graduated sizes, are carefully displayed on low shelves so that children can select their own "work" and return the items when they have finished. The use of the term *work* for these activities conveys the sense of respect for the child that is further exemplified by the soft voices and serious demeanor of the adults as they interact with the children. These ideas have become an accepted part of a developmental approach to early childhood education and can be seen in many programs that do not identify themselves as Montessori schools (Crain, 2005, pp. 65–86). Even among Montessori practitioners, however, there is variation in the extent to which these ideas are followed.

Other models attempt to apply the ideas of theorists whose own work did not prescribe specific educational methods. (Chapter 3 provided an overview of those theories.) For example, Constance Kamii studied with Piaget and has written several books suggesting ways that his theory can be used to help children build their understanding of arithmetic in more appropriate and effective ways. The High/Scope Curriculum is also based on Piaget's theories and has been widely used by child development programs as well as public schools.

Because many curriculum models incorporate elements of several theories, another way to conceptualize differences among them is to look at whether they focus on the individual child's specific skills, on the physical or social context for learning and development, or on the content to be learned. For each of the types discussed below, Figure 12.1 gives an example of a published curriculum for infants and toddlers and another for children ages 3 to 6.

- Some curricula focus on eliciting or supporting the **individual child's specific skills** in each domain of development (e.g., fine and gross motor, cognitive, social, communication, and adaptive or self-help). Teachers assess the children to determine which skills or objectives they have mastered and then follow a prescribed sequence of progressively more challenging activities thought to support the next level of achievement. A target skill for a child who can stand without support, for example, is to take steps while holding on to an adult with two hands. Adults are directed to design particular activities to practice walking or to look for opportunities to embed the practice in the child's daily routines.

- Some curricula focus on establishing a **physical and social context** that supports learning and development. The emphasis can be on a **physical environment** that facilitates children's spontaneous play as the primary means of physical, social, emotional, and intellectual growth. Such a curriculum views the classroom as the textbook and the teacher as both the designer who enriches the textbook and the guide who helps the children get the most from it. The High/Scope approach (based on Piaget's theory of cognitive development) emphasizes the **key experiences** that children should have as a consequence of their interaction with the environment, with their teachers, and with other children. The representation of one's ideas, communicating them to others, is one such key experience; for example, drawing a picture of one's block structure. Other key experiences include classification, language and literacy, and relating to adults and other children.

- Another approach focuses on **content or concepts** to be learned. The **thematic approach** suggests that teachers select a topic (such as farm animals or community helpers) and organize activities or infuse materials related to that topic throughout the classroom. The **project approach** differs from the thematic approach in that neither the topic for investigation nor the length of time devoted to its study is predetermined by the teacher. Once teachers have identified a topic, either because they have observed an interest during the children's play or because they have a hunch it will be exciting for the children, they help the children organize the investigation of that topic. They might begin with a discussion to elicit the children's current knowledge of the topic, as well as their questions and curiosity. They then follow up with field trips, special visitors, or other activities designed to gather more information. Often, small groups of children collect particular bits of information and devise ways to communicate their findings to their classmates. The project culminates in some event or construction that pulls together all of the new understandings the children have acquired.

FIGURE 12.1 *Examples of curricula*

Focus: Individual Child's Specific Skills	
Examples for Infants and Toddlers	**Example for Children Ages 3 through 5**
Cryer, D., Harms, T., & Bourland, B. (1987). *Active learning for ones.* Reading, MA: Addison-Wesley.	Bricker, D., & Waddell, M. (2002). *Volume 4: AEPS curriculum for three to six years.* Baltimore: Paul H. Brookes.
Bricker, D., & Waddell, M. (2002). *Volume 3: AEPS curriculum for three to six years.* Baltimore: Paul H. Brookes.	

Focus: Physical or Social Context	
Examples for Infants and Toddlers	**Examples for Children Ages 3 through 5**
Dombro, A. L., Coker, L. J., & Dodge, D. T. (1999). *The creative curriculum for infants and toddlers* (rev. ed.). Washington, DC: Teaching Strategies.	Dodge, D. T., Coker, L. J., & Heroman, C. (2002). *The creative curriculum for early childhood* (4th ed.). Washington, DC: Teaching Strategies.
Post, J., & Hohmann, M. (2000). *Tender care and early learning: Supporting infants and toddlers in child care settings.* Ypsilanti, MI: High/Scope Press.	Hohmann, M., & Weikart, D. P. (2002). *Educating young children: Active learning practices for preschool and child care programs.* Ypsilanti, MI: High/Scope Press.

Focus: Content or Concepts	
Examples for Infants and Toddlers	**Examples for Children Ages 3 through 5**
O'Brien, M. (1997). *Inclusive child care for infants and toddlers: Meeting individual and special needs.* Baltimore: Paul H. Brookes.	Schickedanz, J. A., Pergantis, M. L., Kanosky, J., Blaney, A., & Ottinger, J. (1997). *Curriculum in early childhood: A resource guide for preschool and kindergarten teachers.* Boston: Allyn & Bacon.
Maguire-Fong, M. J. (1999). *Investigations: A responsive approach to infant curriculum.* Program for Infant Toddler Caregivers. Available online at http://pitc.edgateway.net/lpt/pitc docs/magfonghnd.html.	Helm, J. H., & Katz, L. (2001). *Young investigators: The project approach in the early years.* New York: Teachers College Press.

251

Some educators have begun to move beyond simply adopting a predefined curriculum model, arguing that rigid adherence to any particular model tends to cast teachers in the role of technicians rather than professionals and decision makers. Inspired by the early childhood programs of Reggio Emilia, Italy, they opt instead for an approach that views teachers as researchers, constantly creating and re-creating their own theories of teaching and learning as they observe and document the children's experiences (Goffin & Wilson, 2001). (See, e.g., Curtis & Carter, 1996; Fraser & Gestwicki, 2000; Wurm, 2005.)

The **Reggio Emilia approach** is just that—an approach to early education that has been evolving in the town of that name since the end of World War II, although it did not come to the attention of American educators until the 1980s (e.g., Gandini, 1984) when an exhibition featuring the work of the town's early childhood schools, "The 100 Languages of Children," began touring the United States. It is not a curriculum or a method; one cannot attend training to become a certified "Reggio teacher," nor can a program become accredited as a "Reggio school," although several schools in the United States have established special relationships with the Italian programs over years of study and interaction. Early childhood professionals who have studied the approach speak of being inspired by it and work to adapt its core principles within their own contexts. These core principles, gleaned from writings and conference presentations by educators from Reggio Emilia and their colleagues in other countries, include the following:

- An image of the child as competent and capable, full of questions and theories and having rights as opposed to needs
- Teachers as researchers who partner with children and with parents and learn alongside them
- The environment as a coteacher, where every aspect reflects the values and history of the participants and supports the children and teachers as they explore and learn
- Parents as full participants in the life of the school who contribute as well as learn in meaningful ways
- School as a place where life (not preparation for life) happens, where values and knowledge are constructed, not merely passed on
- Small group work, collaboration, and many forms of expression (or "100 languages") as essential for learning
- Documentation as a process that involves observing children, collecting and analyzing data, reflecting in collaboration with children, colleagues, and families, and finally presenting results in ways that make the learning of all participants visible

The work produced in the Reggio schools is so compelling and the Reggio educators are so passionate and eloquent in their articulation of the philosophy that many early childhood professionals around the world are eager to study and adopt the approach. While that idealistic yearning for excellence is to be applauded, some caution is also warranted. Educators who do not understand the complexity and depth of thought behind each of the principles can mistakenly assume that they will be "doing Reggio" if they purchase certain types of equipment or set up an *atelier* (art studio). They don't realize that adapting this approach takes years of study and reflection, that it is actually a never-ending process because the approach itself is continually evolving.

If you are a new administrator and the teachers you hire have minimal experience in early childhood education, it might make sense to take a more gradual approach. The curriculum resources described in this chapter are only a few examples that you might use to establish a foundation upon which you could build as you learn more about the Reggio approach. For example, both the Creative Curriculum and the High/Scope approaches provide basic guidelines for setting up an environment to facilitate play and exploration. Both offer specific suggestions for scheduling as well as ways teachers can interact with children, ask questions to provoke thought, and set up small or large group learning experiences. There are training opportunities associated with each as well as systems for assessing children's progress toward educational goals.

Within this overall context, teachers can address particular IFSP or IEP goals by drawing on one of the individual, skills-based curricula. Given a rich environment and a consistent daily schedule that allows plenty of time for play in that environment, children will inevitably reveal their ideas and interests. Once they have become comfortable supporting and observing children's play, teachers can begin to notice emerging topics and help children pursue investigations of those topics, using either a thematic or project approach. As you and your teachers collaborate to implement these approaches, to question and reflect on your practice, you can continue to study more about the Reggio approach, gradually moving toward an adaptation of its principles that is uniquely suited to your particular context.

Developmental Principles

In spite of differences in emphasis, many curriculum types can fit under the umbrella of "developmentally appropriate practice" as defined by the NAEYC. Certainly, all professionals want children to learn and to reach their highest human potential. The label on an early childhood program is not as important as whether the interactions support growth in all areas of development—physical, cognitive, social, and emotional. In order to help staff and stakeholders make an informed choice about which curricular approach to use, the manager must have a firm grounding in basic developmental principles:

1. All human development is based on a physiological foundation that is determined genetically at conception and nurtured during the prenatal period and thereafter. Later development builds on early development; that is, nurturing and education must build on this early genetic base and on each preceding stage of development.
2. Development follows a predictable sequence, provided that the environment permits. That is, given the appropriate opportunities, children walk before they run, babble before they speak, and scribble before they draw faces.
3. Children have individual timetables for moving through the sequences of physical, social, cognitive, and emotional development. One child may walk at 8 months, another at 15 months; one gets the first tooth at 4 months, another at 12 months; one speaks a first sentence at 16 months, whereas another is twice that age—but all are within a normal range of development.
4. From large, global behavior patterns, more specific and more complex patterns emerge and combine with others to form increasingly specialized abilities and skills. A child first grasps an object like a crayon in a fist, then uses fingers and thumbs together to pick up tiny objects, and finally masters a keyboard or violin. Each skill is increasingly complex, requiring integration with other skills. Similar examples can be given for development with respect to reasoning, speaking, or getting along with others.
5. Development is influenced by internal and external factors, as well as by interactions between the two. For example, a child may be delayed in walking because of internal factors, such as neural or muscular disorders, or because of external factors, such as a lack of opportunity. A child who experiences both a physical disability and an unsupportive environment is likely to have greater delays.

6. There are dynamic interrelations between areas of development. For example, with the increase in speech development comes an increased ability to play with other children, showing a connection between speech and social development. With increased motor control and the ability to hold a crayon, pencil, or paintbrush, the child can explore and express ideas through drawings and paintings.

7. Various developmental critical periods have been identified. If certain conditions exist during those periods, a child can be prevented from proceeding to more advanced levels. For example, because the first year of life is so important for brain development, good nutrition and freedom from disease are essential during this critical period. Motor performance studies indicated that skills such as running, jumping, and skipping must reach a certain level by age 6 or individuals are very likely to experience difficulty with the games of school age and adolescence (Seefeldt & Haubenstricker, 1982).

8. Individuals generally behave as though they are striving to reach a maximum potential. When deprivation, nutritional or otherwise, is severe, the body shows a strong drive to overcome the deficiency. When avenues for growth are blocked, many individuals find ways around those roadblocks. For example, a sightless child uses all of the other senses to compensate for the deficit. Thus, the individual strives toward health and independence, rather than illness and dependence.

Basic Guides to Program Development

Keeping developmental principles in mind, you can provide an effective educational program for young children if the teachers have adequate training, sufficient protected and paid time to plan carefully, and the manager's support and encouragement. Teachers should make tentative, general plans for their assigned age group, then observe and seek additional information to understand the individual development of each child within the group. The following 10-point guide gives teachers and managers a framework for planning and evaluating their program:

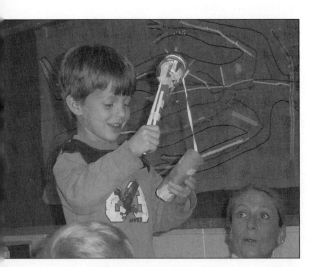

Children ages 3 to 5 enjoy group times that are meaningful—for example, when they share the work they have done on a class project.

1. A good program is planned for the whole child with an emphasis on the child's strengths and potential. Whether the child is from a small or large family, the city or country, an advantaged or disadvantaged home, the program addresses the physical, social, emotional, and fundamental cognitive aspects of development—much more than narrow academic goals.

2. A good program is inclusive. It proactively extends its services to children with or at risk of developing disabilities, and it collaborates with families and other professionals to accommodate the special needs of those children in order to foster their development to the fullest extent possible. This aim is articulated in the program's philosophy and affects every decision—curriculum selection, teaching strategies, environmental arrangement, staff development, and relationships with the families (Delaney, 2001).

3. A good program accepts and treats all children with respect, regardless of race, gender, or ability. Adults teach the children to value who they are, to show empathy for

those who are different from them, and to recognize and stand up against unfairness toward themselves or others. In other words, a good program incorporates the principles of an **antibias curriculum** as outlined by the NAEYC (Derman-Sparks, 1992).

4. A good program begins where the children are in their development. Plans are based on observations made as the children engage in naturally occurring play and interactions, rather than on prescribed or scripted activities.

5. A good program provides balance. Children have opportunities for both active and quiet play. Teachers allow plenty of time for the children to initiate their own activities, and they also introduce their own ideas, or provocations, to stimulate the children's thinking. In large time blocks, the child has the freedom to select the type of activity preferred. The schedule balances the routines of physical care and learning experiences in a logical sequence of events. Recognizing that tension and fatigue interfere with learning, teachers avoid prolonged sitting as well as prolonged physical exertion.

6. A good program recognizes that the "children's emotional and social development is as important to school readiness as their cognitive and language development" (Fenichel, 2001, p. 8). A good program supports emotional development by providing **continuity of care** so that the children, particularly infants, can develop secure relationships with their primary caregivers. For the same reason, the program facilitates the transition from home by welcoming and working closely with the parents as the child acclimates to the new environment (Cryer & Harms, 2000, pp. 356–357). It supports social development by offering materials and activities that invite the children to play with one another, learning through experience to share, to take turns, to interact with individuals and groups, to choose friends and to be chosen. At the same time, the program allows the children to be alone and regroup as needed, to grow in self-direction and independence within the context of appropriate limits on behavior, to learn to make choices that respect the rights of others and to learn the reasons for rules.

7. A good program encourages thinking. It encourages children to think, reason, remember, experiment, and generalize. It engages the children's minds with topics and materials that are both attractive and meaningfully connected to the children's lives and the world they inhabit. It engages the teachers' minds as well, so that they become learners with the children, discovering new ideas about a particular topic as well as about the children in their care. Teachers observe carefully and follow up on the children's interests as they plan experiences.

8. A good program encourages the children's verbal expressions. To learn words and sentence structure, children must have an opportunity to talk. In addition, it supports and encourages the children's use of many "languages" to explore and express their thoughts—graphic art, reading or telling stories, dramatic play, music, and movement are part of every day's activity. Creativity is valued, fostered, and recognized.

9. A good program encourages the children to learn about and care for their bodies. It establishes a routine of washing, eating, resting, and eliminating, and it places priority on safety training, both to protect the children and to teach them to protect themselves. It is action packed with daily opportunities, indoors and outdoors, to exercise the whole body. The classroom is frequently noisy compared to traditional upper-age classes. When bad weather prevents going outdoors, adequate provision is made for gross-motor activities in semisheltered or indoor areas. The reasons why action, noise, and talking are permitted may have to be explained to administrators and others so that the program is not curtailed unnecessarily.

10. A good program includes the parents in partnership with the teachers and children, recognizing the parents' primary importance to their children's growth and development. Communication is two-way with the center actively soliciting and accepting the parents' opinions and ideas, as well as offering support, advice, and appropriate referrals as needed.

Manager's Responsibility for the Educational Program

There are six major ways managers can support the teachers who are delegated the task of producing high-quality programs.

1. *Managers must know what constitutes high quality and appropriate interaction.*

Managers cannot support high quality unless they know what it is. Even those who have been in the field for years must invest time and effort to stay abreast of the rapidly expanding knowledge base. Managers who are well informed have more resources to share as well as greater credibility with the professional teaching staff. Basic child development principles may have stayed the same for many years, but ideas about how those principles should be applied undergo constant transformation as new information becomes available.

Years ago, for example, early childhood teachers believed that reading and writing were matters for elementary school and bemoaned the "pushed-down" curriculum that brought workbooks into programs for young children. As more research about very young children's awareness of print became available, teachers began to think about ways to support this emergent literacy. Those who were stuck in their earlier (justified) resistance to workbooks did not want to hear about writing centers for young children, but those who kept abreast of new developments found that supporting literacy acquisition was very appropriate—and lots more exciting than "teaching prereading skills." Unfortunately, in some programs the emphasis has moved from supporting emergent literacy to literacy instruction, which is so narrowly defined and repetitive that it is actually counterproductive (Neuman & Roskos, 2005).

A similar tension exists between those who feel computers have no place in early childhood programs and those who believe that the program that does not offer this experience is failing to prepare its children for life in the 21st century. Certainly, television and computers have become fixtures in the lives of American children, and child development professionals worry that there has been insufficient research to fully understand the consequences (Anderson & Evans, 2001). The American Academy of Pediatrics recommends no media exposure for children under 2 and a limit of 2 hours per day with careful adult guidance for older children (2002b). Some intervention specialists argue that computers support many forms of assistive technology and adaptive equipment for children, including toddlers, with disabilities (Wilds, 2001).

Where older children are concerned resolution to the debate may have more to do with how, rather than whether, computers are used. Unfortunately, much of the software available for the general population of young children offers little more than an animated workbook exercise. Even the most up-to-date computer will never replace paints, blocks, dramatic play, or the other traditional early childhood activities that belong in all good programs. Most importantly, even the most user-friendly computer cannot replace complex interactions with living, breathing human beings. Still, convincing arguments are being made for the computer's place alongside these time-tested elements of a high-quality program for 3- to 5-year-olds (Scoter, Ellis, & Railsback, 2001).

Perhaps most importantly, well-informed managers are less likely to fall prey to misinterpretations of research that lead to unsound practices. Recent media attention to the importance of the early years for brain development is a case in point. Some individuals have concluded erroneously that babies benefit from intensive "lessons" designed to teach particular concepts when in fact such lessons may actually impede the infant's learning (Lally, 1999, p. 105).

2. *Managers must hire well-prepared staff and work to ensure that they receive adequate compensation.*

The children's specific learning activities are primarily the responsibility of the center's teachers and caregivers. The manager's role begins with the employment of people who have the professional preparation and know-how necessary to plan a high-quality program. Caregivers' formal education and specialized training are major factors influencing program quality. Those who have more formal education and more specialized training pertaining to children (Howes, 1997; Phillipsen, Burchinal, Howes, & Cryer, 1997) offer care that is more stimulating, warm, and supportive. They are also more likely to organize materials and activities into more age-appropriate environments for children, as reflected in higher scores on scales such as the ECERS and ITERS (Cost, Quality, & Child Outcomes Study Team, 1995). Writing job specifications and job descriptions that reflect these facts and hiring well-prepared people are very important steps toward developing a high-quality program. Providing adequate compensation so that highly qualified people can afford to remain in the field is essential (Russell & Rogers, 2005).

3. *Managers must provide the conditions and resources that highly qualified teachers need in order to do their jobs: appropriate group sizes, sufficient support staff, adequate supplies and materials.*

Span of control, a concept discussed in chapter 7, suggests that small groups allow teachers to plan for and interact more effectively with the children as well as with parents. Some state licensing standards set limits on group sizes. The National Day Care Study found that a group size of 18 for 3- and 4-year-olds was optimal. The NAEYC accepts a group size of 20 children with the important proviso that the group has highly qualified staff.

Teachers do not work in a vacuum; they need the support of many others. Some support staff are professionals who render specific services to the center's children and parents. A pediatrician might serve as the child-care health consultant (discussed in chapter 10) to provide guidance and information regarding health issues. A psychologist might be consulted about a particular behavior problem, or a family-life educator might plan and chair a series of parent meetings on topics that parents face during child rearing. Volunteers can do a number of routine chores, extending the energies of the regular staff. All support personnel, paid or volunteer, require training to be really helpful, a responsibility that the manager must assume.

Children need equipment, games, books, and materials that support their desire to explore, discover, try out, talk about, think about, question, and expand their understanding and control of their world. Managers support teachers by making sure that the appropriate items are available in sufficient quantity and at the time and place needed.

4. *Managers must provide opportunities and support for teachers to plan the program.*

Careful planning and preparation for each day are hallmarks of high-quality programs. They help ensure rich experiences for children and increase each teacher's ability to be relaxed and responsive to children's needs and interests. When planning and preparation are adequate, the children are busy and

Managers support curriculum when they provide appropriate equipment and encourage teachers to facilitate children's exploration.

Teachers need protected time to collaborate and plan an effective curriculum.

productive in their classrooms and play yards. A lack of planning can result in programs that are either chaotic or dull and repetitive.

Given the importance of planning, it follows that teachers should be paid for the time it takes. Far too many teachers in today's child-care centers must do what planning they can after working 8 hours with the children. They plan tomorrow's activities in the kitchen while they prepare supper or after they put their own children to bed. Overworked teachers are forced to draw on ideas that have worked in the past, taking little time to develop new ideas or improved approaches. Many do not have much time to confer with their coworkers, sharing ideas and insights. This lack of paid planning time is a major impediment to high-quality educational programming.

Managers must find a way to provide the teachers with a few hours away from the children each week so that they can think, read, organize, confer with colleagues, and develop challenging ideas. The less experienced the teacher, the more time and support for planning are needed. Managers might consider the following alternatives:

- Hire a permanent substitute who can "float" among the classrooms and free each teacher for a block of planning time one or more days per week.
- Take over each classroom for an hour or two each week to personally relieve each teacher to do planning. (This suggestion has important advantages: The manager practices professional skills, maintains credibility with the staff, becomes better acquainted with the children, and understands program problems and needs.)

After you have arranged the teachers' planning time, you may have to help some to use the time effectively, providing resources or guidance and feedback as they discuss options. Teachers may require help focusing on specific children and developing a program that fits their needs. Another aspect of planning involves coordinating the various programs that might serve the same children. Children with disabilities, for example, might spend mornings in special educational or therapeutic settings and afternoons in a child development center. School-age children often move within the same building—from their regular classroom and teacher to another room with another adult for after-school programs. Too frequently, the staff in one program have no idea what happened in the other—whether it is down the hall or across town. High quality demands that all of the adults in a child's life collaborate to provide the best possible program wherever it happens to occur.

As noted in chapter 8, more experienced teachers may be mentors for less experienced teachers with important benefits for each. Your efforts as manager should be diagnostic—observe where and what help is needed and seek to provide it. By observing teachers as they plan, you may learn where professional development efforts should be focused.

In addition to regular planning, the teachers need to plan for times when they may be absent. Assigning coteachers or a teacher and assistant to each group of children makes it easier to carry on in the absence of one of them. As teachers develop more collegial relationships with the other teachers and assistants, planning becomes a shared process, and everyone in the center knows the daily routine, as well as the current topics or projects under way. Thus, when a teacher is out ill, a substitute has many sources of information and support in addition to the written plans she has helped create. In some centers, the classroom assistant moves into the lead teacher's position during her absence, and the substitute fills the assistant role. Furthermore, as programs move toward a play-based program with large blocks of time for the children to initiate their own projects and activities, the need for adult direction decreases. One first-grade teacher reported with pride that, when she returned from a brief illness, the principal (who had substituted for her in her absence) remarked that the children did not seem to need him at all! They entered the room, marked their name on the attendance chart, put a token in the appropriate container to indicate whether they wanted to order a hot lunch, and went to work in the learning centers according to their individual weekly plans. Obviously, routines have to be established in advance in order for the children to function so efficiently.

5. *Managers must support teachers' continued growth with regular, positive feedback and opportunities for professional development.*

Your goal as a manager is to provide the kind of feedback that fosters teachers' feelings of confidence and competence and encourages them to be self-motivated. Suppose, for example, that you and your staff have decided to use displays of photographs and transcripts of the children's comments to convey information about the curriculum to parents. Instead of telling the teachers that they made a "great bulletin board," you might want to tell them that you are aware of the work that went into it and that you have seen several parents stop to look at the photographs and read the captions. This sort of feedback has been referred to as "encouragement," as distinguished from "praise" (Hitz & Driscoll, 1994). Other ways to ensure that teachers receive positive feedback are to suggest that parents visit a classroom to see the work that a teacher has been doing with the children or to suggest that one teacher consult another because of some particular expertise the latter has to offer.

A potential for growth should be one criterion for employee selection. No job stands still, and everyone should be expected to learn and improve. That is why all job descriptions require that the candidate continue learning by participating in courses, workshops, and other professional development activities. Reference materials for early childhood curriculum should be available in your center to serve as guides and as inspiration for the teachers. As manager, you can make it a practice to maintain an up-to-date collection of professional literature for staff. As a result of their professional growth, teachers are motivated to plan more meaningful learning experiences and more appropriate responses based on a greater understanding of children's behavior. Chapter 8 contains several suggestions for professional development activities.

6. *Managers must interpret program practices for parents and other stakeholders and sometime advocate on behalf of staff when practices they know to be developmentally appropriate are questioned or criticized.*

Helping parents and other members of the public appreciate the experiences offered the children in your program should be high on your agenda. As you conduct enrollment interviews with families, you can inform them of what to expect and what they should appreciate about the type of program you offer. Many parents have little background upon which to base an evaluation and may welcome reassurance from you. A parent may pressure a teacher to have children practice correct letter formation; a board member may complain that your teachers "just let children play" rather than preparing them for school. Your job is to articulate (and help your teachers articulate) the reasons behind educational program decisions. Chapters 13 and 14 provide specific suggestions for ways to do this.

Decisions, Decisions. . .

Have the class break into pairs and role-play a situation in which a program manager responds to a parent's objection that the "children don't do anything but play all day in this center." Remember to try to listen carefully to, and really hear, the reasons for the parent's objection before responding. Discuss the feelings experienced by the "managers" and the "parents" during this exercise. What did you learn?

Scheduling

Schedules help the teachers and the support staff know what to expect as they work together. Schedules help the children gain a sense of security as they come to realize that the sequence of events is the same every day. When children know what to do without being told, they grow in self-direction and confidence.

A general schedule should be posted where parents can see it and have some idea of what their children are doing at particular times of the day. This does not mean, however, that the children's movements must be rigidly programmed minute-by-minute throughout the day. A **time block plan** with generous periods set aside for particular types of activity is more realistic and child-friendly. Figure 12.2 is a sample time block plan for 3- to 5-year-old children, with approximate times noted for each block.

Short-day programs use Time Blocks II, III, and IV; full-day programs follow all of the blocks.

Note that the period for self-selected indoor activity in this schedule lasts at least 90 minutes, followed by another hour for self-selected activity outdoors. For individuals without extensive experience with children's programs, this might seem like an overly long period of "just playing." The importance of play for children's development in all domains has been well-documented (Frost, Brown, Sutterby, & Thornton, 2004) and research has shown that longer play periods promote a greater complexity in the children's thinking, as well as in their social interactions (Christie & Wardle, 1992). The Early Childhood Environment Rating Scale (Harms et al., 2005), a widely accepted measure of quality, underscores this concept by requiring not only that programs make particular types of materials available to children, but also that those materials be accessible to children for a "substantial portion of the day" or at least "one-third of the time the children are in attendance" (p. 7).

Self-selected activity or free play does not mean that children are left to their own devices. Teachers are actively involved during this time, working with individual or small groups of children, commenting, questioning, and guiding. As teachers gain experience with facilitating the children's play, they find that they can also use this time to observe the children carefully. Reflecting on these observations and discussing them with colleagues is the best way for teachers to learn to see the possibilities inherent in play. Therefore, we emphasize again that managers must ensure that the teachers have adequate protected time to carry out this important aspect of planning.

Scheduling for Infants and Toddlers

The daily schedule for infants and toddlers will be even more flexible than that for 3- to 5-year-olds, tailoring the flow of events to the individual needs of each child in care. Physical

FIGURE 12.2 *Time block plan for 3- to 5-year-old children*

Time Block I 7:30–8:30 A.M.	**Arrival and Breakfast** Breakfast for those desiring it; self-selected activities (classroom groups may be combined until more children arrive); clean up.
Time Block II 8:30–8:45 or 9:00 A.M.	**Morning Meeting (Arrival for Short-Day Program)** Groups gather in individual classrooms to discuss plans for day; songs, fingerplays, stories (adjust length of time depending on ages and abilities of children; may begin with only 5 or 10 minutes and gradually lengthen as year progresses).
Time Block III 8:45 or 9:00– 10:30 A.M.	**Self-Selected Activity (Indoors)** Small-group work on projects; free play in interest centers (table toys/games/math materials, art, music/movement, blocks, sand/water, dramatic play, science, writing, books); self-serve snack as an option until 10:00.
Time Block IV 10:30–11:45 A.M.	**Transition; Self-Selected Activity (Outdoors)** Clean up; toileting/handwashing; dress for outside; small groups move outdoors with an adult as they are ready; climbing, running, riding toys, balls, sand/water, swings, slides, books, art, dramatic play.
Time Block V 11:45–12:30 P.M.	**Transition to Lunch (Departure for Part-Day Program)** Toileting, handwashing, lunch served family-style, repeat toileting and handwashing; prepare for nap.
Time Block VI 12:30–2:30 P.M.	**Nap** Quiet music, individual or group story, backrubs; quiet play for children who do not sleep.
Time Block VII 2:30–6:00 P.M.	**Self-Selected Activity (Indoors or Outdoors)** Toileting and handwashing as children awaken; snack in small or large group; wash hands and move to interest areas; outdoor or indoor motor activity available as a choice; prepare to go home; combine classroom groups as numbers diminish; teachers set up for following day.

care routines for feeding, diapering, toileting, and sleeping will occupy much of the time. These should never be rushed through in order to get to more programmed activities, but should be treated as valuable opportunities for pleasurable interactions with rich possibilities for learning and development. On the other hand, infant–toddler programs are not only about feeding, diapering, and putting to sleep. Even very young infants benefit when adults make interesting experiences available to them during the times they are awake and alert. When adults take the time to plan interesting experiences, they are often surprised by very young children's sustained engagement. It may seem at first that life in an infant–toddler room is a nonstop sequence of attending to individual needs, but as time goes on, those individual schedules tend to coalesce around a group rhythm of eating, sleeping, and playing together.

Figure 12.3 is one possibility for organizing the flow of time in an infant–toddler program. Note that lunch is scheduled earlier in the day because the smaller stomach capacity of the youngest children means that they get hungry more quickly. They also tire more quickly so the earlier lunchtime avoids both cranky babies and the possibility that one or more will fall asleep face-down in the mashed potatoes.

Note also that there is no formal "group time" scheduled, although this does not mean that group experiences are not valued. The daily schedule for infants and toddlers, therefore, is built around responding to their needs and respecting their competence. Group experiences occur in very natural, unobtrusive ways. Meals are pleasurable occasions for enjoying one another's company and conversation within a rich multisensory encounter. Children also form spontaneous groups around particularly interesting play materials, and with adult support they are able to sustain these interactions for a surprising length of time. Adults can serve as catalysts for such experiences by offering something interesting to do. How many times has a teacher started reading a book to one child and wound up with a lapful of eager listeners? And how different is the experience for the child who is drawn by the story from that of the child who is told to sit and listen because it is group time?

As Dr. Ronald Lally has frequently pointed out, infants and toddlers have their own built-in "curriculum"—a tremendous curiosity and drive to make sense of the people and things in their world. Adults who interrupt that process to "teach" particular concepts at a given moment may or may not be successful at teaching the intended concept but certainly they risk teaching the child that his or her interests and questions are unimportant.

Families' Role in the Educational Program

Some parents may reluctantly enroll their children in your center, feeling forced by the demands of earning a livelihood to forego precious moments with their children during their formative early years. Others are eager to give their children the advantage of early educational opportunities and social experiences with peers. All parents expect you to treat their children kindly, to protect them from harm, and to help them develop to their fullest potential.

A study confirmed the value that parents place on good-quality care for their children; it also revealed, however, that parents consistently overrate the quality of care their children are receiving. Nine of ten parents gave their centers "very good" ratings, while professional observers found the same centers to be "poor" or "mediocre" (Cost, Quality, & Child Outcomes Study Team, 1995). It seems that although parents want the best for their children, they lack the information necessary to help them judge what is best. Perhaps they have not observed enough programs to have a basis for comparison; perhaps they have never seen a high-quality program in operation; perhaps they have been seduced by glossy brochures and an attractive surface appearance, never actually seeing what happens at the center while they are at work.

As manager, you can also contribute to the ongoing education of parents and the public about the components of high-quality early education. Adults who have not studied child development often rely on their own memories of school to form images of what teaching and learning should be like. They may pressure you and your teachers to provide evidence of such "learning" in the form of worksheets, memorized ABCs, rote counting, and a daily "art" project. Depending on the level of their professional backgrounds, your staff may

FIGURE 12.3   *Time block plan for an infant–toddler program*

Time Block I 7:30–9:30 A.M.	**Arrival and Breakfast** Teachers and parent informally share pertinent information as parent helps child settle into classroom; diapering or toileting and handwashing; bottles or breakfast as needed; infants sleep as needed; older children play freely.
Time Block II 9:30–10:00 A.M.	**Morning Snack** Diapering or toileting and handwashing; group snack for children who can sit up; pleasant conversation encouraged; children allowed to leave table, wash hands, and go play when ready.
Time Block III 10:00–11:00 A.M.	**Self-Selected Activity (Indoors or Outdoors)** Mobile children play freely with blocks, manipulatives, dolls, and dramatic play accessories, books, vehicles and pushtoys; climb on loft; adults invite individuals or small groups to use play dough, clay, paint, or play with water. Adults either bring materials to babies or take babies to interesting experiences (e.g., mirrors, balls, books, music). All go outside for varying length of time depending upon weather.
Time Block IV 11:00–11:45 A.M.	**Lunch; Transition to Nap** Diapering or toileting and handwashing for mobile children; group lunch for those who can sit up; conversation encouraged; children allowed to leave table, wash hands, and go to cots when ready.
Time Block V 11:45–2:30 P.M.	**Nap** Diapering, toileting, handwashing as needed; adults sit next to children and help them settle (read storybooks, rub backs, etc.); children who wake before others are allowed to get up, perhaps be taken outside or to another room to play so they don't wake sleepers.
Time Block VI 2:30–3:00 P.M.	**Snack** Diapering or toileting and handwashing; group snack for children who can sit up; pleasant conversation encouraged; children allowed to leave table, wash hands, and go play when ready.
Time Block VII 3:00–6:00 P.M. (parents begin arriving about 4:00 P.M.)	**Self-Selected Activity (Indoors or Outdoors)** Repeat morning sequence of indoor and outdoor activities. Diapering and toileting as needed and before parents arrive.

share these beliefs or feel coerced by parent demands to resort to these stereotyped substitutes for genuine learning experiences.

Many teachers have found, however, that when they provide the parents with evidence that the children are learning, the demands for worksheets and rote skills are replaced by a new enthusiasm for more appropriate experiences. Chapter 13 contains specific suggestions for approaching this issue. Managers who view this kind of public education as part of their job and plan for it accordingly are less likely to feel burned out at the prospect of facing each year's new group of well-intentioned, but uninformed, critics.

In addition to informing families about your educational program, you can invite them to participate in meaningful ways. Consider the following example.

Rebekah, a teacher in a full-day program, had just finished reading the book *Mama, Do You Love Me?* by Barbara Joosse, to her group of 3- to 5-year-olds. At the lunch table that day, she noticed the children giggling over the words with which the mother in the book addressed her child: "dear one." She explained to the children that "dear one" was a special name that the mother gave her child because she loved her. As soon as she suggested that perhaps the children had their own special names that their families called them, the conversation exploded with each child eagerly telling the others about his or her "special name."

Rebekah noted this enthusiasm and, with her colleagues, planned several ways to follow up on it. At group time, she made a large chart listing each child's name and special name—including the child who declared somberly that her given name should be listed in both columns because "her family did not have special names." She made three sets of laminated cards (one set with each of the children's names; one set with each of their pictures; and one set with each of their special names) and put them out in an attractive three-drawer desk organizer so children could explore them. Because Valentine's Day was coming soon and she wanted to downplay the commercial aspects of the holiday, she composed a letter with the children asking families whether their child had a special name and, if so, what was its meaning or origin.

The letters began to arrive, one or two per day, over the next several weeks. At large group, Rebekah invited the child who had brought a letter that day to sit in her lap as she read it aloud and the other children listened with rapt attention. Afterward, Rebekah placed the letter (in a plastic sleeve) in an album alongside a page displaying the child's photograph, name, and special name. Many of the letters were so heartfelt that they brought tears to the eyes of visitors to the classroom. Most importantly, the album became a focal point that children delighted in sharing with their family members during arrival and pick up times. Some insisted on having each page read aloud; others decided to read only the girls' letters one day and the boys' letters the next. Of course, seeing their children's enthusiasm over the "special names book" inspired families who had not yet sent a letter to do so and eventually the album was complete.

The children often looked at the album alone or with one or two classmates. They used it as a reference when sorting and matching the laminated cards. Soon, many could recognize not only their own and their classmates names, but the special names as well. They even noted that the special names were always printed with "funny marks" (i.e., quotation marks) in front and back. The album became part of the classroom culture for many years. As children left the program over the course of each summer, part of the class ritual was to sing the song about new friends and old: "One is silver and the other, gold." Their pages were then moved to an album appropriately trimmed with gold glitter and titled "Old Friends," while incoming families were invited to add their children's pages to the "New Friends" album.

Decisions, Decisions . . .

What do you think the children learned through the "special names" project? How do you think the children and their families felt about their participation? Can you think of other examples where teachers have noticed children's interests and involved families in exploring those interests? Discuss with your classmates.

Planning Experiences for Children

Interesting, enriching experiences for children may "just happen" in the course of your lives together, but they are more likely to occur if teachers plan thoughtfully. Planning must be based on both the goals your educational program has established for children and your observations of the interests and abilities of the children for whom you are planning. The form you select for your educational program may be influenced by several factors. Published curricula often include suggested daily schedules and forms for planning and recording children's experiences. Some state licensing regulations set specific requirements for what plans must include as well as when and where they must be posted. Some educators argue that, rather than post plans that may or may not be followed in a program where children's interests are paramount, it is more appropriate to post detailed descriptions of what in fact happened in a program during the previous week.

Figures 12.4 and 12.5 are examples of weekly planning forms that some programs have found useful. They are intended as a starting point. You will note that the forms assume that certain materials and supplies are available to the children every day. When additions or changes are planned, children are given time to explore new materials fully over the course of the week (or longer) so that they have opportunities to become comfortable and to discover new and more complex ways of using or combining materials. Teachers record pertinent observations that they intend to follow up on and then write in only the changes or additions that they will make to the various interest centers that week. You will note that the topic proposed for investigation is not reflected in every single interest area because it is assumed that play will go on as usual and children will continue to explore many interests in addition to the one the teachers have selected.

Plans for large group in the 3- to 5-year-old classroom are also somewhat open-ended because it is assumed that every large group includes discussion of what the children plan to do or have done, interesting things that have happened, and (in this classroom) reenactment of stories the children have dictated to the teacher during the time block for self-selected activity. The teachers have noted their intention to compose a letter with the children, and this will probably occur on Monday unless other events overshadow their plans that day. They have also indicated their intention to read aloud the letters that families send to school, but because they cannot predict when or how many letters will come in, they have left this as an option for the remainder of the week—and probably for several weeks to come.

Whatever planning form you adopt, it is likely that you and your teachers will find ways to modify it to suit your own needs and style. Ideally, planning experiences for children is a joyful process, one that taps teachers' deep thinking and creativity, not a tedious ritual that must be repeated for its own sake every week.

FIGURE 12.4 *Weekly activity plan for 3- to 5-year-old children*

Week of Oct. 3–7	Observations to follow up on; Possibilities: • Children fascinated with "dear one," the "special name" a child was given by the mother in the book *Mama Do You Love Me?* • Begin collecting children's "special names" and story behind each? (reading, writing, connections with families, self-image)

Possible Changes/Additions to Interest Areas Available Every Day

Art	Blocks	Dramatic Play	Writing/Reading
Refresh paint jars; have children help mix several shades of one color each day; note their descriptive words for various hues.	Continue sketching children's constructions: offer clipboards and pens if they are interested in doing so themselves.	Watch for "special names" as children enact family roles.	List of names and special names to copy; album to collect and display letters from families along with child's picture and printed name/special name.

Table Toys/Math	Sand/Water	Science/Nature	Music/Movement
Three sets of cards to sort and match: children's names, special names, and pictures.	Add clear tubes and funnels to water table.	Look for changes in garden.	Add scarves and tambourines.

Large Group: Reread *Mama, Do You Love Me?*; make a chart listing each child's name and "special name"; compose a letter to send home to families; read individual letters aloud as received.

Family Participation: Ask family to send letter to school giving child's special name and the story of how it came about.

Reminders: Send letters home with children; post a reminder in entrance.

FIGURE 12.5 *Weekly activity plan for mixed-age infant-toddler room*

Week of *Oct. 3–7*

Observations to follow up on

- All fascinated by arrival of 10-week-old Sarah in infant area; talking about "baby"; watching through divider
- Jerome and Keisha walking short distance without hanging on to furniture
- Angie and Heidi pulling open storage bins under cribs in infant area

Possibilities/additions to materials available every day

Books	**Blocks**	**Art Materials**	**Manipulatives**
Books with pictures of babies; invite children to look at their own albums and talk about when they were "babies."	Cardboard "bricks"	Finger paint	Replace items stored in bins with things children can safely explore; household utensils?

Gross Motor Equipment	**Dramatic Play**	**Music/Movement**	**Sand/Water**
Push carts to support independent walking; encourage moving cartloads of toys from one area to another?	Add baby bottles and small blankets to dolls	CD: *Lullabies from around the world*	Baby basin with soapy water and towels for bathing "babies"
			Science/Nature
			Take "babies" outdoors; dress for weather; support A & H's exploration of space and containment

Family Participation: Ask families for wooden or plastic cooking utensils to put in storage bins; request baby pictures for children who enrolled as toddlers (as center does not have earlier images in our documentation files).

Reminders: Take pictures to document Jerome and Keisha's new walking skills; collect examples of what toddlers know about babies.

Conclusion

Serving children and families is the primary reason for a child development program's existence. The manager plays a key role in determining the quality of that service. The programming must be based on sound developmental principles. The manager's job is to hire staff members who are well grounded in those principles, and then to support them as they plan and implement the program. Support includes providing paid planning time, adequate auxiliary staff, sufficient materials and equipment, regular feedback and encouragement, and ongoing opportunities for professional development. The manager also serves as a go-between, interpreting the program for parents and other stakeholders and defending it when necessary.

QUESTIONS FOR REVIEW

1. Discuss high-quality programs from a manager's perspective with respect to decisions about the age of the children, group size, and adult–child ratio.
2. Describe several approaches to curriculum for young children.
3. Define and give an example of a child's growth, development, and maturation.
4. List the 10 guides to program development and provide an example of each.
5. List the six ways a manager can support high-quality programs.

PROFESSIONAL PORTFOLIO

1. Plan a PowerPoint (or other digital imaging technique) presentation on curriculum innovations for a center's staff. Practice giving the presentation to your class, encouraging suggestions for improvement. Improve the presentation for a larger audience, and propose that your workshop be given at a meeting of local early childhood professional organization or at a conference of teachers.
2. Develop an annotated list of at least 10 resources (print, video, or Internet) addressing some aspect of developmentally appropriate programs for children. Give the title, author, publisher, publication date, cost, and purchasing information for each resource. Under each entry, summarize and evaluate the content and describe how you might use it in a center.

RESOURCES FOR FURTHER STUDY

Print

Dodge, D. T., Colker, L. J., & Heroman, C. (2000). *Connecting content, teaching, and learning: A supplement to the creative curriculum for early childhood.* Washington, DC: Teaching Strategies.

Kostelnik, M. J., Soderman, A. K., & Whiren, A. P. (2004). *Developmentally appropriate curriculum: Best practices in early childhood education* (3rd ed.). Upper Saddle River, NJ: Merrill/Prentice Hall.

Sandall, S., McLean, M. E., & Smith, B. J. (2000). *DEC recommended practices in early intervention/early childhood education.* Longmont, CO: Sopris West and Denver, CO: The Division for Early Childhood.

Wurm, J. P. (2005). *Working in the Reggio way: A beginner's guide for American teachers.* St. Paul, MN: Redleaf Press and Washington, DC: National Association for the Education of Young Children.

Internet

National Association for the Education of Young Children

http://www.naeyc.org/accreditation/next_era.asp

Overview and samples of NAEYC Early Childhood Program Standards and Accreditation Performance Criteria

Administration for Children and Families

http://nccic.acf.hhs.gov/statedata/statepro/index.html

Administration for Children and Families website with contact information for agencies involved in early childhood education in each state as well as links to additional state and national resources.

Clearinghouse on Early Education and Parenting

http://ceep.crc.uiuc.edu/poptopics/preschoolcurr.html

The Early Childhood Education Curriculum Debate: Direct Instruction vs. Child-Initiated Learning (written by Ron Banks in 2001, updated June 2004) for the Clearinghouse on Early Education and Parenting; summarizes key points and includes links to numerous resources on the topic.

Municipal Infant–Toddler Centers and Preschools of Reggio Emilia

http://zerosei.comune.re.it/inter/nidiescuole.htm

Website of the Municipal Infant–Toddler Centers and Preschools of Reggio Emilia; describes key features and the rationale behind each.

Family Support

A child development center is an organization designed to provide a service to families. It is part of the human ecological system's social–cultural environment described in Chapter 3. One way to look at the social–cultural environment is to envision a vast network of interconnected parts. The center has a connection with each family whose child is enrolled. Those families have connections to one another, partly as a consequence of their involvement with the center. The center and the families have specific connections with agencies and institutions outside the center, as well as general connections with society as a whole.

Maintaining these connections is essential to the survival of individuals, families, and institutions. One of your major functions as manager is to facilitate the communication between your center, the families you serve, and the rest of the community. To do so, you must use the managerial processes discussed throughout this book: planning, organizing, leading, staffing, and monitoring and controlling for quality. Your success benefits the children in your care, their families, your center, and your community. This chapter examines the ways that child development programs partner with and support families.

Relationships with Families

Children do not exist in a vacuum. Serving children means serving families, and that requires both an understanding of how family systems work and an appreciation for diverse parenting styles. It means forming partnerships with parents and knowing enough about your community to help the families access resources necessary to promote family wellness.

Once parents enroll their children in your center, they become consumers of your service. The most obvious example of the service is the direct care and education you provide for the children, supplementing the parents' time, energy, and know-how. In a deeper sense, however, parents are much more than consumers. The service you provide is a human service, qualitatively different from tuning a car engine or dry-cleaning a family's clothing. It is a long-term commitment of time and energy, unlike cutting someone's hair or giving a manicure.

Because of the unique character of the service you provide, your staff and the families are partners in the important task of nurturing children and supporting their development.

Regulations and Professional Standards

Licensing regulations typically require that child development programs provide families upon enrollment with written policies regarding admission, withdrawal, fees, schedule of operation, health requirements, and discipline or guidance. Once children are in care, centers are expected to keep parents informed via posted menus and written records of accidents or injuries. Centers caring for infants and toddlers must provide records of children's food intake, bowel patterns, and developmental milestones.

The Early Childhood and Infant/Toddler Environment Rating Scales address these issues in the indicators for minimal quality in the provisions for parents. Also at the minimal level, programs are expected to offer "some possibilities" for family involvement. Programs must exceed this standard and encourage family involvement in multiple ways at the "good" level. At the "excellent" level, parents participate in program evaluation and governance (Harms et al., 2005, p. 67; 2003, p. 49). A comparable evaluation tool, the Program Administration Scale (Talan & Bloom, 2004), distinguishes among inadequate, minimal, good, and excellent provisions for family support and involvement based in part upon the number of ways the center responds to family needs: e.g., providing a toy or resource library, extended hours, transportation, scholarships, or referral services (pp. 42–43).

NAEYC Guidelines

The National Association for the Education of Young Children (NAEYC) views establishing reciprocal relationships with families as an essential component of developmentally appropriate practices. This requires moving beyond the traditional "parent education" approach that has often characterized the interactions between child development programs and families. It means asking more of the parents than merely baking cookies for the center's fund-raiser. It means finding new, creative ways to communicate with families who may be too busy and too tired to attend evening workshops. It does not, however, mean turning over all program planning to the families.

The NAEYC offers the following eight guidelines for building partnerships with families:

1. Realize that in order to serve children well, you need the families as much as they need you. Although you or your teachers may disagree with particular families on some matters, if you remember that the goal you have in common is the good of the child, you can respect each other and work to resolve any difficulties.

2. Building a strong relationship requires "regular, frequent, two-way communication" between the partners. As an administrator, you have many opportunities to share program information with the families and to listen to their concerns. It is also your responsibility to encourage your teachers to establish lines of communication with the families and to support their efforts to do so.

3. Family involvement extends beyond the observation of and participation in classroom activities to having a voice in decisions regarding their children's care.

4. Teachers strive continually for balance, honoring what the families want and hope for their children without forgetting or ignoring what they know about child development and early education.

5. Programs offer frequent opportunities for families and teachers to share information about the children through day-to-day encounters, as well as formal conferences.

Families have the final say in decisions involving their children. Teachers and other child development professionals can provide information to help the families make decisions; perhaps more importantly, they can help the families see themselves as capable.

6. Teachers realize that they have only part of the picture. Therefore, they ask the families to share what they know about their children's development and to help plan appropriate programs.

7. Program staff help families access appropriate services, taking into account what the families say they need or want. The staff also help them tap into existing strengths or support networks.

8. Center staff help families navigate the social and health service system. They work with the families to pass along information about a child's development that smoothes the transition from one program to another. (Bredekamp & Copple, 1997, p. 22)

DEC Guidelines

While the NAEYC guidelines are intended to apply to programs serving *all* children, the Division for Early Childhood (DEC) of the Council for Exceptional Children focuses specifically on children with or at risk for developing disabilities. This organization has identified four clusters of recommended practices in early intervention and early childhood special education. A careful review of these recommended practices reveals close parallels with the NAEYC guidelines, suggesting the extent to which these two organizations have communicated and collaborated.

1. *Families and professionals share responsibility and work collaboratively.* Family members and professionals work together to establish goals and work toward their accomplishment; professionals support the families' ability to make informed choices by providing information; and they are sensitive and respectful of each family's unique culture, language, and identity.

2. *Practices strengthen family functioning.* The aim is for families to make choices and access resources in order to reach the goals they set for themselves; professionals support this process by providing information and opportunities for experience in the least disruptive way.

3. *Practices are individualized and flexible.* Services are not provided in a one-size-fits-all format; rather, they are tuned to the priorities and preferences of individual family members; professionals recognize and respect the families' unique characteristics stemming from their cultural, ethnic, and socioeconomic background, as well as the community context; and they take into account the families' beliefs and values.

4. *Practices are strengths- and assets-based.* Rather than seeking to "fix" families' deficits or shortcomings, professionals look for strengths and assets that can be mobilized; they foster family competence and confidence by building on existing strengths and offering the families opportunities to acquire new knowledge and skills. (Sandall, McLean, & Smith, 2000, pp. 45–46)

As facility manager, you have many opportunities to put these guidelines into practice. You can employ teachers who understand and believe in the concept of partnering with families and are sensitive to cultural, social, and linguistic diversity. Staff can acquire these attitudes and skills through a professional development program. Because children with disabilities may spend more time with your teachers than with the specialists who come to the center to provide specific therapies, the teachers can become valuable members of the transdisciplinary team serving those children and families. For example, a teacher might know that a child routinely performs a particular skill at the center even though she has been unable or unwilling to reveal it to the therapist. Documenting such observations helps the team arrive at a more realistic assessment of the child's true abilities, as well as a more appropriate plan for intervention. Teachers can also learn specific strategies and techniques for infusing therapeutic goals into the child's daily life.

Your role as manager is to ensure that the teachers have time for this type of collaboration and teamwork. You may also find it necessary to advocate for your teachers, making sure that their observations are heard and respected by specialists who might have more advanced training. You may have to help the teachers feel confident enough to speak up, or help the visiting specialists find ways to do their work while respecting the ongoing life of the classroom. At the same time, you may have to pave the way for the specialists by helping the teachers understand and value their work and feel comfortable about their presence in the classroom. On a more mundane level, one administrator of a university-based child development program had to negotiate with the university's parking authorities so that the many professionals serving a child with cerebral palsy could park outside the center each week without being ticketed—or paying the substantial annual fee for employee parking.

Decisions, Decisions . . .

Compare the NAEYC and DEC guidelines for involving family members in child development programs with the criteria included in the environmental rating scales and program administration scale. What common themes do you see? Discuss similarities and differences with your classmates.

Understanding Family Systems

Uri Bronfenbrenner's **ecological model of human development** and the **family ecosystems theory,** discussed in Chapter 3, suggested that, just as families provide the context for the individual child's development, they also exist within a network of formal and informal support systems. These systems provide the resources that enable families to nurture their children, physically and psychologically. The child development facility is one such system. It is important to remember that its role is to supplement and support—not substitute or supplant—the families as the primary context for the children's development. The NAEYC guidelines and the DEC's recommended practices are clearly grounded in this ecological view of families and children.

Berns (1989, p. 76) identified five functions common to all families. These functions, which may vary widely in the form they take in individual families, are reproduction, socialization, assignment of social roles, economic production and consumption, and emotional support.

Reproduction involves more than just having babies. In order for society to survive, those babies must be cared for and kept healthy and safe so that they can replace members lost through death. Child development centers share with families the primary function of keeping children healthy and safe, and this is a major concern of the managers. The center may also influence the families' reproduction function in at least two other ways. First, the availability of or lack of high-quality child care may influence a couple's decision to have a child. Second, the center might provide some families with the links they need to access other community services such as family planning, prenatal care, and well-baby clinics—all of which contribute directly to the family's ability to raise healthy, functioning members of society.

Socialization is the process by which "society's values, beliefs, attitudes, knowledge, skills, and techniques" are passed on to children (Hildebrand, Phenice, Gray, & Hines, 2000). Child development centers assist with this function in ways that are perhaps too numerous to list. The center's curriculum, with the specific objectives of helping children acquire knowledge and skills, is only the most obvious example of its socialization function. All of the other aspects of the environment and interactions at the center also embody and pass on certain beliefs and attitudes to children—from the tidy shelves that show the children how materials are valued and treated to the way that caregivers foster independence and competence by encouraging toddlers to pull up their own pants after diaper changing.

Because centers have this impact, the staff must ensure that a dominant culture with its values, beliefs, knowledge, skills, and techniques does not obliterate or teach the children to devalue these same aspects in other cultures. This requires center managers and staff to continually educate themselves about today's family forms and lifestyles and about all of the cultures they contact. Only through open and honest communication can centers help, instead of hinder, families with the socialization of their children.

Regarding the assignment of **social roles,** Berns stated that families pass on to their children racial, ethnic, religious, and socioeconomic identities—each consisting of particular behaviors and obligations. Just as with socialization, centers must take care to respect the diversity of social roles that the children bring to the center. Centers might have a positive impact on this family function by helping the parents of children with disabilities see potentials that they had not previously recognized. They can also help families see the value of maintaining a home culture and language so that children do not become cut off from their heritage as they learn new ways.

Economic production and consumption are vital concerns for your center. Obviously, the existence of high-quality child development centers makes it possible for parents to work and participate to a greater extent in the community's economic life. Centers might also provide information that enables the families to become wiser consumers of everything from laundry detergent to television shows to toys.

Emotional support arises from relationships. Relationships developed at the center build on and extend the relationships that children have with their immediate families, fostering trust, independence, and competence. Parents, too, receive emotional support from their interactions with center staff and other parents. All parents have occasional feelings of being inadequate and overwhelmed by the enormous job of child rearing. In the past, they received support from their extended families and close neighbors. In today's mobile society, the center has become, in the words of Ellen Galinsky, a prominent early childhood professional, "the new extended family" (Galinsky & Hooks, 1977).

Parenting Styles

Psychologist Diana Baumrind (1973, 1977) examined differences in parents' expectation levels for mature behavior, degree of control, amount of communication, and emotional nurturance. She found three distinct profiles, which she labeled authoritarian, permissive, and authoritative. According to Baumrind's scheme, **authoritarian** parents expect very high levels of mature behavior from their children and exert strict control methods, including physical punishment for infractions. They offer little in the way of emotional support, however, and do not spend much time explaining the reasons for their rules. At the opposite extreme, **permissive** parents have low expectations, make few demands, and offer little information to their children about why they should behave in particular ways. They do express high levels of caring and concern and may use this as their only tool for encouraging the children to obey—"I won't like you if you do. . . ."

According to Baumrind's research, neither of these styles is associated with increased social responsibility in children. Both produce children who rely on external controls for their own behavior and often suffer low self-esteem. The happy medium seems to be the **authoritative** parenting style. These parents balance high expectations and firm limits with clear explanations of the reasons for those limits and the consequences for transgression, together with an attitude of caring and support. Children of authoritative parents tend to enjoy high self-esteem and the ability to control their own behavior and act responsibly.

Based on this description, it is easy to see why early childhood professionals are often taught to adopt the authoritative style of interacting with children, and why many parent education programs attempt to teach it to parents. There is an important caveat, however—each of the dimensions examined by Baumrind (control, maturity demands, communication, and nurturance) is highly influenced by many factors, including cultural and individual characteristics and values. What appear as harsh, controlling demands to one person might be perceived as emphatic expressions of care and concern by another. One person's effort to foster independence by letting a toddler feed himself might be seen by another as uncaring or missing an opportunity to teach the toddler the importance of nurturing tenderness. A child accustomed to a sharp tone and brusque demands might experience a teacher's softer voice and milder requests as lacking control and caring.

It seems, then, that the three basic parenting styles described by Baumrind can manifest themselves in as many ways as there are parents. What is the child development professional to make of this information? Recalling the NAEYC and DEC recommendation that programs work in partnership with the families to establish and achieve goals, one use of this information might be to empower families by making them aware of the ways in which their behaviors might impact the outcomes they want for their children. Teachers can also learn from families effective ways to communicate with their particular children.

Decisions, Decisions . . .

Divide your class into groups of three. Assign one member of each team to assume the role of parent, teacher, or director. Role-play the following situation: The teacher is concerned because a 4-year-old girl has been having violent tantrums in the classroom. She has asked to meet with the parents to discuss the problem. The parent responds that the problem stems from the teacher's "soft" approach to discipline and reports that spanking has eliminated similar behavior at home. Following the role-play, have the "parents," "teachers," and "directors" meet in a group to discuss how they felt during the exchange. Report each group's findings to the class as a whole.

Cultural Responsiveness

Given the changing demographics of the United States' population (described in chapter 1), it is likely that as a center manager, you will interact with many people who are different from you in some way. Your staff members, as well as the families you serve, may have different ethnic backgrounds; they may not speak the same language you do. They might have significantly less—or significantly more—education and income than you. Their religious faith or lifestyle might differ from yours. One survey of 450 child-care programs in California found that the overwhelming majority served children from at least two racial or language groups (96 and 81 percent, respectively) (Chang, 1993, p. 65). Your success as a manager depends on your ability to communicate across these cultural lines and to collaborate effectively with different people.

Cultural responsiveness is the term used to denote this ability, and it is an important hallmark of the early childhood professional. Cultural responsiveness, sometimes called cross-cultural competence, refers to "ways of thinking and behaving that enable members of one cultural, ethnic, or linguistic group to work effectively with members of another" (Lynch & Hanson, 1998, p. 492). How, you might wonder, can you be expected to acquire this ability if you are likely to work with so many different groups during your career? On the other hand, if you work in a program where everyone seems to share the same ethnic, cultural, and linguistic background, you might think this is something that doesn't apply to you. Either of these views—that cultural responsiveness is impossible or that it is irrelevant—will hinder your efforts to provide the best possible program for young children and their families.

As an early childhood administrator promoting cultural responsiveness, you must address both interpersonal and structural issues. Interpersonal issues concern your own attitudes and the ways you relate to others, as well as your efforts to support culturally responsive attitudes, skills, and dispositions in your staff. Structural issues include environment, staffing patterns, group sizes, and all of the other ways you set the stage for cultural responsiveness to flourish.

Interpersonal Aspects of Cultural Responsiveness

Cultural responsiveness begins with knowledge—knowledge of your own cultural background and the many ways it has shaped your beliefs. If you happen to be a member of the dominant culture in any community, your culture may be as invisible to you as the air you breathe. All of the notions that you take for granted—how children should behave, what they should learn and when, and how adults should treat them—are products of your cultural upbringing. Someone from another culture might have very different ideas about the same things. The problem is, unless you realize how your culture has shaped your ideas, you might dismiss the other person's ideas as simply wrong. The risk of doing this is increased if your culture is strongly reflected in your professional training. Middle-class Anglo-European values, for example, coincide with much of what early childhood professionals learn as "best practice" in the United States (Lubeck, 1994). Uncovering your own cultural heritage is part of the self-reflective knowledge discussed in chapter 2 and an important first step for you and your staff. Several of the resources listed at the end of this chapter suggest exercises that you can do to begin this process.

Cultural responsiveness also requires another kind of knowledge—knowledge of the cultures represented by the families you serve. You can acquire this knowledge by reading, viewing videotapes, or any of the ways you might study any academic subject (e.g., Hildebrand et al., 2000). No matter how much you learn about any particular group in this way, however, it is important to remember that the members of any particular group are as different from one another as they are from you. It is also possible that individual members of two different racial or ethnic groups have more in common with each other than they do with any set of characteristics associated with their respective groups. The best way to avoid the pitfall of lumping all members of a group into one stereotype is to take the risk and ask questions. Instead of making assumptions, you can say, "I've read that. . . . What do you think about that?" If you ask respectfully, conveying your sincere openness and desire to learn, most people are happy to share information about their culture with you.

Knowledge, then, is a necessary component of cultural responsiveness, but it is not sufficient by itself. Being willing to ask questions and being open to and respectful of different ideas are also matters of attitude or disposition. If you open yourself to this way of learning about other people, you will inevitably make mistakes. The key is to foster, in yourself and in your staff, a willingness to apologize frankly for those mistakes and learn from them for the future. Whether these discussions occur in one-on-one situations or in group settings, when people from different cultures make a sincere effort to work together, mistakes are forgiven and may even be found amusing. One of the authors once lived in an African culture where all references to eating were considered unfit for polite company. In her ignorance, she invited some African colleagues to dinner and was both surprised and grateful when they gently informed her of her faux pas. When conflicts do occur, the parties involved should listen to each other, resolve to think about what they heard, and agree to discuss it again later (Gonzalez-Mena, 1997).

Structural Aspects of Cultural Responsiveness

Although the face-to-face interactions between you, your staff, and the families you serve certainly influence your program's level of cultural responsiveness, there is a great deal that administrators can do to set the stage for those interactions. First, the physical environment can reflect and welcome the cultures represented in a program. This involves more than simply tacking up a few commercial images of people in "native costume." It might mean reflecting the program's community by displaying photographs of family members and people, buildings, or places that play an important role in the families' lives. It might mean creating arrangements of beautiful or meaningful objects from each family that represent some aspect of their heritage or the hopes and dreams they have for their children. It can mean including in your CD or tape collection samples of music that the families enjoy at home.

Administrators structure the social environment to support cultural responsiveness when they employ staff members who share the cultural and linguistic heritage of the families they serve. This strategy makes it easier to provide cultural consistency between home and school, which facilitates the children's identity formation and communication with the families. It is also just as important to have representation of the diverse groups at the management level and on governing boards. Finally, administrators can limit the number of children in any one group, thus reducing the potential number of cultures and making teachers' task of relating to those cultures less daunting (Mangione, 1993).

Family-Friendly Practice

Family-friendly is the term commonly applied to professional practices based on conscious efforts to acknowledge the central role of families in their children's development and to accommodate the particular needs of today's diverse families. Copeland and McCreedy (1998) cited a number of social factors that contributed to the emergence of what David Elkind has termed the "postmodern" or "permeable" family. Many of these were discussed in chapter 1: parents who are much younger or older than the typical child-bearing age of past times; more single-parent- or grandparent-headed households; blended families, juggling the demands of widely disparate age ranges; and the earlier return of mothers to the workforce.

Copeland and McCreedy (1998, pp. 311–313) called for a "paradigm shift"—a radical change in the way child development programs view their obligations to meet family needs. They offered several suggestions for making child development programs more family-friendly. Many of their suggestions for program directors echo the NAEYC and DEC guidelines discussed earlier.

1. **With your teachers, take a hard look at your attitudes and beliefs.** Do you assume that parents who don't read your newsletter or who come late to pick up their

children simply don't care? Is that assumption communicated in a look or gesture that makes the parents feel judged or put down? The first step toward a more helpful attitude is talking to the parents to learn what they are really thinking and experiencing. It is likely that your empathy will grow as you acquire accurate information. From that new stance, you can begin the kind of dialogue that leads to collaboration and mutual support.

2. **Rethink your policies.** Do your enrollment forms seem to deny the existence of blended families, single-parent families, families with gay or lesbian parents? If you have a pay-in-advance fee policy, do you make allowances for the families whose care is subsidized by public funds and is paid after the services are delivered? Do you work with families who experience a financial crisis and must postpone payments? How do you support mothers who wish to breast-feed their babies?

3. **Bend a little.** Find "win-win" solutions when your program's usual practices conflict with the families' needs and wishes. Suppose your custom is to schedule parent conferences during nap time. Many parents' work schedules make it impossible for them to attend; yet, it seems unfair to ask teachers to schedule conferences outside their already long workday. Perhaps you can work with the families to find a way to pay the teachers for this overtime work or to hire substitutes so teachers who hold evening conferences can take compensatory time off at some later date.

4. **Find ways to include the families in decisions that impact their children.** Schedule meetings when most family representatives are able to attend and find ways for the other families to voice their opinions—provide written ballots or put suggestion boxes near the entryway. Let the families know that they have been heard by following up on their ideas and telling them about any adjustments in your newsletter.

5. **Create an environment that welcomes families, as well as children.** Comfortable, adult-size furnishings invite family members to linger a few moments with their children before dashing off to work. Some centers make a variety of time-saving services available to busy parents—for example, assistance with tax preparation or voter registration, or access to the center's copy machine and computer.

6. **Keep families informed.** Display staff photos and names in the entryway so that family members know who's who. Provide name tags for substitutes or visitors. Use newsletters, e-mail, websites, and displays in the classroom to give families a glimpse of the life that goes on in your program.

7. **Help families do their job.** Provide lists of community resources; interesting and timely articles; a place to post carpool requests; and class rosters with names, phone numbers, and birthdays. Create a resource library with books and videos on parenting topics—even a collection of high-quality entertainment videos that families can enjoy together.

Building Partnerships with Families

In a recent interview, Paola Cagliari, a *pedagogista* (education coordinator) for the municipal early childhood programs of Reggio Emilia, Italy, spoke of a new way to conceptualize the relationships between families and schools. "One essential challenge is that of modifying the idea of the teacher, who is no longer the holder of certain knowledge that is simply taught to children and parents, enclosed in the security of an unchangeable and incontestable institution and context." But, she added, "At the same time we try to avoid moving toward the idea of a teacher and a school that merely offer a service modeled on the individual needs of families" (Gambetti & Kaminsky, 2001, p. 3). In other words, neither teachers nor families dictate program content; instead, they collaborate to create something that neither could have created alone.

A growing body of research in the United States has demonstrated that parents' involvement, regardless of their wealth or education, is the most important factor for a child's success in school (U.S. Department of Education, 1994). This involvement begins with the family's first encounter with the educational system. For many of today's children, that means when they are carried into the infant room at their child development center. The way that first encounter between parent and educator is handled can color the entire educational career—and thus, the entire life—of that child (Fenichel, 2001, p. 14).

Unfortunately, few states require early childhood professionals to have course work or training in parent involvement skills (FYI: Professional preparation and family involvement, 1995). This places a heavy responsibility on the center's manager to help staff members develop these skills. Care must be taken to avoid several pitfalls. Some parents may have had bad experiences during their own schooling and, as a result, may feel intimidated or hostile toward representatives of "the system." Others might have the opposite reaction and, relinquishing their own role, depend on you to make all of the decisions as the omniscient expert. Still others might feel that they must compete with center staff for their child's affection and respect.

All of these pitfalls hamper the creation of the kind of partnership that works best for all parties involved. There are, however, concrete steps that you can take, from the beginning of your relationship with each family, to help establish that partnership.

To be approved for NAEYC accreditation, your center must have a functioning system that encourages the parents' involvement in their child's care and education. We have already discussed the NAEYC's general guidelines for establishing reciprocal relationships with families. Translated into more specific strategies, NAEYC recommendations include orientation visits, conferences with parents, daily reports to keep parents informed about their child's progress, and telephone conferences with the parents to gain information regarding parental experiences, observations, and wishes. In fact, the NAEYC's assessment of how well your center performs these functions includes input from the parents. As part of your self-study for the accreditation process, you must survey the parents to get their evaluation of your center's parental involvement component (NAEYC, 2005).

Pre-Enrollment Visits

Parents usually feel better about their choice of a center when they are treated individually during the decision-making stage, rather than being part of a large group of parents. Before enrollment, parents seeking child development services should be encouraged to come to the center without the child for a conference and a tour of the facility. They should be encouraged to sit comfortably and observe the children and teachers in action. They may wish to visit the center for several hours. This is wise from their point of view, for they can see more clearly how the children are treated and how problems are handled. As manager, you should be open to such a visit, even suggest it, especially if parents come without their child. Parents searching for a suitable center for their child may simply drop by, or they may call to schedule an appointment. Are you prepared to be cordial on a moment's notice? An open-door policy builds families' confidence in your center.

An observation period can dispel families' anxieties or raise questions they might like to ask. You must have a procedure in place so families receive answers to questions without disrupting ongoing work. Clearly, the teachers cannot leave their children unattended to talk with the parents of prospective enrollees. Therefore, it must be made clear that any discussion with the child's potential teacher must be scheduled, unless a qualified substitute is available for the teacher's class. Most visiting parents are happy to cooperate if you explain the reason for your policy.

Frequently, parents bring their child along. Depending on the activities under way, it may be unwise to take a visiting child into an ongoing group of children. The children may resent a visitor disrupting their activity. Occasionally, children call a strange child names or make negative or teasing comments that could be taken as unfriendly by the visitors. Thus, waiting until the children have gone outdoors may work best. Alternatively, another time could be arranged for the child's visit—after hours or on a weekend. With no other children in the room, the child can explore the environment uninhibited and without the added need to adjust socially to numerous unfamiliar children. Such exploration generally leaves a favorable impression and the child and parent become eager to enroll.

Handbook for Families

One of your primary tools for communicating with the families is the center's handbook. This provides parents with all of the basic information about your center in one convenient package. Some programs include two copies of the final page, which contains a statement to be signed by the parents, affirming their understanding and agreement to abide by the policies and procedures described in the handbook. Parents return one copy to the center and keep one in the handbook for their records.

As noted earlier, state licensing regulations or funding requirements frequently spell out what must be included in the handbook. Examples include the program's schedule and hours of operation, and its policies regarding admission and withdrawal criteria, immunization and other health issues, discipline, meals, and fees (including late payment penalties). You should include more than the minimum required information, however. The handbook gives you a chance to highlight the qualities that make your center unique. Many handbooks include a brief history of the program's origin and its developments over time, a statement of the program's philosophy, a description of the curriculum and sample daily schedule, and a flowchart or other illustration of the administrative structure. The handbook can also address opportunities for family involvement, and program traditions and rituals such as birthday or seasonal celebrations (including the reasons for those traditions). Figure 13.1 lists the typical contents of a family handbook.

Computer word processing or desktop publishing programs make it easy to create an attractive, professional-looking handbook. Because your philosophy and your policies are likely to evolve over time, you may want to print only a limited supply, perhaps enough for one year's enrollment. You can then revise the content, or at least review it closely, every year to keep your handbook up to date. With the digital imaging techniques available, you can make your handbook more appealing to your readers by incorporating photographs and children's drawings.

Orientation

This is the get-acquainted period for your center and the new family. Ideally, parents have already visited the center to observe the program and have received a copy of the center's parent handbook to read at their leisure. If your center enrolls several families at one time (e.g., the beginning of the school year), you can hold an orientation meeting for the group. If, like most full-day, year-round programs, you enroll new families whenever a vacancy occurs, you must set aside time for an orientation meeting with each family. This is your opportunity to explain the content and purpose of the various application and permission forms that parents are asked to sign, to review your program's philosophy, and to discuss your policies to ensure they are clearly understood. Even though you have provided a written copy of the center's policies and asked the parents to sign statements affirming that they understand and will abide by those policies, the fact is that many families are simply too busy

FIGURE 13.1 *Typical contents of a family handbook*

1. A welcome to parents and families
2. A statement of the program's mission and philosophy
3. Brief history of the center, including accreditation
4. Flowchart of the program's administrative structure
5. Overview of the general curriculum (e.g., goals, methods, rationale)
6. Admission and withdrawal policies
7. Calendar and schedule of operations (e.g., hours, days closed, inclement weather procedure)
8. Sample daily schedule
9. Fee policy, including late-payment policy
10. Food service policy (e.g., meals and times offered, sample menu)
11. Health policies and practices:
    - Children's initial immunization records and updates, physical examination requirements
    - Staff health requirements (TB tests, physical examinations)
    - Communicable diseases among children and/or staff (exclusion from school, requirements for readmission)
    - Diapering and toileting
    - Resting and sleep (individual cots, cribs, bedding, laundry)
12. Discipline or guidance policy
13. Emergency procedures (fire, tornado, or other emergency; serious accident or injury; required family emergency contact information)
14. What to bring and what to leave at home (transition objects)
15. Communication with families and opportunities for involvement
    - Visits and interviews before enrollment
    - Transition period during first week(s) of enrollment
    - Documentation of children's daily experiences
    - Newsletters
    - Conferences
    - Special events, birthday or holiday celebrations
16. Policy for reporting suspected child abuse or neglect
17. Community resources for families
18. Statement of understanding and intent to comply with policies

or distracted to read those policies thoroughly. Investing time in a face-to-face discussion at the beginning puts your relationship with a family on a firm footing and prevents unpleasant surprises later on.

Phased Enrollment

If your center operates on a school-year schedule, you can phase in the start-up by having a few children arrive with their parents each day until the maximum capacity is achieved, perhaps by the end of the week. Phasing in makes it easier for the staff to deal with problems than if large groups of children arrive at once. Children can receive more individual attention. Parents can observe their child playing with other children and interacting with the teachers until the child feels comfortable enough to be left at the center.

Programs that operate on a year-round, full-day schedule can practice phased enrollment as well. First, they can encourage parents to spend as much time as possible at the center with their child during the first week. They can also ask that parents plan for their child to attend only part time for the first few days. One program suggests that, for a few days, a new 3- or 4-year-old child come for the morning and go home with mom or dad right after lunch. Frequently, these new children initiate the move to a longer day themselves by telling their parents that they want to stay for a nap with their friends. During this phase-in period, parents can gradually decrease their time at the center, perhaps stepping out for a cup of coffee or running an errand after the child is settled into play—always with the reassurance that they will be back shortly. Gradually, the "errand time" grows longer until the family can bring the child to the door, say good-bye, and leave secure in the knowledge that the child is playing happily. The parents know that the staff will call if the child seems to need them.

The benefits of this phasing-in process are numerous. Children feel more secure with their parents present and feel free to explore the materials and activities your program offers. The more they explore and engage themselves, the easier it becomes for them to separate from their families later on. Children who are forced to adapt to a new environment without this supportive transition period often spend so much time and energy missing their absent parents that they cannot focus on anything else. Parents and teachers benefit because they become acquainted and comfortable with one another over the course of the week. Because the parents get to see the program in operation, they have a mental image to call on when they find themselves wondering what their child is doing or feeling. Often, the parents themselves have some anxiety that should be recognized. Teachers benefit because they learn from the parents the particular, subtle ways they relate to their children. How does this baby like to be held for feeding? What does this child mean by a particular word or phrase? Parents and teachers both get a chance to ask questions that neither may have thought of during the initial interview. In short, the parent, the child, and the teacher begin to develop trust, an essential ingredient of a productive relationship. Although such procedures may require effort and coordination, the children are better adjusted and the center receives good publicity when the parents tell others that you are a person-oriented manager who really has the child's and parents' interests at heart.

Of course, a gradual initiation to full-day care presents challenges. Many parents do not have the luxury of taking a week off work even if they want to do so. Others find it hard to see the value of this investment of their time. As the administrator, you must be flexible as you plan with the families. One thing is certain, however, you should make your expectations known before enrollment and ask the families for their commitment to the best possible beginning for their child.

Decisions, Decisions . . .

Discuss with your classmates or the manager of a child development center the idea of having parents spend the first week or month with their child at the center. Would you be comfortable doing your job with parents present? How would you make them feel welcome? How would you structure a gradual transition to the point where the child attends the center alone?

Home Visits

A home visit can be the foundation for developing your center's harmonious relationship with the children and their families. Arranging a visit to the child's home before the child begins attending helps strengthen the home–school bond. A short visit is all that is required to give the child a more secure feeling and provide the teachers with bits of information (e.g., about siblings, pets, and family lifestyle). This visit helps the child adjust to being without the family in the new environment. A picture of the child taken during the visit can be displayed in the child's locker, on the bulletin board, or in a book about the children.

Home visits are a common practice for many programs that operate on a school-year calendar. The practice is rare for full-day, year-round programs with budgets typically based on what parents can pay. Those centers seldom have the luxury of extra staff members to supervise the children while directors or lead teachers make home visits during regular hours of operation. The alternative of asking teachers to make such visits on their own time, after long days at school, is both unfair and unwise because it risks overtaxing teachers' energy and creating burnout. One option is to hire a person whose specific role is to visit the home of each new child to get acquainted with the child, the family, and the neighborhood. This same staff member should visit the child's classroom at the center a few times, providing a familiar face to help bridge home and center. If home visits have been so helpful for 3- and 4-year-old children, how much more beneficial might they be to the younger child who is about to spend so much more of her life in your center over the next few years?

Families Visit the Center

Just as your home visits begin to forge relationships with families, welcoming them in the center reciprocates their hospitality and helps to nourish and maintain those relationships. Informal visits so that the families can observe the program in action should be encouraged—with no prior notice required—so long as everyone understands that the teacher's first priority is with the children. If questions or concerns arise that require the teacher's input, it may be necessary to ask family members to schedule an appointment at a more convenient time. Or a teacher could offer to call the parents during nap time or later that evening.

In addition to impromptu visits, centers may also plan specific times for parents to come to school—such as inviting mothers, dads, or a substitute parent to lunch on different occasions. Centers often hold potluck meals at the center—parents bring a dish to share and have an opportunity to meet other parents and their children. The children can proudly show off "my school" to their parents and siblings during these times.

Safety Concerns. One caveat in regard to family visits concerns the center's responsibility for the safety of all children. As program manager, you must be aware at all times and have control over who comes and goes from the center. In a larger facility, that can mean having a lock system that allows entry only to individuals who have the code. Even without such a system, you and your staff should feel comfortable asking any visitors you don't know on sight to identify themselves and state their business. Family members will be reassured by your vigilance.

Some children are in child-care facilities because they have been abused in their families. Spending time in the program can be a valuable way for those family members to learn more appropriate ways of dealing with children. Centers will have to exert extra precautions to balance that benefit with the need to keep all children safe. At the most basic level, they would have to ensure that no person with a history of abuse or neglect is ever left alone with children.

It is not uncommon for a divorced or separated parent to obtain court orders prohibiting the noncustodial parent from contact with the child. As program manager, you would need evidence of the court order in order to comply with the prohibition. Without it you normally would have no legal right to restrict a parent's contact with his or her child.

Conferences

In addition to planning these group events for family members, you should arrange frequent opportunities for individual encounters between the teachers and the families. Many people think of parent conferences as those hurried, somewhat formal events, scheduled at the end of each semester where teachers go over children's grades and point out areas needing improvement. Too often, conferences that occur at other times are precipitated by some misbehavior or serious difficulty the child is having. How can conferences be used more positively? It helps to think of conferences in a broader context and realize that every contact you or your staff has with a family can be a "mini-conference," an opportunity to exchange information that helps you both do a better job of nurturing and educating the child.

Of course, such exchanges cannot occur unless family members and your staff speak the same language, literally as well as figuratively. If you are unable to hire staff who share a language with the families you serve, perhaps you can find volunteers from the community to serve as interpreters. These same volunteers might be willing to perform the same service with any written materials you send home. Teachers and caregivers also must refrain from using jargon when they communicate with family members.

As manager, you set an example for your staff by making it a point to know each child's family members well enough to greet them by name and make pertinent comments or inquiries—"How do you like your new job?" or "Is Melinda's grandmother feeling better?" This type of exchange makes the family feel welcome and provides you with valuable information—it may explain why Melinda has seemed so fretful lately.

By scheduling adequate staff and informing staff members that the relationships with the families are part of their job and not just idle chatter, you can ensure that the primary caregivers have a moment or two to share information informally at drop-off and pick-up times. Encourage the staff to call the families or send notes home to share bits of the child's daily life at the center. And, of course, you can provide paid time for the staff to plan and conduct regular, more formal conferences at times when parents are available.

Comfortable, adult-size seating, a quiet corner, and perhaps some coffee or fruit juice set the stage for a relaxed, friendly conversation. Some teachers find it helpful to send a note to the families that explains what they hope to discuss in the conference and asks the families to write down any particular questions they might have. When both parties have given thought to the conference beforehand, precious time is not wasted. (See Seplocha, 2004, for an example of a chart that could be sent home to families to set the stage for a productive conference.)

Many teachers and parents find it useful to have actual examples that illustrate the child's growth. For infants, this might be an album or diary that includes photographs taken at the center and written anecdotes about specific incidents. For slightly older children, these materials can be augmented by drawings and writing samples, photographs of block constructions or dramatic play episodes, or lists of favorite books. These concrete examples are more meaningful to parents than abstract developmental checklists, which can be unconvincing if teachers fail to notice a child doing something that she does quite well at home. This **portfolio method** of assessing and recording the children's development is described in chapter 15 (see Shores & Grace, 2005).

A Family Affair.   You could also make the conference a family affair. One school made a practice of inviting family members to schedule an appointment for "muffin day" every six months or so. The family selected a date in consultation with the teacher, who recorded it on the classroom calendar. Appointments were limited to afternoons when the classroom was quiet because children were outside playing and to days when there were enough adults on hand to allow the teacher to spend this one-on-one time with the family. (An alternative would have been to meet with the families after the center closed.) The children, who could recognize their names, knew the significance of the calendar notation and kept track of the progression of days with great anticipation. They sent notes to the cook requesting that she buy a particular flavor of muffin mix and on the morning of the appointed day, they helped to mix and bake the muffins. When they awoke from their naps, they helped spread a pretty cloth over an art table where they set out the pitcher of juice and basket of muffins.

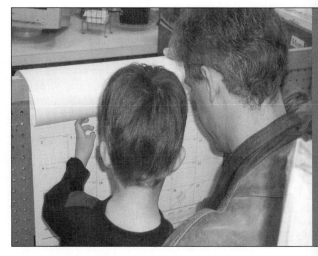

Children eagerly check the calendar with their families in anticipation of "muffin day."

Sometimes one parent attended; other times the group included two parents, a grandparent, and perhaps an older sibling. The child's portfolio provided a focus for the get-together, often with the child narrating particular sections. Usually, the child moved away from the table after a short time, either to play or to give a guided tour of the classroom to a family member, giving the teacher an opportunity for a more detailed conversation with the parent. If either the teacher or parent had a serious concern to discuss, they arranged a more private time to get together.

Decisions, Decisions . . .

Imagine you are the manager of a child development program where one of the toddler teachers has come to share with you her concern that a child in her classroom seems far behind the others in language development. What further information would you want from the teacher? What suggestion(s) would you make for a course of action? Discuss your ideas with your classmates.

Parent Meetings

The manager should establish a policy for parent meetings, give the teachers guidance and support as they plan for the meetings, and assign support staff to provide logistical services—arrange the seating, prepare snacks and beverages, and clean up afterward. A manager wisely stays in the background, encouraging the teachers and caregivers to strengthen their ties with parents. Providing child care during parent conferences and meetings will make it possible for more families to participate.

Parent meetings have a number of functions in the child development center. Parents can be gathered to receive general information on center procedures and policies. Meetings can facilitate the parents' becoming acquainted with one another. An outgrowth of this

Muffin day has arrived! This child helps make the muffins and, after her nap, helps to set the table for her parents and her teacher while the other children play outside. After the snack, everyone enjoys reviewing the portfolio together.

objective is that many parents begin to support one another—for example, babysitting, sharing a car pool, or teaching a skill.

Some meetings are specifically designed to give parents information about parenting and child development. In some centers, an extension-type program includes classes on English as a second language, nutrition and cooperative food buying, driver's education, and cultural renewal or the history of the parents' culture. Meetings may serve to update parents about recent center activities or to show the children's art exhibits or offer a singing presentation by the children.

If the parents do the planning for educational meetings, the topics are far more likely to fit their needs. A designated parent educator may help plan some meetings or the regular staff may help. Parents generally want their child's teacher to be present at meetings even when general topics are on the agenda. They like to meet with their child's teacher for answers to certain questions. In large centers serving many children, general parent meetings are often poorly attended simply because the parents realize that specific information about their child cannot be obtained. Though personal counseling cannot take place at a public meeting, a casual conversation may solve a problem or an appointment can be made for future individual conferences.

Remember that a child with divorced parents may have two homes and two sets of parents. Children of lesbian or gay parents might have two mothers or two fathers. All of the suggestions for inviting families to meetings and conferences apply to every family, however it may be configured.

The parents in cooperatives actually operate the school, while other centers may have ad hoc committees that provide a formal avenue for expressing parental concerns, planning programs, and advising the manager or policy board. Participating in a parent group has opened new career vistas for many parents, especially as parents began to see the breadth and depth of the early childhood education field. Well-organized parent groups have helped more than one program threatened with reduced or discontinued funding. Head Start actually survived during one administration thanks to the countrywide outcry by parents who rallied to its support. Parent groups are organized for various reasons, and political strength is one of them.

Newsletters, E-Mail, and Web Pages

A newsletter is a useful communication device that can be produced weekly, or less often. In a page or two, you can give short accounts of class activities and can update parents on future plans and events. A page of the children's favorite songs and poems helps get parents involved reading and singing with their children. Hints can be given for holiday activities or places they can take their children to visit, such as a dairy or cider mill. Of course, secretarial help and some expenses are necessary for this activity and must be arranged by the manager. Desktop publishing programs make it easier to produce eye-catching, professional-looking newsletters.

Given the growing number of families with computers and Internet access, some centers are moving from paper-based communication to electronic forms. If you know that every family has access to e-mail, you can distribute your newsletter that way. If you adopt this method, it is essential that you provide paper copies of all communication for families without such access. Many teachers send a daily or weekly e-mail to families, sometimes including photographs, to let them know what went on in their classrooms. Other centers post such information on their web pages and protect the confidentiality of children and families by establishing password access for those enrolled in the program. We will discuss web pages as a tool for marketing and public relations in the following chapter.

Documentation and Display

Most families are eager to learn about what their children are doing while in your care all day. Many child development programs in the United States have a tradition of using photographs and displays of children's work to share information with families. The early childhood programs of Reggio Emilia, Italy, have inspired even more powerful and effective uses of such displays. Documentation panels (displays of photographs and descriptions of what goes on in the classrooms) draw family members into the life of the school and give them something to talk about with their children beyond the usual "What did you do in school today?" Documentation panels are aesthetically appealing and profoundly reflective products of an ongoing process in which teachers observe children, collect and analyze data, and add their own reflections about the meaning of what they observe (Rinaldi, 2001). Family members enjoy seeing such evidence of their children's thinking. The children themselves often serve as guides, escorting families around the displays and explaining the details (e.g., Gennarelli, 2004).

Family Resource Corner

Many programs set aside a room or part of a room where materials of interest to parents are made available. A collection of books or videos about child development, early education, discipline, healthy nutrition, and other topics make useful information readily available. Organizations like Zero to Three and the NAEYC offer a number of inexpensive books and pamphlets that child development programs could share with families. Many can be downloaded at no cost from the organizations' websites and duplicated for families. (For example, *The Magic of Everyday Moments*, a series of booklets describing development at successive stages in the child's first years and offering suggestions to families for maximizing learning, is available at http://www.zerotothree.org/magic/.)

Family members will also appreciate information not directly related to parenting and child development. You could provide information about families' rights to child-care tax credits or subsidy payments. You might post notices of important community events or put out a basket to collect grocery store coupons for products that one family might not use while another does. In short, this is a space that invites family members to spend a few extra moments at the center and to begin to see the program as not just a drop-off point for their children, but also as support for the entire family.

Home Activities

Home activities have long been prescribed by child development centers, often as a way of influencing parents to spend more time and energy with their children or teaching them what child development professionals consider more effective or appropriate ways of interacting with children. Some families may be unaware of the need to read to their children, for example, or they may simply be too busy. A workshop on effective ways to read to children, along with a book-lending program, might be helpful. Give pep talks about the benefits of the public library and information about the activities it sponsors. Several articles and books on the reading list at the end of this chapter contain suggestions for other ways to share appropriate activities with families.

Care must be taken, however, to avoid creating undue stress for the children or parents by asking families to spend precious time on activities that are, at best, trivial and, at worst, so much like school that parents resort to the methods they remember being used with them as young children in school. They might feel pressured to send back completed "homework" or demand that their children take part in activities that hold no interest for either the children or the parents.

It is more helpful to provide tactful suggestions of ways that families can enhance learning by including their young children in their daily lives (Dunst, Hamby, Trivette, Raab, & Bruder, 2001). You might suggest that they ask a 4-year-old to find the items that match cost-saving coupons when they go to the grocery store, for example, or that toddlers be given a collection of clean empty margarine or yogurt containers to stack while the older family members prepare a meal. You and your staff could brainstorm such a list simply by thinking about every room in a house and imagining the kinds of learning experiences a child could have there. Water play in the bathtub, for example, is a sound way of learning about objects that float and sink. Dorothy Rich (1992) compiled an extensive array of activities that are both age-appropriate and related to important life skills.

When Conflicts Arise

Sometimes, families may want to discuss some concern or complaint with you, and you must make it clear that you are available for this. Although you may find it challenging, it is essential that you convey an openness to listen to the parents' concerns without becoming defensive or prejudging the situation. Assure the parents that you will investigate and take action if necessary. Follow through as quickly as possible, and report back to the parents promptly. If the concern involves staff members, take care to express the same openness and willingness to listen to them as well. It may be helpful to schedule a meeting with the parent and staff member together where you can facilitate communication.

The same advice would hold if the complaint originated from a staff member regarding something a family member had done. Consider the following scenario:

> Just as the manager arrives at the center one morning, Janelle, one of the teachers, enters her office fuming. She announces that Mrs. Jones was 20 minutes late picking up Olivia the previous night and that she had been late several times already in recent weeks. She says that when this happens, she is late getting home, which upsets the evening routine for her entire family. The situation is becoming so stressful for her that it is affecting her ability to be patient and positive with the children in her room.

What can the manager do? Recall the steps for conflict resolution presented in chapter 8:

Step 1: Name the problem and decide to address it. In the situation described above, let's assume that the problem is not occurring in more than one classroom, so rather than bringing it up at a parent meeting the manager schedules an appointment to meet with Olivia's mother and the teacher together. She says, "Mrs. Jones, our sign-out sheet shows that you have been 15 or 20 minutes late picking up Olivia three times this month. This is a problem for Janelle (Olivia's teacher) and for our center because we want to take good care of Olivia and all our children, but we can't do that if we don't also take care of our staff. I'm hoping you will be able to help us think of a solution."

Step 2: Listen to both sides. Mrs. Jones might say that the 6:00 deadline for pick-up is simply unrealistic. "I'm supposed to get out of work at 5:00, but often my boss has last-minute requests. As a new employee, I just don't feel I can refuse to put in a little extra time. And then I have the drive across town at the height of rush-hour traffic. I really try, but sometimes I just can't make it on time. I'm really worried that you'll ask me to withdraw Olivia from the center and then I'll have to give up my job because I have no child care." Janelle explains that she loves her job and cares a lot about Olivia. She says, "I feel sad for her when she is the last one waiting to be picked up. I don't mean to let my feelings show so obviously, but I'm exhausted at the end of the day and looking forward to getting home to my own family. I need to get supper on the table and then try to squeeze in all my housework along with helping kids with homework and studying for my own classes."

Step 3: Recap. Summarize each person's point of view. "Both of you are feeling stressed because of this issue. Mrs. Jones, you are caught between the demands of your job and our expectation that you pick up Olivia by 6:00. Janelle, you also feel stretched beyond your limits when your work hours spill over into time that you need for your family and yourself."

Step 4: Brainstorm several possible alternatives. As one party offers a suggestion, the other should be given a chance to react frankly and constructively. In our example, Mrs. Jones might suggest that the center move the deadline for pick-up time from 6:00 to 6:30. Janelle could counter that this would mean she got home late every night instead of just occasionally. Janelle might propose that Mrs. Jones arrange with a parent of another child at the center to pick up Olivia on nights when Mrs. Jones must work late. An objection to this idea could be that Mrs. Jones doesn't feel she knows any of the other parents well enough to ask (or trust) them to do this. If neither can develop potential solutions, the manager might make some tentative suggestions. The same idea might be presented more than once before it is agreed upon. No one should leave the conversation feeling coerced into an unacceptable solution.

Step 5: Agree on a workable solution and plan methods to carry it out. In this situation, the three participants might arrive at a plan that involves paying overtime to one center staff member who voluntarily agrees to work until 6:30. (This can be one person who works this schedule regularly, or the teachers could agree to rotate the duty among themselves, with one person staying late on Monday, one on Tuesday, and so forth.) The designated staff member will care for the child whose parent is late in that child's classroom, or in the event that more than one parent is late, she will bring the children together in a designated classroom. The stipulation is that parents who are late must call to let the center know and they must pay an agreed-upon late fee to cover the overtime pay for the staff member. Under this arrangement, all the other teachers are free to leave at their scheduled times.

Step 6: Acknowledge the work that each individual contributed to the problem-solving process. The manager thanks both Mrs. Jones and Janelle for listening to each other and for persevering to map out a solution.

Step 7: Follow up. In this example, the manager puts the plan into place after checking with teachers and finding that the idea of working an extra half-hour one regularly scheduled night per week for overtime pay was acceptable even to Janelle. The manager also explains the new policy to families, in writing and at a parent meeting. At the next month's staff meeting, the manager learns that the plan is working well. Teachers are pleased to know that their workday will end as scheduled. The manager also includes a short survey in the monthly newsletter to solicit families' perceptions of the new system.

Of course, not every conflict will end so peacefully. Most managers of any business have experienced difficult encounters with customers, and child development programs are no exception. Failure to pay fees, behaving in a disrespectful manner toward staff, constantly criticizing the program, and spreading malicious gossip among other parents are just a few examples of things parents can do to make a manager's life difficult. Confronting the individual calmly and courteously may enable you to discover the root of the problem and work toward a solution. If that doesn't work, it may be time to explain that your program may not be the best fit for the family's needs and to suggest some other alternatives.

Sometimes managers have to do things that parents might perceive as making their life difficult. Certainly, reporting suspected abuse or neglect would be high on that list. Consider, also, the following scenarios:

1. A teacher reports that 2-year-old Jeremy has just not been himself all day. He seems listless, pale, and did not eat lunch or snack. You agree that they should call his mother at work. She comes to pick him up, but she protests that the child is not sick. Later she calls you to report that the pediatrician found nothing wrong. She is very upset because she missed work and feels that the staff believes she is not a good mother.

2. A woman you have never seen arrives at the center. She tells you that she is a neighbor who has been asked to pick up 3-year-old Brittany because her mother is out of town and her father has had to work late. When you check Brittany's file, you find that the parents have given no authorization for any other than themselves to pick up their child.

In each of these situations, your job as manager will be easier if you have made your program's policies very clear in advance. Families need to know in advance that you will report suspected abuse or neglect. They need to know your policies on exclusion of sick children, and what you expect of them should their child become ill while in your care. They need to know that you will not release a child to anyone without their written authorization. If you put these policies in writing and explain them during the orientation, you can remind families that they heard about and agreed to them when an occasion to invoke them arises. During orientation you can acknowledge frankly that they might be inconvenienced or upset by the policies at some point, and you can emphasize that your primary goal is to protect their child.

Families as Human Resources for the Center

Communication and relationships are two-way affairs. The center is a resource for the families whose children are enrolled, and those family members are a rich source of human capital for the center. As mentioned earlier, programs such as Head Start have long made a practice of hiring staff members from within the population they serve. What better way of ensuring that your center's policies and practices are in tune with the cultural backgrounds of the children? In some centers, such as parent cooperatives, the staff consists almost entirely of unpaid parent volunteers who take turns assisting the paid teacher.

Even when they are not regular staff members, parents provide valuable information and support for the teachers and caregivers. Child development staff may know about children in general, but the family knows more about its own particular child. Furthermore, the burden of being the all-knowing "expert" can be a heavy one. When center staff members value the contributions that family members make, everyone gains.

In addition to the expertise they bring about their own children, families provide a center with a rich pool of professional expertise from which to draw. Someone with advanced computer skills might help you set up a system for maintaining the center's health and financial records and train a staff member to use the system. Carpenters, plumbers, electricians, landscape gardeners, or carpet cleaners might contribute a few hours to a special improvement project. People who do not work outside their home might agree to sew new curtains or make a slipcover for the easy chair in your reading corner. A corporate executive might agree to consult on some aspect of the center's management. The list of possibilities is limited only by your imagination.

Besides contributing directly to your center's day-to-day operation, family members can serve the center as leaders and policy makers. This type of family involvement is recognized as an indication of very high quality in the environmental and program rating scales discussed earlier in this chapter. In addition to all of the professional skills they might bring, parents can help you see things from the perspective of your customers, which is a key element of today's quality management. (Policy boards and advisory boards are discussed in Chapter 5.)

Community Resources to Promote Family Wellness

Creating links with agencies in your community benefits the families and children you serve. Many centers keep a file of community agencies and resources for referrals. Such referrals are more productive if you have established contacts in the various agencies and can suggest that families ask for a particular person by name. Your agency contacts might also bring specific resources to the center where they are more accessible to the families. Some centers have health department representatives offer immunization clinics on-site at certain times during the year. Others might invite a parenting expert from the community mental health clinic to conduct workshops for interested family members. Your local child-care resource and referral agency is a good place to begin looking for what is available in your community.

Conclusion

Child development centers, as organizations designed to provide a service to families, comprise part of the social–cultural environment of the human ecological system. To provide high-quality programs, center managers must cultivate effective communication and positive relationships with the families of the children they serve, as well as with the people and institutions in the larger community who serve as resources for those families. In order to accomplish these aims, administrators and staff must have an understanding of family functions and diverse parenting styles. They must cultivate cultural responsiveness and family-friendly practices. Professional standards for high-quality child development centers, including NAEYC accreditation criteria, place a priority on the parents' involvement. Programs build relationships with families through initial contacts, visits to the center, home visits, enrollment procedures, conferences, and parent meetings. Policies that are clearly stated in advance, open discussion of difficulties and conflict resolution strategies can help prevent or resolve disagreements between families and providers. It is important for centers to recognize the potential that families offer as human resources for the program and to help link families with community resources that promote family wellness.

QUESTIONS FOR REVIEW

1. List NAEYC guidelines for family involvement in child development programs; give examples of how programs might apply the guidelines.
2. List DEC guidelines for family involvement in programs for children with disabilities; give examples of how programs might apply the guidelines.
3. Why do child development professionals believe that interaction with all parents is essential?
4. List the five functions of families as identified by Berns and indicate how teachers or managers may be involved with each function.
5. List and describe in detail at least five ways child development programs initiate and build solid relationships with families.
6. In what ways can families contribute human resources to child development programs?
7. What are the dangers of asking parents to do school-like activities with children? What alternatives might be more appropriate? Why?

PROFESSIONAL PORTFOLIO

1. Accompany a child and family member on a trip to the grocery store, the library, or during some other household task. With permission, use a digital camera to record the sequence of events. Add a narrative that describes what happened and explains its significance to the child's learning. Create a booklet or display panel that shows other families how learning is embedded in everyday activities. (If you choose the display panel option, you can include the components separately in your portfolio.)
2. Create a plan to promote meaningful family involvement in a child development program. Describe at least three specific strategies and explain why you think they would be effective.
3. Use a desktop publishing program to develop a brochure for family members on some aspect of child development. Study several professional articles on a topic such as art for preschool children, biting, or toilet training. Summarize what you have learned and offer suggestions that families can use at home. Have your classmates review the brochure and offer suggestions. Revise and polish it so that it is both appealing to readers and easy to understand.

RESOURCES FOR FURTHER STUDY

Print

Beginnings Workshop: Meeting the needs of today's families. *Exchange, 163* (2005, May/June), pp. 37–51.

Coppel, C. (2003). *A world of difference: Readings on teaching young children in a diverse society.* Washington, DC: National Association for the Education of Young Children.

Fagan, J., & Palm, G. (2004) *Fathers and early childhood programs.* Albany, NY: Delmar.

Pulido-Tobiassen, D., & Gonzalez-Mena, J. (1999). *A place to begin: Working with parents on issues of diversity.* Sacramento: California Tomorrow.

Stephens, K. (2004, July/August). Sometimes the customer *isn't* always right: Problem solving with parents. *Exchange 158*, pp. 68–74.

Internet

Zero to Three

http://www.zerotothree.org/ztt_parents.html

Parents' section of Zero to Three website; available in English and Spanish; provides information of parenting topics "A–Z," a "tip of the week," and access to other resources.

National Association for the Education of Young Children

http://www.naeyc.org/families/

Family section of the NAEYC website; includes "Early Years Are Learning Years," a series of short articles available in PDF format for programs to download and distribute with newsletters (provided they properly credit the NAEYC). Topics include Choosing a Preschool, Singing as a Teaching Tool, What to Do about Biters, and others.

Parenting Exchange

https://secure.ccie.com/catalog/cciecatalog.php?cPath=53

Parenting Exchange, a series of columns addressing parent concerns on a variety of issues that purchasers may reprint for parents in their program; available for purchase on CD or via subscription.

CHAPTER FOURTEEN

Marketing and Public Relations

No matter how wonderful your program is, it cannot survive without children to serve, and families are unlikely to bring their children to you unless they are aware of two things: that your program exists and that your program offers something that meets their needs. Getting that information out to the families is what marketing is all about. Although this may seem obvious if you are the manager of a for-profit program that depends on parent fees for its existence, it is no less true for nonprofit and publicly funded programs that must market their programs to attract and keep potential funders. A child development program is a service, but it is also a business. No business can survive without a steady supply of customers.

Marketing, then, is the process by which you make your presence known and inform the community about the benefits of your services. Once potential customers inquire about the program, you must apply all of the techniques described in the previous chapter to create and sustain a relationship with the families. Some marketing experts assert that these activities are a continuation of your marketing process—once you attract a customer, you work to satisfy and retain that customer, and, ultimately, to enhance the quality of your relationship (Bitner, 2000, p. 38). Attracting new customers is only one purpose of marketing; other purposes might be to convince a corporation to purchase your services for its employees or to persuade a charitable agency to fund a scholarship program so that homeless children can attend your center.

Public relations is a broader, but related, concept. Although the target audience for marketing is potential customers, public relations efforts attempt to reach the wider community to build a positive image of the program in the public mind (Clarke, 2000, p. 143). Businesses cultivate good public relations the way farmers cultivate the soil—they create conditions for the seeds of marketing to take root and flourish. Marketing and public relations both entail all of the management processes you have studied: planning, organizing, staffing, leading, and monitoring for effectiveness.

Marketing: Attracting and Retaining Customers

As noted, marketing involves specific activities designed to bring your program's unique service to the attention of those people most likely to want that service. Before you can design the marketing activities, you must know—and be able to communicate clearly and concisely—exactly what makes your service unique. This means knowing something about your competition; that is, the programs that offer similar services. In addition, you must know something about your potential customers—who they are, where they are likely to be reached, and what they value. Once you have a clear picture of this background information, you can begin to devise steps to connect the two sides of the marketing equation: the service you offer and the customers who want it.

Begin your marketing by thinking about your program's strongest assets. Is your program NAEYC accredited? Can you highlight the education and experience levels of your staff? Have you adopted an innovative curriculum? Have you found a way to keep the children with a specific teacher for all or most of their years at your program? Consider asking currently enrolled families for their perspectives on these questions. A key element of effective marketing is addressing the potential customer's point of view. Remember, if people are going to enroll their children in your center, they must know that you exist and that your facility might match their needs regarding location, price, hours, services, and quality indicators. To be effective, that information must be stated briefly, accurately, and positively.

Next, take a look at the other programs and services for families and children in your area. Bush (2001, p. 81) distinguishes between direct and indirect competitors: Direct competitors are all of the other centers serving the same population; indirect competitors include facilities such as family child-care homes, public school preschool and after-school programs, and individual babysitters. What makes your program stand out from all of these alternatives? Why should a parent seeking child care choose you?

The answers to these questions, when boiled down to a few key phrases, comprise the kernel of the public image you want to develop for your program—something you emphasize in all of your advertising and promotional materials. Using a consistent design to convey this information builds program recognition and maximizes marketing effectiveness. If you have the funds, invest in professional help to design your publicity materials. Even if your budget does not allow this, you can tap other resources. A local advertising agency might be looking for a worthy cause to support as part of its own public relations effort. A college student—or an entire class—might adopt your program for an assignment and design an entire public relations campaign.

Communicating Your Message

Marketing expert Harry Beckwith recommends that all of your promotional materials convey, immediately and clearly, your "Key Claim" and your "Key Proof" (2000, p. 207). In other words, a prospective client or customer should be able to determine at once what your program does and what evidence you have to support that assertion:

> *Key Claim:* Rainbow Child Development Center provides peace of mind for the working parents of children ages 6 weeks to 6 years.

> *Key Proof:* Our program, accredited by the National Association for the Education of Young Children, features home-cooked, nutritious meals; small group size; and individualized care and education from experienced teachers whose education exceeds the norm for child-care programs in this community.

You should consider all of the avenues available as you plan this phase of your marketing strategy: the Internet, printed material, mass media, and person-to-person oral communication. You might ask your staff to brainstorm ideas for a logo and the content to be covered by publicity efforts. Be sure to have your staff and policy board help with the final editing of anything you make public.

Decisions, Decisions . . .

Divide your class into groups of three or four students. Assign each group a different type of child development program (e.g., infant–toddler, part-day preschool, after-school program, summer day camp for elementary school children, program for hospitalized children). Ask each group to write a key claim and key proof for its particular service. Share each group's results with the rest of the class.

Websites. According to the U.S. Department of Commerce (2004), the percentage of U.S. households with computers has increased from 36.6 in 1997 to 61.8 in 2003, and it is safe to assume that this upward trend is continuing. More than 5 out of 6 homes with computers also have Internet access. When shopping for goods or services, people may still follow the old Yellow Pages slogan, "Let your fingers do the walking," but they are likely to have a computer mouse in those fingers and to be using an Internet search engine instead of a paper telephone directory. Married couples and families with children—groups very likely to be in need of child care services—are also more likely to use computers and the Internet. If your program does not have a presence on the Internet, you are missing an important opportunity.

You probably already have such a presence at the most basic level if your program is included in the online directories of licensing and resource and referral agencies. While these listings would let prospective clients know you exist, they will probably give only minimum information about your program, such as licensing status, ages served, and contact information. To really take advantage of the Internet's potential you could create a website, a virtual "place" with an address or uniform resource locator (URL) where people could visit to learn more about your program.

Typically, websites have a home page with links to additional pages, created in HyperText Markup Language (HTML). Each page consists of text, graphics, and often links to other websites. The cost of developing a website varies. If you have the skills or are willing and have the time to learn, you can create your own pages. If you have the funds, you can hire a professional to do the job. If, like most child-care managers, you are strapped for both time and funds, you may be able to tap some volunteer resource: a parent, board member, or local college student majoring in computer technology. In addition to costs associated with developing the site, you will have to pay for registering your domain name (or URL) and for making your site available through an Internet service provider (ISP). Tap your network with community businesses or chamber of commerce to get recommendations for reputable providers that are reliable and reasonably priced.

Probably a good way to decide what you want your website to look like is to visit those of other child development programs or comparable services. You will probably get lots of good ideas as well as learn some things that you definitely want to avoid. Because your website is likely to be a family's all-important first impression of your program, you will want to create one that looks professional and is easy to navigate. Too much print to fit easily on a screen, hard-to-read typefaces, and inconsistent format from one page to the next can frustrate potential clients. "Cute" clip art or other graphics, clashing colors, misspelled words, or inaccurate information will cast doubt on your program's quality. Many of the suggestions given below for writing brochure content will apply to composing text for your website.

At a minimum, your website should include your mission statement and program philosophy, your location (with a map), photographs of your facility, a description of your curriculum, your schedule of operation and fees, information about available openings and waiting lists, enrollment policies, and a link to contact you via e-mail. Many programs include photographs, brief biographies, and resumes of staff members as well as galleries of images and descriptions of projects or children's art. (Be sure to have written permission of families before including children's pictures on your website.) You might add a calendar of coming events, testimonials from satisfied customers, and links to your handbook, newsletter, and registration forms.

Brochures.   While computer and Internet use is growing nationwide, a completely paperless marketing strategy would be unwise. Many people simply prefer to get their information in paper and print format. And there is still a substantial population with limited access to these tools—a situation referred to as the "digital divide." Percentages of computer and Internet users among Black and Hispanic families, those with lower incomes and less education, and those living either in rural or inner-city areas are far lower than the percentage of White, upper-income, college-educated, metropolitan residents (Newburger, 2001). Thus you will need to get your message across on paper as well as electronically.

Printed brochures can convey much of the information you include in your website. Like web pages, they must be carefully planned with up-to-date and accurate information. The writing must be clear and interesting to convey the message that your program is a stimulating place for children. Computer software packages often include templates for 2- or 3-column brochures that can be printed on both sides of standard letter- or legal-size paper. Pictures from the center add visual appeal and augment the information in the text. Remember to give specific, concrete information and avoid using an educator's abstract vocabulary.

The brochure should state the center's name, address, and telephone number, along with a brief description of the age groups served, prices of the service, hours of operation, philosophy, typical activities, additional services such as meals or transportation. Driving directions or nearby bus routes for those parents without private means of transportation are helpful.

Advertisements.   The most basic form of advertisement is a listing in the local telephone company's Yellow Pages. Schon (1998, p. 336) recommended listing the center under several headings because families may be looking for day care, nursery school, preschool, child care, or some other term. Your listing in the telephone book is an investment that lasts all year—until the next edition is printed.

You can supplement the telephone listing by advertising in your local newspaper on a regular basis. The least expensive ad consists of a few lines in the classified section. You can make both the classified ad and the telephone listing stand out by

Desktop publishing programs and digital photography make it easy and economical to produce an attractive, professional-looking brochure.

paying for extras (e.g., bold print) or by including a slogan or motto that captures your program's best qualities.

Here is an example of a center's advertisement that is brief and to the point:

The Edgewater Little People's Child Development Center, NAEYC-accredited, is enrolling 3- and 4-year-old children for the fall term. Call 555-1111 to learn more about this innovative child development program.

This type of notice may appear in a newspaper classified advertisement, on a television or newspaper community calendar, or on a laundry room bulletin board. It informs parents of an available service and it tells them where to get more information. Using the phrase *innovative child development program* indicates that there are quality differences between centers that parents may wish to investigate.

A more expensive form of advertising is the display ad. Display ads (like web pages) must strike a balance between formats that catch the reader's eye and those that appear cheap because they are overdone. A successful layout and headline should hold readers' attention for about 3 seconds, long enough to get them to spend another 20 seconds reading the rest of the ad (Schon, 1998). Put yourself in the reader's place when composing your ad and try to address his or her interests. Your ad in the Yellow Pages remains in place for a year, but your newspaper ads last only as long as the particular edition of the paper in which they appear. Because families might be scanning the paper for child-care leads at any time, it is important to repeat your ads and to place them in the papers most likely to reach your target audience.

Identifying and Reaching Potential Customers

In addition to thinking about what you have to offer and how to package that information, you must think about the audience you are trying to reach—who they are, where to reach them most effectively, and how to enlarge that audience. The answer to the first question involves creating a customer profile: "a description of a typical customer . . . [including] age, income level, education, profession, geographic area, lifestyle, or interests" (Bush, 2001, p. 82). Schon and Neugebauer (1998, pp. 324–325) suggested that programs analyze their potential customer base by considering four angles: the characteristics of the parents who want or need the service, the characteristics of the children you are prepared to serve, the type of program you offer, and the way your program operates. A program designed to provide a low-cost, partial-day educational experience for 3- and 4-year-old children with stay-at-home mothers has a different customer profile than one serving dual-career, upper-income families seeking a full-day or after-school care for children from infancy through early school years.

The fit between a potential customer and a service provider can also involve personal characteristics or "natural affinity" (Beckwith, 2000, pp. 170–180). Suppose you are a free-spirit, highly creative and artistic with a flair for the dramatic, and your program reflects those qualities with its loose schedule and emphasis on messy activities. The button-down, success-oriented parents who want their child to "learn discipline" are not likely to be happy with you, nor you with them. Being clear about who you are and communicating this at the outset will avoid many future difficulties. The concept of natural affinity leads to a corollary—that no one can satisfy everyone. Your unique characteristics determine your customer profile as much as the wants and needs of your potential clients.

Once you have identified your customer profile, the next step is to determine the best way to reach that particular group. As we will discuss a little later, you need to reach the entire community for public relations purposes. For marketing purposes, however, you must target your efforts more precisely.

Most communities have a Child Care Resource and Referral (CCR&R) agency that provides families with information about existing programs and guidelines for choosing between them. (You can locate your community's CCR&R agency at the website of the National Association of Child Care Resource and Referral Agencies, at http://www.naccrra.org.) These CCR&R agencies are likely to advertise themselves in the community in a number of ways, and you can take advantage of that groundwork by ensuring that your program is listed with them. The NAEYC, in addition to setting the criteria and administering the accreditation process, has also worked to inform the public about the components of high-quality children's programs and the significance of accreditation as a mark of excellence. If your center is accredited, its name appears on the list of accredited programs in your community.

Although NAEYC accreditation and the CCR&R agencies have become recognized in recent years, not all families are aware of their existence or think about them when searching for child care. For those reasons, managers must seek other avenues of reaching potential customers, including the ads in the Yellow Pages and newspapers described previously. Brochures can be given to a community Welcome Wagon or placed in the chamber of commerce, pediatricians' offices, businesses, churches, labor union offices, schools, and other places of public access.

Making the Most of First Contacts

Marketing does not end with getting your name in front of potential customers. If they have been sufficiently intrigued by your advertisements, brochures, or recommendations from satisfied customers, the families will take the next step and call about your program. Not every family who calls follows up by enrolling a child, but you can increase the chance of that happening. Neugebauer (1998b) has provided numerous suggestions. First, ensure that callers are greeted in a professional manner. "ABC Child Development Center. How may I help you?" said in a pleasant, professional tone lets the caller know who you are and that you welcome the call. A harsh or whining tone, interruptions in conversation, or nervous speech habits (e.g., um, you know) all convey the opposite impression. Speaking very softly and smiling as you speak are recommended techniques to improve the effectiveness of your telephone communication.

The next few minutes provide a marketing opportunity: Find out what the caller needs and explain how your service fulfills those needs. Being able to state, in capsule form, your program's strongest points and most attractive qualities is part of the payoff for all your work preparing marketing materials. If you delegate the task of answering the telephone, prepare that person by reviewing the points in advance and post a list of key points near the telephone.

Just as the headline and format of the display ad must entice the reader to continue reading the ad, one of your goals when handling a telephone inquiry is to get the caller to spend more time learning about your program. Parents seeking child development services may be unskilled in requesting the information they need. You can help by suggesting that they visit the program and by offering specific options for when they might do that. Scheduling that visit during the first telephone contact is more likely to result in follow-up than leaving the matter vague.

Not every call is going to lead to an enrollment, or even to an appointment to visit the center. Nevertheless, the way you handle the call gives the callers a lasting impression about your center's helpfulness. A good marketing strategy is to take the names and addresses of all callers and routinely mail them a copy of your program's brochure. This is additional evidence of your professionalism and friendly interest. It is also an efficient use of your resources because it puts your marketing material in the hands of a self-identified target audience. Your postage and printing costs might be repaid by a new enrollment, or you might simply reap the benefits of a heightened public awareness of your program's positive image.

Decisions, Decisions . . .

Divide the class into teams of two and role-play a telephone conversation between a center manager and a parent seeking child care. Let half of the teams try using the techniques described in this section and the other half deliberately violate these concepts. Ask a volunteer team from each group to demonstrate for the entire class. Discuss.

Service Environment as Marketing Tool

Marketing theorists have coined the term **servicescape** to include the physical, or built, environment, as well as the social environment, where a particular service is obtained (Bitner, 2000, p. 37). As you recall from the discussion of the human ecological system in chapter 3, the human-built environment comprises everything that human beings have constructed or altered to fit their needs; in this case, it is the center's building, grounds, and furnishings. The **social–cultural environment** includes other people— the teachers, support staff, parents, and children who interact within the center. Earlier chapters examined these elements from the perspective of their connection to program goals and quality of care. Now, we turn our attention to the role of the servicescape in marketing.

Bitner (2000, pp. 40–41) suggested that the servicescape fills at least four important marketing functions:

1. It **packages** the service you provide, conveying a particular image and evoking certain emotional or intellectual responses, just as the wrappings associated with more tangible products do. Imagine yourself as a parent in search of child care. You walk up a beautifully landscaped, curving walkway to the center's entryway. As you open the door, you are greeted by the aroma of fresh-baked bread and the pleasant hum of active children, punctuated by giggles. The staff members are wearing neatly pressed slacks and attractive smocks. One of them welcomes you with a smile and invites you to be seated on a wicker settee in a foyer decorated with healthy green plants and carefully framed children's artwork. Contrast this experience with another: You approach a dilapidated modular unit from a barren asphalt parking lot. As you open the door, your nostrils are assailed by the unmistakable odor of dirty diapers, which penetrates the mask of disinfectant spray. You hear children crying and adults speaking in loud, harsh tones. There is no place to sit or feel that you are not in the way, and no one approaches to greet you. Which "package" appears to contain the quality of program you want for your child?

By carefully displaying framed photos of each child's family, this center hopes to create a servicescape that emphasizes awareness of the importance of families in their children's lives.

2. It **facilitates** the delivery of the service you provide. In other words, it makes it easier for employees to do their jobs and for customers to get what they need. As a consequence, staff members and families are more likely to experience pleasure and satisfaction. This means that their interactions with one another will be more positive, leading to still greater levels of pleasure and satisfaction. Consider this example: In one center, the teachers noticed that the children had an easier time saying good-bye to their parents in the morning if they could wave and blow kisses to them through the window. The windows, however, were too high for the children to reach, and the center's location made it impossible to lower them. The program evolved a custom of letting individual children stand on a countertop just below the window, watching until their parents were out of sight. Because a staff member stood next to them for safety reasons, this meant one less adult to help greet the children at the busy start of the morning. When the center had the opportunity to purchase a new loft, the staff decided to remove the wall cabinets under the window, so the loft could be installed in front of it. Because the loft and stairway leading up to it were enclosed, the children could independently position themselves to wave good-bye and the teachers were free to do other things. This simple change in the servicescape reduced the stress and increased the satisfaction for parents, children, and teachers.

3. It **socializes** both customers and employees, sending a message about how they are expected to act and relate to each other in that space. An infant–toddler classroom equipped with a comfortable adult-size sofa invites staff members, as well as parents, to take time to snuggle with the children. It also says that adults are respected, that their need for comfort is as important as that of the children. Walls adorned with striking photographs of children and teachers engaged in playful activities speak volumes about what happens in a space. The room arrangement lets the children know whether to run and jump or to sit quietly with a puzzle. Thoughtfully placed, adequate storage space encourages staff members to maintain an orderly, harmonious environment. Steps leading up to the diapering surface suggest that children are participants in their own caregiving routines, as well as a concern for the caregiver's back muscles.

4. It **differentiates** your program from others offering similar services. The look and feel of the servicescape tells people whether to expect a fast-food menu of hamburger, fries, and soft drink or a gourmet five-course repast. Even in fast-food outlets, the décor and color scheme of each distinguishes it from all of the others. In the world of child care, some large chains purposely cultivate a uniform corporate image so that potential customers recognize the logo on signs or even the particular type of architecture. When this is done purposefully, it serves the marketing purpose of promoting brand recognition and consumer comfort. When a particular center looks like every other one simply because all equipment is purchased from the same catalogs and all are decorated with items from the same teacher-supply store, it fails to tap the servicescape's potential. Making a center stand out from the crowd and give potential customers reasons to choose it over competitors need not cost a fortune. In fact, it could be less expensive to build equipment tailored to your particular needs and to decorate with homelike objects that reflect the lives of the families who use the center than to purchase commercial materials.

An important aspect of the servicescape is its aesthetic quality or the general attractiveness of its design. Wagner (2000, pp. 69–70) argued that a well-designed service environment communicates information about the quality of the service and increases the pleasure and satisfaction that customers derive from their experience in that environment. Thus, attention to form, shape, light, color, and texture is an investment that pays doubly. Not only does it contribute to a higher quality experience for the children and caregivers, but it also helps you "sell" your program.

Decisions, Decisions. . .

Think of a store where several members of your class like to shop or a restaurant where they like to eat. Describe the servicescape of the place(s) you select. How do the stores work to attract customers and enhance their satisfaction with the service?

Increasing Customer Satisfaction

Probably one of your best referral sources for new customers is word-of-mouth advertising done by enrolled families who are satisfied with your services. Many centers ask new parents how they heard about the center, and the most common answer is that they have a friend, neighbor, or coworker who uses the center and is highly satisfied with its service. Some programs capitalize on this marketing resource by offering a discount on one month's tuition to families who refer someone who enrolls a new child. A good way to ensure that your current customers sing your praises is to apply basic concepts of customer service.

Principles of Customer Service

Small-business expert William Franklin (1998) listed eight principles that we have adapted and applied to the business of child development programs:

Understand What You Are Selling. Child development programs struggle with the public's perception that they are selling a babysitting service where incidental learning takes place—all too often, the teachers buy into that perception as well. Actually, high-quality, developmentally appropriate programs are providing an educational service that also happens to fill the function of keeping children safe and happy while their parents work. Consider the example of a company that produces high-quality fountain pens (Clarke, 2000, pp. 48–49). When the company markets its product as simply a writing implement, it competes with mass-produced, even disposable, ballpoint pens. When, on the other hand, it sells a luxury gift item that happens to double as a writing implement, it appeals to an entirely different market, one likely to be willing to pay much higher prices.

Ask What the Customers Want. This shows your concern and pinpoints what they actually need. A single parent faced with getting to work on time or losing her job may want to know more about your program's hours of operation and proximity to public transportation than its Piaget-based curriculum. This doesn't mean that program quality is unimportant, just that it might not be uppermost in the parent's mind at the moment. You can always find ways to communicate that aspect of your service later.

Focus on Relationships. When you accept a child for care in your program, you are embarking on a relationship with that child's family that will last, ideally, for years. Think of the trust that the families must have to leave their children in your care and think of how much that trust will grow as you and the families get to know each other—as your relationship strengthens. The previous chapter described a number of strategies that programs can use to build a strong foundation for that relationship. Those strategies not only help you serve the families better, but they also make good business sense.

Focus on What You *Can* Do to Help.   You may not be able to solve every problem, but you can take some steps to help. For example, your concern for the teachers who want to get home to their own families may mean that you are unwilling to bend your program's rule about picking children up on time. But, you can help the families work out "buddy systems" so that parents who are unavoidably detained can make emergency arrangements easier.

Don't Pass the Buck. Ensure the Customer Connects with the Person Who Can Help with a Problem.   For program managers, this might mean following through to find out what happened to a child's lost mittens and reporting back to the irritated parent on the telephone, rather than just letting the caller languish on hold until a busy teacher can come to the phone.

Look for the Reason for Anger and Deal with That Instead of Becoming Defensive.
Parents who are angry that their child has come home with a case of head lice don't want to hear that such occurrences are "part of being in child care." They want to know that you understand their concern and share their determination that it does not happen again.

Work Toward Agreeing on a Plan for Action.   Suppose some parents are upset and believe their toddler has regressed in his toilet training progress since entering your program. Simply telling them that you will instruct the staff to invite the child to sit on the toilet at regular times during the day is not likely to appease them. Suggesting that strategy and asking for their opinion before embarking on it is more likely to make them feel a part of the decision making.

Go the Extra Mile and Let the Families Know About It.   This advice applies to businesses that absorb the cost when a mistake by one of their employees creates an inconvenience or dissatisfaction. Most child development programs operate on a tight budget that does not allow such an option. Nevertheless, there are many ways that the programs and their employees can provide service above and beyond the customers' expectation. The teacher who brings her own guitar and shares her musical gifts with the children is an example. So is the manager who shops for better food prices in order to provide more nutritious meals, or the cook whose ingenuity adds "gourmet" touches to make those meals more attractive. None of these extra measures of quality are readily apparent to the families—you have to tell them.

Public Relations: Impacting Perceptions and Opinions

Forward-thinking managers are concerned with more than enlarging their customer base. They also strive to become—and to be recognized as—important members of the community at large. A building contractor might contribute lumber for a playground structure. A financial institution's president might serve on an arts council board. A manufacturing firm might give employees paid leave time to volunteer in schools or hospitals, or it might match any monetary contributions those employees make to specific community organizations. They do these things, not simply for an immediate or direct payoff in increased sales, but because they view themselves as corporate citizens, contributing money, employee time, and expertise to enhance the quality of life in their communities. In other words, they cultivate good **public relations.** Of course, those corporate citizens hope to reap the benefits of their good works in the form of increased business or some other desirable outcome, so the line

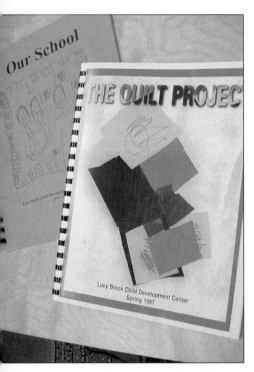

Documentation of projects completed as part of the curriculum can become marketing and public relations tools, conveying important information about a program's curriculum and basic philosophy.

between public relations and marketing can become blurred. In fact, what we are calling public relations is sometimes termed "community marketing" (e.g., Wassom, 2001).

Public relations has been defined as "the shaping of the broader context within which the public in general—or, more likely, specific target publics, forms opinions and makes decisions" (Saffir, 2000, p. 7). Like all communication, public relations is a two-way street. Skillful opinion shapers do not work in a vacuum; they attempt to gauge current public perceptions and to predict how those perceptions might change in various circumstances. Understanding how this works—and how important it is—is what Saffir called **public relations literacy.** His term for the ability to apply that knowledge skillfully is **public relations competency** (2000, pp. xii–xiii). The practice of public relations, then, is "the art and science of analyzing trends, predicting their consequences, . . . and implementing planned programs of action which will serve both the organization's and the public's interest" (Newsom & Carroll, 1998, p. 5).

Saffir predicted that public relations will emerge in the 21st century "as the dominant force in what is fundamental to success in business and politics" (2000, p. xiii). With this in mind, early childhood administrators are wise to follow the lead of their counterparts in the business world. Consider the many "publics" whose opinions directly influence child development programs. At the most local level, more than one manager has been faced with disgruntled individuals who would like to see the center shut down or moved. They might be neighbors who object to the noise from the playground or church members who resent what they see as messy rooms.

Corporate executives, looking for ways to contribute to their community for their own public relations purposes, can become program benefactors only if they know about the work the programs do. From a broader perspective, members of the governing bodies that make decisions about subsidy rates are likely to question proposals for increases if they are unaware of the true costs and benefits of high-quality child care. A public that perceives child care as menial work will not support licensing standards requiring higher levels of teacher education or salaries commensurate with those qualifications.

Everything that you do to promote a public awareness of your program also contributes to a public awareness of the benefits of high-quality programs and the risks of poor-quality care. Gradually, you might also help people understand the dilemma faced by managers who try to balance high-quality care with affordability and fair compensation for their staff.

This awareness benefits the children, the families, and the early childhood professionals because people become more willing to invest personal and government resources in paying for high-quality care. One of the findings of the four-state study called *Cost, Quality, and Child Outcomes in Child Care Centers* was that "inadequate consumer knowledge . . . reduces incentives for some centers to provide good-quality care" (Cost, Quality, and Child Outcomes Study Team, 1995, p. 9). In other words, parents, although they value good-quality care, do not have sufficient information about what constitutes high quality. One effective method of conveying this information to parents is the NAEYC accreditation system. According to a study, accredited centers were able to charge more for their services than other centers (Neugebauer, 1995, p. 14).

In general, neither the parents nor the government agencies pay rates that reflect a quality difference between centers. This means that, as a manager striving to provide high-quality care and fair compensation for your staff, you will have a harder time making ends meet than the manager who is less conscientious. Stronger licensing regulations could reduce this financial advantage for mediocre centers. According to the Cost, Quality, and Child Outcomes Study, "states with more demanding licensing standards have fewer poor-quality centers" (Cost, Quality, and Child Outcomes Study Team, 1995, p. 4). But, it takes an informed public to demand those stronger standards and to invest the resources necessary for their consistent enforcement.

Clearly, wise managers see to it that as many people as possible have been informed of all the good that their program accomplishes. Does this mean that you must factor the cost of an expensive PR representative into your already strapped budget? We think not. Much public relations work is simply an extension of what you already do to forge relationships with the families and the community and to foster professional development in yourself and your staff. It requires only that you make a conscious effort to make the most of your efforts. Once you have done that, you can take additional steps to make your program more visible and more highly regarded in your community.

Family Members as PR Representatives

View every family you serve as a potential ambassador for your program. We have already mentioned the role families play in marketing through word-of-mouth advertising. When they are informed, these same families can also carry your message about the value of highly qualified staff, better adult–child ratios, and other elements of quality to the community at large. They can help prospective customers understand why the lower rates at another center are not necessarily a better bargain. They can become advocates when, for example, a building owner moves to evict a center or when funding and licensing safeguards are threatened by government cutbacks.

Note that the key to tapping this resource is education. The more clearly you communicate what you do and why you do it to the families you serve, the more prepared they are to take that message to the entire community. This suggests that all of the strategies discussed in the previous chapter for building strong relationships with the families are public relations strategies as well. Furthermore, you do not have to reinvent the wheel to educate. You have powerful allies in the NAEYC and your community's CCR&R agency. Both of these organizations can provide you with a wealth of materials that present information about high-quality child care and its importance in attractive, readable formats. You need only serve as the conduit to get these materials into the hands of your program's families.

Expanding the Audience

Of course, you cannot rely entirely on families to carry your message to the community. You must do so directly. Again, begin with what you are already doing instead of adding a huge new undertaking to your busy schedule. Think of all of the ways you currently communicate with family members. Then, think of how these same efforts can be extended to the community at large.

Spread the News (letter).   You have already invested time and energy to create an attractive, professional-looking newsletter, chock full of substantive information about your curriculum and other program aspects. For a few pennies each, you can print several (or several dozen) extra copies and distribute them to key individuals or organizations in your community. Potential "subscribers" include the chief executive officer of the company where many of your parents work, your local CCR&R agency, the loan officer or president of the bank that holds the mortgage on your building, or parents of program "alumni" who may hold influential positions in the community. You can probably think of several others.

Create a database of names and addresses and add to it as you meet other people who might be encouraged to develop an interest in your center. Remember to delete the names of those individuals who have moved, changed jobs, or indicated that they do not wish to receive your newsletter. Each time you print the newsletter, generate labels from your database to streamline the mailing process.

Open Up Your Parent Meetings.   Again, you and your staff invest considerable time and energy planning and preparing for parent meetings. Some of those meetings will be of concern only to currently enrolled families. Other meetings might appeal to a broader audience. Advertising that meeting lets people know your program exists, enhances your program's prestige by establishing a connection with a professional organization, and broadens the scope of services identified with your program from "just" child care to parenting education for the larger community. Of course, this ad also fills a marketing function by putting your name and telephone number into the hands of potential customers who may save it for future reference. Figure 14.1 is an example of a public service announcement that you could use to advertise with the local newspaper or radio or television station. Most of these media outlets have "community calendar" features that carry such announcements at no charge.

Agency Links

Cultivating links with the agencies in your community can benefit your center in numerous ways. Licensing representatives can often offer advice and information to help you meet or exceed regulatory requirements. Instead of dreading the annual inspection visit and becoming defensive when problems are noted, assume that you and the licensing agent are both working toward the same goal—protecting the health and well-being of the children in your care. Licensing representatives are human, and like you, enjoy a friendly reception. They are likely to view sincere requests for advice as a welcome change from tedious checklists and reports.

Centers that have established good contacts with their community health services have experts to call when, for example, an outbreak of head lice occurs. Public health agencies can provide literature on this and other topics that you can distribute to families. They might also have experts on staff who can speak at your professional development meetings or visit your center to help you evaluate its health and safety practices. As noted in chapter 10, you should work with a health professional to review your program's health policies and procedures.

Your local CCR&R agency is your link to a large pool of prospective customers, as well as a possible resource for staff training. Many CCR&R programs sponsor workshops for child development staff on such topics as room arrangement or behavior guidance. Some have specialists on staff who can provide on-site technical assistance and consultation.

FIGURE 14.1   *Sample public meeting announcement*

TALK ON PARENTING: On April 15 at 8 P.M. at the Edgewater Little People's Child Development Center, Dr. James Service, noted child development specialist, will discuss "Problem-Solving Techniques to Use with Your Young Child." All community parents are invited. Edgewater Child Development Center, 123 Child Way, Watertown. Child care is provided for young children during the meeting. Call 555–1111 for more information.

Maintaining close ties with the public and private schools in your service area benefits all concerned. Families appreciate the smooth transition when their children move from child care to kindergarten and the children thrive when the teachers from both levels communicate with each other (with the permission and participation of families, of course). Teachers find it helpful to know something about the children they will have in their class, and the children and their families will be more comfortable entering the new school environment if you have helped them learn about it in advance. Schools can also be a source of referrals for your program. Families new to a community may turn to school personnel for information about available options for after-school care or the care of younger siblings. The more the school personnel know about your program and its quality, the more likely they are to mention its name.

If all of these reasons are not sufficiently convincing, networking with other agencies in your community can ultimately have a financial payoff. It puts you in a position to hear about new funding sources or requests for proposals offered by corporate or charitable foundations. Representatives of those agencies may be able to provide letters of support when you do submit grant proposals. Finally, the representatives of those agencies might serve on committees formed to evaluate the proposal merits.

Publicizing Events and Accomplishments

Every high-quality child development program has countless stories that deserve a wider audience. Telling your program's stories to that wider audience can be accomplished in several ways. You might get acquainted with a reporter who likes to do stories about children and give a standing invitation to her to visit your center. Or, you can write a press release and submit it to the local paper when the children in your program undertake an interesting project or field trip. A press release is most effective when typed, double-spaced, and brief. It should answer the journalist's questions—who, what, when, where, why—within the first paragraph. Clearly indicate the date of intended release, and include a name, e-mail address, and telephone number of someone to contact for further information.

The paper might print your release as written, or the editor might send a photographer or reporter to develop a more extensive human interest piece. If the paper does print your release, it may be shortened to fit available space. Because editors may accomplish this by deleting sentences or paragraphs at the end of the story, it is important to get all essential information as close to the beginning as possible.

Remember to thank the people who help put your story before the public. A letter to the editor, or directly to the reporter (with a copy to his supervisor), builds good will and paves the way for event future coverage. On the other hand, calling or writing to complain when your story is not published is likely to have the opposite effect (Stephens, 1998).

Accreditation

One of the best publicity stories for your center is about becoming fully accredited by the NAEYC. The very process of working toward accreditation raises public awareness because it involves surveying the parents of your program's children, calling attention to what you are trying to achieve. When you inform the public about your accomplishment, you raise the public's awareness of the importance of high-quality early childhood programs. In this way, you generate positive effects for children, families, and child-care professionals far beyond those directly involved in your center. Plan the story well in advance—have photos available and top the story off with a photo of your certificate! Frame the certificate and place it in a conspicuous place in your center. The interested newspapers and television stations should know that accreditation signifies that you have met national criteria as an outstanding child development center with a high-quality program. Thereafter, remember to add a note about the accreditation to your public relations materials, brochures, and your letterhead.

Staff Development as a Public Relations Vehicle

You are engaging in public relations work whenever you or your staff members participate with or appear before other groups. For example, you speak to a church group about child care. The people gain impressions about you and about your center from how well you are prepared and the manner of your presentation. Be sure to share opportunities to represent your center with the staff. This approach encourages them to learn new things and become more reflective about their practice. It also makes them feel good and shows the public that you value your teachers' abilities. These benefits also are realized when you encourage your staff to be active in local, state, and national professional associations. Thus, your center gains professional recognition at the same time you and your staff members grow professionally.

You and your staff can initiate appearances on conference programs. The NAEYC, for example, publishes a call for presentation proposals in *Young Children* about a year before its annual meeting. Your state and local associations may work in the same way, perhaps within a shorter time frame. A presentation has most of the same components as writing a good feature article.

You or your teachers may wish to publish professional articles in local, state, or national journals. Many practitioners have innovative ideas that may be useful to others. Submitting those ideas to a journal read by other teachers is another way for you and your staff to reflect on what you do and clarify your thinking.

Writing good feature articles entails four steps according to Richardson and Callahan, as adapted by Burckhardt (1984). You must visualize your audience, analyze your problem, organize your thinking and material, and dramatize your presentation. Before you start to write, study issues of the magazine or journal to determine the nature, style, and length of its articles. Many professional journals (e.g., *Young Children*) include their publication guidelines on their website. Prepare your article, writing and rewriting until it is clear and interesting. Type it neatly, double spaced. Professional journals want authors' names on a separate page from the article, and they may want two or three copies of each article to speed up the review process.

Magazines require that you enclose a self-addressed return envelope and postage to facilitate the article's return should the editors find it not suitable for their publication. If the article is returned, look it over for errors or outdated material, improve wording where possible, and submit it to another magazine or journal. Persistence pays off, so never give up after the first rejection slip. Your byline should include information about your center, which adds to public recognition of your center.

Networking

Even if you do not choose to present a topic at a professional conference, you and your staff can take advantage of opportunities to meet with people with similar interests and problems. Successful managers actively cultivate a wide network of professional contacts—people you can turn to (or who can turn to you) for advice, information, recommendations, referrals, or other types of assistance. Thus, it is important not only to attend conferences sponsored by professional organizations, but to join those organizations and become actively involved in their projects and governance. The NAEYC, with its various local, state, or regional affiliates, is a good starting point for all child development professionals. Administrators are also likely to benefit from organizations more particularly tailored to their role, such as a local director's support group or the National Association of Child Care Professionals (http://www.naccp.org).

A simple tool to help make the most of your networking efforts is the business card. Like your brochure and print advertisements, a business card should have an identifiable "look" that conveys an image of quality. In addition to essential information (e.g., the program's name and website URL, your name and title, address, telephone, fax, and e-mail), the card might also contain a logo or very brief phrase that communicates something about your program's mission. Exchanging cards with people you meet at professional gatherings is one way to help both of you remember each other's names after the event. The next step is to organize the contacts so they are accessible when you need them. This might mean creating categories instead of filing cards alphabetically by the name of company or individual.

The World Beyond Child Care

So far, we have examined ways that your public relations efforts can piggy-back on your ongoing efforts to communicate with families and to develop professional capabilities in yourself and your staff. Once you have these initiatives in place and begin to see their advantages, you are ready to move into the world beyond child care.

Making Connections

Remember that the word "public" in public relations actually has a broad connotation—every organization has many publics, each with a different perspective on what the organization does. Corporations gain a competitive edge in recruiting highly qualified employees if they can point to excellent child-care facilities in the community—but they may need your help to realize this potential benefit. Think of all of the other seemingly unrelated entities that stand to benefit from the existence of your program—real estate agents and others with an interest in "selling" a neighborhood or community, or taxpayers with an interest in welfare-to-work programs. Your goal is to reach each of those publics in a way that speaks to their interest.

Take Stock of Your Community.   Bagin and Gallagher (2001, pp. 137–138) suggested compiling a list of key contacts who can serve as liaisons with community organizations. They can provide feedback about the opinions held by their members and help convey your message. They suggested considering the following group categories: civic (e.g., Rotary, Lions Club), cultural (e.g., arts or humanities councils), economic (e.g., labor unions, retail merchants' associations), fraternal (e.g., Knights of Columbus), governmental (e.g., health or recreation departments), patriotic (e.g., American Legion, veterans groups), political (e.g., League of Women Voters), professional (e.g., doctors' or lawyers' associations), religious, retirees, and youth (e.g., YMCA, YWCA., 4-H Clubs).

Reach Out.   In addition to joining organizations with a focus on children or child care, consider joining organizations that bring you into contact with people with other interests, skills, and connections. Your community's chamber of commerce and the League of Women Voters are two examples. Use the listed categories to think about all of the groups that exist in your community. By participating in these "outside" groups, you learn a great deal about issues impacting your center, and you can bring your unique perspective as a child development professional to the discussions. As you become more comfortable and take a more active role in these organizations, you gain respect for yourself, as well as for your program and the profession in general.

Join Hands. Work with community partners to do things that benefit you both. Wassom (2001) suggested providing copies of articles on parenting topics (stamped with your program's name, web address, and phone number) to businesses where parents are likely to spend time waiting (e.g., hair salons). Once that relationship is established, she suggested that the center and salon could collaborate further by arranging on-site haircuts during center hours for the children of busy parents. On a broader scale, child development programs can partner with a number of community agencies or businesses to hold events that draw in a larger number of families than any single program could attract. For example, children's fairs celebrate the Week of the Young Child in many communities. In one town, child development programs set up booths with simple activities for the children, the Public Health Department offers immunizations, other helping agencies provide information about their programs, and businesses sponsor refreshments or provide small gifts for those attending.

Decisions, Decisions . . .

With your classmates, brainstorm a list of organizations in your community with which a child development program manager might make networking contacts.

"Double Duty" in Public Relations

Developing a sound public relations strategy pays off in numerous ways. The preparation of one type of information may be useful as you develop other types of public information. For example, carefully prepared talks to parents can form the nucleus for professional articles, or vice versa. Carefully stated objectives can enhance your written reports to the policy board, as well as serve as key statements on a public information brochure. Pictures taken for publicity pieces make delightful books for children. They can be arranged on tough cardboard and labeled with short descriptive phrases that children can soon "read."

Many materials serve several purposes; therefore, you must develop a system for carefully filing all of the materials you develop. With an adequate filing system, you can quickly locate a previous piece that might serve a present need when updated.

Countering Negative Publicity

A common lament among child development professionals is that negative stories about child care always receive more extensive and prominent coverage than all of their positive efforts. News of a child-care provider who has been convicted of molesting a child overshadows the fact that countless others provide safe, loving care day in and day out. It is small comfort that this seems to be true in every arena. Sensational news sells newspapers and attracts viewers, and sensational news is, more often than not, bad news.

Sometimes the effects of negative publicity can spill over even when your program is not directly involved. When a prominent researcher was quoted in the national press comparing sanitation conditions in child care to life in the middle ages, the follow-up by local television crews in one city could have put directors on the defensive. Because they had good health practices in place, however, and because they could keep cool under pressure, the directors could explain what they did to prevent the spread of infection and to keep the children healthy. As a consequence, the news that night showed children washing their hands and staff members cleaning tables with a bleach solution.

Of course, your first defense against negative publicity is the prevention of incidents that might trigger it—in other words, good management. From the initial planning to monitoring and controlling for quality, the manager's first goal is to protect the children's health and well-being. No amount of "spin doctoring" can make up for negligence, and it is unethical to suggest otherwise. But negative incidents happen in the best of programs, and wise managers have a plan in place to minimize the damage when they do occur.

That plan should clearly designate the spokesperson for the program who is responsible for handling all contacts with media representatives. In most cases, this duty falls on your shoulders. Although staff members should be kept informed of the situation, they should not communicate their version of events, which may be incomplete or inaccurate, to reporters. Rather, they should be instructed to decline all comment and to refer any questions to you. This is not an effort at secrecy, merely a precaution to help eliminate confusion and ensure the clear communication of complete information.

By communicating all of the facts as clearly and quickly as possible, you can avoid the appearance of having something to hide or defend. Often, this strategy helps defuse a story before it is blown out of proportion. Dorothy Hewes (1998, p. 346) related a story of a director confronted with questions about a suspected child molester who had, at one time, been a volunteer at the center. The director was able to inform the reporter that the individual in question had done only maintenance work and that had occurred many years earlier. The director also took the proactive measure of informing her employer and staff in anticipation of further questions. As the result of her quick action, the story mentioned the center only in passing and other news coverage focused on the center's policies for protecting children.

When presenting information to the news media, the *how* is often as important as the *who* and the *what*. All of your preparation for positive publicity will stand you in good stead here. Your printed materials will give reporters accurate information about the name of your program and its essential features. Your practice writing press releases that lead with the essentials will remind you to concentrate on getting the facts stated at the outset because your interview is likely to be edited down to only a sentence or two. Speak slowly and distinctly, look at the reporter, and focus as much on the positive as possible. If it turns out that your program was wrong, a sincere apology will probably do more to repair your image than a barrage of excuses.

You may agree in your heart with the joke that equates an executive's definition of a bad day as any day in which a secretary announces that the *60 Minutes* camera crew is waiting outside. And, in fact, you may never achieve a high level of comfort handling negative publicity. Still, it does not make sense to pretend that it cannot happen to you. Accepting and planning for the possibility are part of the manager's job.

Conclusion

Child development programs occupy a particular niche of the business landscape because their "product" is an intangible service. Program administrators are learning that, just like the managers of other service businesses, they must cultivate effective communication and positive relationships with people and institutions in the larger community, as well as with the families they serve. In order for their programs to survive and thrive, they must learn the skills of marketing and public relations to broaden their customer base, attract funding sources, and develop a pool of potential advocates. They must form links with community agencies to help the program operate smoothly and effectively, as well as to create a network of resources to which the families can turn for assistance. Child development programs can promote a public awareness of the hallmarks and advantages of high-quality care, as well as the liabilities of mediocre care, and, in so doing, help create a demand for excellence in all services for young children.

QUESTIONS FOR REVIEW

1. Define marketing and explain how it differs from public relations.
2. What is a customer profile and why is it important to marketing a service?
3. Define the terms key claim and key proof. Give an example of each.
4. List three tools a child development program can use to put its message before the public.
5. Describe an effective way to handle telephone inquiries.
6. Define servicescape and describe the four functions it fulfills in a service organization.
7. List the four steps for writing a good feature article.
8. How does the concept of public relations relate to a child development program's efforts to communicate with families and support the professional development of staff members?

PROFESSIONAL PORTFOLIO

1. Evaluate the websites of several child development programs (or other types of small businesses). Then, collaborate with a small group of your classmates to design a web page for a hypothetical child development program. Decide what information you should include and how it should be organized so that the site is easily navigated. Consider adding links to sites that provide other types of information your prospective clients might want or need. Pay attention to the aesthetic aspects of layout, background, and design. Print out a hard copy of your home page for inclusion in your portfolio.

2. Design a brochure or create a sample newsletter for a child development program. Include information about the program that is of interest to parents, as well as informative to people who may not have firsthand knowledge of your program. Make sure that your publication is attractive and reader-friendly and that it can be easily and inexpensively reproduced.

3. Plan an event for a child development program to which key public officials and community leaders are invited. Describe the event and explain what you hope to accomplish with it. When and where will the event be held? Write a letter of invitation and list those to whom you will send it. Explain your rationale for each decision.

RESOURCES FOR FURTHER STUDY

Print

Arnold, M. (2005). *Effective communication techniques for child care*. Clifton Park, NY: Delmar.

Kinder, J. A. (2000). *A short guide to school public relations*. Bloomington, IN: Phi Delta Kappa Educational Foundation.

Internet

Webopedia

http://www.webopedia.com

Free dictionary and search engine for computer and Internet technology definitions.

Research-Based Web Design and Usability Guidelines

http://usability.gov/guidelines/

Web design and usability guidelines regarding content, graphics, accessibility, and so forth, compiled by the National Cancer Institute.

Web Style Guide

http://www.webstyleguide.com

Web Style Guide, 2nd edition. Yale University Center for Advanced Instructional Media. Patrick Lynch and Sarah Horton. Also available in hard copy from Yale University Press.

HTML Goodies

http://www.htmlgoodies.com/introduction/intro/

A "non-technical" introduction to website design including discussion of content, style, function, and ease of maintenance.

CHAPTER FIFTEEN

Assessment and Evaluation

The fifth major management function is to monitor and control for quality. The manager is charged with knowing the standards, establishing systems to meet those standards, assessing and evaluating the program against the accepted standards, and when performance falls short, taking action to correct the problem. Monitoring and controlling for quality involve appraising the performance of individual staff members (including the manager), as well as evaluating the function of the program as a whole. They involve looking at intangible indicators (outcomes) of program effectiveness, such as the children's or families' satisfaction with the services, as well as the concrete elements of the physical facility that contribute to those outcomes.

In 1995, the Cost, Quality, and Child Outcomes in Child Care Centers Study captured national attention with its finding that "child care at most centers in the United States is poor to mediocre, with almost half of the infants and toddlers in rooms having less than minimal quality." The study also found that states with more stringent licensing regulations had fewer poor-quality centers and that those centers that were able to provide better than average care had access to outside resources through donations, employer sponsorship, or public funds (Cost, Quality, and Child Outcomes Study Team, 1995, pp. 2–5).

As discussed in chapter 3, child development programs are part of the social–cultural environment, and this study clearly demonstrated how a governmental system, as part of that environment, impacts center quality. Other elements of the social–cultural environment that either establish or impact center standards include professional organizations, market forces, and public opinion. All of these elements interact to raise or lower the level of quality deemed acceptable for out-of-home child care.

For example, child development professionals might advocate for more stringent standards regarding the educational qualifications of child-care workers, but if the public does not understand or concur with the importance of such qualifications, parents are likely to object to the higher rates centers must charge in order to attract and retain highly qualified staff with adequate salaries. Nor do governmental bodies recognize the need to subsidize such centers. Finally, when centers violate the higher standards, regulatory agencies are unable to secure the needed enforcement support from the judicial system if the rules are perceived as unfair or too stringent.

When quality is viewed from the perspective of the ecological systems framework, it becomes clear that monitoring in the child development center must go hand in hand with establishing good relations with parents and the public and professional advocacy on behalf of the children and families. Those areas are discussed in detail in chapters 13, 14, and 16, respectively.

Standards

Standards are defined as the designated level or degree of quality that is proper and adequate for a specific purpose. They are the measuring sticks used to determine how well the center is accomplishing its aims. As discussed in previous chapters, standards for child development programs are set by a number of different bodies, each with a particular focus. State governments, for example, establish licensing agencies to act on behalf of the public and enforce rules that protect children's safety and welfare. These rules are considered minimum standards and govern the amount of space and equipment a program must provide, the number of staff and their qualifications, health practices, fire safety, and many other areas.

Ideally, a state legislature mandates that such standards be created and delineates the broad areas that the standards regulate. Then, the legislature authorizes a particular agency, such as the health or social services department, to write the detailed standards with the help of experts in child development, fire safety, sanitation, and transportation, and input from parents and child-care providers. During the lengthy process, the proposed rules are reviewed many times and modified so that the end product represents the best thinking of the entire community about children's basic safety and welfare needs. Some states have established a tiered system, awarding higher levels of licensing to programs that meet more stringent standards, such as the indicators of quality set forth in environmental rating scales for early childhood, infant/toddler, school age, and family child-care settings (Harms et al., 2005; 2003; 1995; 1989).

Child development programs in public school settings usually must meet an additional set of standards regarding what children should know and be able to do set by the state's Department of Education (Scott-Little, Kagan, & Frelow, 2005). These standards, too, are often developed with public input at many levels. Head Start programs, which are federally funded, must follow the *Head Start Program Performance Standards*. Because one of those standards requires that staff possess the Child Development Associate credential, Head Start staff must also meet *CDAC Competency Standards* (Council for Early Childhood Professional Recognition, 1992).

The American Public Health Association and the American Academy of Pediatrics (APHA/AAP) have collaborated to establish national standards for health and safety in child-care programs (APHA/AAP, 2002). The American Consumer Product Safety Commission has established guidelines for playground equipment and surfacing. The National Life Safety Fire Code provides standards for the safe storage and use of hazardous materials and the protection from "conditions hazardous to life or property in the occupancy of buildings or premises" (Children's Foundation, 1995).

As you have read many times, the National Association for the Education of Children's *Developmentally Appropriate Practice in Early Childhood Programs Serving Children from Birth through Age Eight* (Bredekamp & Copple, 1997) provided a comprehensive set of high standards for any child development center. The NAEYC standards also have been adapted for school-age child-care programs (Albrecht & Plantz, 1991).

Program managers who accept "developmentally appropriate" as the degree of quality that is proper and adequate for their purpose can use the NAEYC's guidelines to establish quality levels in all program areas. They can also use the guidelines to assess the appropriateness of their efforts to respect and affirm cultural differences and to include children of all abilities (Derman-Sparks, 1992; Fox, Hanline, Vail, & Gallant, 1994). The Division for Early Childhood (DEC) of the Council for Exceptional Children has developed guidelines for serving children with special needs (Sandall, McLean, & Smith, 2000) and tools for evaluating and assessing the quality of those programs (Hemmeter, Joseph, Smith, & Sandall, 2001).

Accreditation

Any center, whether funded by a government agency or private tuition, can elect to meet an additional set of standards that is designed to establish a benchmark of quality beyond the minimum welfare and safety considerations of licensing regulations. These centers can work toward achieving accreditation from the NAEYC, the largest organization of early childhood professionals in the United States.

Accreditation is a distinction awarded to early childhood schools and child-care centers that have met a majority of the criteria related to 10 program standards and completed the outside validation procedure in a voluntary process supervised by the National Academy of Early Childhood Programs, a division of the NAEYC. Originally established in 1985, the standards were revised in 2005 and may be found at the NAEYC website: http://www.aeyc.org/accreditation/performance criteria/complete.asp. These standards were reviewed by early childhood professionals and parents from across the nation before they were accepted by the NAEYC board. One section of criteria pertains to center administration.

Accreditation, then, is a voluntary system that provides policy boards, managers, and staff members an incentive to work toward a high level of program development and the appropriate recognition when the center reaches that high-quality standard. In addition, the accreditation designation informs parents and the general public that early childhood programs have various levels of quality. When choosing an accredited center, parents can be assured that the center has been investigated and found to be of high quality. Large numbers of schools and centers have now been accredited through this voluntary system. Centers providing developmentally appropriate programs should strive for the public recognition that comes with accreditation. (Information about accreditation is available on the NAEYC website: http://www.naeyc.org.)

The Manager's Role

Monitoring and **controlling** are defined as the evaluative and action functions of maintaining high quality in the promised services. *Monitoring* requires being alert to and continuously observing for compliance with applicable standards. *Controlling* requires that you state the standards you expect each program component to achieve, measure the performance against the standards, and either correct any deviations from the established standards and plans or modify any standards that prove unrealistic or inappropriate (DuBrin, 2000, p. 332). Monitoring and controlling for quality are functions that each staff member must be concerned about daily, hourly, and moment to moment. In short, after a manager has developed a plan and put that plan into action, she must check regularly to determine whether the plan is being implemented properly and meeting its intended aims.

Monitoring and controlling are already a part of your life. Consider this example: When you are driving your car, you continually monitor speed, road conditions, time, and dozens of other factors. You have standards to meet in the form of traffic regulations, common courtesy, a schedule, and personal ideas about efficiency or the beauty of the selected route. As you drive, you measure your performance against those standards and correct any deviations: adjusting your speed, turning the steering wheel when the road curves, or deciding to take another route if there is too much traffic. A child-care center manager makes similar observations and adjustments to maintain efficiency and quality.

Managers establish personal standards that are based on professional knowledge and individual experience; they also observe the standards established by outside sources. Wise managers understand that the rules are minimum standards, the results of a collaborative effort of many people just like themselves. They ensure that their centers adhere to the rules and do not try to get around them. They also understand that they have a voice in improving the rules as new needs arise or new information develops. In other words, a center manager works in partnership with the licensing agency to establish a baseline of quality.

Having determined which standards apply to your center and why, your ability to maintain high quality depends, in part, on encouraging each staff member to take responsibility for his performance and to make adjustments whenever inadequacies occur. It is easier to encourage this type of responsibility if you select your staff carefully, orient and train them thoroughly, and provide feedback on their performance.

You must, however, make it easy for them to comply by structuring the environment, providing needed supplies, and ensuring that other supports are in place. A staff member left alone with too many crying infants, for example, may be tempted to take shortcuts when it comes to sanitizing a diapering table in between changes. Similarly, if there is no running water nearby or no hand lotion to soothe chapped hands, busy caregivers are less likely to be conscientious about handwashing.

Steps in the Monitoring and Controlling Process

The manager's first step in the monitoring and controlling process, then, is to *understand the requirements thoroughly.* Managers who lack this in-depth understanding are likely to be so consumed with the petty details of meeting the letter of the law that they quickly become candidates for burnout.

Next, the manager must *communicate the standards clearly* so that every staff member understands the importance of the standards and her responsibility for meeting them.

Third, the manager must *monitor compliance with the standards and act to maintain high performance standards in every center unit.* One phrase that describes this activity is "managing by walking around," but this should not be construed as casually meandering through the facility when the whim strikes. To be effective, you must have a purpose in mind, make notes of what you see, and follow through by sharing your observations of problem areas with the people who can do something to correct the situation (Albrecht, 1998).

Fourth, the manager must *listen to and understand others' views.* When leading staff members toward high-quality performance, it is essential to practice good communication skills. It is not enough to realize that some employees are failing to comply with established standards—you should know why. In other words, until you understand the problems they experience, you cannot begin to solve them. The most direct—and effective—way to accomplish this is to ask. Staff members who believe that their views are respected are more likely to become partners in the program's quality enhancement effort (Johnston, 1998). When this happens, everyone's stress is reduced—yours and your staff's.

Finally, the manager must *strive to maintain objectivity when evaluating problems and issues.* It is certainly a challenge to confront problems in a cool, calm manner, but it helps if a manager develops the habit of seeking information before leaping into action. Covey (1992, p. 139) recommended asking four questions: "(1) Where are we? (2) Where do we want to go? (3) How do we get there? (4) How will we know when we have arrived?" He cautioned that strong emotions can often color one's perceptions regarding the first two questions, leading to premature and energy-draining battles over the third. Consider the following example:

> In a small center, a teacher in the infant–toddler classroom became upset with the teacher of the 3-to-5-year-old group over sharing the playground. "For the past several days," she fumed, "she has brought the older kids outside within a few minutes of the time I have arrived with the babies. That means that, after all of the time we have spent bundling our children up for outdoor play, we have to turn around and go back inside—or run the risk of having the babies trampled by the big kids. I thought we had agreed on a schedule!" Instead of solving the problem by decree, the director asked the two teachers to discuss it with her at the weekly staff meeting devoted to administrative issues. The discussion became heated almost immediately, as one teacher defended herself from what felt like an attack. "We can't always stick to a precise schedule for coming outside," she said. "Sometimes we finish our group time early, or the children just seem more restless than usual." The other teacher reacted by emphasizing her point even more strongly, and both voices rose in volume. The director intervened, reminding them that the goal was to find a solution that worked for everyone. After much discussion, they decided that what they really needed was a fence to create a protected space for the babies so that both age groups could be outside at the same time. The director agreed to apply for a grant to provide the needed funds, and the two teachers found a way to coordinate their schedules in the meantime. The older children were fascinated with the construction of the fence, calling it the "baby cage!" and the subsequent interactions between older and younger children through the fence have been a joy for the adults and children on both sides.

In this example, the answers to the questions "Where are we?" and "Where do we want to go?" were somewhat distorted by the teachers' strong feelings. One was exasperated at working so hard to get outside, only to have to come right back in; the other was equally frustrated at the prospect of being chained to a rigid time schedule. Both leapt to the conclusion that the only answer to "where do we want to go" was the enforcement of that rigid schedule, and the conversation turned to confrontation as they argued about how to get to that point. Once they understood that they both agreed on the importance of outdoor play *and* a flexible schedule, they could begin to work toward a "win-win" solution.

Decisions, Decisions . . .

Your center has a policy of sending a brief note home when children get scrapes and bumps on the playground. You have noticed that these are occurring more frequently of late and worry that a more serious accident could occur. How can you monitor the quality of the care children receive on the playground? List the factors you want to consider.

Evaluation of the Educational Program

Monitoring and controlling the children's program is a central concern of administrators. All of the other components (e.g., food service, safety and sanitation, health practices) exist in order to support that program. At least five groups of people may provide helpful information regarding the center's program quality.

Children Evaluate

A child development program has many customers: Parents who enroll their children are purchasing a service; society at large expects the programs to keep children safe and prepare them for later life. Certainly, one of the customers is the person who experiences the service firsthand—the child. If the aim of quality management is customer satisfaction, then managers must be concerned with the way their young customers experience the program. Are they happy to come to school in the morning? Are the classrooms filled with the pleasant hum of busy children constructively engaged in a variety of intriguing activities? Do they seem clean, rested, and well fed? Do the adults and children seem to enjoy each other's company? All are signs of satisfied customers that managers can observe as they walk around the center each day.

In contrast, managers should be alert for the signs of dissatisfied customers: lots of crying, children wandering listlessly, adults whose interactions with the children are limited to telling them what to do or reprimanding them for failing to do it. Katz (1998) referred to this approach as a "bottom-up" view of program quality.

Of course, a "snapshot" of a few children here or there does not give you a picture of what the program is like for all of the children or what it is like for one particular child over a longer span of time. You should augment this informal checkup with some systematic data collection. You might, for example, choose one or more children to shadow for a day or a week, noting such things as the child's activity, mood, and partners in play or conversation at regular, predetermined intervals.

This approach puts you in the child's shoes, so to speak, and helps you see the program through his eyes. Are you greeted pleasantly when you arrive? Or are you left to find your own way to enter the play of other children? How much of your day is spent hurrying to keep up with others or waiting for others to catch up with you? How much time is spent wandering and how much constructively engaged? How much time is devoted to teacher-directed crafts or games and how much to projects that you and the other children instigate?

Another way the children can give you a broad picture of how your center is doing is through their own development. You can record the child's baseline information to have a standard for comparing later growth and development. NAEYC accreditation criteria require that programs establish procedures for regular assessment of children's learning and development for the purposes of planning and improving services. The results of such assessments are to be used only for the benefit of children, never to label or stigmatize a child or family. In collaboration with the National Association of Early Childhood Specialists in state Departments of Education, NAEYC asserts that, "Tools for assessing young children's progress must be clearly connected to important learning. . .; must be technically, developmentally, and culturally valid; and must yield comprehensive useful information" (NAEYC and NAECS/SDE, 2002, p. 7). Rather than resorting to formal testing, you can provide parents with much more meaningful information about their child's development if you keep dated notes of your observations and samples of the child's drawings and other work. This way parents can readily see how much their child has changed over the months at the center.

Decisions, Decisions . . .

Looking over the notes of your day's observation of 4-year-old Tanya, you see that at least four times during the day, she cried for several minutes—when another child took something she was using, when she could not get her boots on, when she fell on the playground, and when she was told to lie on her cot at nap time. No adult approached her during any of these incidents, and each time she gradually stopped crying and went on to some other activity. What does this behavior suggest to you? As center manager, what should you do? Discuss your ideas with your classmates.

Teachers Evaluate

The teachers evaluate their planning, organizing, and interacting with the children, measuring their actions against professional standards such as those shown in Figure 15.1. Teachers make adjustments to correct shortcomings. They are wise to monitor, evaluate,

FIGURE 15.1   *Program evaluation*

Program Guidelines	Fair	Good	Excellent
The Program I Observed			
1. Was planned from the point of view of the whole child in the immediate environment.	☐	☐	☐
2. Valued the child's healthy, happy, responding, secure approach to living.	☐	☐	☐
3. Provided for the emotional growth of the child.	☐	☐	☐
4. Balanced active and quiet activities.	☐	☐	☐
5. Provided appropriate opportunities for children to grow in self-direction and independence.	☐	☐	☐
6. Established and maintained limits on behavior for protection of individuals, groups, and the learning environment.	☐	☐	☐
7. Challenged children's intellectual powers.	☐	☐	☐
8. Provided media of self-expression.	☐	☐	☐
9. Encouraged children's verbal expressions.	☐	☐	☐
10. Provided opportunities for social development.	☐	☐	☐
11. Helped children learn to understand their bodies.	☐	☐	☐
12. Provided opportunities for each child to play outdoors every day.	☐	☐	☐
13. Provided opportunities for vigorous action.	☐	☐	☐
14. Was fun for the children.	☐	☐	☐
15. Considered the interests and needs of parents as well as children.	☐	☐	☐

Remarks:

_____

_____

_____

_____

_____

_____

Source: V. Hildebrand, *A laboratory workbook for introduction to early childhood education* (Upper Saddle River, NJ: Prentice Hall, 1991), p. 125.

and control from moment to moment. For example, if they present a learning task to the children and notice that some are unable to perform the task, they may conclude that the task is too difficult. That is an evaluation. The standard of performance is in the teacher's mind, based on prior knowledge and experience with children of this age. Using an instant evaluation, the teacher has at least two alternatives. The activity can be postponed until a later date when the children are more mature and able to do the activity or the rules can be modified to enable the children to accomplish some minimum success with the activity. Children deserve to be cared for in groups that are small enough to allow this type of close observation by their teachers. A teacher's participation and encouragement make it more likely that children will enjoy a new activity.

If teachers keep a daily diary, they can review the problem areas from time to time and search for solutions. For example, if they note that the transition from outdoor play to lunch is frequently chaotic and stressful for teachers and children alike, they can explore options to manage this. They might decide to gather everyone on the carpet and sing a few songs while the children wash their hands and move to the lunch tables a few at a time.

Teachers evaluate the program and make adjustments to meet the needs of individual children. Sometimes that means offering just enough help so that a child can use scissors successfully.

Teachers can make a summary of the experiences offered to children over the course of the week, month, or year. Of course, knowing what the group was offered does not indicate what an individual child chose to do just as knowing the cafeteria menu does not identify what a child selected for lunch. Thus, the teachers must also regularly record information on individual children. They can routinely go through their list of children and think about what they have observed each child doing. Planning to make notes on a few different children each day helps ensure that no child is ignored or forgotten. These observations can be added to each child's portfolio along with dated samples of drawings, attempts at writing, and photographs of block or clay creations. Like the portfolio of an artist or model, a child's portfolio contains representative samples of her work. Because young children are constantly developing, representative samples of their work saved at regular intervals can dramatically capture the process. Writing samples collected over a year's time, for example, may well progress from marks that look like "scribbling" to the uneducated eye to work that begins to resemble conventional script.

Teachers can collect these samples in legal-size file folders, large resealable plastic bags, or manila envelopes. Once they have mastered the technique of routinely collecting observations and work samples, teachers can move on to organizing portfolios. The portfolios should have sections for physical, social, emotional, and cognitive development so that the teachers can be sure that they are truly observing and documenting the growth of the whole child. (See, for example, Shores & Grace, 2005.) When it is time for a parent conference,

Decisions, Decisions . . .

Michael, a 3-year-old with Down syndrome, had been coming to Rainbow Child Development Center for 2 months. The lead teacher in his classroom has observed that Michael has never joined in during large-group songs and games. Instead, he sits somewhat listlessly a little behind the others, his gaze wandering toward the ceiling. Discuss what the teacher should do. What should the manager do?

Parents evaluate the program when they see their children enjoying activities or when they have an opportunity to review a portfolio of the child's work with the teacher.

the teacher has a cumulative record of observations that can be discussed. Parents feel trust and confidence when the teacher can cite specific examples. A brief conversation with a parent when he picks up his child could let the parent know what the child has done of interest during the day. This information often helps parents engage their child in conversation, and the child will tell the parents more than "We just played" when asked about school.

How can a manager help teachers appreciate the value of watching a child closely? How can managers ensure that there is enough time for teachers to make the necessary observations? Keeping records helps the teachers show parents and others that the children are achieving developmental milestones. Teachers' observations are also an important part of the assessment process for children with disabilities or developmental delays. Observations form the basis of planning for the individual needs of all children (Curtis & Carter, 1996).

The teachers in charge of each group must meet to discuss goals, evaluate programs, and settle on the best plans for the future. Discussing an individual child's needs and preparing strategies to meet those needs requires planning opportunities. This coordination of effort is difficult in those centers where the staff have staggered hours, but time must be found if a high-quality program is to be achieved.

Families Evaluate

The parents' evaluation of their satisfaction becomes apparent when your center gets admission requests from families who are friends and acquaintances of those families with children already enrolled. On the other hand, if parents take their child out of your center because they are dissatisfied, this decision is also an evaluation and may hurt your image in the community. Monitoring admissions, dropouts, and the reasons for both can help you gain clues about the parents' evaluation of your center's program and service.

Decisions, Decisions . . .

Two families abruptly withdrew their children from your center last week. They did not say anything to you, but another parent with whom you have a long-standing relationship has suggested that they were unhappy because it seemed their children had a different teacher every week. Your center *has* undergone several staff changes recently: One teacher had a baby and decided to stay at home, another found a higher-paying job in the public school system, and one of the new teachers you hired just did not work out. What should you do as manager?

The parents' opinions and suggestions should be solicited periodically to learn how the program is meeting their needs and those of their children. Many questions can be answered during a private conference—it is easier to get more elaboration on a point than if only written questionnaires are used. You can ask such questions as "Do the hours fit your family's needs?" "Are your needs for consulting with the teacher being met?" "What changes would you suggest?" A questionnaire such as that in Figure 15.2 might be developed to get some helpful feedback. A questionnaire may also draw the parents' attention to the high-quality features of your service.

FIGURE 15.2 *Parents' program rating sheet*

Dear Parents:

Please rate your child's center experience on each of the items listed below. Use the following numeric scale.

Rating Scale: 4—Very Satisfactory 2—Unsatisfactory
   3—Satisfactory 1—Very Unsatisfactory

Your rating, keeping your own child in mind:

____ 1. Amount and quality of warmth and understanding received?

____ 2. Amount of individual attention given?

____ 3. Amount of planning and effort teachers invest in the program?

____ 4. Amount of diversity of experiences and materials available?

____ 5. Amount of activities fostering creativity?

____ 6. Amount of activities enriching intellectual ability?

____ 7. Amount of activities enriching language development?

____ 8. Amount of activities encouraging your child's social development—making friends, being with children, etc.?

____ 9. Amount of activities enhancing motor skills such as running, climbing, throwing, catching, and the like?

____ 10. Amount of activities helping your child feed good about himself or herself?

____ 11. The amount of encouragement given for your child to take care of himself or herself and become more independent?

____ 12. Number of children in the class?

____ 13. Number of adults helping in the class?

____ 14. Amount of space available in the classroom and play yard?

____ 15. Amount, type, and quality of equipment in the yard?

____ 16. Communication network for keeping parents informed?

____ 17. Opportunity you have had to visit the classroom or teacher?

____ 18. Your child's overall progress this year?

   19. Write below or on the back of this page your concerns that do not seem to be covered by the questions above.

_____

_____

_____

_____

_____

The Community and Professionals Evaluate

As noted earlier, some outside evaluations take place because they are required by law or a center's funding source, including licensing personnel or representatives of a state's Department of Education. Others are solicited voluntarily, such as the final evaluation of a center's application by the accrediting commission of the National Academy of Early Childhood Programs, the accreditation arm of the NAEYC. People from the community also form evaluative opinions about the center based on what they see and hear around the community.

Some managers find it valuable to exchange evaluation services with other centers. They often gain helpful perspectives when they see how others handle similar functions. For example, during a visit to another center, Rachel, a manager, observed a smoothly operating session with the adults helping the children get dressed in their outdoor winter clothing. Five or six children took their boots and snowsuits to the middle of the playroom, where an adult sat on a small chair. Sitting on the floor near the adult, the children dressed themselves, with the assistance of a few verbal suggestions and a tug on a boot here or there. Rachel recorded the smooth operation and vowed to make some changes in the system she operated. She had gained a new perspective during the exchange visit. She commended the center when discussing her observation with them.

The Manager Evaluates

As manager, you must monitor the program to compare its performance to your stated goals and with current professional standards. Informal spot checks can be done daily. Periodically, more formalized procedures are necessary—checking lesson plans, taking detailed notes in each group, or using checklists.

The evaluations, standards, and feedback systems must be established with teacher input and carried out in an agreeable, supportive way so as to increase the teacher's confidence, motivation, and ability. The teachers' evaluation checklist in Figure 15.1 should be coordinated with the planning guidelines suggested in chapter 12 because there is an important relationship between planning, monitoring, and controlling. Remember that when you expect to monitor or evaluate the teachers or others on aspects of program quality, you must communicate this information early to allow planning and development time. It is unfair to staff members to add new items to the evaluation without notice.

Ideally, the elements of quality to be evaluated are established together with your teachers and other center stakeholders. Recall from the discussion of management techniques that staff are more likely to follow through on goals for which they feel some ownership. When they do, the manager can evaluate by serving more as a mirror than as a judge. Carter (1998) devised an evaluation form on which the manager objectively notes whether the agreed-upon performance indicators are observed "Frequently, Occasionally, or Never" and provides some specific examples.

Instead of saying that a staff member does an "excellent" job providing a variety of art experiences for the children, the manager might indicate that this is observed only occasionally, adding that the same watercolors and manila paper have been put out on the art table every day for the last several weeks.

Managers evaluate the program—and are evaluated—for evidence that children and teachers have the time and materials to become deeply engaged in experiences.

This type of remark gives the teachers an opportunity to explain that they were trying to make sure that every child had an opportunity to waterpaint or that they wanted the children to explore additional possibilities with the same media. Another explanation might be that the teachers lacked other materials and did not know how to go about requesting them. Of course, it is possible that a teacher just had no other ideas about what art experiences to offer the children. In a conference discussing the evaluation, the manager might learn something about the wisdom of offering the children repeated opportunities to experience materials, or the manager might take action to provide different materials and ensure that the teachers know how to get what they need. In the last scenario, the evaluation becomes a training tool if the manager and teacher collaborate to establish a goal for the next evaluation and a plan of action for meeting that goal.

Of course, the possibility remains that a teacher's performance simply is not acceptable, in which case it is the manager's job to make this clear and state any expectations for improvement, as well as any consequences for the failure to do so. Ongoing professional development activities help the teachers become more effective partners in this aspect of their evaluation. As discussed in chapter 8, the manager must document the results of all evaluations as well as warnings and steps taken to help an employee improve. When a teacher fails to improve in spite of these efforts, dismissal is the only option.

Monitoring Other Units

All of the center's units must be the focus of the manager's monitoring and controlling function. That is, you must set minimum standards for each and make corrections when deviations are observed. For example, it is appropriate to evaluate the policy board's decision-making process, the method used to present items to the board, how professionalism is increased, how to serve more children and families, and ways to increase the board's effectiveness. If any item does not measure up to the predetermined standards, you must initiate corrective action.

Any deviations from the staff's standards should be brought to their attention immediately, especially matters having an effect on the children. Hiring new staff is very expensive; therefore, improving the performance of those who have been hired is desirable. It is reasonable to expect people to be punctual and to carry out the job as explained by the job description. Following the standards set by the profession or service is also to be assumed. Like teachers, food service, maintenance, and clerical personnel are expected to comply with professional standards. Staff members can help set the criteria or standards by which they will be judged. To be fair, the criteria for pay raises, promotions, or dismissal should be set early and communicated to the staff, rather than when it is time to make a judgment at the end of a year.

The Financial Area

Money management must continuously be evaluated. You are responsible for careful, accurate, and honest accounting in collecting fees and paying expenses. Both profit and nonprofit organizations should stick to their budgets. In profit-making centers, figuring in a reasonable percentage for profit is necessary. Establishing an accounting system with the assistance of a competent accountant is essential. Financial control is discussed in chapter 6.

The Physical Plant

The safety, sanitation, security, and aesthetics of the entire physical plant might be your responsibility, or you may have only a portion of a building as your concern. We discussed specific requirements for establishing facilities that are safe and inviting in previous chapters. Monitoring and controlling for quality in these areas means that the manager establish a regular schedule for completing specific tasks as well as a regular schedule for verifying that standards are being maintained. When deficiencies are noted, the manager must work with staff members to correct them. For example, when staff focus on children's needs (as they should), they may lapse into habits of leaving items out instead of putting them away. If you notice this occurring, you might evaluate the situation to see whether a change in the storage arrangements or additional storage space is needed.

The security of your facility during nights, weekends, and vacations must be planned and controlled. Many centers have difficulty preventing the older neighborhood children from coming into the playground after hours to play on, and possibly damage, the equipment. This may dictate choosing heavier or more substantial equipment than the size and age of the center's enrollees requires. Security locks are also essential. Some of the "visitors" might be of the four-legged variety, so you should cover outdoor sandboxes when they are not in use to prevent them from becoming unsanitary litter boxes.

Food Service

Items to evaluate in the food service area (discussed in chapter 11) include the following:

1. Do meals offer sufficient quantity, variety, and nutritive content to meet the recommended daily allowances?
2. Are the children's attitudes toward meals, manners, and nutrition education positive?
3. Are the foods adequate for staff?
4. Are the kitchen and dining areas arranged efficiently?
5. Are noise levels low?
6. Is the space adequate to attend to an individual child's needs?
7. Are good sanitation procedures strictly adhered to?
8. Are all food workers healthy, clean, and dressed to deliver clean, healthful food?
9. Does the interaction between the teachers and food service staff facilitate the use of food in classroom learning activities?
10. Is information on the children's food intake and nutrition being disseminated to their parents?
11. Are the midmorning and midafternoon snacks nutritious, adequate, and attractive?
12. Are teachers receiving a nutrition break?
13. Have you monitored the food shopping with regard to cost, waste, and leftovers?

Children's Health and Safety

Items requiring evaluation in this category (discussed in chapter 12) include the following:

1. Have all of the parents filed immunization records?
2. Are your records clear as to who is available to pick up a child if he becomes ill during the day?
3. Do all staff members know where these records are filed?
4. Have you arranged a place to keep a sick child comfortable, quiet, and away from the others until she can be taken home?
5. Have you made arrangements for continually monitoring the children's health to be aware of the signs of illness?

6. Do you require a medical clearance to readmit a child following an absence?

7. Is your nap room space adequate, free of drafts, and accessible to exits in case of fire?

8. Are sufficient staff available during nap time to evacuate the building in case of fire?

9. Does each staff member know his role in an emergency evacuation—for example, taking the children's emergency information and an attendance list; calling for help and giving directions to the center?

10. Are evacuation plans known and practiced?

11. Is the nap time length communicated to the parents?

12. Are provisions adequate for those children who will not sleep?

13. Do you have sources of medical advice that can guide you or your staff on a moment's notice in case of emergency?

14. Are those medical advisers' phone numbers posted by each phone?

15. Is the temperature of your building correct for active children?

16. Have all appropriate precautions been taken to prevent child abuse of any kind?

Parental and Public Relations

As noted, there is some overlap in evaluating those actions that affect parents and evaluating those that affect the general public. Careful attention to the following areas is necessary (additional information appears in chapters 13 and 14):

1. Are telephone calls answered politely?

2. Are letters answered politely and promptly?

3. Are the parents' needs being met?

4. Are advertisements, brochures, and newsletters adequate and up to date?

5. Are you making and carrying out plans to communicate with the parents?

6. Are publications available to lend to parents to help them with their parenting questions?

7. Do the parents understand your procedures for dealing with a sick child and their responsibility to pick up the child and return the child after the illness is over?

8. Do all staff have a clear understanding of who should speak with the parents, the public, or media representatives when complaints or criticisms arise?

9. Are staff members who fill leadership roles in the community well prepared to represent the center?

10. Are parents informed about your food service and health policies?

11. Do parents know your routine during emergencies?

Evaluation of Management

As manager, you must regularly seek an evaluation of your own performance from the policy board and staff so that you might improve your management and operation of the enterprise. You can work with the board and staff to set up the evaluation process. You should learn much from it in a friendly, cooperative, and harmonious fashion, just as you expect your staff to learn from their evaluations. Figure 15.3 is a suggested form for a manager's evaluation.

FIGURE 15.3 *Evaluation of the manager*

Please rate the manager of the XYZ Child Development Center using the following numeric scale.

4—Very Satisfactory	2—Unsatisfactory
3—Satisfactory	1—Very Unsatisfactory

_____ 1. Knowledgeable regarding policies, procedures, and regulations?

_____ 2. Establishes goals and objectives that are realistic and appropriate?

_____ 3. Effective in the development, evaluation, and revision of programs, plans, and procedures?

_____ 4. Seeks advice and consultation on goals, programs, plans, and procedures?

_____ 5. Decisions reflect overall goals and plans?

_____ 6. Delegates and organizes units to facilitate conduct of programs?

_____ 7. Carries out systematic assessment of qualifications, abilities, and achievements of staff members?

_____ 8. Is effective in recruitment of competent staff members?

_____ 9. Makes effective staff assignments?

_____ 10. Carries out objective evaluation of the performance of staff members?

_____ 11. Makes effective use of all nonhuman resources—money, equipment, buildings?

_____ 12. Is objective in evaluating problems and issues?

_____ 13. Acts promptly, but not in undue haste?

_____ 14. Has ability to listen and to understand others' views?

_____ 15. Maintains constructive relationships with others?

_____ 16. Anticipates future developments in areas of responsibility?

_____ 17. Facilitates staff development?

_____ 18. Exercises leadership essential to a manager's role?

_____ 19. Provides up-to-date leadership in professional activities in the community, state, and nation?

20. Other: Discuss other criteria and rate the manager on those items you feel are important. Write at the bottom or on the back of this page.

_____

_____

_____

_____

_____

_____

Evaluating Administrative Practice

By now it should be clear that maintaining high quality at the classroom level depends on the overall quality of a program's administrative practices. The Program Administration Scale (Talan & Bloom, 2004) is a tool for assessing that quality. It is analogous to the environment rating scales that we have mentioned several times throughout this book, but broader in scope. The authors state that they were specifically interested in tapping "organizational practices that foster collaboration, diversity, cultural sensitivity, and social justice" (p. 1). Like the ECERS-R (Harms et al., 2005), the Program Administration Scale (PAS) uses a 7-point scale, from inadequate to excellent, to rate 25 items in 10 areas or subscales. The subscales are: human resources development (including supervision and performance appraisal); personnel cost and allocation; center operations; child assessment; fiscal management; program planning and evaluation; family partnerships; marketing and public relations; technology; and staff qualifications.

When Evaluations Yield Negative Results

Monitoring and controlling for quality is an ongoing process. There will inevitably be times when a program fails to meet one or more particular standards, whether its own or those established by an outside agency. In general, such occasions should be handled as an opportunity to correct the problem and improve services. Becoming defensive may be tempting, particularly if the deficiency impacts the program's licensing status or funding, but it usually just wastes precious energy. It may help to step back and put the particular deficiency into perspective. Failing to meet one criteria does not necessarily mean the program is "bad." NAEYC accreditation standards, for example, identify criteria that all centers must meet (e.g., supervision; no corporal punishment), but beyond that the expectation is that centers will achieve compliance with 80 percent of the criteria associated with program standards. It is also possible to achieve a "good" or "excellent" overall score on the environmental rating scales with less than perfect scores on each individual item.

On the other hand, failure to meet some standards can have serious consequences for children, as well as legal or funding implications for the program. Unless a problem presents an immediate danger for children, licensing agencies generally give programs a period of time to correct the situation. Your job is to make the correction and submit documentation that you have done so to your licensing representative.

Finally, because evaluators are human, they can sometimes be in error. If you feel that this has happened to your program, it is important to approach the situation calmly and professionally. Present evidence that your program does in fact meet the criteria in question and request a reevaluation. If you are unsuccessful, find out what options you have for appeal or mediation and follow through.

Conclusion

Monitoring and controlling for quality are major concerns for a manager. By setting standards, measuring performance, and leading staff to correct problems, the manager performs essential monitoring and controlling functions. Local and state rules form the basis for minimum standards, but most managers want their center to have higher standards. NAEYC accreditation is a distinction that centers and schools can earn for producing high-quality programs.

Every aspect of the center must come under regular scrutiny and the resulting information must be put to use to improve program quality. Various publics share in the monitoring or evaluating function: the board, the teachers, the manager, other staff members, the parents, the community, and, most of all, the children, who reveal by their enjoyment of the activities and willingness to attend the center that they are happy with the nurturing and educating they are receiving.

QUESTIONS FOR REVIEW

1. Define the monitoring and controlling process. Explain how this process relates to a center's operation.

2. Explain how the monitoring and controlling function relates to standards, licensing, and accreditation.

3. Define the "bottom-up" approach to evaluating a program's quality. What would a "top-down" approach involve?

4. Discuss the ways that each of the following people evaluate a center:
   a. the children enrolled
   b. the parents of the children enrolled
   c. the professionals and others in a community
   d. the manager

PROFESSIONAL PORTFOLIO

1. Locate an instrument (other than the example given in this chapter) that evaluates overall program quality. Describe how you might use the instrument and give specific examples of what you should do with your findings.

2. Assume that you are the manager of a child development center that has received a "poor" rating from the licensing consultant because staff failed to wash their hands at required times—before preparing and serving food, after diapering, or after helping children wipe their noses. Develop a plan to correct this problem. Describe who will take what action when and how.

3. Develop a questionnaire to evaluate parent satisfaction with a child development program. Describe when and how often you might administer the questionnaire, how to encourage responses, and what you should do with the findings.

RESOURCES FOR FURTHER STUDY

Print

Child and program assessment: Tools for reflective educators (2004, January). *Young Children, 59*(1), entire issue.

Freeman, N. K., & Brown, M. H. (2000, September). Evaluating the child care director: The collaborative professional assessment process. *Young Children, 55* (5), 20–28.

Internet

Organizational Climate Assessment
http://cecl.nl.edu/technical/oca.htm
Description and ordering information for the Organizational Climate Assessment developed by the McCormick Tribune Center for Early Childhood Leadership at National-Louis University in Wheeling, Illinois; home page includes a link to subscribe to a free monthly e-bulletin.

Making Learning Visible
http://www.pz.harvard.edu/mlv/
Website for Making Learning Visible, a collaborative effort of Project Zero at the Harvard Graduate School of Education and the Municipal Preschools and Infant–Toddler Centers of Reggio Emilia, Italy; includes detailed examples of documentation that reveal children's learning as individuals within groups.

16

Leadership

T hink about the leaders you followed as a child, as a student, and as an adult. What characteristics did they possess? Why were those leaders important in your life?

Now look at yourself as a potential leader. What talents do you bring to the leader's role in a child development program? If you have managed a classroom, you certainly have had some experience planning, organizing, and monitoring. The classroom represents a microcosm of the entire program, and many of the skills you honed there can be applied to the director's role. But directing a program is not the only leadership opportunity available to seasoned early childhood professionals. You can also consider being the principal of a school, the manager of a Child Care Resource and Referral agency or some other human services unit such as a United Fund agency, a senior citizen center, or a family planning agency. Leadership in the various human service organizations requires many similar skills.

Leading means being out in front of a working unit. Leading can be contrasted with driving, which is done from behind the energy source. For example, you drive a horse from behind and lead it from the front. Leading tends to be democratic and cooperative, whereas driving tends to be autocratic. Leadership in a child development center requires a person who can plan, organize, and delegate work appropriately. Leading in a center requires skills in interpersonal relations—the ability to develop rapport and motivation among all employees in order to provide high-quality services.

Your professional preparation and experience undoubtedly have helped you understand that people prefer to be treated as human beings, not as cogs in a wheel. To be a successful manager, you must develop attitudes that show an interest in, friendliness toward, and support of the members of your staff. People are certainly more effective as workers if they sense these positive attitudes than they are if they feel you are uninterested, hostile, or unsupportive.

To be an effective leader, you must be a good decision maker who can gain the support of your staff by involving them in democratic decision-making processes. Decision making requires an intelligent gathering of facts and initiative on the part of the leader.

Leaders must possess intelligence, vision, initiative, maturity, decisiveness, and self-assurance. They must also develop credibility with their employees. Your training, publications, and experience as a teacher can help you build this credibility. You maintain and enhance this credibility through professional courses, internships, reading, and continued experience.

Managing and Leading Differ

Leading is defined as the process of inspiring "confidence and support among the people who are needed to achieve organizational goals" (DuBrin, 2000, p. 232). It is one of the basic functions of management, but it is not synonymous with managing (Freeman & Brown, 2000). According to DuBrin, management is the rational and methodical application of specific strategies to situations, regardless of context. Leadership, on the other hand, deals more in the realm of feelings and imagining possibilities. "Management involves getting things done through other people. Leadership places more emphasis on helping others do the things they know need to be done to achieve the common vision" (DuBrin, 2000, pp. 232–233).

Management consultant Stephen Covey asserted that leaders must have the necessary vision to focus on the larger picture, anticipate trends, and set new goals, while managers concentrate on finding the most efficient ways of accomplishing established goals (Covey, 1989, p. 101). He painted a scenario in which the workers clear a path through a jungle as the managers survey the site and procure better tools to accomplish the task. Meanwhile, the leader climbs a tree to discover that the entire group is in the wrong jungle! In short, the leader has a vision, not just a mission.

According to Margie Carter and Deb Curtis, a mission addresses the way things are, while a vision conveys how we would like them to be (Carter & Curtis, 1998, pp. 18–19). Extending Covey's analogy, one could argue that for too long, too many early childhood professionals have been good workers and managers, trying to clear better and faster paths through the jungle, making do with fewer and fewer resources. Occasionally, though, a leader emerges—someone like Loris Malaguzzi, the Italian thinker and prominent early childhood educator whose fundamental premise was that children are competent and powerful and deserve the finest equipment and materials, the most beautiful spaces, and the best thinking of the best minds. As a result of his leadership, the early childhood programs of Reggio Emilia have flourished for 30 years and provide models of excellence for the world (Katz, 1998). In a similar way, leaders in the United States and other countries are challenging our old ideas about curriculum, professional development, and ways of serving all children regardless of race, ethnicity, gender, income, or ability.

Decisions, Decisions . . .

What trends do you think a center manager should be thinking about today?
List the three trends you consider most important. Compare your list with your classmates'.

Types of Leadership

Leadership has become the focus of increasing attention in the early childhood profession. There is also growing recognition that many existing leadership models do not really fit in the context of early childhood organizations. According to Kagan and Hallmark (2001), traditional leadership theories assume that leaders, usually male, sit alone at the head of a large hierarchical corporation. They got there, and they maintain their position, by beating out the competition. The world of early care and education contradicts each of these elements: Most programs are small and power is shared between several leaders—usually women—who operate in a collaborative mode. Leadership theory is catching up to early childhood practice, however, by adopting a systems perspective and recognizing the need for power sharing and collaboration. The concept of servant-leadership, developed by Robert K. Greenleaf in the 1970s, is said to have revolutionized workplaces around the world with its idea that true leadership grows out of serving the needs of others—employees, customers, and community (Spears, 1998, pp. 1–3). Such leaders are said to have a passion to serve and to view their work as a calling rather than just a livelihood or career. These ideas add a spiritual and ethical dimension to the concept of leadership that seems particularly compatible with the early childhood profession, as is evident in these questions posed by Greenleaf as the true test of a servant-leader:

> Do those served grow as persons? Do they, while being served, become healthier, wiser, freer, more autonomous, more likely themselves to become servants? And what is the effect on the least privileged in society; will they benefit, or, at least, not be further deprived? (1998, p. 19)

A recent NAEYC publication identified five types of leadership needed in the field of early care and education: pedagogical, administrative, advocacy, community, and conceptual (Kagan & Bowman, 1997).

Pedagogical Leadership

Pedagogy is the science of teaching. Pedagogical leadership requires a program manager not only to be a good teacher, but also to have the ability to explain the reasons for particular teaching practices to other teachers, parents, and the public. Rather than slavishly following a particular curriculum, a pedagogical leader is knowledgeable about, and able to apply, current theories and research findings in early childhood education. Research is inconclusive regarding the superiority of one curriculum model over another. In chapter 12, you encountered a number of approaches to early childhood curricula. Few programs offer "pure" examples of any single approach. Most blend many approaches, using what makes sense for their group, or groups, of children at any given time. Furthermore, popular and professional opinion about what is best for children shifts with time. Recently, some have argued that a rigid adoption of a particular curriculum model is incompatible with the movement toward greater professionalism in the early childhood field. If we expect teachers to draw on a broad knowledge base, responding with flexibility, creativity, and sensitivity to the needs of individual children, can we also expect rigorous compliance with preconceived models (e.g., Goffin & Wilson, 2001, pp. 216–217)?

The pedagogical leader's job, then, is to steer a course through this shifting landscape, guided by a firm understanding of basic child development principles, selecting and applying the most promising information. The leader must also interpret pedagogical theory and research for staff members, families, and others who may not share the same depth of knowledge about young children.

A pedagogical leader applies knowledge and experience to help families enjoy their children. At every stage of life, children

Managers exercise pedagogical leadership when they explain the reasons for particular teaching practices to other teachers, parents, and the public.

have some negative characteristics that may bother their parents, especially those who do not understand children's growth and development very well. Policy makers often impose unrealistic expectations for academic achievement because they do not understand the enormity of the children's accomplishments in other areas. Simply by sharing news of a child's achievements you can inspire the parents and others to look more closely and notice things they may have taken for granted. Sharing information about child development and how to cope with the various stages can make life in many homes less stressful for both parents and children. Many centers have discovered the power of attractive displays that document the children's work with photographs, drawings, and samples of their conversations. An added benefit of such displays is that the audience gains new respect for the children's thinking and the work that teachers and caregivers do.

Administrative Leadership

A manager who has achieved administrative leadership has grown beyond competence to excellence in all of the areas discussed throughout this text. Jorde-Bloom (1998) suggested that managers move through a hierarchy of skills as they grow into leaders. *Technical competency* involves handling budgets, developing policies, and meeting regulatory requirements. *Staff relations competency*, essentially the ability to get staff to work together to accomplish program goals, is grounded in effective communication skills. The following 10 rules for good communication can help you avoid the human tendency to do all of the talking when approached with a problem or complaint:

1. Stop talking so you can really hear the other person.
2. Make the other person feel at ease and free to talk.
3. Show an interest in what the other person has to say.
4. Keep your eyes on the person who is talking.
5. Reflect the feelings the other person is expressing.
6. Put yourself in the other person's position.
7. Avoid expressing anger or arguing.
8. Allow plenty of time without hurrying.
9. Avoid all distractions.
10. Stop talking and listen to learn and understand. Many times people resolve their complaints on their own if you listen attentively and reflect the feelings expressed.

Managers exercise administrative leadership when they hire sensitive teachers and organize staff schedules so that those teachers have time to give children individual attention.

Neither the technical competency nor the staff relations competency requires specialized knowledge about children and families or about early education and care. These skills can be acquired through general management training or business experience. Yet, both are fundamental to the operation of a child development program and must be in place before the manager can progress to the higher-level competencies: *educational programming*, *public relations*, and *symbolic*. Clearly, the administrator who has risen from the ranks of teacher has some expertise in educational programming. At the managerial level, however, excellence in educational programming implies the ability to exercise a staff relations competency so that everyone supports a common vision. Once this competency is in place, directors can begin carrying their message to the world outside their center (public relations competency). Finally, at the highest level, those directors with symbolic competency "serve as a symbol for the collective identity of the group by articulating a vision, clarifying and affirming values, promoting reflection and introspection, and creating and sustaining a culture built on norms of continuous improvement and ethical conduct" (Jorde-Bloom, 1998, p. 36). It is at this level that the director moves from competence to excellence, from manager to leader.

Advocacy Leadership

Advocacy is a natural outgrowth of administrative leadership and professionalism. As a program director, you are in a pivotal position to advocate for children. You have seen many families firsthand. You are in touch with them and are aware of their needs and concerns. You have credibility and expertise because your center is an important support service for families in your community.

Goals of Child Advocates.   Advocates strive to "improve the landscape for children and families" by garnering public and private support for staff training, strong licensing standards, accreditation, fair compensation for child-care professionals, and systems to help families locate and recognize high-quality care (Blank, 1998, p. 39). Effective advocates understand the human ecological system framework described in chapter 3 and the ways in which the ripple effect works: When you change one factor in the system, it affects and changes other things. Here are just three examples: An increase in the unemployment rate quickly causes children to drop out of child development centers because parents cannot pay the tuition when they are unemployed. A rise in the cost of living causes more women to seek employment outside the home, thus influencing them to seek child care. The need to make child care affordable means lower wages for staff, which means that as soon as they acquire some expertise, many workers leave the field for better paying jobs. Therefore, centers must perpetually divert energy and other resources to recruiting and training staff, and the children are continually in the position of being "practiced on" by neophytes in the profession. Figure 16.1 lists several issues of concern to advocates for children and families. If you reflect on your community's concerns, perhaps you can think of others.

Decisions, Decisions . . .

If there were one thing you could change for the children in your community, what would it be? Compare your answer with those of your classmates and explain why you think your issue is important.

Work of the Advocate.   Advocacy requires that you become committed to joining those discussions and actions that support a cause that you think needs community attention. You learn about it, work for it, and persuade others to join you. You acquire this insight from your professional education and experience and your daily interactions with the families your center serves. You see parents in happy and depressed moods. You see them hurrying to work and hurrying home again. You see children, who have just become comfortable and happy, having to leave because their parents can no longer afford the tuition, and your center cannot make ends meet without it. You see caregivers working hard to provide a high-quality program for other people's children, while earning a salary that does not allow them to provide the same experience for their children.

FIGURE 16.1   *Sample advocacy issues*

Adoption and foster care
Advertising and young children
Before- and after-school care
Blended or step families
Bottle feeding
Breast-feeding
Child abuse
Child care
   Cost
   Quality
   Availability
Childhood obesity
Children with disabilities
   AIDS
   Autism
   Blindness
   Cerebral palsy
   Chronic illness
   Down syndrome
   Fetal alcohol syndrome
   Mental retardation
   Orthopedic problems
   Prenatal drug exposure
   Speech impairment
Children and fitness
Children's access to nature
Children's libraries
Children's museums
Children's television
Computers and children
Curriculum reform (learning standards)
Diets/prenatal/children
Disciplinary methods
Diversity
   Ability
   Economic
   Ethnic
   Gender
   Lifestyle
   Racial
   Religious
Educational reform/child care
Emergent literacy
English-language learners in early childhood programs

Family planning
Family privacy rights
Family wellness
Fathers as primary caregivers
Foster care
Full-day kindergarten
Gender roles
Homeless children
Hunger
Immigrant families
   Supporting home language and culture
   Rights/needs
Immunization campaigns
Inclusion of children with disabilities
Legal rights of children and families
Licensing standards
National health insurance
Nonviolent conflict resolution
One-child family
Organized sports for young children
Outdoor play; natural environments and
   children
Parenting education
Play, children's right to
Peace education
Poverty and family support programs
Population/ecological balance
Prenatal care
Lamaze/other birth preparation
Professional recognition for child-care workers
Quality, compensation, and affordability in
   child care
Reproductive rights
Second language education
Sexual abuse
Single-parents (fathers, mothers, adoptive)
Staffing crisis in child care
Testing children
Violence in children's lives
   Communities
   Domestic
   Television
Worthy wages for child-care personnel
Year-round school

You also have the broad perspective developed from your philosophy, education, and experience with many children and parents over the years. You have a strong belief that something can be done about most things if enough ideas and energy are brought to bear. As you advocate for an individual child, a group of children, or all of the children in our global village, you show your optimistic view that, with effort, a better future is possible. You add your voice to those belonging to a long line of visionary leaders throughout history and around the world, using the time-honored democratic process to bring about the kinds of progress that modern societies increasingly seek to provide. Most importantly, you keep in mind that using the talents and ideas of everyone leads to more progress.

Providing or Locating Information.   One important advocacy task is to provide information essential to wise decision making. You should be comfortable with this role, especially when it involves facts about children's development and the early childhood profession. You know about available information sources and where to look for them. You may use many means to get the facts to the people, from one-to-one conversations to the use of various types of mass media.

Getting People to Work Together.   Cooperation grows when people know each other. Within your center, you can facilitate a social exchange between the families to aid their cooperation. First, parents must become acquainted with each other and must become aware of their common concerns. They must realize where time, energy, or money can be invested most effectively to serve their children better. Many of your activities and arrangements involve specific goals to help people become acquainted and cooperate. Parents who meet one another while their children attend your program often become lifelong friends, forming a support network and carrying their zeal to participate in their children's education into elementary school and beyond.

Reaching Decision Makers.   Your target population for advocacy consists of the general public, business leaders, and government decision makers. Decision makers are usually political beings, responsive to a constituent group. They must have solid information, and often advocacy groups provide it. Advocates must also analyze the power dynamics of any organization they wish to influence. Getting the support of only one powerful leader may be all that is necessary to get a policy changed. Advocates must take the time to analyze the dynamics of situations to know who the leaders are and to seek out the best people to influence those leaders.

Shepherd (1991) suggests six principles of message construction to aid persuasive communication:

1. *Know your audience.* Who are you writing for and speaking to? What do they do for a living? Where will you meet them? What type of language and examples will they understand?

2. *Capture attention.* Analyze the audience to determine what appeals to them. Can they identify with your topic and approach from a personal perspective? Can they translate their own experiences into the experiences of their children? How can you make a strong argument for a beneficial outcome?

3. *Enhance comprehension.* Small bites of information are remembered better than large ones. Think of the short sound bite used by the television world. Break your large message into many smaller messages. Use "how to" examples from everyday life.

4. *Promote acceptance.* Show how people with credibility are advocating this approach—use some local leaders' opinions or experiences. The medical authorities are usually among the most credible. Be sure you address and work through the

points of resistance in your community. Tailor your messages to anticipate and respond to opposing arguments.

5. *Make your message easy to remember.* High-imagery words arouse your audience to see your point and remember it. To help stir readers' reactions, use good true-to-life examples of the type that might have occurred down the street. Organize information so it is easily recalled. You can use a poem, joke, or gimmick that ties several points together and aids memory.

6. *Encourage action.* You want the audience to decide to act on the information you have provided. Chart their actions step-by-step; tell them precisely what their choices are. Walk them through it verbally. Like the television marketer, tell them to "Go to the phone, dial the number, and ask for. . . ." Discuss the great outcomes that will occur if everyone listening decides to act. Be persuasive, positive, and pleasant.

These principles of persuasive communication can be used for articles, talks, brochures, and books, and even for preparing to testify before a community or legislative body.

Steps in Advocacy. At a workshop for women leaders, *advocacy* was defined as "pursuing specific activities to reach a vision" (Etchart, 1995). Potential advocates were encouraged to follow five steps to reach that vision:

1. Know what you want to say about an important issue.
2. Decide who should hear your message.
3. Decide how to say it in a way that captures the audience's attention and promotes positive responses.
4. Get help from groups with common goals.
5. Develop a plan of action.

Advocating on Behalf of Early Childhood Professionals. A child advocate also works indirectly to improve children's lives by developing higher professional standards and better working conditions for the center's staff. Women workers have been exploited throughout history, and it is time to call a halt to it. Men working in the child development services field also suffer because of the prevailing attitude that classifies child care as women's work. We expect professionalism in our employees; therefore, they should be paid the same as those individuals with comparable education and responsibility. Center employees should earn far more than parking lot attendants.

Center managers who want to raise their voices and help the NAEYC bring about better compensation for center employees can begin by using the suggestions from the Center for the Child Care Workforce (Whitebook & Bellm, 1999) and participate in programs such as the TEACH Early Childhood Scholarship project (Russell & Rogers, 2005) as discussed in Chapter 6.

Community Leadership

Leaders in the early childhood profession are visible outside their programs, using their knowledge, passion, and vision to mobilize the entire community to improve the lot of children and families. This type of leadership takes time to build and depends on personal characteristics and professional expertise. The essential activity is "making meaning, or connecting with what people already have in their minds and hearts" (Crompton, 1998, p. 51). This process begins by establishing a common ground with your audience about what should be. Then, you must show them how reality deviates from that shared ideal and explain why that deviation is important. Most people agree that all children deserve to be safe, healthy, and loved. If you can show how many, or how often, children in your community are deprived of these basic rights, and if you can explain what this situation means in the long run—for the children and for your community—your audience will be prepared to take the next step: thinking about how they can help turn what *should be* into what *is*. There are several ways that early childhood leaders become community leaders.

Providing Publicity on Issues Related to Children.   You can encourage a television station to run a special series for parents—and you can organize discussion groups around the series. You can inform parents and the public when one of your staff members completes a new credential or college degree. You can participate in and spread the word about national celebrations (e.g., Week of the Young Child or Worthy Wage Day). You can encourage the various media organizations to cover programs appropriate for families by calling or writing to them or by encouraging parents to comment to the media.

Managers exercise community leadership when they collaborate with agencies so that all children have access to developmentally appropriate programs.

Forging Links between Systems on Behalf of Children.   Parents and teachers who have become increasingly concerned about the warlike toys being sold to children have banded together to protest to toy manufacturers and distributors. This effort links the home, school, and business communities. Some advocates may seek to use legal means to regulate the sale of war toys, arguing for renewed restrictions on advertising during children's television programs.

Other types of links are being forged in states throughout the country as community colleges and 4-year institutions seek to establish matriculation agreements that allow child development professionals to move on to higher levels of education without starting over. In the same vein, advocates are calling for the agencies that confer teaching credentials to coordinate their requirements with those agencies that license child-care centers, recognizing that all young children need nurturing and education.

Encouraging Development of New Services.   Being aware of children's needs helps you develop recommendations for important new services. In recent years, children's science museums have started to provide hands-on activities that help children learn more than they could just by looking and listening. Drop-in child care in churches, airports, and shopping centers is a response from sensitive businesspeople who realized that being a child in these settings is tiring and not much fun. Businesses have been persuaded that children's needs are better served in a child-appropriate playroom that provides a place to rest, a snack, and other children. It takes creative people to conceptualize helpful new services, and it takes people knowledgeable about child development to ensure that they are appropriate places for children, not just brightly decorated parking lots.

Conceptual Leadership

According to Kagan and Neuman (1997), conceptual leadership transcends even the visionary leadership described here. Visionary leaders focus on their own organizations, while conceptual leaders are concerned about broad issues of social justice and human betterment.

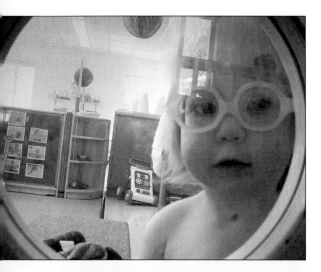

Conceptual leaders look at the world through the eyes of children. They expect their programs, and their communities, to support every child's right to be safe, healthy, and happy, and they work hard to find ways to measure up to that goal.

Kagan and Neuman identify five key characteristics of conceptual leaders: "They (1) think in terms of the whole field; (2) are responsive to diverse perspectives; (3) think long term; (4) push the what-is to the what-might-be—thinking possibility, invention, and vision; and (5) seek to impact the social good." At the national level, two examples of conceptual leadership are found in the work of the NAEYC's antibias task force and in the legislation protecting the rights of individuals with disabilities. At a global level, entities such as the Organization for Economic Cooperation and Development (OECD) work to establish international consensus on the basic rights and needs of children everywhere.

The goals of the antibias curriculum advocated by the NAEYC represent a proactive approach toward protecting the civil rights of children and families. They include fostering a healthy self-image in all children, cultivating empathy and respect for others, recognizing unfairness, and standing up for oneself and others when unfairness exists (Derman-Sparks, 1992). Clearly, the center that embraces these goals is contributing toward the protection of civil rights in ways that reach far beyond the center's walls.

The Americans with Disabilities Act requires that every center make reasonable efforts to accommodate the special needs of children with disabilities. Here again, as a leader and advocate, you can take a proactive stance and make the extra effort necessary to access community resources and devise creative solutions to meet those special needs. You can enthusiastically encourage the enrollment of children with special needs, knowing that all children—not only those with disabilities—benefit from such inclusion.

The Organization for Economic Cooperation and Development sponsored studies in several countries to assess the quality of early care and education and make policy recommendations. The team assigned to study the United States concluded that the system was fragmented and that inadequate attention was paid to issues such as quality, accessibility, affordability, and staff compensation. Their report, a clear example of conceptual leadership, recommended the following goals:

1. Creating a comprehensive, coordinated, and stable system of early care and education.
2. Adopting a more universal approach through collaboration with public education.
3. Taking a proactive stance toward child poverty and diversity.
4. Creating an effective staff training and professional development system.
5. Introducing paid parental leave.
6. Creating a stable research framework and a long-term research agenda.
   (OECD, 2000, July)

Values

Values are statements of what "ought" to exist or "ought" to be done. They influence everything you do. You have been developing your values throughout your life. Very early in a leadership position, you may confront values that differ from your own. For example, your values may differ from those held by the board members who control your operation. Parents, the consumers of your service, may adhere to still other values. Figure 16.2 lists some examples of values that might govern an early childhood educator's practice. Some

FIGURE 16.2 *Value orientations*

The discussion of values in this chapter has posed several questions to which there are only very individual answers. As a manager, you might be asked to make decisions that involve values and you must understand and explain the value issues at stake.

This exercise helps you focus on and better understand some value orientations. It has been used in research and as a device to start people thinking and talking about values. The nine stories draw attention to some of the philosophical differences that may exist in child development centers as different teachers apply their preferred values about early childhood education. The primary value orientation in each story is as follows:

1. socialization	4. aesthetics	7. freedom
2. intellect	5. authority	8. individuality
3. morality	6. health	9. economics

(As you read each of the nine stories, feel free to use "he" or "she." We used feminine pronouns consistently in order to avoid introducing possible bias based on gender and to reflect the reality that early childhood teachers are predominantly female.) After reading all of the stories, select the one that illustrates a value that you would rank most important to you and one that you would rank least important. Try to explain the reasons for your selections.

1. Teacher A thinks it important for children to learn to get along with others. She feels that children should learn to get along, help each other, and share through having the freedom to interact. Her classroom is usually a beehive of activity. She willingly puts off a science lesson if there is a spontaneous group activity in progress at the moment. Teacher A makes friends with the children and their parents and arranges situations so that each child can know and make friends with all of the others. When difficulties arise, she prefers to let the children work out the problem, intervening only as a last resort. She sometimes helps parents arrange their children's play groups during weekends or vacations.

2. Teacher B believes that children should be well prepared for "real school." Her classroom schedule is arranged so that she gets lots of basic learning material covered each day. She avoids getting sidetracked during a class project; therefore, she is able to carry out her lesson plans completely. She believes she must teach the children a good deal of information, including ABCs, colors, shapes, and numbers. Her children frequently achieve above average on standardized tests, which indicates to her that they are learning the material. Her talks with the parents focus on the children's preparation for first grade. She participates in lectures and seminars to increase her own learning whenever available.

3. Teacher C is concerned that the children develop a sense of morality and good judgment. She often discusses with them how they ought to behave. She tells them her own views and introduces religious stories and ideas. The children are taught what is right and wrong and are expected to behave accordingly. Manners and saying "please" and "thank you" are stressed. Teacher C discusses any topic that is of interest to the children, especially if she feels it will aid their character development. She encourages them to correct each other if they feel someone is doing something wrong.

4. Teacher D keeps her classroom looking attractive at all times. She takes special care that the colors are harmonious and that various artifacts are displayed in the room. The children's art objects and paintings are carefully mounted and labeled. Creative movement and music, including works of the great composers, are a part of the program. Well-written children's literature is used regularly. Teacher D wears colorful and fashionable clothing. She helps the children arrange their hair and clothing to look their best.

(Continued)

FIGURE 16.2   *Continued*

5. Teacher E's schedule and activities are outlined by the school's director, and she carefully follows the guidelines. She is grateful for the leadership of her school's director and values the opinions of fellow teachers and parents. At the beginning of each year, the director distributes a list of policies and regulations that give Teacher E a guide for administering her classroom. She believes that the director is a competent administrator and knows a lot about running the class. She is pleased when the director brings in new learning programs for her to use.

6. Teacher F likes the children to have lots of fresh air and sunshine. She carefully checks to see that the children have sufficient light, correct temperature, and chairs and tables of suitable height. Each morning, she checks up on their habits: good breakfast, daily bath, toothbrushing, and proper rest. She checks throats and chests for signs of contagious disease and has the children taken home when they seem ill. Routines of toileting and handwashing are frequent in her schedule. Nutritious foods are always available for snacks.

7. Teacher G feels that the children should really plan their own program. She avoids thinking ahead about what the children might be doing each day, but brings toys out as the children arrive and indicate their interests. She may choose an activity because she particularly wants to do it that day. She tries to respond to the children's needs of the moment and avoids pushing them into organized learning tasks. She emphasizes spontaneous learning, picking up on some project that the child seems interested in. Her schedule is completely flexible, and rarely do the children follow the same schedule 2 days in a row.

8. Teacher H believes that each child learns in a different way. She considers the child a person first and a student second. Her program is arranged so that each child can express his individuality. A supportive atmosphere prevails that allows the child to feel free to venture into new experiences, but it is not one of indulgence. Teacher H strives to plan a rich variety of experiences with fresh views of familiar scenes, excursions to new places, or walks in the parks. She uses many methods of motivation and novel ways of sparking the children's imaginations.

9. Teacher I stresses protecting the school property and conserving materials. She teaches the children to use supplies, such as paint, paper, and glue, sparingly. She searches for "found" materials to supplement her supplies and utilizes any volunteer service available. She shows the children how to use all of their paper for a picture even if they paint a small spot and start to leave. Teacher I is also concerned with saving time. She works at being efficient and expects to teach the children these traits. She thinks education is a way of improving one's station in life and a way of making a good living.

Source: V. Hildebrand, *Guiding young children* (Upper Saddle River, NJ: Prentice Hall, 1980), pp. 394–397. See also V. Hildebrand, "Value orientations for nursery school programs," *Reading Improvement, 12*(3) (Fall 1975), pp. 168–173. (Hildebrand's study found that parents and experienced professional teachers chose Story 8, which stresses individuality, as the most desired; Story 1, stressing socialization, was their second choice.)

general understanding of values is needed in order for your center to function effectively. Without some consensus about basic values, dealing with conflicts constructively will be difficult.

Decisions, Decisions . . .

Read the vignettes in Figure 16.2 and rank the values expressed by each in order of their importance to you. Compare your list with those of your class-mates. Discuss.

The values expressed in the U.S. Constitution, the freedom of speech, assembly, and religion and the right to due process, are just as applicable to child development programs as the halls of Congress. Recognizing and affirming these values can help guide your decisions.

Decisions, Decisions . . .

A student teacher assigned to a child development laboratory at a state university noticed that the center had a practice of saying a nondenominational "grace" before snack. She asked whether the policy was appropriate in a state-sponsored facility. What do you think? What would you think if the prayer were addressed to "Allah" or "Krishna" instead of "Lord"?

What are your values regarding family life and parental rights? A child-care center generally is designed as a support system for families. A public school may focus its objectives to educate the children and not include the family. Is this as it "ought" to be? What right does a parent have to make decisions about the early education the child receives?

Parental involvement was one of the innovations of Project Head Start. Parents participated at various levels to help bring about changes that benefited the whole family, but particularly the children. What are your values regarding parental involvement? What if your teachers or the children's parents have another view?

What are your values about a teacher's right to choose the philosophical approach to be implemented in a classroom that is part of the center you manage? What would you do if the governing board demanded a philosophical approach that you strongly disagree with?

What are your values regarding the children's early years? That is, are children expected to have full lives in all areas of human development during these years, or are these years only cognitive stepping stones to the more important years in "real" school and beyond? Curriculum planning differs depending on your values. Your interaction with the children and parents also varies depending on your values.

What are your values regarding the children's learning about right and wrong? Do you believe children are testing you when they do wrong? Do you believe that reward and punishment are the best means of developing "right" behavior in children? What is "right" behavior, anyway? What happens when your definitions of "right" and "good" differ from those of the parents?

What are your values regarding cultural, racial, and ethnic diversity? Should a child development center staff value the breadth of vision needed to achieve the equality ideals embodied in the Constitution? Do these ideals of equality help our pluralistic society become a happier home for all families? Is equality a significant part of the American dream?

Leadership and Accreditation

Leadership is related to many aspects of the NAEYC's center accreditation project. Leaders in the organization initiated the concept; they developed and disseminated the initial draft and invited responses from hundreds of early childhood professional leaders several times before approving and publishing the final version. Leaders in individual schools or centers make the decision to pursue accreditation, which is voluntary. As they guide their programs through the process, they exert administrative leadership by raising the overall quality of their service. They also demonstrate community leadership: As more programs become accredited, the public's awareness of the importance of high quality to early childhood care and education programs grows. Therefore, would-be leaders should know and implement the accreditation standards, work toward accreditation for their centers, assist others to become accredited, and help educate the public about the standards of high-quality early childhood education.

Professional Support

It may seem contradictory when your day is filled with children, staff, families, and dozens of other people, but early childhood administrators often feel alone, just as parents who stay home with young children all day feel alone. In both cases, it seems that one person is responsible for meeting the needs of many who depend on him, and no one is there to help shoulder the burden. Meeting with other directors to share common problems and learn new ideas can recharge your energy and help prevent burnout. You can take a leadership role in this support network by inviting your local Association for the Education of Young Children, the Association for Childhood Education International, or your local managers' group to meet in your facility. (The appendix provides a list of organizations and their journals.)

Professional Research and Writing

Many leaders in the profession gain prominence through their research and writing. Because people read their work to become informed on a subject, writers should exercise care to present facts accurately and objectively and to draw responsible conclusions.

As a manager, you may offer your center as the site of a research study conducted by a university faculty researcher. Such activities often stimulate staffers to work hard, learn together, and maintain professional interest and enjoyment. Research participation may inspire a staff member to go back to college to take a course or finish a degree. Even without university participation, you can design research studies that involve your staff members as contributors, and all of you may share authorship if the results are published.

You can encourage your staff to develop investigations and become part of a growing trend toward action research in teacher education (Black & Huss, 1995). Recall that careful observation and reflection are primary avenues for professional development. Margie Carter, a respected teacher educator, stated, "As teachers get more intrigued with children's play, they become more intentional and appropriate in their actions in the classroom" (1993, p. 48).

Consulting

Assuming the role of consultant may seem remote if you are just beginning to study management, but as you observe and assist more experienced professionals, you are building your own expertise. Soon, you may find that others ask for your help with problems in their programs—perhaps as you network at conferences and professional meetings. A university or community college might hire you to supervise teaching interns in your region and, as you visit their field placement sites, you may find yourself offering guidance to the directors, as well as to the interns. In the process of helping other professionals do their jobs more effectively, your own understanding of the management process becomes more focused. At some point, you may decide to move from salaried internship supervisor to independent entrepreneur and start your own business as an early childhood program consultant.

Making such a leap might seem risky, but the opportunities for consultants are increasing. More and more corporations, service groups, churches, and government agencies have taken an interest in early childhood care and education. Whether they have done so for self-interest reasons (attracting and retaining employees) or altruism (just doing something good for children), they may have to look outside of their organization for the expertise they need. That is where you come in. By doing so, you are following in the footsteps of the leaders who helped establish model programs under the 1941 Lanham Act during World War II and those who shaped Head Start during the War on Poverty.

One way to get started as a consultant is to become involved in the NAEYC's accreditation process. With training, you can join a team that visits programs to assess whether they meet the criteria associated with program standards. If you are employed as a teacher or program manager, your employer might agree to give you released time with pay as you perform this service for your community and profession. After all, they stand to benefit when you bring back fresh ideas gleaned from the other programs. Presenting at professional conferences is another way to build your reputation as a source of useful expertise.

When potential clients approach, it is essential that you have a clear idea of what they need, what you can offer, and what you should charge for your service. Do they need help with the "nuts and bolts" of operating a program? With parent involvement? With training neophyte teachers or motivating jaded employees? Do they want you to help plan a new state-of-the-art facility or write a grant to fund their project? Are you meeting with three key people or with the entire teaching staff of a corporate franchise program? Are there many meetings over a period of weeks or months, or is this a "one-shot" effort? What exactly are the outcomes you are expected to produce? Investing enough time to clarify the answers to these questions at the outset greatly increases your chance for a successful business relationship.

Conclusion

Not every manager is a leader. Leadership requires vision, sensitivity to others, and a level of excellence in all management functions. Although leaders have been traditionally characterized as hierarchical and competitive, leadership in the field of early care and education is more likely to be collaborative and compatible with a model of servant-leadership. Leaders in this field exhibit five types of leadership: pedagogical, administrative, advocacy, community, and conceptual. Leadership is involved in many aspects of NAEYC's accreditation project, from its conceptualization to its implementation in individual programs. Managers find that accreditation assures parents of a center's high quality and stimulates interest in centers by government policy makers and industrial leaders.

Values shape the decisions and actions of leaders, their followers (staff members), and the families they serve. True leadership depends on a reflective awareness of one's own value orientation, as well as a willingness to listen, understand, and respect that of others. This means that leaders must be able to listen to others, as well as express their ideas clearly and convincingly.

Your educational experience, professional work with children and their families, and, most importantly, your commitment to children and families prepare you well for becoming a leader in your own program, in your community, in your profession, and—ultimately—in society at large.

QUESTIONS FOR REVIEW

1. Define leading. Give examples of how leading applies to the manager's role in a child development center.
2. Explain how managing and leading differ.
3. List and give examples of five types of leadership.
4. Discuss how leadership and NAEYC accreditation are related.
5. Define values and describe how they relate to conceptual leadership.
6. List the 10 rules for communicating with staff and others. Give an example of each rule from the perspective of a center manager.
7. State the goals of advocacy for children and families.
8. State Shepherd's six principles of message construction and relate each principle to advocacy in a child development center.

PROFESSIONAL PORTFOLIO

1. Select an advocacy issue of importance in your community that interests you (perhaps from the list given in Figure 16.1). Outline an advocacy program that you and your professional association might present to a local or regional decision-making body.
   - Define the issue and goal or outcome desired.
   - Describe the audience.
   - Describe the steps for getting your message across.
   - Outline the decision-making process.
   - Propose the action desired.

2. Write a letter to the editor of your local newspaper about an issue concerning children and families.
3. Select a topic in which recent research findings have important implications for child development professionals (e.g., brain development). Plan a presentation for a workshop at a professional conference in which you interpret the findings and offer suggestions for ways practitioners can apply them.
4. Write a 250- to 500-word article interpreting the same research findings for an audience consisting primarily of parents and others who might be unfamiliar with child development theory. Use the Shepherd criteria.

RESOURCES FOR FURTHER STUDY

Print

Derman-Sparks, L., Phillips, C. B., and Hillard, A. G. (1997). *Teaching/learning anti-racism: A developmental approach.* New York: Teachers College Press.

Jorde-Bloom, p. (2003). *Leadership in action: How effective directors get things done.* Lake Forest, IL: New Horizons.

Leadership in early childhood education (2005, January). *Young Children, 60*(1), entire issue.

Wheelock College Institute for Leadership and Career Initiatives (2000). *The many faces of leadership;* also *The power of mentoring.* Boston: Author.

Internet

McCormick Tribune Center for Early Childhood Leadership
http://cecl.nl.edu

McCormick Tribune Center for Early Childhood Leadership offers training and technical assistance for administrators, including online coursework and hosted discussions with nationally recognized experts.

Clearinghouse on Early Education and Parenting
http://ceep.crc.uiuc.edu

The Clearinghouse on Early Education and Parenting (CEEP), part of the *Early Childhood and Parenting (ECAP) Collaborative*, at the University of Illinois at Urbana-Champaign; provides publications and information worldwide.

Children's Defense Fund
www.childrensdefense.org

The Children's Defense Fund is a nonprofit advocacy organization with a particular focus on the needs of poor and minority children and those with disabilities. The site provides information and guidelines for advocates in several areas. For example, a link to Early Childhood Development connects with a menu of resources, including "State Fact Sheets on Early Childhood Development," which provides a state-by-state summary of statistics regarding poverty level, child-care quality, Head Start participation, and prekindergarten initiatives.

RESOURCES FOR PROFESSIONAL SUPPORT

Professional Organizations and Their Journals

Adult Education Association
1225 19th St., NW
Washington, DC 20036
Publishes *Adult Learning, Adult Education Quarterly,* and
  AAACE Online.
http://www.aaace.org

American Association of Family and Consumer Sciences
  (AAFCS)
400 N. Columbus St., Suite 202
Alexandria, VA 22314
Publishes *Journal of Family and Consumer Sciences.*
http://www.aafcs.org

American Association for Gifted Children (AAGC)
Duke University
PO Box 90270
Durham, NC 27708-0270
http://www.aagc.org

American Montessori Society (AMS)
281 Park Ave. South
New York, NY 10010
Publishes *Montessori Life* (quarterly).
http://www.amshq.org

American Public Health Association (APHA)
800 I St., NW
Washington, DC 20001-3710
Publishes *American Journal of Public Health* and *The Nation's
  Health.*
http://www.apha.org

Association for Childhood Education International (ACEI)
17904 Georgia Ave., Suite 215
Olney, MD 20832
Publishes *Childhood Education.*
http://www.acei.org

Association for Supervision and Curriculum
  Development (ASCD)
1703 N. Beauregard St.
Alexandria, VA 22311
Publishes *Education Leadership.*
http://www.ascd.org

Child Welfare League of America, Inc.
440 First St., NW, 3rd floor
Washington, DC 20001
Publishes *Child Welfare.*
http://www.cwla.org

Children's Defense Fund
25 E St., NW
Washington, DC 20001
http://www.childrensdefense.org

Council for Exceptional Children
1110 North Glebe Rd., Suite 300
Arlington, VA 22201
Publishes *Exceptional Children* and *TEACHING Exceptional
  Children.*
http://www.cec.sped.org

Council for Professional Recognition
2460 16th St., NW
Washington, DC 20009-3575
Operates Child Development Associate (CDA) Credentialing
    program; Head Start fellowships; U.S. Military School Age
    Credential; and Reggio Children USA.
http://www.cdacouncil.org

Division for Early Childhood of The Council for
    Exceptional Children
27 Fort Missoula Rd., Suite 2
Missoula, MT 59804
Publishes *Journal of Early Intervention* and *Young Exceptional
    Children.*
http://www.dec-sped.org

Families and Work Institute
267 Fifth Ave., Floor 2
New York, NY 10016
http://www.familiesandwork.org

International Reading Association
800 Barksdale Rd.
PO Box 8139
Newark, DE 19714-8139
Publishes *The Reading Teacher.*
http://www.reading.org

National Association of Child Care Professionals
An organization for child-care owners, directors, and
    administrators.
http://www.naccp.org

National Association for the Education of Young Children
    (NAEYC)
1509 16th St., NW
Washington, DC 20036-1426
Publishes *Young Children* and *Early Childhood Research Quarterly.*
http://www.naeyc.org
Provides links to alphabetical listing of other national early
    childhood organizations at
http://www.naeyc.org/ece/links.asp.

National Association of Elementary School Principals
1615 Duke St.
Alexandria, VA 22314-3483
Publishes *Leading Early Childhood Learning Communities: What
    Principals Should Know and Be Able to Do.*
http://www.naesp.org

National Association for Gifted Children
1707 L St., NW, Suite 550
Washington, DC 20036
Publishes *Gifted Child Quarterly* and *Parenting for High
    Potential.*
www.nagc.org

National Association for Multicultural Education
733 Fifteenth St., NW
Washington, DC 20005
http://www.nameorg.org

National Child Care Association
2025 M St., NW, Suite 800
Washington, DC, 20036-3309
http://www.nccanet.org

National Coalition for Campus Children's Centers
119 Schindler Education Centr
University of Northern Iowa
Cedar Falls, IA 50614
http://www.campuschildren.org

National Council on Family Relations
3989 Central Ave., NE, #550
Minneapolis, MN 55421
Publishes *Family Relationships* and *Journal of Marriage and
    the Family.*
http://www.ncfr.org

National Education Association (NEA)
1201 16th St., NW
Washington, DC 20036
Publishes *NEA Today* and *Tomorrow's Teachers.*
http://www.nea.org

National Science Teachers Association
1840 Wilson Blvd.
Arlington VA 22201-3000
Publishes *Science and Children.*
http://www.nsta.org

North American Reggio Emilia Alliance
c/o Inspired Practices in Early Education, Inc.
2040 Wilson Ridge Court
Roswell, GA 30075
http://www.reggioalliance.org

Organisation Mondiale pour l'Education Prescolaire (OMEP)
(World Organization for Early Childhood Education)
U.S. Representative
PO Box 66
Garrett Park, MD 20896
Publishes *International Journal of Early Childhood.*
http://www.omep-usnc.org

Society for Research in Child Development
5801 Ellis Ave.
Chicago, IL 60637
Publishes *Child Development* and *Child Development Abstracts
    and Bibliography.*
http://www.srcd.org

Southern Early Childhood Association
5403 Brady Station
Little Rock, AR 72215
Publishes *Dimensions.*
http://www.southernearlychildhood.org/raising_intro.html

Zero to Three
National Center for Infants, Toddlers, and Families
2000 M St., NW, Suite 200
Washington, DC 20036
Publishes *Zero to Three.*
http://www.zerotothree.org

Additional Early Childhood Periodicals

Children's Environments
City University of New York
Graduate Center
365 Fifth Ave.
New York, NY 10016
Published 1984–1995; back issues available at
http://web.gc.cuny.edu/che/journal.htm

Early Child Development and Care
Taylor & Francis Group, Ltd.
http://www.tandf.co.uk/journals/titles/03004430.asp

Early Childhood Research and Practice
Bilingual Internet journal on development, care,
   and education of young children.
http://ecrp.uiuc.edu

Exchange
PO Box 3249
Redmond, WA 98073
http://www.childcareexchange.com

*Innovations in Early Education: The International Reggio
   Exchange*
The Merrill-Palmer Institute
71-A E. Ferry Ave.
Detroit, MI 48202
http://www.mpi.wayne.edu

Texas Child Care
PO Box 162881
Austin, TX 78716-2881
http://www.childcarequarterly.com

Early Childhood Discussion Groups on the Internet

ECENET-L (Early Childhood Education Net)
E-mail to: listserv@listserv.uiuc.edu

ECEOL-L (Early Childhood Education on Line)
E-mail to: lists@maine.edu

REGGIO-L (Reggio Emilia Approach to Early Education)
SAC-L (School-age care planning, resources, funding and related topics)
E-mail to: listserv@listserv.uiuc.edu

Send a message via e-mail to the address indicated for the group you want to join. Put the address in the "To" section and your own e-mail address in the "From" section. In the body of the message, write the following: Subscribe ECENET-L (or whatever list you are joining). Then, put your full name. You will get a message back confirming the fact that you have joined the list, as well as instructions for posting messages and signing off the list, should you want to do so.

Administration for Children and Families (2004, August). *Fact Sheet: Office of Family Assistance.* U.S. Department of Health and Human Services. Retrieved July 5, 2005, from http://www.acf.hhs.gov/opa/fact sheets/tanf_factsheet.html

Albrecht, K. (1998). Managing teacher performance while walking around. In B. & R. Neugebauer (Eds.), *The art of leadership: Managing an early childhood organization* (pp. 266–267). Redmond, WA: Exchange Press.

Albrecht, K. M., & Plantz, M. C. (Eds.). (1991). *Developmentally appropriate practice in school-age child care programs.* Alexandria, VA: Project Home Safe, American Home Economics Association.

American Academy of Pediatrics (2002a). Caring for children within a medical home. *Healthy Child Care America: Promoting optimal health for America's children.* Summary Report 1997–2001, p. 9. Retrieved July 21, 2005, from http://www.healthychildcare.org/pdf/summaryreport.pdf.

American Academy of Pediatrics (2002b). *Television—How it affects children.* Retrieved on August 5, 2005, from http://www.aap.org/healthtopics/mediause.cfm.

American Public Health Association & American Academy of Pediatrics (APHA/AAP). (2002). *Caring for our children: National health and safety performance standards: Guidelines for out-of-home child care programs.* Washington, DC and Elk Grove, IL: Authors.

Anderson, Daniel R., & Evans, Marie K. (2001, October/November). Peril and potential of media for infants and toddlers. *Zero to Three, 22*(2), 10–16.

Bagin, D., & Gallagher, D. R. (2001). *School and community relations* (7th ed.). Boston: Allyn & Bacon.

Bailey, D. B., & Wolery, M. (1992). *Teaching infants and preschoolers with disabilities* (2nd ed.). Upper Saddle River, NJ: Merrill/Prentice Hall.

Barnett, S., Brown, K., & Shore, R. (2004, April). The universal vs. targeted debate: Should the United States have preschool for all? *Preschool Policy Matters.* Available online at http://www.nieer.org

Barnett, S., Hustedt, J. T., Robin, K. B., & Schulman, K. L. (2004). *The state of preschool: 2004 state preschool yearbook.* National Institute for Early Education Research http://nieer.org

Baumrind, D. (1973). Current patterns of parental authority. *Developmental Psychology Monographs, 4*(1).

Baumrind, D. (1977). Some thoughts about childrearing. In S. Cohen & T. J. Comiskey (Eds.), *Child development: Contemporary perspectives.* Itasca, IL: F. E. Peacock.

Beckwith, H. (2000). *The invisible touch: Four keys to modern marketing.* New York: Warner Books.

Bellm, D., Gnezda, T., Whitebook, M., & Breunig, G. S. (1994). Policy initiatives to enhance child care staff compensation. In J. Johnson & J. B. McCracken (Eds.), *The early childhood career lattice: Perspectives on professional development* (pp. 161–169). Washington, DC: National Association for the Education of Young Children.

Benfari, Robert C. (1999). *Understanding and changing your management style.* San Francisco: Jossey-Bass.

Berns, R. M. (1989). *Child, family, community.* Fort Worth, TX: Harcourt Brace Jovanovich.

Birch, L., Johnson, S. L., & Fisher, J. (1995, January). Children's eating: The development of food acceptance patterns. *Young Children, 50*(2), 71–78.

Bitner, M. J. (2000). The servicescape. In T. A. Swartz & D. Iacobucci (Eds.), *Handbook of services marketing and management* (pp. 37–50). Thousand Oaks, CA: Sage Publications.

Black, C., & Huss, R. (1995, Spring). Teacher as researcher projects: A constructive process. *Journal of Early Childhood Teacher Education, 16*(2), 3–7.

Blank, H. K. (1998). Advocacy leadership. In S. L. Kagan & B. T. Bowman (Eds.), *Leadership in early care and education* (pp. 39–45). Washington, DC: National Association for the Education of Young Children.

Bloom, P. J. (1999). Building director competence: Credentialing and education. *Journal of Early Childhood Teacher Education, 20*(2), 207–214.

Bloom, P. J. (2005, July/August). Dedication doesn't have to mean deadication. *Exchange, 164,* pp. 74–76.

Bowman, B. T., Donovan, M. S., and Burns, M. S. (Eds.). (2001). *Eager to learn: Educating our preschoolers.* Washington, DC: National Academy Press.

Brauner, J., Gordic, B., and Zigler, E. (2004). Putting the child back into child care: Combining care and education for children ages 3–5. *Social Policy Report,* XVIII:III. Retrieved on June 16, 2005, from http://www.srcd.org/Documents/Publications/SPR/SPR183.pdf

Bredekamp, S. (Ed.). (1987). *Developmentally appropriate practice in early childhood programs serving children from birth through age 8.* Washington, DC: National Association for the Education of Young Children.

Bredekamp, S. (Ed.). (1991). *Accreditation criteria and procedures of the National Academy of Early Childhood Programs.* Washington, DC: National Association for the Education of Young Children.

Bredekamp, S. (1994, November 30). *Advanced remarks: Lessons from Reggio.* Address given at annual NAEYC Conference, Atlanta, GA.

Bredekamp, S., & Copple, C. (Eds.). (1997). *Developmentally appropriate practice in early childhood programs* (rev. ed.). Washington, DC: National Association for the Education of Young Children.

Bredekamp, S., & Willer, B. (1992, March). Of ladders and lattices, cores and cones: Conceptualizing an early childhood professional development system. *Young Children, 47*(3), 47–50.

Brown, N. H., & Manning, J. P. (2000). Core knowledge for directors. In M. L. Culkin (Ed.), *Managing quality in young children's programs: The leader's role* (pp. 78–96). New York: Teachers College Press.

Bryson, K., and Casper, L. M. (1999) Coresident grandparents and grandchildren. *Current Population Reports, Special Studies* (May). Washington, DC: U.S. Census Bureau.

Bubolz, M. M., & Sontag, M. S. (1993). Human ecology theory. In P. G. Boss, W. J. Doherty, R. LaRossa, W. R. Schumm, and S. K. Steinmetz (Eds.), *Sourcebook of family theories and methods: A contextual approach* (pp. 419–448). New York: Plenum.

Burckhardt, A. (1984). *Writing about food and families, fashion and furnishings.* Ames: Iowa State University Press.

Bush, J. (2001). *Dollars and sense: Planning for profit in your child care business.* Albany, NY: Delmar.

Caldwell, B. M. (2001, July). Déjà vu all over again: A researcher explains the NICHD study. *Young Children, 56*(4), 58–59.

California Department of Education. (1994). *Just kids: A practical guide for working with children prenatally substance-exposed.* Sacramento, CA: Author.

Campbell, D. M., Cignetti, P. B., Melenyzer, B. J., Nettles, D. H., & Wyman, Jr., R. M. (1997). *How to develop a professional portfolio.* Boston: Allyn & Bacon.

Capizzano, J., & Adams, G. (2000). The hours that children under five spend in child care: Variation across states. In *Assessing the new federalism policy brief* (B–8). Washington, DC: The Urban Institute.

Carter, M. (1993). Catching teachers "being good": Using observation to communicate. In E. Jones (Ed.), *Growing teachers: Partnerships in professional development* (pp. 38–53). Washington, DC: National Association for the Education of Young Children.

Carter, M. (1995, July/August). Developing strong self-images—It's important for teachers, too! *Child Care Information Exchange, 104,* 60–62.

Carter, M. (1998). Evaluating staff performance: A valuable training tool. In B. & R. Neugebauer (Eds.), *The art of leadership: Managing early childhood organizations* (pp. 272–274). Redmond, WA: Exchange Press.

Carter, M., & Curtis, D. (1998). *The visionary director: A handbook for dreaming, organizing, and improvising in your center.* St. Paul, MN: Redleaf.

Caspar, L. M. (1997). *Who's minding our preschoolers? Fall 1994 (Update).* (U.S. Census Bureau, Current Population Reports, Series P70-62). Washington, DC: U.S. Government Printing Office.

Center for Child Care Workforce (1998). *Creating better child care jobs: Model work standards for teaching staff in center-based child care.* Washington, DC: Author.

Center for Early Childhood Leadership (Spring 2004a). Research Notes: *The role of technology in early childhood program administration: Results of the 2004 directors' technology survey.* Wheeling, IL: National-Louis University.

Center for Early Childhood Leadership (Summer 2004b). Research Notes: *Directors' perceptions about male involvement in early childhood programs.* Wheeling, IL: National-Louis University.

Center for Universal Design (1997). *Principles of universal design.* Retrieved July 19, 2005, from http://www.design. ncsu.edu:8120/cud/univ_design/princ_overview.htm

Centers for Disease Control (2005, May 27). *Morbidity and Mortality Weekly Report (MMWR) 54*(20); 513–516. Retrieved December 10, 2005, from http://www.cdc.gov/mmwr/preview/mmwrhtml/mm5420a5.htm

Ceppi, G., & Zini, M. (Eds.). (1998). *Children, spaces, relations: Metaproject for an environment for young children.* Reggio Emilia, Italy: Reggio Children s.r.l.

Chang, H. N. (1993). *Affirming children's roots: Cultural and linguistic diversity in early care and education.* San Francisco: California Tomorrow.

Chen, X., Sekine, M., Hamanishi, S., Yamagami, T., & Kagamimori S. (2005, July). Associations of lifestyle factors with quality of life (QOL) in Japanese children: A 3-year follow-up of the Toyama Birth Cohort Study. *Child: Care, health and development, 31*:4, 433–440.

Child Care Action Campaign (2001). *Business outreach. Some facts about business and child care.* Retrieved from www.childcareaction.org

Child Care Bureau (n.d.). *What congregations should know about federal funding for child care.* http://www.acf.hhs.gov/programs/ccb/providers/faithbased.htm

Child Mental Health Foundations and Agencies Network (FAN). (2000, September 6). *A good beginning: sending America's children to school with the social and emotional competence they need to succeed.* Retrieved from www.naeyc.org/childrens_champions/reports_research/good_beginning

Children's Defense Fund. (2001). *Yearbook 2001: The state of America's children.* Washington, DC: Author.

Children's Defense Fund (2005a). *Head Start basics 2005.* Washington, DC: Author. http://www.childrensdefense.org/earlychildhood/headstart/headstartbasics2005.pdf

Children's Defense Fund (2005b). *Head Start: A formula for success threatened by the president's proposed budget.* Washington, DC: Author. Retrieved December 15, 2005, from http://www.childrensdefense.org/earlychildhood/headstart/headstartbudget2005.pdf

Children's Foundation. (1995). *Child day care center licensing study.* Washington, DC: Author.

Christie, J. F., & Wardle, F. (1992, March). How much time is needed for play? *Young Children, 47,* 28–32.

Clarke, G. (2000). *Marketing a service for profit: A practical guide to key service marketing concepts.* London: Kogan Page Limited.

Cohen, A. J. (1999). Smart questions to ask your insurance agent. In Child Care Information Exchange. *Inside child care: Trend report 2000* (pp. 87–89). Redmond, WA: Exchange Press.

Copeland, M. L., & McCreedy, B. S. (1998). Creating family-friendly policies. In B. & R. Neugebauer (Eds.), *The art of leadership: Managing early childhood organizations* (pp. 311–313). Redmond, WA: Exchange Press.

Cost, Quality, and Child Outcomes Study Team. (1995). *Cost, quality, and child outcomes in child care centers.* Public Report (2nd ed.). Denver: Economics Department, University of Colorado at Denver.

Council for Early Childhood Professional Recognition. (1992). *CDAC competency standards.* Washington, DC: Author.

Council for Professional Recognition. (2001, October). Helping children cope with disaster. *Council News and Views,* 8–9.

Covello, J., & Hazelgren, B. (1998). *Your first business plan* (3rd ed.). Naperville, IL: Sourcebooks.

Covey, S. R. (1989). *The seven habits of highly effective people.* New York: Simon & Schuster.

Crain, W. (2005). *Theories of development: Concepts and applications.* Upper Saddle River, NJ: Prentice Hall.

Crompton, D. A. (1998). Community leadership. In S. L. Kagan & B. T. Bowman (Eds.), *Leadership in early care and education* (pp. 49–55). Washington, DC: National Association for the Education of Young Children.

Cryer, D., & Harms, T. (2000). *Infants and toddlers in out-of-home care.* Baltimore: Paul H. Brookes.

Culkin, M. L. (Ed.). (2000). Managing quality in young children's programs: The leader's role. New York: Teachers College Press.

Curtis, D., & Carter, M. (1996). *Reflecting children's lives: A handbook for planning child-centered curriculum.* St. Paul, MN: Redleaf.

Curtis, K. F. (1995). On entering and staying in the teaching profession. *Childhood Education, 71*(5), 288–F.

Dahlberg, G., Moss, P., & Pence, A. (1999). *Beyond quality in early childhood education and care: Postmodern perspectives.* London: Falmer Press.

Daly, D. L., & Dowd, T. P. (1992). Characteristics of effective, harm free environments for children in out of home care. *Child Welfare, 71*(6), 87–96.

Delaney, E. M. (2001, September). The administrator's role in making inclusion work. *Young Children, 56*(5), 66–70.

Derman-Sparks, L. (1992). Reaching potentials through anti-bias, multicultural curriculum. In S. Bredekamp & T. Rosegrant (Eds.), *Reaching potentials: Appropriate curriculum and assessment for young children* (pp. 114–127). Washington, DC: National Association for the Education of Young Children.

Downs, B. (2003, October). *Fertility of American women: June 2002.* (U.S. Census Bureau: Current Population Reports, Series P20-548). Washington, DC: U.S. Government Printing Office. Available online at http://www.census.gov/population/www/socdemo/fertility.html

DuBrin, A. J. (2000). *The active manager: How to plan, organize, lead and control your way to success.* London: International Thompson Publishing.

Dunst, C., Hamby, D., Trivette, C. M., Raab, M., & Bruder, M. B. (2000). Everyday family and community life and children's naturally occurring learning opportunities. *Journal of Early Intervention, 23*(3), 151–164.

Edwards, C. P. (2002, Spring). Three approaches from Europe: Waldorf, Montessori, and Reggio Emilia. *Early Childhood Research and Practice, 4* (1). Retrieved August 5, 2005, from http://ecrp.uiuc.edu/v4n1/edwards.html

Ehrle, J., Adams, G., & Tout, K. (2001). Who's caring for our youngest children? Childcare patterns of infants and toddlers. In *Assessing the new federalism policy brief* (Occasional Paper Number 42). Washington, DC: The Urban Institute.

Elkind, D. (1994). *Ties that stress: The new family imbalance.* Cambridge, MA: Harvard University Press.

Endres, J. B., & Rockwell, R. E. (1990). *Food, nutrition, and the young child* (3rd ed.). Upper Saddle River, NJ: Merrill/Prentice Hall.

Etchart, N. (1995, June). Cairo, Beijing & beyond! *Association for Women in Development Newsletter, 9*(3), 15.

FYI: Professional preparation and family involvement. (1995, March). *Young Children, 50*(3), 9.

Feeney, S., & Freeman, N. (1999). *Ethics and the early childhood educator: Using the NAEYC Code.* Washington, DC: National Association for the Education of Young Children.

Feeney, S., & Kipnis, K. (2005). *Code of ethical conduct and statement of commitment.* Washington, DC: National Association for the Education of Young Children.

Fenichel, E. (Ed.). (1992). *Learning through supervision and mentorship to support development of infants, toddlers, and their families: A source book.* Washington, DC: Zero to Three.

Fenichel, E. (2001, April/May). From neurons to neighborhoods: What's in it for you? *Zero to Three, 21*(5), 8–15.

Fiene, R. (2002). *13 indicators of quality child care: Research update.* Report to Office of the Assistant Secretary for Planning and Evaluation and Health Resources and Services Administration/Maternal and Child Health Bureau, U.S. Department of Health and Human Services. Retrieved August 11, 2005, from http://aspe.hhs.gov/hsp/ccquality-ind02/#Child

Filippini, T. (1994). The role of the pedagogista. In C. Edwards, L. Gandini, & G. Forman (Eds.), *The hundred languages of children: The Reggio Emilia approach—advanced reflections* (pp. 127–137). Norwood, NJ: Ablex.

Finkelhor, D., Williams, L. M., Kalinowski, M., & Burns, N. (1988). *Sexual abuse in day care: A national study.* Durham, NH: Family Research Laboratory, University of New Hampshire.

Fox, L., Hanline, M. F., Vail, C. O., & Gallant, K. R. (1994, Summer). Developmentally appropriate practice: Applications for young children with disabilities. *Journal of Early Intervention, 18*(3), 243–257.

Franklin, W. H. (1998). Who cares? Eight principles for dealing with customers. In B. & R. Neugebauer (Eds.), *The art of leadership: Managing early childhood organizations* (pp. 329–331). Redmond, WA: Exchange Press.

Fraser, S., & Gestwicki, C. (2000). *Authentic childhood: Exploring Reggio Emilia in the classroom.* Albany, NY: Delmar.

Freeman, N. K., & Brown, M. H. (1999). How soon can you close the center? A story of survival. *Journal of Early Childhood Teacher Education, 20*(1), 49–58.

Frieman, B. B., & Settel, J. (1994, Summer). What the classroom teacher needs to know about children with chronic health problems. *Childhood Education, 70*(4), 201.

Frost, J. L., Brown, P-S, Sutterby, J. A., and Thornton, C. D. (2004). *The developmental benefits of playgrounds.* Olney, MD: Association for Childhood Education International.

Galinsky, E., & Hooks, W. (1977). *The new extended family: Day care that works.* Boston: Houghton Mifflin.

Gambetti, A., & Kaminsky, J. A. (2001, Spring/Summer). The fundamental role of participation in the experience of the Reggio Emilia municipal infant–toddler centers and preschools: An interview with Paola Cagliari. *Innovations in Early Education: The international Reggio exchange, 8*(3), 1–6.

Gandini, L. (1984, Summer). Not just anywhere: Making child care centers into "particular" places. *Beginnings,* 17–20.

Gennarelli, C. (2004, January). Communicating with families: Children lead the way. *Young Children, 59*(1), 98–100.

Gilliam, W. S., & Marchesseault, C. M. (2005, March 30). *From Capitols to classrooms, policies to practice: State-funded prekindergarten at the classroom level.* The National Prekindergarten Study. Yale University Child Study Center. Retrieved July 5, 2005, from http://nieer.org/resources/files/NPSteachers.pdf

Goffin, S. G., & Wilson, C. (2001). *Curriculum models and early childhood education: Appraising the relationship* (2nd ed.). Upper Saddle River, NJ: Merrill/Prentice Hall.

Goleman, D. (1995). *Emotional intelligence: Why it can matter more than IQ.* New York: Bantam Books.

Gonzalez-Mena, J. (1997). *Multicultural issues in child care* (2nd ed.). Mountain View, CA: Mayfield.

Gordon, T. (1970). *P.E.T.: Parent effectiveness training.* New York: Wyden.

Gordon, T. (1974). *T.E.T.: Teacher effectiveness training.* New York: Wyden.

Gordon, T. (1978). *Leadership effectiveness training: L.E.T.* New York: Bantam.

Greenleaf, R. K. (1998). Servant-leadership. In L. C. Spears (Ed.), *Insights on leadership: Service, stewardship, spirit, and servant-leadership* (pp. 15–20). New York: Wiley.

Greenspan, S. I., & Wieder, S. (1998). *The child with special needs.* Reading, MA: Addison-Wesley.

Hansen, K. A., & Bachu, A. (1995, August). *The Foreign-Born Population: 1994.* (Current Population Reports P20-486). Washington, DC: U.S. Census Bureau.

Harms, T., & Clifford, R. (1989). *Family Day Care Rating Scale (FDCRS) (1989).* New York: Teachers College Press.

Harms, T., Clifford, R. M., & Cryer, D. (2005). *Early childhood environment rating scale* (rev. ed.). New York: Teachers College Press.

Harms, T., Cryer, D., & Clifford, R. M. (2003). *Infant/toddler environment rating scale* (rev. ed.). New York: Teachers College Press.

Harms, T., Jacobs, E. V., & White, D. R. (1995). *School-age care environment rating scale.* New York: Teachers College Press.

Hatch, M. J. (1997). Organization theory: modern, symbolic, and postmodern perspectives. New York: Oxford University Press.

Haugen, Kirsten (n.d.). Chart: *Steps for adapting materials for use by all children.* Retrieved July 19, 2005, from http://www.childcareexchange.com/library/5016101.pdf

Hayden, J. (1995, July/August). Applying early childhood principles in extraordinary circumstances. *Child Care Information Exchange, 104,* 64–66.

Head Start Bureau (2001). Head Start Child Outcomes Framework. *Head Start Bulletin, 70,* 44–50.

Hearron, P., & Hildebrand, V. (2005). *Guiding young children* (7th ed.). Upper Saddle River, NJ: Merrill/ Prentice Hall.

Hemmeter, M. L., Joseph, G. E., Smith, B. J., & Sandall, S. (2001). *DEC recommended practices: Program assessment.* Longmont, CA: Sopris West and Denver, CO: DEC.

Hemmeter, M. L., Joseph, G. E., Smith, B. J., & Sandall, S. (Eds.). (2001). *DEC recommended practices in program assessment: Improving practices for young children with special needs and their families.* Denver, CO: Division for Early Childhood, Council for Exceptional Children.

Hewes, D. W. (1994, July/August). TQ what? Applying total quality management in child care. *Child Care Information Exchange, 98,* 20–24.

Hewes, D. (1998). When shaming fingers point: Dealing with negative publicity. In B. & R. Neugebauer (Eds.), *The art of leadership: Managing early childhood organizations* (pp. 345–347). Redmond, WA: Exchange Press.

Hildebrand, V. (1993). *Management of child development centers* (3rd ed.). Upper Saddle River, NJ: Merrill/Prentice Hall.

Hildebrand, V., Phenice, L., Gray, M., & Hines, R. P. (2000). *Knowing and serving diverse families* (2nd ed.). Upper Saddle River, NJ: Merrill/Prentice Hall.

Hill-Scott, K. (2000). Leadership in child development programs: Prospects for the future. In M. L. Culkin (Ed.), *Managing quality in young children's programs: The leader's role* (pp. 203–220). New York: Teachers College Press.

Hines, R. P. (1983, May/June). Techniques for preparing people to work with young children. *Illinois Teacher, 26*(5), 186–187.

Hiss, T. (1987, June 22 and 29). Experiencing places, *New Yorker* (pp. 45–68, 73–86). Cited in J. Greenman (1988), *Caring spaces, learning places: Children's environments that work.* Redmond, WA: Exchange Press.

Hitt, M. A., Middlemist, R. D., & Mathis, R. L. (1986). *Management: Concepts and effective practice.* St. Paul, MN: West.

Hitz, R., & Driscoll, A. (1994, Spring). Give encouragement, not praise. *Texas Child Care, 17*(4), 2–11.

Hogan, N., & Graham, M. (2001, Winter). Helping children cope with disaster. *A.C.E.I. Focus on Pre-K & K, 14*(2), 1–6, 8.

Howes, C. 1997. Children's experiences in center-based child care as a function of teacher background and adult:child ratio. *Merrill-Palmer Quarterly 43,* 404–425.

Huettig, C.I., Sanborn, C.F., DiMarco, N., Popejoy, A., & Rich, S. (2005 March). The O generation: Our youngest children are at risk for obesity. *Young Children, 59*(2), 50–55.

Johnston, J. M. (1998). Assessing staff problems: Key to effective staff development. In B. & R. Neugebauer (Eds.), *The art of leadership: Managing early childhood organizations* (pp. 268–271). Redmond, WA: Exchange Press.

Jorde-Bloom, P. (1998). Commentary. In S. L. Kagan & B. T. Bowman (Eds.), *Leadership in early care and education* (pp. 34–37). Washington, DC: National Association for the Education of Young Children.

Kagan, S. L., & Bowman, B. T. (Eds.). (1997). *Leadership in early care and education.* Washington, DC: National Association for the Education of Young Children.

Kagan, S. L., & Hallmark, L. G. (2001, July/August). Cultivating leadership in early care and education. *Child Care Information Exchange, 140,* 7–12.

Kagan, S. L., & Neuman, M. J., Conceptual leadership. In S. L. Kagan & B. T. Bowman (Eds.), (1997) *Leadership in early care and education* (pp. 59–64). Washington, DC: National Association for the Education of Young Children.

Kamerman, S. B., & Kahn, A. J. (1988). *Mothers alone: Strategies for a time of change.* Dover, MA: Auburn House.

Kamerman, S. B., & Kahn, A. J. (1994). *A welcome for every child: Care, education, and family support for infants and toddlers in Europe.* Washington, DC: Zero to Three.

Kamii, C. (1982). *Number in preschool and kindergarten.* Washington, DC: National Association for the Education of Young Children.

Katz, L. (1994). Pedagogical leadership. In S. L. Kagan & B. T. Bowman (Eds.), *Leadership in early care and education* (pp. 17–20). Washington, DC: National Association for the Education of Young Children.

Katz, L. (1998). Looking at the quality of early childhood programs. In B. & R. Neugebauer (Eds.), *The art of leadership: Managing early childhood organizations* (p. 287). Redmond, WA: Exchange Press.

Katz, L. (1998). What can we learn from Reggio Emilia? In C. Edwards, L. Gandini, & G. Forman (Eds.), *The hundred languages of children: The Reggio Emilia approach—advanced reflections* (pp. 27–45). Greenwich, CT: Ablex.

Katz, L. G. (1984). Developmental stages of preschool teachers. In M. Kaplan-Sanoff & R. Yablans-Magid (Eds.), *Exploring early childhood* (pp. 478–482). Upper Saddle River, NJ: Prentice Hall.

Katz, L. G., & Chard, S. C. (2000). *Engaging children's minds: The project approach* (2nd ed.). Stamford, CT: Ablex.

Kauerz, K., and McMaken, J. (2004, June). *No Child Left Behind policy brief: Implications for the early learning field.* Denver, CO: Education Commission of the States.

Kohn, A. (1994, December). The risks of rewards. ERIC Digest, EDO-PS-94-14. Urbana, IL: ERIC Clearinghouse on Elementary and Early Childhood Education.

Kostelnik, M. J., Whiren, A. P., Soderman, A. K. Stein, L. C., & Gregory, K. (2001). *Guiding children's social development: Theory to practice* (4th ed.). Albany, NY: Delmar.

Lally, J. R. (1999). Brain research, infant learning, and child care curriculum. In *Child Care Information Exchange, Inside child care: Trend report 2000* (pp. 105–108). Redmond, WA: Exchange Press.

Lally, J. R. (2005, January). The human rights of infants and toddlers: A comparison of child-care philosophies in Europe, Australia, New Zealand, and the United States. *Zero to Three, 25*(3), 43–46.

Larsen, L. J. (2004, August). *The foreign-born population in the United States: 2003.* (Current Population Reports P20–551). Washington, DC: U.S. Census Bureau.

Larson, K., Artz, G., Hegland, S., Kuku, Y., & Otto, D. (2005). *Child care, parents, and work: The economic role of child care in Iowa.* Iowa State University Extension, Center for Family Policy. Retrieved December 17, 2005, from http://www.extension.iastate.edu/cd-dial/pdf/ChildCareParents.pdf

Lazar, I., Darlington, R., Murray, H., Royce, J., & Snipper, A. (1982). Lasting effects of early education. *Monographs of the Society for Research in Child Development, 47* (1–2, Serial No. 194). Chicago: University of Chicago Press.

Lemak, D. J. (2004). Leading students through the management theory jungle by following the path of the seminal theorists: A paradigmatic approach. *Management Decision, 42*(10), 1309–1325. Retrieved June 13, 2005, from http://0-miranda.emerald-library.com.wncln.wncln.org/vl=8916427/cl=21/nw=1/rpsv/cw/www/mcb/00251747/v42n10/contp1-1.htm

Lubeck, S. (1994). The politics of developmentally appropriate practice: Exploring issues of culture, class, and curriculum. In B. L. Mallory & R. S. New (Eds.), *Diversity and developmentally appropriate practices: Challenges for early childhood education.* New York: Teachers College Press.

Lumeng, J. (2005 January). What can we do to prevent childhood obesity? *Zero to Three, 25*(3), 13–19.

Lynch, E. W., & Hanson, M. J. (1998). *Developing cross-cultural competence: A guide for working with children and their families* (2nd ed.). Baltimore: Paul H. Brookes.

Mallory, B. L. (1994). Inclusive policy, practice, and theory for young children with developmental differences. In B. L. Mallory & R. S. New (Eds.), *Diversity and developmentally appropriate practices: Challenges for early childhood education.* New York: Teachers College Press.

Mallory, B. L., & New, R. S. (Eds.). (1994). *Diversity and developmentally appropriate practices: Challenges for early childhood education.* New York: Teachers College Press.

Mangione, P. L. (1993). Child care video magazine. *Essential connections: Ten keys to culturally sensitive child care.* Sacramento, CA: Far West Laboratory/California Department of Education.

Martin, J. A., Hamilton, B. E., Sutton, P. D., Ventura, S. J., Menacker, F., & Munson, M. L. (2003) *National Vital Statistics Reports, 52*(10). Retrieved June 16, 2005, from http://www.cdc.gov/ncha/data/nvsr/nvsr52/nvsr52_10.pdf

Maslow, A. H. (1954). *Motivation and personality.* New York: Harper & Row.

McBride, B. A., & Hicks, T. (1999). Teacher training and research: Does it make a difference in lab school program quality? *Journal of Early Childhood Teacher Education, 20*(1), 19–27.

McCormick Tribune Center for Early Childhood Leadership (June 2005 eBulletin). *NAEYC Code of ethical conduct supplement for program administrators* (Draft 3: 6-27-05). Retrieved July 1, 2005, from http://cecl.nl.edu/naeyc/code/ethics.pdf

McGinnis, J. R. (2000). *Children's outdoor environments: A guide to play and learning.* Raleigh: NC Partnership for Children.

McKey, R. H., Condelli, L., Ganson, H., Barrett, B., McConkey, C., & Plantz, M. (1985). *The impact of Head Start on children, families, and communities.* Washington, DC: U.S. Department of Health and Human Services.

Meisels, S. J., and Atkins-Burnett, S. (2004, January). The Head Start National Reporting System: A Critique. *Young Children, 59*(1), 64–66.

Michigan Department of Civil Rights. (1986). *Pre-employment inquiry guide.* Detroit: Author.

Mitchell, A., & David, J. (Eds.). (1992). *Explorations with young children: A curriculum guide from the Bank Street College of Education.* Mt. Rainier, MD: Gryphon House.

Morgan, G. G. (2000). The director as a key to quality. In M. L. Culkin (Ed.), *Managing quality in young children's programs: The leader's role* (pp. 40–58). New York: Teachers College Press.

National Association for the Education of Young Children. (2005). *NAEYC Early Childhood Program Standards.* Retrieved July 29, 2005, from http://www.naeyc.org/accreditation/performancecriteria/program_standards.html

National Association for the Education of Young Children and National Association of Early Childhood Specialists in State Departments of Education (2002, November). *Early learning standards: Creating the conditions for success.* Washington, DC: Author. Available online at www.naeyc.org/about/positions/pdf/positionstatement.pdf

National Association of State Boards of Education. (2005). *Right from the start.* Alexandria, VA: Author.

National Child Care Information Center (2004, October). *Tiered quality strategies: definitions and state systems.* Child Care Bureau, Department of Health and Human Services. Retrieved July 8, 2005, from http://nccic.org/pubs/tiered-defsystems.pdf

National Education Goals Panel (1995). *Reconsidering children's early development and learning: Toward common views and vocabulary.* Goal 1 Technical Planning Group. S.L. Kagan, E. Moore, & S. Bredekamp (Eds). Washington, DC: U.S. Government Printing Office.

National Governors' Association Center for Best Practices. (1997, April 30). *Issue Brief: Highlights of national and state initiatives for young children.* Available online at www.nga.org/Pubs/IssueBriefs/default.asp

National Governors' Association Center for Best Practices. (2000, January 21). *Serving children and youth through the Temporary Assistance for Needy Families Block Grant.* Available online at www.nga.org/Pubs/IssueBriefs/default.asp

Neugebauer, R. (1995, May/June). Public and private purchasing practices drive quality down. *Child Care Information Exchange, 103,* 12–14.

Neugebauer, R. (1998a). Step-by-step guide to team building. In B. Neugebauer & R. Neugebauer (Eds.), *The art of leadership: Managing an early childhood organization* (pp. 250–254). Redmond, WA: Exchange Press.

Neugebauer, R. (1998b). Ma Bell and child care: Handling telephone inquiries. In B. Neugebauer & R. Neugebauer (Eds.), *The art of leadership: Managing early childhood organizations* (pp. 332–335). Redmond, WA: Exchange Press.

Neugebauer, R. (1999). The cost of center-based child care. In Child Care Information Exchange. *Inside child care: Trend report 2000* (pp. 27–30).

Neugebauer, R. (2000a, March/April). Non-profit child care: A powerful worldwide movement. *Child Care Information Exchange, 132,* 6–12.

Neugebauer, R. (2000b, May/June). Religious organizations taking proactive role in child care. *Child Care Information Exchange, 133,* 18–20.

Neugebauer, R. (2000c, September/October). Looking back: Events that have shaped our current child care delivery system. *Child Care Information Exchange, 135,* 35–38.

Neugebauer, R. (2000d, November/December). Looking ahead: Trends that will shape early care and education. *Child Care Information Exchange, 136,* 7–11.

Neugebauer, R. (2005a, January/February). The US military child care system: A model worth replicating. *Child Care Information Exchange, 161,* 31–32.

Neugebauer, R. (2005b, March/April). Employer child care providers stalled, but optimistic. *Child Care Information Exchange, 162,* 66–68.

Neuman, S., & Roskos, K. (2005, July). Whatever happened to developmentally appropriate practice in early literacy? *Young Children, 60*(4), 22–26.

Newburger, E. C. (2001, September). *Home computers and Internet use in the United States: August 2000.* Current Population Reports. U.S. Census Bureau. Retrieved August 12, 2005, from http://www.census.gov/prod/2001pubs/p23-207.pdf

Newsom, D., & Carroll, B. (1998). *Public relations writing: Form and style* (5th ed.). Belmont, CA: Wadsworth.

North Carolina Department of Health & Human Resources, Division of Child Development (1998, September 30). *North Carolina early childhood administration credential: Minimum standards for completion of portfolio assignments* (revised). Raleigh, NC: Author.

Odom, S. L., & Diamond, K. E. (1998). Inclusion of young children with special needs in early childhood education: The research base. *Early Childhood Research Quarterly, 13*(1), 3–25.

Olds, A. R. (2001). *Child care design guide.* New York: McGraw Hill.

Olsen, G. (1993, July/August). The exit interview: A tool for program improvement. *Child Care Information Exchange, 92,* 71–75.

Organization for Economic Cooperation and Development (OECD). (2000, July). *OECD country note: Early childhood education and care policy in the United States of America.* Paris: Author.

Paolucci, B., Hall, O. A., & Axinn, N. (1977). *Family decision making: An ecosystem approach.* New York: Wiley.

Papert, S. (1993). *The children's machine: Rethinking school in the age of the computer.* New York: Basic Books.

Pastalan, L. (1971, December). *How the elderly negotiate their environment.* Paper prepared for Environment for the Aged: A Working Conference on Behavioral Research, Utilization, and Environmental Policy. San Juan, Puerto Rico.

Petrash, J. *Understanding Waldorf education: Teaching from the inside out.* Beltsville, MD: Gryphon House.

Phillipsen, L. C., Burchinal, M. R., Howes, C., & Cryer, D. (1997). "The Prediction of Process Quality from Structural Features of Child Care." *Early Childhood Research Quarterly 12,* 281–303.

Pinson, L., & Jinnett, J. (1999). *Anatomy of a business plan* (4th ed.). Chicago: Dearborn Financial Publishing.

Poelle, L. (1993). I'll visit your class, you visit mine: Experienced teachers as mentors. In E. Jones (Ed.), *Growing teachers: Partnerships in staff development* (pp. 118–134). Washington, DC: National Association for the Education of Young Children.

Porter, S. (1982, March 8). Hard questions for neophytes. *Lansing (MI) State Journal,* p. 8B.

Pugach, M. C. (2001, Summer). The stories we choose to tell: Fulfilling the promise of qualitative research for special education. *Exceptional Children, 67*(4), 439–453.

Raver, C. C., & Zigler, E. F. (2004, January). Another step back? Assessing readiness in Head Start. *Young Children, 59*(1), 58–63.

Rich, D. (1992). *Megaskills.* Boston: Houghton Mifflin.

Rinaldi, C. (1994). Staff development in Reggio Emilia. In L. Katz & B. Cesarone (Eds.), *Reflections on the Reggio Emilia approach* (pp. 55–60). Urbana, IL: ERIC Clearinghouse on Elementary and Early Childhood Education.

Rinaldi, C. (2001). Documentation and assessment: What is the relationship? In C. Giudici, C. Rinaldi, &

M. Krechevsky (Editorial Coordinators), *Making learning visible: Children as individual and group learners.* Cambridge, MA: Project Zero, Harvard Graduate School of Education and Reggio Emilia, Italy: Reggio Children, pp. 78–89.

Rinker, L. (2001, November/December). Raising the bar. *Child Care Information Exchange, 142,* 14–18.

Rose, E. (1999). *A mother's job: The history of day care 1890–1960.* New York: Oxford University Press.

Rous, Beth (1994). Perspectives of teachers about instructional supervision and behaviors that influence preschool instruction. *Journal of Early Intervention, 26*(4), 266–283.

Ruopp, R., Travers, J., Glantz, F., & Coelen, C. (1979). *Children at the center: Final report of the National Day Care Study* (Vol. 1). Washington, DC: Department of Health, Education, and Welfare.

Russell, S., & Rogers, J. (2005 March/April). T.E.A.C.H. Early Childhood: Providing strategies and solutions for the early childhood workforce. *Child Care Information Exchange, 162,* 69–73.

Ryan, S. (1974). *A report on longitudinal evaluations of preschool programs* (pp. 1–13). Washington, DC: Department of Health, Education, and Welfare.

Saffir, L. (2000). *Power public relations: How to master the new PR* (2nd ed.). Lincolnwood (Chicago), IL: NTC Business Books.

Sandall, S., McLean, M., & Smith, B. (Eds.). (2000). *DEC recommended practices in early intervention/early childhood special education.* Longmont, CA: Sopris & Denver: DEC.

Santora, Marc. (2005, January 30). U.S. is close to eliminating AIDS in infants, officials say [Electronic version]. *New York Times,* p. 1.

Schon, B. (1998). Promoting your center with advertisements. In B. & R. Neugebauer (Eds.), *The art of leadership: Managing early childhood organizations* (pp. 336–337). Redmond, WA: Exchange Press.

Schon, B., & Neugebauer, R. (1998). Marketing strategies that work in child care. In B. & R. Neugebauer (Eds.), *The art of leadership: Managing early childhood organizations* (pp. 324–328). Redmond, WA: Exchange Press.

School of the 21st Century. (1998). Retrieved from www.yale.edu/21C

Schumacher, R. B., & Carlson, R. S. (1999). Variables and risk factors associated with child abuse in day care settings. *Child Abuse & Neglect, 23*(9), 891–898.

Scoter, J. V., Ellis, D., & Railsback, J. (2001, June). *Technology in early childhood education: Finding the balance.* Northwest Regional Educational Laboratory. Retrieved August 5, 2005, from http://www.nwrel.org/request/june01/ByRequest.pdf

Scott-Little, C., Kagan, S. L., & Frelow, V. S. (2005, March). *Inside the content: The breadth and depth of early learning standards.* Greensboro, NC: SERVE (available online at http://www.serve.org/downloads/publications/insidecontentfr.pdf

Seefeldt, V., & Haubenstricker, J. (1982). Patterns, phases, or stages: An analytical model for the study of developmental movement. In J. A. Kelso & J. E. Clark (Eds.), *The development of movement control and coordination* (pp. 309–318). New York: Wiley.

Seibert, K. W., & Daudelin, M. W. (1999). *The role of reflection in managerial learning: Theory, research, and practice.* Westport, CT: Quorum Books.

Seplocha, H. (2004, September). "We": The most important feature of a parent-teacher conference. *Young Children, 59*(5), 98.

Shareef, I., & Gonzalez-Mena, J. (1997, May/June). Training and staff development in early childhood education: Beneath the veneers of resistance and professionalism. *Child Care Information Exchange, 115,* 6–8.

Shellenbarger, S. (2001, September 26). Quality child care protected kids caught in terrorist attacks. *New York Times,* p. B1.

Shepherd, S. K. (1991, November/December). Principles of message construction. *Food and Nutrition News, 63*(5), 1–3.

Shonkoff, J. P., & Phillips, D. A. (2000, April/May). From neurons to neighborhoods: The science of early childhood development—an introduction. *Zero to Three, 21*(5), 4–8.

Shore, R. (1997). *Rethinking the brain: New insights into early development.* New York: Families and Work Institute.

Shores, E. F., & Grace, C. (2005). *The portfolio book.* Upper Saddle River, NJ: Prentice Hall.

Smith, K, (2000). *Who's minding the kids? Child care arrangements: Fall 1995.* (U.S. Census Bureau, Current Population Reports, Series P70-70). Washington, DC: U.S. Government Printing Office.

Spears, L. C. (Ed.). (1998). *Insights on leadership: Service, stewardship, spirit, and servant-leadership.* New York: Wiley.

Staley, C. C., Ranck, E. R., Perrault, J., & Neugebauer, R. (1986, January). Guidelines for effective staff selection. *Child Care Information Exchange, 47,* 23.

Stephens, K. (1998). Courting the media with special events. In B. & R. Neugebauer (Eds.), *The art of leadership: Managing early childhood organizations* (pp. 340–344). Redmond, WA: Exchange Press.

Swain, B. (1994, March/April). Your workplace: An emotional battlefield? *Child Care Information Exchange, 96,* 73–76.

Talan, T. N., & Bloom, P. J. (2004). *Program administration scale: Measuring early childhood leadership and management.* New York: Teachers College Press.

Thomas, R. M. (1992). *Comparing theories of child development.* Belmont, CA: Wadsworth.

Tobin, J. J., Wu, D. Y. H., & Davidson, D. H. (1989). *Preschool in three cultures.* New Haven, CT: Yale University Press.

U.S. Bureau of Labor Statistics (1996). Cited in Whitebook, M. and Bellm, D. (1999). *Taking on turnover: An action guide for child care center teachers and directors.* Washington, DC: Center for the Child Care Workforce, p. 38.

U.S. Census Bureau. (2001). Current Population Reports, Series P23–205. *Population profile of the United States: 1999.* Washington, DC: U.S. Government Printing Office.

U.S. Census Bureau (2003, January 24). Survey of income and program participation (SIPP), 1996 Panel, Wave 10. PPL Table 6. *Who's minding the kids? Child care arrangements: Spring 1999.* Retrieved on June 7, 2005, from http://www.census.gov/population/www/socdemo/child/ppl-168.html

U.S. Consumer Product Safety Commission (1997). *Handbook for public playground safety,* Pub. No. 325. Washington, DC: Author. Available online at http://www.cpsc.gov

U.S. Department of Agriculture Food Safety and Inspection Service (1998, February). *Salmonella questions and answers.* Retrieved December 10, 2005, from http://www.fsis.usda.gov/OA/background/bksalmon.htm

U.S. Department of Commerce, Economics and Statistics Administration, National Telecommunications and Information Administration (2004, September). *A nation online: Entering the broadband age.* Retrieved December 15, 2005, from http://www.ntia.doc.gov/reports/anol/NationOnlineBroadband04.htm# Toc78020933

U.S. Department of Education. (1994). *Strong families, strong schools: Building community partnerships for learning.* Washington, DC: U.S. Government Printing Office.

U.S. Department of Labor. (1988). *Child care: A workforce issue.* Washington, DC: U.S. Government Printing Office.

U.S. Department of Labor (2004). *Employment characteristics of families in 2003.* USDL 04-719. http://www.bls.gov/cps/

U.S. Department of Labor, Bureau of Labor Statistics. (1998, August). *Issues in labor statistics: Employer-sponsored childcare benefits.* Summary 98-9. Available in PDF format at www.bls.gov/opub/ils

U.S. Department of Labor, Bureau of Labor Statistics. (1999, April). *Employee benefits in small private establishments, 1996.* Bulletin 2507. Retrieved from http://stats.bls.gov/ebshome

U.S. Department of Labor, Bureau of Labor Statistics. (1999, September). *Employee benefits in medium and large private establishments, 1997.* Bulletin 2517. Retrieved from www.bls.gov/ncs/ebs/home.htm

U.S. Department of Labor, Bureau of Labor Statistics. (2000, December). *Employee benefits in state and local government, 1998.* Bulletin 2531. Retrieved from www.bls.gov/ncs/ebs/sp/ebb10018.pdf

U.S. Department of Labor, Bureau of Labor Statistics. (2000, December 28). *Monthly labor review: The editor's desk.* Retrieved from www.bls.gov/ebs/home

VanderVen, K. (1999). The dual functions of director competencies and leadership: A model for early childhood teacher education. *Journal of Early Childhood Teacher Education, 20*(2), 193–199.

VanderVen, K. (2000). Capturing the breadth and depth of the job: The administrator as influential leader in a complex world. In M. L. Culkin (Ed.), *Managing quality in young children's programs: The leader's role* (pp. 112–131). New York: Teachers College Press.

Ventura, S. J., Mosher, W. D., Curtin, S. C., Abma, J. C., & Henshaw, S. (2001). Trends in pregnancy rates for the United States, 1976–1997: An update. *National Vital Statistics Reports, 49*(4). Hyattsville, MD: National Center for Health Statistics.

Wagner, J. (2000). A model of aesthetic value in the servicescape. In T. A. Swartz & D. Iacobucci (Eds.), *Handbook of services marketing and management* (pp. 69–85). Thousand Oaks, CA: Sage Publications.

Walker, T., & Donohue, C. (2005, January/February). Decoding technology: Program management tools. *Child Care Information Exchange, 161,* 33–36.

Wassom, J. (2001, May/June). Community marketing made easy. *Child Care Information Exchange, 139,* 18–20.

Whitebook, M., & Bellm, D. (1999). *Taking on turnover: An action guide for child care center teachers and directors.* Washington, DC: Center for the Child Care Workforce.

Widerstrom, A. H., Mowder, B. A., & Sandall, S. R. (1997). *Infant development and risk: An introduction.* Baltimore: Paul H. Brookes.

Wilds, M. (2001, October/November). It's about time! Computers as assistive technology for infants and toddlers with disabilities. *Zero to Three, 22*(2), 37–41.

Winter, S. M. (2005, Summer). The importance of No Child Left Behind policies for teacher educators. *Focus on Teacher Education, 5*(4), 1–3.

Wolery, M., & Wilbers, J. S. (1994). Introduction to the inclusion of young children with special needs in early childhood programs. In M. Wolery & J. S. Wilburs (Eds.), *Including children with special needs in early childhood programs: Research monograph of the National Association for the Education of Young Children* (vol. 6, pp. 1–22). Washington, DC: NAEYC.

Wurm, J. (2005). *Working in the Reggio way: A beginner's guide for American teachers.* St. Paul, MN: Redleaf Press and Washington, DC: National Association for the Education of Young Children.

Xavier, S. (2005) Are you at the top of your game? Checklist for effective leaders [Electronic Version]. *The Journal of Business Strategy, 26*(3), pp. 35–42.

Yaven, L. (2005). *Documentation, assessment, and the digital: Teaching interpretation in design education.* Retrieved August 17, 2005, from http://futurehistory.aiga.org/resources/content/2/2/6/8/documents/l_yaven.pdf

Zeece, P. D. (1998). Power lines—The use and abuse of power in child care programming. In B. & R.

Neugebauer, *The art of leadership: Managing early childhood organizations* (pp. 29–33). Redmond, WA: Exchange Press.

Zigler, E. F., & Lang, M. E. (1991). *Child care choices: Balancing the needs of children, families, and society.* New York: The Free Press.